Cetasikas

by Nina van Gorkom
Zolag 2014
Second Edition

Second edition published in 2014 by
Zolag
32 Woodnook Road
Streatham
London
SW16 6TZ
www.zolag.co.uk

ISBN 978-1897633-30-4

British Library Cataloguing in Publication Data
A CIP record for this book is available from the British Library
Printed in the UK and USA by Lightningsource.

Table of Contents

Preface 1

1 Introduction 3

PART I: The Universals 9

2 Contact 11
- 2.1 Contact (phassa) 11
  - 2.1.1 Questions 16

3 Feeling 17
- 3.1 Feeling (vedanā) 17
  - 3.1.1 Questions 24

4 Perception 25
- 4.1 Perception (saññā) 25
  - 4.1.1 Questions 31

5 Volition 33
- 5.1 Volition (cetanā) 33
  - 5.1.1 Questions 39

6 Volition in the Cycle of Birth and Death 41
  - 6.0.1 Questions 45

7 Concentration 47
- 7.1 Concentration (ekaggatā) 47
  - 7.1.1 Questions 50

8 Vitality and Attention 51
- 8.1 Vitality (jīvitindriya) 51
- 8.2 Attention (manasikāra) 52
  - 8.2.1 Questions 55

PART II: The Particulars 57

9 Applied thinking and Sustained thinking **59**
9.1 The Particulars (pakiṇṇakā) 59
9.2 Applied thinking (vitakka) 59
9.3 Sustained Thinking (vicāra) 62
9.3.1 Questions 65

10 Determination and Energy **67**
10.1 Determination (adhimokkha) 67
10.2 Energy (viriya) 69
10.2.1 Questions 72

11 Right Effort of the eightfold Path **75**
11.0.1 Questions 79

12 Enthusiasm **81**
12.1 Enthusiasm (pīti) 81
12.1.1 Questions 87

13 Zeal **89**
13.1 Zeal (chanda) 89
13.1.1 Questions 93

PART III: Akusala Cetasikas **95**

14 Introduction to Akusala Cittas **97**

15 Ignorance, Shamelessness, Recklessness and Restlessness **101**
15.1 Moha 101
15.2 Shamelessness and Recklessness 104
15.3 Restlessness 106
15.3.1 Questions 107

16 Attachment **109**
16.1 Attachment (lobha) 109
16.1.1 Questions 116

17 Wrong View **117**
17.1 Wrong View (diṭṭhi) 117
17.1.1 Questions 122

18 Conceit 125
18.1 Conceit (māna) 125
18.1.1 Questions 128

19 Aversion 129
19.1 Aversion (dosa) 129
19.1.1 Questions 133

20 Envy, Stinginess, Regret 135
20.1 Introduction 135
20.2 Envy (issā) 135
20.3 Stinginess (macchariya) 136
20.4 Regret (kukkucca) 140
20.4.1 Questions 143

21 Sloth, Torpor and Doubt 145
21.1 Sloth (thīna), Torpor (middha) 145
21.2 Vicikicchā 149
21.2.1 Questions 151

22 Different Groups of Defilements Part I 153
22.0.1 Questions 157

23 Different Groups of Defilements Part II 159
23.0.1 Questions 165

24 Different Groups of Defilements Part III 167
24.0.1 Questions 173

PART IV: Beautiful Cetasikas 175

25 Beautiful Cetasikas 177
25.1 Introduction 177

26 Confidence 185
26.1 Confidence (saddhā) 185
26.1.1 Questions 190

27 Mindfulness 191
27.1 Mindfulness (sati) 191
27.1.1 Questions 198

28 Moral Shame and Fear of Blame 199
28.1 Moral Shame (hiri) and Fear of Blame (ottappa) 199
28.1.1 Questions 202

29 Non-Attachment 203
29.1 Non-Attachment (alobha) 203
29.1.1 Questions 207

30 Non-Aversion 209
30.1 Non-Aversion (adosa) 209
30.1.1 Questions 215

31 Equanimity 217
31.1 Equanimity (tatramajjhattatā) 217
31.1.1 Questions 221

32 Six Pairs of Beautiful Cetasikas 223
32.0.1 Questions 231

33 The Three Abstinences 233
33.1 The Three Abstinences (virati-cetasikas) 233
33.1.1 Questions 239

34 Compassion and Sympathetic Joy 241
34.1 Compassion (karuṇā) and Sympathetic Joy (muditā) 241
34.1.1 Questions 246

35 Understanding 247
35.1 Understanding (paññā) 247
35.1.1 Questions 251

36 The Stages of Insight 253
36.0.1 Questions 260

37 Wholesome Deeds 263

38 Appendix to Chapter 2 275
38.1 The Feelings which accompany the different cittas 275

39 Appendix to Chapter 5 .... **279**

39.1 Cetanā as a link in the "Dependant Origination" 279

40 Appendix to Chapter 8 .... **281**

40.1 The cittas which are accompanied by vitakka and vicāra 281

41 Appendix to Chapter 9 .... **283**

41.1 Cittas which are accompanied by viriya 283

42 Appendix to Chapter 11 .... **285**

42.1 The different cittas accompanied by pīti 285

43 Appendix to Chapter 12 .... **287**

43.1 The cittas accompanied by chanda, zeal or wish-to-do 287

44 Appendix to Chapter 20 .... **289**

44.1 Summary of Akusala Cetasikas 289

44.1.1 Summarizing the fourteen akusala cetasikas, they are: 289

44.1.2 Summary of the Akusala Cittas and their accompanying Cetasikas 289

45 Appendix to Chapter 31 .... **293**

45.0.1 Nineteen Sobhana Cetasikas accompanying each Sobhana Citta 293

45.0.2 Six Sobhana Cetasikas which do not accompany each Sobhana Citta: 294

46 Appendix to chapter 34 .... **297**

46.1 Three stages of "tender insight" (taruṇa vipassanā): 297

46.2 Eight Stages of Principal Insight (Mahā-Vipassanā ñāṇa): 297

47 Glossary **299**

Books **315**

Books written by Nina van Gorkom 315

Books translated by Nina van Gorkom 315

Preface

This book deals with the operations of the mind, citta, and its accompanying mental factors, cetasikas. A detailed study of the many types of cetasikas will help the reader to know his own defilements and to develop good qualities and eventually, to eradicate all defilements. Defilements and good qualities are different types of cetasika. In this study I refer to my book *Abhidhamma in Daily Life* which deals with the basic points of the Abhidhamma. It is useful to read this book first in order to understand my study on cetasikas.

The reader may wonder what the purpose is of the many Pāli terms used in this book. In the course of his study he will see that the Pāli terms are helpful for precision of understanding. I have used the Pāli terms next to their English equivalents but the English terms often have a specific meaning in the context of Western psychology or philosophy. We should try to understand the correct meaning rendered by the Pāli terms.

In this study on cetasikas I have quoted from the first book of the Abhidhamma, the *Dhammasangaṇi* (Buddhist Psychological Ethics). I also used Buddhaghosa's commentary to this book, the *Atthasālinī* (in English: The Expositor) and his encyclopedia on Buddhism, the *Visuddhimagga* (in English: The Path of Purification). Buddhaghosa's commentaries date from the fifth century A.D. He edited in Sri Lanka old commentary works with utmost conscientiousness and translated them from Singhalese into Pāli. The reader will be impressed by the discriminative, refined knowledge of all the details of the Buddha's teachings and by the vivid way he illustrates points of the teachings with examples. He continuously points to the goal: the development of insight in order to see realities as they are. I quoted from the suttas texts which deal with the development of all kinds of kusala, comprising the development of calm and the development of insight. These texts can encourage us to keep in mind the purpose of our study. Some people believe that the Abhidhamma, the teaching on ultimate realities, is not the original teaching of the Buddha. The Buddhist scriptures, the Tipiṭaka, consist of the Vinaya (book of Discipline for the monks), the Suttanta (discourses) and the Abhidhamma. The Abhidhamma enumerates all realities and the different conditions for the phenomena which arise. In order to show that the different parts of the scriptures are one, that they are the Buddha's teaching, I quoted also from the suttas texts which deal with ultimate realities. There is also Abhidhamma in the suttas. In the suttas we read time and again that the Buddha spoke about ultimate realities appearing through the senses and through the mind-door. In order to understand the suttas some basic knowledge of the Abhidhamma is indispensable. As we study the Abhidhamma we will become more convinced that the Abhidhamma pertains to our daily life, that it teaches about the phenomena we can experience at this moment. As we continue with the study of the Abhidhamma we will be impressed by the depth of its teaching. No ordinary person could conceive such a detailed exposition of everything which is real, except an Enlightened One.

The reader may find this book technical, but as he proceeds he will find that a detailed study of realities helps him to understand his daily life.

I wish to express my deepest thankfulness to Ms. Sujin Boriharnwannaket in Bangkok, who greatly assisted me in understanding the Dhamma and its application in daily life. I based my study of cetasikas on the lectures she held in the Saket Temple in Bangkok. I also wish to express my appreciation to the "Dhamma Study and Propagation Foundation" and to the publisher Alan Weller. With their help the publication of this book was possible. All the texts from which I quoted have been printed by the Pāli text Society.

I will now continue with a general introduction in order to help the reader to have more understanding of the nature of the cetasikas which accompany the different types of cittas.

1 Introduction

`Not to do evil, to cultivate good, to purify one's mind,`
`this is the teaching of the Buddhas.`

`Dhammapada, vs. 183`

The mind cannot be purified if we do not thoroughly investigate it. When we try to analyse the mind it seems to escape us, we cannot grasp it. The mind is variable, it changes very rapidly. At one moment there is a mind with attachment, at another moment a mind with generosity, at another moment a mind with anger. At each moment there is a different mind. Through the Buddhist teachings we learn that in reality the mind is different from what we mean by the word "mind" in conventional language. What we call mind are in reality different fleeting moments of consciousness succeeding one another very rapidly. Since "mind" has in psychology a meaning different from "mind" according to the Buddhist teaching, it is to be preferred to use the Pāli term citta (pronounced: chitta). Pāli is the language of the Buddhist scriptures of the Theravāda tradition. Citta is derived from the Pāli word for thinking (cinteti). All cittas have in common that they "think" of an object, but we have to take thinking here in a very general sense, meaning, being conscious of an object, or cognizing an object.

The Buddha's teachings explain in a very precise way the objects which, each through the appropriate doorway, can be cognized by citta. For example, colour or visible object can be known through the eye-door, sound through the ear-door. Through each of the senses the corresponding object can be known. Through the mind-door all kinds of objects, also concepts and ideas, can be known. Before we studied the Buddhist teachings we had a vague, general idea of a thinking mind and we did not have a precise knowledge of objects which are cognized each through their appropriate doorway. Citta is varied because of the different kinds of objects it experiences. Seeing is totally different from hearing.

Citta is varied because of the different mental factors or adjuncts which accompany it in various combinations. The Pāli term cetasika (pronounce: chetasika) is to be preferred to the English translations of this term which vary in different textbooks. Cetasika means literally: belonging to the mind (ceto). There are fiftytwo different cetasikas which each have their own characteristic and function. Later on I will explain the rationale of these cetasikas and their classification. There is only one citta at a time, cognizing one object, and each citta is accompanied by several cetasikas which also experience the same object, but which each perform their own function while they assist the citta in cognizing that object. They arise and fall away together with the citta.

Citta and cetasika are mental phenomena, nāma, which are real in the ultimate sense. Ultimate realities or paramattha dhammas have each their own characteristic, their own function, they are true for everybody.

There are four paramattha dhammas:

- citta

- cetasika
- rūpa
- nibbāna

Citta, cetasika and rūpa are saṅkhāra dhammas, conditioned dhammas; they do not arise by themselves, each of them is conditioned by other phenomena. Citta for example, does not arise by itself, it is conditioned by the accompanying cetasikas. Nibbāna is the unconditioned dhamma, visaṅkhāra dhamma or asaṅkhata dhamma; it does not arise and fall away. Nibbāna is the object of the supramundane citta, lokuttara citta, arising at the moment of enlightenment. What we call in conventional language a "person" is in the absolute or ultimate sense only citta, cetasika and rūpa. There is no lasting person or "self", there are only citta, cetasika and rūpa which arise and then fall away immediately. Citta and cetasika are both nāmas, realities which can experience something, whereas rūpa does not experience anything.

Citta and cetasika arise together, but they are different types of paramattha dhammas. In order to explain the difference between citta and cetasika the commentary to the first book of the Abhidhamma, the *Atthasālinī*, uses the simile of the king and his retinue. The king is the chief, the principal, and his retinue are his attendants. Even so are the cittas which arise in our daily life the leaders in cognizing the object, and the cetasikas are the assistants of citta. The cetasikas have to perform their own tasks and operate at each moment of citta. Citta with its accompanying cetasikas arise each moment and then they fall away immediately.

The reader may wonder what the use is of knowing the details about citta and cetasikas. Citta and cetasikas are not abstract categories, they are active at this very moment. We could not see, hear, think, act, be angry or have attachment without cetasikas. Seeing, for example, is a citta. It is the citta which cognizes colour or visible object. In order to perform its function it needs the assistance of cetasikas, such as contact, which contacts visible object, or one-pointedness, which focuses on the object. It is important to have more understanding of cetasikas. We should know that defilements are cetasikas and that good qualities are cetasikas. They arise in daily life and when they appear we should investigate their characteristics. Otherwise we would not know what is right and what is wrong. We would not know when defilements arise and how deeply rooted they are. If the Buddha had not taught in detail about defilements we would only have a vague idea about them. How could we see the danger of defilements when they are unknown to us? How could we develop what is wholesome if we would not know the characteristics of wholesome cetasikas and the different ways of good deeds? There is a great variety of cetasikas accompanying the different cittas. Akusala cittas are accompanied by cetasikas which are defilements, whereas kusala cittas are accompanied by cetasikas which are good qualities. Apart from defilements and good qualities there are also cetasikas which accompany cittas which are unwholesome, cittas which are wholesome and cittas which are neither wholesome nor unwholesome.

Citta and its accompanying cetasikas are closely associated and they condition one another. There is a relationship and interdependence between them. Citta conditions cetasikas. When the citta is wholesome, kusala, all accompanying cetasikas are also kusala, even those kinds of cetasikas which can arise with each type of citta. When the citta is unwholesome, akusala, all the accompanying cetasikas are akusala. Feeling, for example, is a cetasika which accompanies each citta. When there is pleasant feeling, it can accompany kusala citta or akusala citta rooted in attachment, but its quality is different in each case. Cetasikas condition the citta they accompany, and the cetasikas which arise together also condition one another. For example, the cetasika understanding, paññā, conditions the citta and the other cetasikas it accompanies. When the citta with generosity is accompanied by paññā which realizes that generosity is kusala, the degree of kusala is higher than in the case of kusala citta without paññā.

When there is generosity, there is no person who is generous, generosity is a cetasika performing its function while it assists the kusala citta. When there is attachment, there is no person who is attached, attachment is a cetasika performing its function. The cetasikas which accompany the citta experience the same object as the citta while they each perform their own function. At one moment there can be attachment to colour which is experienced through the eye-door, at another moment there can be attachment to sound which is experienced through the ear-door, at another moment there can be attachment to the concept of a person which is an object experienced through the mind-door. Citta and its accompanying cetasikas arise and fall away extremely rapidly. When right understanding has not been developed we cannot distinguish between different objects experienced through the different doorways. We are inclined to join different realities together into a "whole", and thus we cannot realize their arising and falling away, their impermanence, and their nature of non-self. Through the study of the Buddhist teachings there can first be more understanding of the true nature of realities on the theoretical level. Only through the development of direct understanding of realities will one know the truth through one's own experience.

There is no abiding ego or self who can direct the operations of the mind. There is a different citta all the time and it is accompanied by different cetasikas. They arise because of their own conditions. We are so used to thinking in terms of a mind belonging to the human person. It is difficult to understand that there is no ego who can direct his mind, who can take his destiny in his own hands and shape it. If everything is beyond control where is the human dignity? If one walks the Buddha's Path one will know the difference between what is true in the ultimate sense and what is only imagination or a dream. There will be less delusion about the truth and there will eventually be elimination of all that is impure and unwholesome. This is mental emancipation and is that not the highest good one could attain?

The reader may find it cumbersome to know which types of cetasikas can accompany which types of citta, and to learn the different classifications of the groups of defilements. Such details, however, help us to be able to see the danger of unwholesomeness and the benefit of wholesomeness. When we know with what types of citta the various cetasikas are combined we will come to understand the underlying motives of our actions, speech and thought. Detailed knowledge will prevent us from taking for kusala what is akusala.

In order to help the reader to understand the variety of cetasikas which accompany different cittas, I shall first summarize a few basic points on citta I also dealt with in my *Abhidhamma in Daily Life.*

Cittas can be classified in many ways and one of these is the classification by way of "jāti" (literally birth or nature). Cittas can be of the following four jātis:

- akusala
- kusala
- vipāka (result)
- kiriya (inoperative, neither cause nor result)

The cetasikas which accompany citta are of the same jāti as the citta they accompany. Some cetasikas accompany cittas of all four jātis, others do not.

Cittas arise and fall away very rapidly and we often do not know that a different citta of another jāti has arisen after the present citta has fallen away. For example, we may think that the present citta is still vipākacitta, the result of kamma, when it is actually akusala citta with attachment or with aversion on account of the object which is experienced. Seeing, for instance, is vipākacitta. The moment of seeing is extremely short. Shortly after it has fallen away, cittas rooted in attachment, aversion or ignorance may arise and these are of a different jāti: the jāti which is akusala.

Cittas perform different functions. For example, seeing is a function (kicca) of citta. Seeing-consciousness which performs the function of seeing arises in a process of cittas; it is preceded and followed by other cittas which perform their own functions. Whenever there are sense-impressions there is not merely one citta, but several cittas arising in a process, and each of these cittas performs its own function. It is the same with cittas arising in a mind-door process. As for cittas which do not arise in either sense-door process or mind-door process, they also have to perform a function. The rebirth-consciousness (paṭisandhi-citta), the life-continuum (bhavanga-citta) and the dying-consciousness (cuti-citta) do not arise in a process of citta[1]. There are bhavanga-cittas in between the different processes of citta.

Summarizing the cittas which perform their functions in a sense-door process and then in the mind-door process[2] when a rūpa impinges on one of the sense-doors:

- atīta-bhavanga (past bhavanga)
- bhavanga calana (vibrating bhavanga)
- bhavangupaccheda (arrest bhavanga, the last bhavanga arising before the object is experienced through the sense-door)
- five-sense-door-adverting-consciousness (pañcadvārāvajjana citta)
- sense-cognition (dvi-pañcaviññāṇa, seeing-consciousness, etc.)
- receiving-consciousness (sampaṭicchana-citta)
- investigating-consciousness (santīraṇa-citta)

---

[1] See Abhidhamma in Daily Life, Chapter 12.
[2] Ibidem, Chapter 15.

- determining-consciousness (votthapana-citta)
- 7 javana-cittas (kusala cittas or akusala cittas in the case of non-arahats),
- 2 registering-consciousness (tadārammaṇa-cittas which may or may not arise).

Then there are bhavanga-cittas and the last two of these, arising before the object is experienced through the mind-door, are specifically designated by a name. The process runs as follows:

- bhavanga calana (vibrating bhavanga)
- bhavangupaccheda (which is in this case the mind-door through which the cittas of the mind-door process will experience the object)
- mind-door-adverting-consciousness (mano-dvārāvajjana-citta)
- 7 javana-cittas
- 2 tadārammaṇa-cittas (which may or may not arise).

After the mind-door process has been completed there are bhavanga-cittas again.

I think that it is useful for the reader to review the enumeration of cittas I have given above, since I, in the following chapters on cetasikas, shall refer to cittas performing different functions in processes and to cittas which do not arise in a process. All these cittas are accompanied by different types of cetasikas.

The study of cetasikas will help us to have more understanding of the intricate operations of the mind, of citta and cetasikas. It will help us to understand in theory that citta and cetasikas act according to their own conditions, and that an abiding agent who could direct mental activities is not to be found. The study of the realities as taught by the Buddha can remind us to investigate them when they appear in our daily life. Theoretical understanding of the truth is a foundation for the development of direct understanding of realities as they present themselves one at a time through the six doors, through the senses and the mind. Since the aim of the study of the Abhidhamma is the development of right understanding of the realities of our life, I refer in this book time and again to its development. Right understanding of nāma and rūpa is developed by being mindful of them when they appear. Sati, mindfulness or awareness, is a wholesome cetasika which is non-forgetful, aware, of the reality which appears at the present moment[3]. At the very moment of sati the reality which appears can be investigated, and in this way right understanding will gradually develop. Eventually nāma and rūpa will be seen as they are: as impermanent and non-self. We should not forget that also awareness, sati, is a cetasika arising because of its own conditions. If we have understood this we shall not force its arising or try to direct it to particular objects, such as this or that cetasika. The study of the Abhidhamma can prevent wrong ideas about the development of the Buddha's Path. The realities of our life, including our defilements, should be understood as not self. So long as we take defilements for self or "mine" they cannot be eradicated. The direct understanding of realities as non-self is the condition for not doing evil, for cultivating the good and for purifying one's mind.

---

[3] I shall deal with sati in Chapter 26.

In the chapters which follow I shall deal with fiftytwo different types of cetasikas. I shall first refer to seven types of cetasikas which accompany every citta. These are the *Universals.* Then I shall refer to six types of cetasikas which can arise with cittas of four jātis, cittas which are kusala, akusala, vipāka and kiriya (neither cause nor result), but which do not accompany each citta. These are called the *Particulars.* After that I shall deal with the *Akusala Cetasikas* and finally with the *Beautiful (sobhana) Cetasikas.*

PART I: The Universals

2 Contact

2.1 Contact (phassa)

A citta cannot arise alone, it has to be accompanied by cetasikas. When there is seeing citta cognizes visible object and the cetasikas which accompany the citta also experience visible object. The citta is the "leader", while the cetasikas which share the same object perform each their own task. The cetasikas have each their own characteristic (lakkhaṇaṃ: specific or generic attribute), function (rasa: function or achievement), manifestation (paccupaṭṭhāna: manifestation, appearance or effect) and proximate cause (padaṭṭhānaṃ)[1]. There are many conditions for the different phenomena which appear, but the "proximate cause" or immediate occasion is mentioned in particular when the cetasikas are defined in the commentaries, the *Atthasālinī* (Expositor) and the *Visuddhimagga.* There are seven cetasikas which have to arise with every citta; they are called the "universals" (sabbacitta-sādhāranā). Some cittas are accompanied only by the universals, others are accompanied by several more cetasikas in addition. Thus, every citta is accompanied by at least the seven universals.

The universals arise with every citta and thus they arise with all the cittas of the four jātis: with akusala citta, kusala citta, vipākacitta and kiriyacitta. They arise with all cittas in all planes of existence where there is nāma: with the cittas of the woeful planes, in the human being plane, in the deva planes, in the rūpa-brahma planes, except the asañña-satta plane (the plane where there is only rūpa not nāma)[2] and in the arūpa-brahma planes. They arise with all cittas of all planes of consciousness: with kāmāvacara-cittas (sensuous plane of citta), with rūpāvacara cittas (plane of rūpa-jhānacittas), arūpāvacara cittas (plane of arūpa-jhānacittas) and with lokuttara cittas (cittas which experience nibbāna)[3].

Contact, in Pāli: phassa, is mentioned first among the universals. Phassa arises together with every citta; it "contacts" the object so that citta can experience it. When seeing experiences visible object, phassa which accompanies seeing-consciousness also experiences visible object but it performs its own function. At that moment phassa "contacts" visible object and conditions seeing-consciousness to see.

The *Atthasālinī* (Expositor, Part IV, Chapter I, 108) states about contact:

> Contact means "it touches". It has touching as its salient characteristic, impact as its function, "coinciding" (of the physical base, object and consciousness) as its manifestation, and the object which has entered the avenue (of awareness) as proximate cause[4].

The *Visuddhimagga* (Path of Purification XIV, 134) gives a similar definition.

---

[1] Expositor I, Part II, Chapter I, 65

[2] See my Abhidhamma in Daily Life, Chapter 20

[3] Ibidem, Chapter 19

[4] See Dhammasangaṇi (the first book of the Abhidhamma), par 2. This book has been translated by the Pāli Text Society under the title of Buddhist Psychological Ethics.

Phassa is different from what we mean in conventional language by physical contact or touch. When we use the word contact in conventional language we may think of the impingement of something external on one of the senses, for example the impingement of hardness on the bodysense. We may use words such as touching or impingement in order to describe phassa, but we should not forget that phassa is nāma, a cetasika which arises together with the citta and assists the citta so that it can experience the object which presents itself through the appropriate doorway. When hardness presents itself through the bodysense there is phassa, contact, arising together with the citta which experiences the hardness. Phassa is not the mere collision of hardness with the bodysense, it is not touch in the physical sense. Impact is the function of phassa in the sense that it assists the citta so that it can cognize the object.

Phassa is manifested by coinciding or concurrence, namely, by the coinciding of three factors: physical base (vatthu), object and consciousness.

When there is seeing, there is the coinciding of eye (the eyebase), visible object and seeing-consciousness; through this concurrence phassa, which is in this case eye-contact, is manifested.

We read in the 'Discourse of the Honey-ball' (Middle Length Sayings I, no. 18) that Mahā-Kaccāna explained to the monks concerning contact:

> This situation occurs: that when there is eye, your reverences, when there is visible object, when there is visual consciousness, one will recognise the manifestation of sensory impingement (phassa)...

When there is the concurrence of the ear, sound and hearing-consciousness, there is the manifestation of ear-contact. When there is the concurrence of body-sense, a tangible object such as hardness and the experience of hardness, there is the manifestation of body-contact. Eye-contact is different from ear-contact and different from body-contact. At each moment of citta there is a different phassa which conditions the citta to experience an object.

Phassa is not the doorway through which citta experiences an object. In the case of a sense-door process the rūpa which is one of the senses is doorway and in the case of a mind-door process nāma is doorway, namely the last bhavanga-citta arising before the mind-door adverting-consciousness, the first citta of the mind-door process[5].

In the planes of existence where there are nāma and rūpa, cittas have a physical base or place of origin, the vatthu[6]. The vatthu is rūpa. In the case of the 'pañca-viññāṇas' (seeing, hearing, etc.) the vatthus are the 'pasāda-rūpas' (the rūpas which are capable of receiving visible object, sound, etc.). In the case of the pañca-viññāṇas the pasāda-rūpa functions as both vatthu and doorway, 'dvāra'. For example, the rūpa which is eyesense (cakkhuppasāda-rūpa) is both doorway and vatthu for seeing-consciousness. Although it is one and the same rūpa, the functions of dvāra and vatthu are different. The dvāra is the means through which citta experiences an object, and the vatthu is the physical base for the citta. Only

[5] See Introduction.

[6] Abhidhamma in Daily Life, Chapter 17

for the pañca-viññāṇas are the dvāra and the vatthu one and the same rūpa. For the other cittas of the sense-door process the dvāra and the vatthu are different rūpas; they have as their vatthu another kind of rūpa which is in the commentaries called the 'heart-base' (hadaya-vatthu)[7]. The cittas which arise in the mind-door process also have as their vatthu the 'heart-base'. The vatthu is the physical base not only of citta, but also of the cetasikas which accompany the citta. When seeing-consciousness arises at the eye-base (cakkhu-vatthu), phassa and the other cetasikas which accompany seeing-consciousness arise also at the eye-base. Thus, citta and the accompanying cetasikas arise together at the same vatthu; they share the same object and they fall away together.

The different cittas with their accompanying cetasikas arise when there are the appropriate conditions for their arising. Even when our eyes are open, there is not seeing all the time. There are many different types of cittas which arise one at a time. When there is, for example, hearing or thinking there cannot be seeing at the same time. When there are the appropriate conditions for seeing-consciousness, it arises. Then there is the concurrence of the eye, visible object and seeing. Eye-contact performs its function so that seeing can experience visible object.

Contact 'supports' the citta and the other cetasikas which accompany the citta. There must be contact arising with the citta in order that it can cognize its object. Contact also supports the other cetasikas it arises together with: without contact there could not be feeling, perception (saññā) or volition (cetanā). The *Atthasālinī* (108) compares phassa with a pillar in a palace which is a strong support to the rest of the structure. In the same way contact is a strong support to the citta and the accompanying cetasikas.

Is there contact now? There is the experience of an object right now and thus there has to be contact as well. There are seeing, hearing or thinking occurring time and again. We think that it is 'I' who sees, hears or thinks, but in reality there are different cittas conditioned by different factors. Knowing more about the different factors through which realities are conditioned will help us to understand that there is no self who experiences an object. Seeing is a nāma which arises because of the concurrence of different factors and it cannot stay, it has to fall away again. We cannot force it to arise nor can we force it to stay.

When we are busy with our work, there are different realities presenting themselves through the senses, but we are usually forgetful of them. When hardness presents itself, phassa performs its function so that citta can experience the object. There is no self who experiences hardness. Considering realities can condition the arising of mindfulness, no matter whether we walk, stand, sit or lie down.

When we study cetasikas we should not forget that cetasikas never arise alone; they have to arise together with citta. They arise with the cittas of our daily life, they are not abstract categories. Since citta and cetasikas which arise together condition one another, the cetasikas and thus also phassa have different qualities when they arise with different types of citta. Phassa which arises with akusala citta is also akusala; phassa which arises with kusala citta is also kusala. When phassa

[7] Ibidem. It is the material support for all cittas other than the pañca-viññāṇas. There is no need to specify its exact location.

arises with lokuttara citta phassa is also lokuttara: at that moment it 'contacts' nibbāna, the object of the lokuttara citta.

Phassa accompanies each of the cittas which arise in different processes: in the sense-door processes and in the mind-door processes[8]. Phassa also accompanies the cittas which do not arise in a process of cittas[9], it accompanies the paṭisandhi-citta (rebirth-consciousness) the bhavanga-citta (life-continuum)[10] and the cuti-citta (dying-consciousness). Although these cittas do not arise in a process, they experience an object: the same object as experienced by the last javana cittas arising before the cuti-citta of the previous life[11]. Phassa which accompanies these cittas contacts that object.

When there is seeing, visible object is experienced through the eyesense and at that moment there is *eye-contact* (cakkhu-samphassa). Phassa is eye-contact only at the moment of seeing-consciousness[12]. The phassa accompanying hearing-consciousness (sota-viññāṇa) is *ear-contact* (sota-samphassa). The phassas arising with the five sense-cognitions (pañcaviññāṇa) are named after the relevant sense-base[13].

When the cittas of the sense-door process have fallen away, the object is experienced through the mind-door. When the mind-door-adverting-consciousness (mano-dvārāvajjana-citta) adverts to the object through the mind-door the phassa accompanying the mano-dvārāvajjana-citta contacts that object. The mano-dvārāvajjana-citta is succeeded by the javana-cittas which experience the same object and the phassas accompanying the javana-cittas contact that object.

The javana-cittas are, in the case of the non-arahat, either akusala cittas or kusala cittas. Most of the time the javana-cittas are akusala cittas; since we have accumulated many kinds of defilements akusala cittas are bound to arise. When we, for example, see a pleasant object, we are likely to be attached to it and to have pleasant feeling on account of the object. However, attachment does not arise at the moment of seeing-consciousness. Seeing-consciousness is vipākacitta (citta which is result) and it is invariably accompanied by indifferent feeling. The phassa which accompanies the seeing-consciousness is also vipāka. When we like what we see there are javana-cittas which are lobha-mūla-cittas (cittas rooted in attachment) and these may be accompanied by pleasant feeling or by indifferent feeling. The phassa which accompanies akusala citta is also akusala. The phassas which accompany different kinds of citta are different and the feelings which accompany the cittas are different as well. The following sutta in the *Kindred Sayings* (IV, Saḷāyatana-vagga, Kindred Sayings on Sense, Third Fifty, Chapter III, par 129, Ghosita) deals with realities as elements and it is explained that different phenomena which arise

---

[8] Abhidhamma in Daily Life, Chapter 13

[9] Abhidhamma in Daily Life, Chapter 17

[10] Bhavanga-cittas arise all through life, in between the processes of cittas

[11] Abhidhamma in Daily Life, Chapter 15

[12] At all the other moments of citta during the eye-door process phassa is "mind-contact", mano-samphassa.

[13] The phassas accompanying all the cittas other than the five sense-cognitions are called mano-samphassa.

have different conditions. The sutta does not mention each moment of citta in the process of cittas. It is understood that the pleasant feeling and unpleasant feeling referred to do not arise at the moment of seeing-consciousness, but later on in the process. We read:

> Once the venerable Ānanda was staying at Kosambī in Ghosita Park.
>
> Then the housefather Ghosita came to see the venerable Ānanda. Seated at one side he said this to the venerable Ānanda:
>
> '"Diversity in elements! Diversity in elements!" is the saying, my lord Ānanda. Pray, sir, how far has diversity in elements been spoken of by the Exalted One?'
>
> 'When the elements of eye and objects that are pleasing and eye-consciousness occur together, housefather, owing to the pleasurable contact there arises pleasant feeling. When the elements of eye, objects that are displeasing and eye-consciousness occur together, owing to the unpleasant contact resulting there arises painful feeling. When the elements of eye, objects that are of indifferent effect and eye-consciousness occur together, owing to neutral contact resulting, there arises feeling that is neutral.
>
> So when the elements of ear...nose...tongue... body...when the elements of mind and objects that are pleasurable and mindconsciousness occur together.
>
> When mind and objects that are displeasing...or mind and objects that are of indifferent effect occur together, owing to the contact resulting, whether it be pleasing, displeasing or neutral, there arises feeling that is pleasing, displeasing or neutral.
>
> Thus far, housefather, diversity in elements has been spoken of by the Exalted One.

When we read this sutta we can be reminded to see phenomena as elements which arise dependent on conditions. Sometimes the object which phassa contacts is pleasant, sometimes unpleasant; this is beyond control. Because of our defilements, attachment, aversion and ignorance arise time and again. If we learn to see the events of our life as conditioned elements, right understanding will develop.

We have different contacts through the eyes and through the ears. When we are at the opera, we may dislike the sight of someone who is singing but we may like the sound. There are different objects and different contacts; there can be like and dislike at different moments. In reality there is no singer nor is there a person who can look at him and listen to his singing at the same time. There are only different elements, nāmas and rūpas, which each have their appropriate conditions for their arising and can only be experienced *one at a time.*

The citta and the accompanying cetasikas which experience visible object arise at one moment; the citta and the accompanying cetasikas which experience sound arise at another moment, in another process of cittas. The dislike of visible object cannot arise at the same time as the attachment to the sound; they arise in different processes of cittas. Cittas succeed one another very rapidly and at each moment there is a different contact accompanying the citta. Because of ignorance we do not know the reality which is experienced at the present moment. We do not know whether it is sound, visible object or a concept. We think that all these realities can appear at the same time. We think most of the time of concepts instead of being aware of realities as they appear one at a time.

The study of phassa cetasika can remind us that at each moment a different citta arises, dependant on different conditions. When there is seeing phassa cannot contact any other object but visible object. Seeing can experience only visible object; it cannot experience a person in the visible object. When there is hearing, phassa cannot contact any other object but sound. Hearing cannot experience a person in the sound. When there is thinking of a concept there is a different citta with a different phassa which contacts the object citta is thinking of. There cannot be more than one contact at a time.

A detailed knowledge of different cittas and their accompanying cetasikas will help us to understand the realities of our daily life as they appear one at a time. It is important to have more understanding of realities such as seeing or hearing. They are cittas arising time and again in daily life. They experience pleasant or unpleasant objects and on account of these objects kusala cittas or akusala cittas arise, but mostly akusala cittas. Through the Abhidhamma we acquire a more precise knowledge of realities, but the knowledge should not stay at the level of theory. When we study the Abhidhamma we can be reminded to be aware of whatever reality appears at the present moment, and in this way the study will lead us to realize fully the aim of the Buddha's teachings: right understanding of realities.

2.1.1 Questions

1. How can we prove that there is contact?
2. Through how many doors is there phassa?
3. Is phassa nāma or rūpa?
4. What is the difference between eye-contact and the eye- door?
5. Are 'mano-samphassa' (mind-contact) and the mind-door different from each other?
6. Why is there not eye-contact every moment our eyes are open?
7. What kind of object does phassa contact when there is bhavanga-citta?
8. When a loud noise hurts our ears, through which doorway is it felt? What kind of object is experienced at that moment? Can other realities apart from sound be experienced through the ear-sense?
9. Why is it useful to know that phassa contacts only one object?
10. Is a concept an object that phassa can contact?
11. Why must there be phassa with every citta?

3 Feeling

3.1 Feeling (vedanā)

Feeling, in Pāli vedanā, is another cetasika among the seven 'universals'. Feeling accompanies every citta, there is no moment without feeling.

We may think that we all know what feeling is and we believe that it is easy to recognize pleasant feeling and unpleasant feeling. However, do we really know the *characteristic of feeling* when it appears or do we merely think of a concept of feeling? Throughout our life we have seen ourselves as a 'whole' of mind and body; also when we consider our feelings we think of this 'whole' which we take for 'self'. When someone asks us: 'How do you feel?' and we answer, for example, 'I am happy', we do not know the characteristic of happy feeling, which is a mental phenomenon, a nāma; we cling to the 'whole' of mind and body. Thus we only know concepts, not realities.

Is there feeling now? We think that we can recognize pleasant feeling or unpleasant feeling, but are we not mixing up feeling with bodily phenomena? Feeling is nāma, quite different from rūpa. So long as we do not distinguish nāma from rūpa we cannot know the characteristic of feeling as it is.

When we study the Abhidhamma we learn that 'vedanā' is not the same as what we mean by feeling in conventional language. Feeling is nāma, it experiences something. Feeling never arises alone; it accompanies citta and other cetasikas and it is conditioned by them. Thus, feeling is a conditioned nāma. Citta does not feel, it cognizes the object and vedanā feels.

Feeling accompanies all cittas of the four jātis: akusala citta, kusala citta, vipākacitta and kiriyacitta. Feeling is of the same jāti as the citta it accompanies. The feeling which accompanies, for example, akusala citta is also akusala and entirely different from the feeling which accompanies vipākacitta. Since there are many different types of citta there is a great variety of feeling. Although there are many kinds of feeling, they have one characteristic in common: they all are the paramattha dhamma, non-self, which feels.

All feelings have the function of *experiencing the taste, the flavour of an object* (*Atthasālinī*, I, Part IV, Chapter I, 109). The *Atthasālinī* uses a simile in order to illustrate that feeling experiences the taste of an object and that citta and the other cetasikas which arise together with feeling experience the taste only partially. A cook who has prepared a meal for the king merely tests the food and then offers it to the king who enjoys the taste of it:

> ...and the king, being lord, expert, and master, eats whatever he likes, even so the mere testing of the food by the cook is like the partial enjoyment of the object by the remaining dhammas (the citta and the other cetasikas), and as the cook tests a portion of the food, so the remaining dhammas enjoy a portion of the object, and as the king, being lord, expert and master, eats the meal according to his pleasure, so feeling, being lord, expert and master, enjoys the taste of the object, and therefore it is said that enjoyment or experience is its function.

Thus, all feelings have in common that they experience the 'taste' of an object. Citta and the other accompanying cetasikas also experience the object, but feeling experiences it in its own characteristic way.

Feelings are manifold and they can be classified in different ways. When they are classified as *three feelings*, they are:

- pleasant feeling (sukha)
- unpleasant feeling (dukkha)
- indifferent (or neutral) feeling (adukkhamasukha: neither painful nor pleasant)

There is no moment without feeling. When there is not pleasant feeling or unpleasant feeling, there is indifferent feeling. It is difficult to know what indifferent feeling is. So long as we cannot distinguish nāma from rūpa we cannot know precisely the characteristic of feeling and thus we cannot know indifferent feeling either. When mental feelings and bodily feelings are taken into account, feelings can be classified as *fivefold:*

- pleasant bodily feeling (sukha)
- painful bodily feeling (dukkha)
- happy feeling (somanassa)
- unhappy feeling (domanassa)
- indifferent feeling (upekkhā).

Pleasant bodily feeling and *painful bodily feeling* are nāmas. We can call them 'bodily feeling' because they are conditioned by impact on the bodysense. When, for example, temperature which is just the right amount of heat or cold impinges on the bodysense, the body-consciousness (kāya-viññāṇa) which experiences it is accompanied by pleasant bodily feeling. Body-consciousness is vipākacitta and in this case kusala vipākacitta[1]. The pleasant bodily feeling which accompanies this kusala vipākacitta is also kusala vipāka. Pleasant bodily feeling cannot accompany any other kind of citta but the body-consciousness, kāya-viññāṇa, which is kusala vipāka. Thus we see that not every kind of feeling can arise with all types of citta.

Painful bodily feeling accompanies only the kāya-viññāṇa which is akusala vipāka. When, for example, temperature which is too hot or too cold impinges on the bodysense, kāya-viññāṇa which is akusala vipākacitta experiences this unpleasant object. This akusala vipākacitta is accompanied by painful bodily feeling. Painful bodily feeling cannot accompany any other kind of citta but the kāya-viññāṇa which is akusala vipāka.

Bodily feelings arise because of impingement of a pleasant or unpleasant object on the bodysense. The kāya-viññāṇa cognizes the pleasant or unpleasant object which impinges on the bodysense, phassa 'contacts' the object and vedanā experiences the "taste" of the object. The feeling which accompanies kāya-viññāṇa is either *pleasant feeling* or *painful feeling*, it cannot be indifferent feeling. In the case

[1] The five sense-cognitions are vipākacittas, results of kamma. When they experience a pleasant object, they are the result of kusala kamma, a wholesome deed, and when they experience an unpleasant object, they are the result of akusala kamma, an unwholesome deed.

of the other pañca-viññāṇas[2] which are seeing, hearing, smelling and tasting, the accompanying feeling is always indifferent feeling, no matter whether the vipākacitta which experiences the object is kusala vipākacitta or akusala vipākacitta.

The Paramattha Mañjūsā, a commentary to the *Visuddhimagga* (XIV, note 56) explains why kāya-viññāṇa is accompanied by either pleasant feeling or unpleasant feeling. This is because of the 'violence of the impact's blow'; there is the direct impact of tangible object on the bodysense. Tangible objects which are experienced through the rūpa which is the bodysense are the following rūpas: solidity, appearing as hardness or softness, temperature, appearing as heat or cold, and motion, appearing as oscillation or pressure. By way of a simile the difference is explained between the impact of tangible object on the bodysense and the impact of the other sense objects on the relevant senses. When a man places cottonwool on an anvil and strikes it with an iron hammer, the hammer goes right through the cottonwool because of the violence of the impact. In the case, however, of the other pañca-viññāṇas, the impact is gentle, like the contact between two pieces of cottonwool. Thus, they are accompanied by indifferent feeling. The 'impact' of visible object on the eye-sense is gentle when compared with the direct physical contact of tangible object with the bodysense.

We may believe that bodily feeling can be indifferent, but this is not so. The moment of body-consciousness (kāya-viññāṇa) is extremely short; it is only one moment of vipāka and after it has fallen away akusala cittas or kusala cittas arise. Body-consciousness is accompanied either by pleasant bodily feeling or by painful bodily feeling. The akusala cittas or kusala cittas which arise shortly afterwards are accompanied by feelings which are different from bodily feeling. They can be accompanied by happy feeling, unhappy feeling or indifferent feeling.

Somanassa, happy feeling, can arise with cittas of all four jātis, with kusala citta, akusala citta, vipākacitta and kiriyacitta.

Somanassa is of the same jāti as the citta it accompanies. It does not arise with every citta. Somanassa cannot accompany dosa-mūla-citta which has aversion towards an object and it cannot accompany moha-mūla-citta, citta rooted in ignorance. Somanassa can accompany lobha-mūla-citta but it does not always accompany lobha-mūla-citta. Lobha-mūla-citta can be accompanied by somanassa or by upekkhā, indifferent feeling. When somanassa accompanies lobha-mūla-citta, somanassa is also akusala. There can be pleasant feeling when one likes a pleasant visible object, a beautiful sound, a fragrant odour, a delicious taste or a soft touch. We would like to have pleasant feeling all the time, it often seems to be the goal of our life. However, pleasant feeling cannot last and when it is gone we are sad. We find it very important what kind of feeling we have, but feelings are beyond control, they arise because of conditions. Lobha accompanied by somanassa is more intense than lobha accompanied by upekkhā.

Lobha-mūla-citta accompanied by somanassa arises when there are the appropriate conditions; there is no self who can prevent this. If we study the different types of feeling and the cittas they accompany it will help us to recognize akusala

[2] The five pairs of sense-cognitions, seeing, hearing, etc. One of each pair is kusala vipāka and one akusala vipāka.

cittas. If we would not know that somanassa may accompany lobha-mūla-citta we would think that it is good to have happy feeling. One may see the disadvantage of unhappy feeling but does one recognize the disadvantage of all kinds of akusala, also when they are accompanied by somanassa? Somanassa does not stay. When we do not get the pleasant objects we are longing for our attachment conditions aversion which is always accompanied by unhappy feeling. If we realize the danger of all kinds of akusala, it can remind us to be aware of the reality which appears. This is the way leading to the eradication of akusala.

Somanassa can accompany kusala citta, but it does not accompany each kusala citta. When we perform dāna (generosity), observe sīla (morality) or apply ourselves to mental development, there can be somanassa or upekkhā, indifferent feeling, with the kusala citta. We would like to have kusala citta with somanassa, but for the arising of somanassa there have to be the right conditions. One of these is strong confidence in the benefit of kusala. Confidence (saddhā) is a wholesome cetasika which accompanies each kusala citta, but there are many degrees of confidence. When one has strong confidence in kusala, one will perform it with joy. We read in the *Atthasālinī* (I, Part II, Chapter I, 75) that:

> 'abundance of confidence (saddhā), purity of views, seeing advantage in kusala, should be understood as factors of this consciousness in making it accompanied by joy'.

When someone has right view of realities, right view of kusala and akusala, of kamma and its result, he will be firmly convinced of the benefit of kusala and this is a condition to perform it with somanassa.

The pleasant feeling which accompanies kusala citta is quite different from the pleasant feeling which accompanies lobha-mūla-citta. When we give a present to someone else and there is pleasant feeling, we may think that there is one kind of feeling which lasts, but in reality there are different moments of feeling accompanying different cittas. There can be a moment of pure generosity accompanied by pleasant feeling, but there are bound to be many moments of attachment after the kusala cittas have fallen away. We may be attached to the person we give to or to the thing we give, or we may expect something in return; we want to be liked by the person who receives our gift. Such moments of attachment may be accompanied by somanassa. Somanassa which is kusala and somanassa which accompanies lobha are different kinds of somanassa arising closely one after the other, and it is difficult to distinguish one from the other. It seems that there is one kind of somanassa and that it lasts. Without right understanding we cannot tell whether the somanassa which arises is kusala or akusala. Since there are many more akusala cittas arising than kusala cittas, there are many more moments of somanassa which are akusala than moments of somanassa which are kusala. We cling to somanassa but we cannot choose our own feelings. Who can control which feeling arises at a particular moment? Feelings arise when there are the right conditions for their arising, they are anattā, non-self. When a certain feeling appears it can be known as only a kind of experience, no self in the feeling.

Somanassa can accompany kāmāvacara cittas, cittas of the sense-sphere, rūpāvacara cittas (rūpa-jhānacittas) and lokuttara cittas. As regards rūpa-jhānacittas, somanassa accompanies the cittas of four stages of jhāna, it does not accompany the cittas of the fifth and highest stage of jhāna. At this stage the citta is accompanied by upekkhā, which is more refined and tranquil than somanassa.

Domanassa, unhappy feeling, arises only with cittas of the jāti which is akusala; it always arises with dosa-mūla-citta, it does not arise with lobha-mūla-citta or with moha-mūla-citta. It depends on one's accumulations whether dosa-mūla-cittas arise or not. When an unpleasant object such as a disagreeable flavour presents itself, dosa-mūla-cittas are likely to arise. If there is, however, wise attention to the unpleasant object, kusala citta arises instead of akusala citta.

Dosa-mūla-citta can arise only in the sensuous planes of existence, it cannot arise in the higher planes of existence where those who cultivate jhāna can be reborn. In the sensuous planes there is clinging to the sense objects and this conditions dosa. When one does not obtain pleasant sense objects dosa is likely to arise. Those who have cultivated rūpa-jhāna and arūpa-jhāna[3] have suppressed attachment to sense objects. They can be reborn in higher planes of existence, in rūpa-brahma-planes and in arūpa-brahma planes and in these planes there are no conditions for dosa. However, when they are reborn in sensuous planes where there are conditions for dosa, dosa-mūla-cittas accompanied by domanassa arise again so long as they have not been eradicated. We dislike domanassa and we would like to get rid of it, but we should understand that dosa can only be eradicated by the development of the wisdom which sees realities as they are. There is no other way. Only the ariyan, the noble person, who has attained the third stage of enlightenment which is the stage of the anāgāmī (non-returner), has eradicated clinging to sense objects and, thus, he has no more conditions for dosa. Since dosa does not arise for the anāgāmī and the arahat, they never have any more unpleasant feeling.

Dosa and domanassa always arise together. It is difficult to distinguish between these two realities , but they are different cetasikas. Domanassa is feeling, it experiences the taste of the undesirable object. Dosa is not feeling, it has a different characteristic. Dosa does not like the object which is experienced. There are many degrees of dosa, it can be a slight aversion, anger or hate. But in any case dosa does not want the object and domanassa feels unhappy. We know so little about the different realities which arise. We may have a backache. Is it painful bodily feeling which appears, or is it the characteristic of domanassa which accompanies dosa-mūla-citta?

Upekkhā, indifferent feeling, is different from somanassa and from domanassa; it is neither happy nor unhappy. Upekkhā can arise with cittas of all four jātis, but it does not arise with every citta. When there is no awareness many moments of feeling pass unnoticed. There is feeling with every citta and when we do not notice any feeling there is still feeling: at such moments there is indifferent feeling. We may not feel either glad or unhappy while we are busy with our work or while

---

[3] See Abhidhamma in Daily Life, Chapter 22. In the development of samatha, tranquil meditation, stages of rūpa-jhāna and arūpa-jhāna can be attained by those who have accumulated the right conditions. Rūpa-jhāna, fine-material jhāna, is still dependent on materiality, whereas arūpa-jhāna, immaterial jhāna, is not dependant on materiality and thus more tranquil.

we are thinking. Then there is indifferent feeling. Indifferent feeling accompanies vipākacittas such as seeing or hearing. It can accompany lobha-mūla-citta; this type of citta can be accompanied either by pleasant feeling or by indifferent feeling. Do we notice clinging which is accompanied by upekkhā? When we walk or when we get hold of different things we use in our daily life, such as a pen or a book, there is bound to be clinging even when we do not feel particularly glad. We cling to life and we want to go on living and receiving sense-impressions. We are attached to sense-impressions such as seeing and hearing. There are many moments of seeing and hearing and shortly after they have fallen away there are bound to be lobha-mūla-cittas even when we do not have happy feeling. After seeing has fallen away there is a mind-door process of cittas which experience visible object through the mind-door and then there can be other mind-door processes of cittas which think of concepts. We may think of a person, a car or a tree. We *like* to notice a person, a car or a tree, these are concepts we are familiar with. We *like* to think and even when we do not feel glad there can be clinging with indifferent feeling, but we do not notice this. It is useful to know that lobha can be accompanied by upekkhā. Through the Abhidhamma we can come to know our many defilements. It is better to know realities than to mislead ourselves with regard to them.

Upekkhā can accompany mahā-kusala cittas, kusala cittas of the sense-sphere. We may help others, observe sīla or study Dhamma with upekkhā. Feeling is a conditioned reality, we cannot force ourselves to have pleasant feeling while we apply ourselves to kusala. Upekkhā arises with kāmāvacara cittas (cittas of the sense-sphere), rūpāvacara cittas (rūpa-jhānacittas), arūpāvacara cittas (arūpa-jhānacittas) and lokuttara cittas. As regards rūpa-jhānacittas, only the cittas of the fifth and highest stage of rūpa-jhāna are accompanied by upekkhā. At that stage there is a higher degree of calm than at the lower stages; the upekkhā which accompanies that type of jhānacitta is very subtle. All the arūpa-jhānacittas are accompanied by upekkhā.

There are many different kinds of feeling and therefore we should not imagine that it is easy to recognize feelings. When we study the Abhidhamma we realize better what we do not know. It is difficult to distinguish *painful bodily feeling* from rūpa, or from domanassa. When we have pain, we 'feel' that something is hurting and we may think that it is easy to discern bodily painful feeling. However, we may not be able to distinguish the painful feeling which is nāma from the rūpa which is impinging on the body-sense. We are usually thinking of the spot which is hurt and then we are thinking of a concept. The thinking is a reality which can be known when it appears, the concept is not a reality. It is important to know the difference between ultimate realities and concepts. A precise knowledge of the different nāmas and rūpas which arise each because of their own conditions will help us to be less deluded about our life.

When hardness impinges on the body-sense, the kāya-viññāṇa cognizes the hardness and the accompanying feeling experiences the 'taste' of the hardness. Time and again vipākacittas arise which experience pleasant or unpleasant objects through the bodysense. There are hardness or softness, heat or cold impinging on the bodysense, no matter whether we are walking, standing, sitting or lying down. There is the experience of hardness or softness time and again when we touch things or take hold of them, but we are so absorbed in what we want to get or want to do that we are unaware of the different experiences through the senses. The feeling which is vipāka is different from feeling which is associated with attachment or aversion. Pleasant bodily feeling which is vipāka is not associated with attachment, and painful bodily feeling is not associated with aversion. At the moment of pleasant bodily feeling there is no attachment to the object; pleasant bodily feeling merely experiences the pleasant object. At the moment of painful bodily feeling there is no dislike of the object; painful bodily feeling merely experiences the unpleasant object. After the vipākacittas which experience pleasant or unpleasant objects have fallen away, akusala cittas which are rooted in lobha (attachment), dosa (aversion) or moha (ignorance) are bound to arise. Akusala cittas arise very often, because we have accumulated many defilements. On the other hand, when there are conditions for 'wise attention'[4] to the object, kusala cittas arise instead of akusala cittas. There may be, for example, after the experience of tangible object, mindfulness of nāma or rūpa.

We have considered the characteristics of pleasant bodily feeling, painful bodily feeling, happy feeling (somanassa), unhappy feeling (domanassa) and indifferent feeling (upekkhā)[5] . Although all of them are the cetasika which is feeling (vedanā), they are different kinds of feeling with different characteristics. At every moment feeling is different, because at every moment there is a different citta. For example, upekkhā (indifferent feeling) which accompanies vipākacitta is different from upekkhā which accompanies akusala citta or upekkhā which accompanies kusala citta. Upekkhā which accompanies the jhānacitta of the fifth stage is different again. All these feelings are upekkhā, but they are conditioned by different cittas and accompanying cetasikas.

Since there is such a variety of feelings, it is useful to know more classifications of feeling. Feelings can be classified by way of contact through the six doors of the eyes, ears, nose, tongue, body-sense and mind. Cittas experience objects through six doors and through these doors pleasant and unpleasant objects are experienced. On account of a pleasant object there is often lobha-mūla-citta which can be accompanied by somanassa or upekkhā, and on account of an unpleasant object there is often dosa-mūla-citta which is accompanied by domanassa. If we understand that the experience of pleasant and unpleasant objects and the different feelings which arise on account of them are conditioned we will attach less importance to the kind of feeling which arises at a particular moment.

The experience of pleasant or unpleasant objects through the senses is vipāka conditioned by kamma, and the kusala cittas or akusala cittas arising on account of the objects which are experienced are conditioned by our accumulated tendencies. There is no self who can exercise power over any reality which arises, there are only nāma and rūpa which arise because of conditions. Sometimes there are condi-

[4] Abhidhamma in Daily Life, Chapter 9

[5] For details about the different feelings which accompany different cittas, see Visuddhimagga XIV, 127-128, and my Appendix 1.

tions for indifferent feeling, sometimes for pleasant feeling, sometimes for unpleasant feeling[6].

Cittas arise and fall away very rapidly, succeeding one another; there never is a moment without citta and never a moment without feeling. We cling to happy feeling, somanassa, but we know so little about ourselves and thus we may not recognize the different kinds of happy feeling. When we are laughing there is happy feeling with lobha-mūla-citta, but we may not realize that there is happy feeling which is akusala. We should not try to suppress laughing, but it is useful to know the different types of realities which arise. When we see someone else there can be happy feeling arising with attachment or happy feeling arising with kusala citta. The cittas which think of the person we meet are akusala cittas when there is no dāna (generosity), sīla (good moral conduct), or bhāvanā (mental development).

Feeling is *saṅkhāra dhamma*, a conditioned dhamma. Feeling is conditioned by the citta and the other cetasikas it accompanies. Feeling which arises, falls away immediately, it does not stay. Feeling is a *khandha*, it is one among the five khandhas, namely, vedanākkhandha[7]. We cling to feeling and we take it for self. If our knowledge of feeling is merely theoretical we will not know feeling as it is. When there is awareness of feeling when it appears it can be known as only a type of nāma and not self.

3.1.1 Questions

1. Through how many doors can pleasant mental feeling experience an object?
2. There is a great variety of feelings, but all feelings have something in common. What is the characteristic they have in common?
3. Feeling accompanies every citta. Can any kind of feeling accompany all cittas?
4. Can everybody know the reality of pleasant feeling or of unpleasant feeling?
5. Why is body-consciousness (kāya-viññāṇa) never accompanied by indifferent feeling?
6. Which jāti is painful bodily feeling?
7. Which jāti is unhappy feeling (domanassa)?
8. When an unpleasant tangible object impinges on the body-sense, can kusala cittas accompanied by somanassa arise which cognize that unpleasant object?

---

[6] Feelings can be classified in several more ways. See Kindred Sayings IV, Saḷāyatana-vagga, Kindred Sayings about Feeling, par 22, where feelings are classified as hundred and eight.

[7] See Abhidhamma in Daily Life, Chapter 2. Conditioned realities can be classified as five aggregates or khandhas: the khandha of rūpas, of feelings, of perceptions (saññā), of "formations" or "activities" (all cetasikas other than feeling and saññā) and of consciousness.

4 Perception

4.1 Perception (saññā)

Saññā, which can be translated as perception, recognition or remembrance, is another cetasika among the seven 'universals' which accompany every citta. Saññā accompanies every citta, there is no moment without saññā. Saññā experiences the same object as the citta it accompanies but it performs its own task: it 'perceives' or 'recognizes' the object and it 'marks' it so that it can be recognized again.

The *Atthasālinī* (I, Part IV, Chapter 1, 110) states about saññā:

> ...It has the characteristic of noting[1] and the function of recognizing what has been previously noted. There is no such thing as perception in the four planes of existence without the characteristic of noting. All perceptions have the characteristic of noting. Of them, that perceiving which knows by specialized knowledge has the function of recognizing what has been noted previously. We may see this procedure when the carpenter recognizes a piece of wood which he has marked by specialized knowledge...

The *Atthasālinī* then gives a second definition:

> Perception has the characteristic of perceiving by an act of general inclusion, and the function of making marks as a condition for repeated perception (for recognizing or remembering)[2], as when woodcutters 'perceive' logs and so forth. Its manifestation is the action of interpreting by means of the sign as apprehended, as in the case of blind persons who 'see' an elephant[3]. Or, it has briefness as manifestation, like lightning, owing to its inability to penetrate the object. Its proximate cause is whatever object has appeared, like the perception which arises in young deer mistaking scarecrows for men.

The *Visuddhimagga* (XIV, 130) gives a similar definition. We can use the words perceiving, noting, recognizing and 'marking' in order to designate the reality which is saññā, but words are inadequate to describe realities. We should study the characteristic and function of saññā.

Saññā is not the same as citta which is the 'leader' in cognizing an object. As we have seen, saññā recognizes the object and it 'marks' it so that it can be recognized

---

[1] In Pāli: sañjānāti, cognizing well.

[2] I am using the translation of the Ven. Nyanaponika, Abhidhamma Studies, page 69, BPS, Kandy, 1976

[3] Here I use the English translation of the Visuddhimagga, XIV, 130, instead of the English text of the Atthasālinī. The commentary refers to a story in the "Udāna" (Verses of Uplift, Minor Anthologies, 68-69) about blind people who touch different parts of an elephant. Each of them interprets in his own way what an elephant is like: the person who touches the head believes that the elephant is like a pot, since he remembers what a pot is like; the person who touches the tusks believes that it is like a ploughshare, and so on. Thus, there is recognizing of a sign or label which was made before.

again. This is explained by way of a simile: carpenters put tags or signs on logs so that they can recognize them at once by means of these marks. This simile can help us to understand the complex process of recognizing or remembering. What we in conventional language call "remembering" consists of many different moments of citta and each of these moments of citta is accompanied by saññā which connects past experiences with the present one and conditions again recognition in the future. This connecting function is represented by the words 'recognition' and 'marking'[4]. When the present experience has fallen away it has become past and what was future becomes the present, and all the time there is saññā which performs its function so that an object can be recognized. If we remember that saññā accompanies *every* citta, we will better understand that the characteristic of saññā is not exactly the same as what we mean by the conventional terms of 'recognition', 'perception' or 'marking'. Each citta which arises falls away immediately and is succeeded by the next citta, and since each citta is accompanied by saññā which recognizes and 'marks' the object, one can recognize or remember what was perceived or learnt before.

The *Atthasālinī* mentions as a manifestation of saññā:

'briefness, like lightning, owing to its inability to penetrate the object'.

Saññā merely recognizes and 'marks' the object. Saññā is different from citta which is the 'chief' in knowing an object and different from paññā which can know the true nature of realities[5] .

The proximate cause of saññā is an object, in whatever way that appears. The object can be a paramattha dhamma, i.e. nāma or rūpa, or a concept (paññatti). Whatever object citta cognizes, saññā recognizes and marks it.

Saññā performs its function through each of the six doors. There is saññā at this moment. When there is seeing there is saññā and it recognizes and marks visible object. When there is hearing there is saññā which recognizes and marks sound. There is saññā when there is smelling, tasting, touching or when there is the experience of objects through the mind-door. Cittas experience objects through the six doors and the saññā which accompanies citta experiences the object through the same doorway and performs its function accordingly. When we recognize someone's voice, this is actually the result of different processes of cittas which experience objects through the sense-door and through the mind-door. At each moment there is saññā which performs its function. There are moments of hearing of what appears through the ears, of sound, and when we think of someone's voice there are cittas which experience concepts. The hearing conditions the thinking, we could not think of a voice if there were not hearing. It is the same when we think we 'see' a person. There is thinking of a concept, but this thinking is conditioned by the seeing of

---

[4] See Abhidhamma Studies, by the Ven. Nyanaponika, 1976, page 70, where it is explained that the making of marks and remembering is included in every act of perception.

[5] The Visuddhimagga (XIV, 3-5) explains the difference between saññā, citta and paññā by way of a simile. Saññā is like the mere perception of a coin by a child who does not know its value. Citta is like the villager who knows its value. Paññā is like the money-changer who penetrates its true characteristics.

visible object. The recognition of a person is the result of many different processes of citta and each moment of citta is accompanied by saññā. There is seeing which experiences visible object and after the eye-door process has been completed visible object is experienced through the mind-door. There are other mind-door processes of cittas which experience concepts.

Saññā accompanies every citta and also when citta experiences a concept saññā marks and remembers that object. When we are engaged in the activities of our daily life, do we notice that there is recognition or remembrance? We remember how to use different objects, how to eat with fork, knife and spoon, how to turn on the water tap, how to write or how to find our way when we walk in our house or on the street. We take it for granted that we remember all these things. We should know that it is saññā which remembers. When we are reading it is due to saññā that we recognize the letters and know their meaning. However, we should not forget that when we are reading there are also moments of seeing and at such moments saññā performs its function as well. It seems that we see and recognize what we see all at the same time, but this is not so. When we recognize letters and words and remember their meaning, this is not due to one moment of saññā but to many moments of saññā accompanying the cittas which succeed one another in the different processes. The study of saññā can remind us that cittas arise and fall away extremely rapidly.

Countless moments of saññā succeed one another and perform their function so that we can remember successive events such as sentences we hear when someone is speaking. There are moments of hearing and the saññā which accompanies hearing-consciousness merely perceives the sound, it does not know the meaning of what is said. When we understand the meaning of what has been said there are cittas which experience concepts and the saññā which accompanies those cittas remembers and 'marks' a concept. Because of many moments of saññā we can follow the trend of thought of a speaker or we ourselves can reason about something, connect parts of an argument and draw conclusions. All this is not due to 'our memory' but to saññā which is not self but only a kind of nāma. What we take for 'our memory' or 'our recognition' is not one moment which stays, but many different moments of saññā which arise and fall away. Because of saññā past experiences and also concepts and names are remembered, people and things are recognized.

Also when we do not remember something or we mistake something for something else, there is saññā which accompanies the cittas at such moments. If we have forgotten something, we did not think of the object we wanted to think of but at that moment we were thinking of another object and this was remembered and marked by saññā. For example, if we go to the market and forget to buy lettuce because we suddenly notice tomatoes and our attention turns to the tomatoes, we say that we have forgotten to buy lettuce. In reality there are moments of saññā all the time since it accompanies each citta, and saññā performs its function all the time. It depends on conditions what object is remembered at a particular moment, it does not always turn out the way 'we' want it. Also when we in vain try to remember a name, there is still saññā, but it remembers and 'marks' an object which is different from the concept we think we should remember. We may have aversion because of our forgetfulness and also then there is citta accompanied by saññā which performs its function.

Saññā accompanies cittas which arise in a process and it also accompanies cittas which do not arise in a process, namely the paṭisandhi-citta (rebirth-consciousness), the bhavanga-citta (life-continuum) and the cuti-citta (dying-consciousness). When we are sound asleep and not dreaming there are bhavanga-cittas and also in between the different processes of cittas there are bhavanga-cittas. The object of the paṭisandhi-citta, the bhavanga-citta and the cuti-citta is the same as the object experienced by the javana-cittas which arose shortly before the cuti-citta of the previous life[6]. 'We', or rather the cittas which are thinking at this moment, do not know what that object is. However every time the bhavanga-citta arises in between the processes of cittas it experiences that object and the saññā which accompanies the bhavanga-citta remembers that object.

Saññā never arises alone, it has to accompany citta and other cetasikas and it is conditioned by them. Saññā is *saṅkhāra dhamma,* conditioned dhamma. Saññā arises with the citta and then falls away with the citta. Saññā is a *khandha,* it is one among the five khandhas. We cling to saññā, we take it for self.

Saññā arises with all cittas of the four jātis. Saññā is of the same jāti as the citta it accompanies and thus saññā can be akusala, kusala, vipāka or kiriya.

Saññā can be classified according to the six kinds of objects which are experienced through the six doors and this reminds us that saññā is different all the time. We read in the *Gradual Sayings* (Book of the Sixes, Chapter VI, par9, A Penetrative Discourse):

> "Monks, perceptions are six: perceptions of visible objects, sounds, smells, tastes, touches and ideas."

The perception of visible object is not the perception of sound and it is not the perception of a concept. When we for example talk to someone else there is saññā which perceives sound, there is saññā which perceives visible object, there is saññā which perceives tangible object, there is saññā which perceives a concept. All these saññās are completely different from one another and they arise at different moments. Objects appear one at a time through the different doorways and different saññās mark and remember these objects. When we understand this it will help us to see that our life actually is one moment of citta which experiences one object through one of the six doors. The ultimate truth is different from conventional truth, namely, the world of people and things which seem to last.

Saññā which arises with akusala citta is also akusala. Saññā may arise together with wrong view. When one takes for permanent what is impermanent the citta with wrong view is also accompanied by saññā which remembers the object in a distorted way. It is the same when one takes for self what is not self. We read in the *Gradual Sayings,* Book of the Fours, Chapter V, par9, Perversions) about four perversions (vipallāsas) of saññā, citta and diṭṭhi:

> Monks, there are these four perversions of perception (saññā), four perversions of thought (citta), four perversions of view (diṭṭhi). What four?

[6] Abhidhamma in Daily Life, Chapter 15

> To hold that in the impermanent there is permanence, is a perversion of perception, thought and view. To hold that in dukkha there is not-dukkha, is a perversion of perception, thought and view. To hold that in the not-self there is self, is a perversion of perception, thought and view. To hold that in the foul there is the fair, is a perversion of perception, thought and view. These are the four perversions of perception, thought and view...

So long as we have not attained to the stage of paññā which knows the impermanence of nāma and rūpa, we may still think that people and things can stay, be it for a long or a short time. Nāma and rūpa are impermanent and thus they are dukkha, they cannot be true happiness. We still take what is dukkha for happiness and we still cling to the concept of self. We also take the foul for the fair. The body is foul, it is not beautiful. However, we cling to our body and take it for something beautiful. So long as one has not attained the first stage of enlightenment, there are still the perversions of saññā, citta and diṭṭhi. The sotāpanna, who has attained the first stage of enlightenment, has eradicated diṭṭhi, wrong view, and thus he has no more perversions which are connected with diṭṭhi. But he has not eradicated all perversions since they are eradicated in different stages. The sotāpanna still clings to objects and therefore he can still have the perversions of citta and saññā while he takes for happiness what is not happiness and takes for beautiful what is foul.

When we think of a concept such as a flower, we may take the flower for something which lasts. The ariyans, those who have attained enlightenment, also think of concepts but they do so without wrong view. When they recognize a flower, they do not take that moment of recognizing for self. Neither do they take the flower for something which lasts.

So long as defilements have not been eradicated we are subject to rebirth, we have to experience objects through the senses and on account of these objects clinging arises. We tend to become obsessed by the objects we experience. We read in the *Middle Length Sayings* (I, no. 18, Discourse of the Honey Ball) about the origin of perceptions and obsessions and their ending. Mahā-Kaccana gave to the monks an explanation about what the Buddha had said in brief:

> ...Visual consciousness, your reverences, arises because of eye and visual object; the meeting of the three is sensory impingement (phassa); feelings are because of sensory impingement; what one feels one perceives; what one perceives one reasons about; what one reasons about obsesses one; what obsesses one is the origin of the number of perceptions and obsessions which assail a man in regard to visual object cognisable by the eye, past, future, present...

The same is said with regard to the other doorways. Is this not daily life? We are obsessed by all the objects which are experienced through the six doors, objects of the past, the present and the future. It is due to saññā that we remember what we saw, heard, smelled, tasted, touched and experienced through the mind-door. We attach so much importance to our recollections, we often are dreaming about them. However, also such moments can be object of awareness and thus the thinking can be known as only a kind of nāma which arises because of conditions, not self. When realities are known as they appear one at a time through the six doorways, one is on the way leading to the end of obsessions. When all defilements have been eradicated there will be no more conditions for rebirth, no more conditions for being obsessed by objects.

Saññā is conditioned by the citta and the other cetasikas it accompanies and thus saññā is different as it accompanies different types of citta. When we listen to the Dhamma and we remember the Dhamma we have heard there is kusala saññā with the kusala citta. Remembering what one has heard and reflecting about it again and again are important conditions for the arising of sati which is mindful of what appears now. The saññā which accompanies mindfulness of the present moment is different from the saññā accompanying the citta which thinks of realities. Saññā does not only arise with kāmāvacara cittas (cittas of the sense-sphere), it arises also with cittas of other planes of consciousness. When one develops samatha saññā recognizes and 'marks' the meditation subject of samatha. When calm is more developed, one may acquire a 'mental image' (nimitta[7]) of the meditation subject. The saññā which remembers a 'mental image' of a meditation subject is different from the saññā which arises all the time in daily life and perceives sense-objects. When one attains jhāna, saññā accompanies the jhānacitta and then saññā is not of the sensuous plane of consciousness. When saññā accompanies rūpāvacara citta (rūpa-jhānacitta) saññā is also rūpāvacara and when saññā accompanies arūpāvacara citta (arūpa-jhānacitta) saññā is also arūpāvacara. The saññā which is arūpāvacara is more refined than the saññā which is rūpāvacara.

The fourth stage of arūpa-jhāna is the 'Sphere of neither perception nor non-perception' (n'eva-saññā-n'āsaññāyatana)[8]. The saññā which accompanies the arūpāvacara citta of the fourth stage of jhāna is extremely subtle. We read in the *Visuddhimagga* (X, 50):

> . . . the perception here is neither perception, since it is incapable of performing the decisive function of perception, nor yet non-perception, since it is present in a subtle state as a residual formation, thus it is 'neither perception nor non-perception. . . '[9]

Saññā accompanies lokuttara citta which experiences nibbāna and then saññā is also lokuttara. Nibbāna cannot be attained unless conditioned realities are known as they are: as impermanent, dukkha and anattā. We read in the *Gradual Sayings* (Book of the Tens, Chapter VI, par6, Ideas) about ten kinds of saññā which are of great fruit and are leading to the 'deathless' , which is nibbāna. The Pāli term saññā is here translated as 'idea'. We read about the ten 'ideas' which should be developed:

> Monks, these ten ideas, if made to grow and made much of, are of great fruit, of great profit for plunging into the deathless, for ending up in the deathless. What ten ideas?

---

[7] Abhidhamma in Daily Life Chapter 21.
[8] Abhidhamma in Daily Life Chapter 22
[9] Abhidhamma in Daily Life Chapter 22

> The idea of the foul, of death, of repulsiveness in food, of distaste for all the world, the idea of impermanence, of dukkha in impermanence, of not-self in dukkha, the idea of abandoning, of fading, of ending.
> These ten ideas, monks, if made to grow. . . are of great profit for plunging into the deathless, for ending up in the deathless.

4.1.1 Questions

1. Saññā accompanies each citta, but it falls away completely with the citta. How can we still remember things which happened in the past?
2. When we see a house, through which doorway does saññā perform its function?
3. When we mistake something for something else, how can there still be saññā at such a moment?
4. When we recognize a house, can there be perversion of saññā?
5. Can the sotāpanna think of concepts and recognize people and things?
6. Give examples of akusala saññā.
7. How can one develop 'perception of impermanence' (anicca saññā)?

5 Volition

5.1 Volition (cetanā)

Cetanā, volition, is another cetasika among the 'universals', the seven cetasikas which accompany every citta. Cetanā is often translated as 'volition', but we should not be misled by the conventional term which designates the reality of cetanā. Cetanā accompanies, together with phassa (contact), vedanā (feeling), saññā (remembrance) and the other 'universals', all cittas of the four jātis. Thus, cetanā accompanies kusala citta, akusala citta, vipākacitta and kiriyacitta. When we intend to steal or when we make the resolution not to kill, it is evident that there is cetanā. However, also when we are seeing or hearing, and even when we are asleep, there is cetanā since it accompanies every citta. There is no citta without cetanā.

The *Atthasālinī* (I, Part IV, Chapter I, 111) states about cetanā that its characteristic is coordinating the associated dhammas (citta and the other cetasikas) on the object and that its function is 'willing'. We read:

> ...There is no such thing as volition in the four planes (of citta) without the characteristic of coordinating; all volition has it. But the function of 'willing' is only in moral (kusala) and immoral (akusala) states...It has directing as manifestation. It arises directing associated states, like the chief disciple, the chief carpenter, etc. who fulfil their own and others' duties.

The *Visuddhimagga* (XIV, 135) gives a similar definition[1]. The characteristic of cetanā is coordinating. It coordinates the citta and the other cetasikas it accompanies on the object. Citta cognizes the object, it is the leader in knowing the object. The cetasikas which accompany citta share the same object, but they each have to fulfil their own task. For example, phassa contacts the object, vedanā feels, experiences the "taste" of the object, and saññā "marks" and remembers the object. Cetanā sees to it that the other dhammas it arises together with fulfil their tasks with regard to the object they all share. Every cetanā which arises, no matter whether it accompanies kusala citta, akusala citta, vipākacitta or kiriyacitta, has to coordinate the tasks of the other dhammas it accompanies.

The cetanā which accompanies kusala citta and akusala citta has, in addition to coordinating, another task to perform: 'willing' or 'activity of kamma'[2]. According to the *Atthasālinī*, as to activity in moral and immoral acts, cetanā is exceedingly energetic whereas the accompanying cetasikas play only a restricted part. Cetanā which accompanies kusala citta and akusala citta coordinates the work of the other cetasikas it arises together with and it 'wills' kusala or akusala, thus, it makes a "double effort". The *Atthasālinī* compares the double task of cetanā to the task of

---

[1] See also the Dhammasangaṇi par5. The translator of the Atthasālinī writes: four planes of existence, but meant is: the four planes of citta, namely: cittas of the sense sphere, rúpa-jhånacittas, arúpa-jhånacittas and lokuttara cittas

[2] āyūhana which means 'striving' or pursuing, is translated in the English text of the Atthasālinī as conation, and in the English text of the Visuddhimagga as accumulation.

a landowner who directs the work of his labourers, looks after them and also takes himself an equal share of the work. He doubles his strength and doubles his effort. Even so volition doubles its strength and its effort in moral and immoral acts.

As regards the manifestation of cetanā which is directing, the *Atthasālinī* compares cetanā with the chief disciple who recites his own lessons and makes the other pupils recite their lessons as well, with the chief carpenter who does his own work and makes the other carpenters do their work, or with the general who fights himself and makes the other soldiers take part in the battle, "...for when he begins, the others follow his example. Even so, when volition starts work on its object, it sets associated states to do each its own."

The cetanā which accompanies vipākacitta and kiriyacitta merely coordinates the tasks of the other dhammas it accompanies, it does not 'will' kusala or akusala and it does not motivate wholesome or unwholesome deeds. For example, seeing-consciousness, which is vipākacitta, the result of kamma, is accompanied by cetanā and this cetanā is also vipāka. The cetanā which accompanies seeing-consciousness directs the tasks which the accompanying dhammas have to fulfil with regard to visible object. It directs, for example, phassa which contacts visible object, vedanā which feels and saññā which marks and remembers visible object.

Cetanā which accompanies kusala citta or akusala citta has a double task, it is 'exceedingly energetic'. Apart from coordinating the other dhammas, it 'wills' kusala or akusala and when it has the intensity to motivate a deed through body, speech or mind, it is capable of producing the result of that deed later on. When we speak about kusala kamma or akusala kamma we usually think of *courses of action* (kamma pathas) which can be performed through body, speech or mind. However, we should remember that when we perform wholesome or unwholesome deeds it is actually the wholesome or unwholesome *volition or intention* which motivates the deed and this is the activity of kamma which is accumulated and can produce its appropriate result later on. Thus, *akusala kamma and kusala kamma are actually akusala cetanā and kusala cetanā.*

Akusala cetanā and kusala cetanā can have many intensities, they can be coarse or more subtle. When they are more subtle they do not motivate kamma pathas, courses of action, through body, speech or mind. For example, when we like our food there is lobha-mūla-citta and it is accompanied by akusala cetanā. Although the lobha-mūla-citta does not motivate an unwholesome course of action, it is not kusala but akusala; it is different from kusala citta with generosity, from kusala citta which observes sīla or from kusala citta which applies itself to mental development. Whenever we do not apply ourselves to dāna, sīla or bhāvanā, we act, speak or think with akusala cittas. Thus, there is likely to be akusala citta very often in a day, since the moments we apply ourselves to kusala are very rare. There is likely to be akusala citta when we take hold of objects, eat, drink or talk. When we laugh there is lobha-mūla citta. We may not realize that there is akusala citta when the degree of akusala does not have the intensity of harming others, but in fact there are countless moments of akusala citta.

When we are lying or slandering the degree of akusala is more coarse and at such moments akusala cetanā motivates akusala kamma patha (course of action) through speech. The akusala cetanā directs the other dhammas it accompanies so that they perform their own tasks and it 'wills' akusala. Moreover, it is able to produce the appropriate result of the bad deed later on, since the unwholesome volition or kamma is accumulated. Each citta which arises falls away but it conditions the succeeding citta. Since our life is an uninterrupted series of cittas which succeed one another, unwholesome and wholesome volitions or kammas are accumulated from moment to moment and can therefore produce results later on.

There are ten kinds of akusala kamma patha, courses of action, which are performed through body, speech or mind[3]. They are: killing, stealing, sexual misbehaviour, lying, slandering, rude speech, frivolous talk, covetousness, ill-will and wrong view. The akusala cetanā (or akusala kamma) which motivates such a deed is capable of producing akusala vipāka in the form of rebirth in an unhappy plane of existence or it can produce akusala vipāka which arises in the course of one's life, vipākacittas which experience unpleasant objects through the senses.

Kamma patha can be of different degrees and thus its result is of different degrees. Kamma patha is not always a 'completed action'. There are certain constituent factors which make kamma patha a completed action and for each of the kamma pathas these factors are different. For example, in the case of killing there have to be: a living being, consciousness that there is a living being, intention of killing, the effort of killing and consequent death (*Atthasālinī*, I, Part III, Chapter V, 97). When a large animal is killed the degree of akusala kamma is higher than when a small animal is killed. The killing of a human being is akusala kamma which is of a higher degree than the killing of an animal.

In the case of slandering, there are four factors which make it a completed action: other persons to be divided; the purpose: 'they will be separated', or the desire to endear oneself to another; the corresponding effort; the communication (*Atthasālinī*, same section, 100). We read:

> "But when there is no rupture among others, the offence does not amount to a complete course; it does so only when there is a rupture."

Akusala kamma patha which is a "completed action" is capable of producing an unhappy rebirth. Some akusala kammas which are very powerful such as killing a parent produce an unhappy rebirth in the immediately following life. Some akusala kammas produce results in this life, some in following lives. There are many intensities of akusala kamma and they produce their results accordingly.

We read in the *Gradual Sayings* (Book of the Eights, Chapter IV, par10, Very trifling) about different results which are produced by akusala kammas. The 'very trifling result' which is mentioned in the sutta is the unpleasant result which arises in the course of one's life. We read:

> Monks, taking life, when pursued, practised, increased, brings one to hell, to an animal's womb, to the Peta realm[4]; what is the very trifling result of taking life is the shortening of a man's life.

[3] Abhidhamma in Daily Life Chapter 5

[4] Peta is translated as 'ghost'. It is a being of an unhappy plane.

> Monks, stealing, when pursued. . . , brings one to hell. . . ; the very trifling result is a man's loss of wealth.
>
> Monks, fleshly lusts when pursued. . . , bring one to hell. . . ; the very trifling result is a man's rivalry and hatred.
>
> Monks, lying when pursued. . . , brings one to hell. . . ; the very trifling result is the slandering and false-speaking for a man.
>
> Monks, backbiting, when pursued. . . , brings one to hell. . . ; the very trifling result is the breaking up of a man's friendships.
>
> Monks, harsh speech, when pursued. . . , brings one to hell. . . ; the very trifling result is an unpleasant noise for a man.
>
> Monks, frivolous talk, when pursued. . . , brings one to hell. . . ; the very trifling result is unacceptable speech for a man.
>
> Monks, drinking strong drink, when pursued, practised, increased, brings one to hell, to an animal's womb, to the Peta realm; what is the very trifling result of drinking strong drink is madness for a man.

When kusala kamma patha is performed, kusala cetanā "wills" kusala, and it also coordinates the tasks of the other dhammas it accompanies. Kusala cetanā is capable of producing its appropriate result later on in the form of rebirth in a happy plane or it can produce its result in the course of life in the form of pleasant experiences through the senses.

Kusala kamma can be classified as dāna (generosity), sīla (morality or virtue) and bhāvanā (mental development). Dāna comprises, apart from giving gifts, many other forms of kusala. Included in dāna are, for example, appreciating the kusala cittas of others and 'sharing one's merits'. As to the sharing of one's merits, when someone has done a wholesome deed and he gives others the opportunity to rejoice in the kusala he has performed, it is a way of dāna; at such a moment he helps others to have kusala cittas as well. The observance of the precepts which is sīla, can also be considered as a way of dāna. We read in the *Gradual Sayings*, (Book of the Eights, Chapter IV, par9, Outcomes of Merit) that going for refuge to the Buddha, the Dhamma and the Sangha leads to happy results and that there are further five gifts which lead to happy results. These are the following[5]:

> Herein, monks, a noble disciple gives up the taking of life and abstains from it. By abstaining from the taking of life, the noble disciple gives to immeasurable beings freedom from fear, gives to them freedom from hostility, and freedom from oppression. By giving to immeasurable beings freedom from fear, hostility and oppression, he himself will enjoy immeasurable freedom from fear, hostility and oppression. . .
>
> Further, monks, a noble disciple gives up the taking of what is not given. . . . . . gives up sexual misconduct. . . . . . gives up wrong speech. . . . . . gives up intoxicating drinks and drugs causing heedlessness, and abstains from them. By abstaining from intoxicating drinks and drugs, the noble disciple gives to immeasurable beings freedom from fear, freedom

[5] Translated by Ven. Nyanaponika, in Anguttara Nikāya, An Anthology III, Wheel publication 238-240, BPS. Kandy, 1976.

from hostility and freedom from oppression. By giving to immeasurable beings freedom from fear, hostility and oppression, he himself will enjoy immeasurable freedom from fear, freedom from hostility and freedom from oppression...

When we abstain from ill deeds we give others the opportunity to live in safety and without fear.

Sīla is abstaining from ill deeds which are committed through body or speech, but apart from abstaining from ill deeds there are many other aspects of sīla[6]. When one abstains from killing it is kusala sīla. But also when there is no opportunity for killing there can be kusala sīla: someone can make the resolution to spare the lives of all living beings, even of the smallest insects he can hardly see. Even so, someone can make the resolution to abstain from other kinds of akusala kamma, even when the opportunity to commit them has not arisen. For example, when a person has found out that intoxicating drinks have a bad effect, kusala cetanā may take the resolution to refrain in the future from intoxicating drinks. The wholesome intention at such a moment can be a condition for abstaining later on when there is an opportunity for drinking. However, kusala citta is not self, it arises when there are conditions for it. A moment later akusala citta may arise and our good intentions are forgotten. We may be annoyed that we do not live up to our good intentions, but we should remember that kusala citta and akusala citta arise because of their own conditions. Akusala citta arises because of conditions which are entirely different from the conditions for the kusala citta which made the resolution to observe sīla. We all have accumulated tendencies to kusala and to akusala and it depends on conditions whether we perform kusala kamma or akusala kamma. When there is no development of mahā-satipaṭṭhāna it is very difficult to observe the precepts.

The *Visuddhimagga* mentions in the section on sīla (Chapter I, 53-60) the "guarding of the sense-doors", because this can be considered as an aspect of sīla. When there is mindfulness of, for example, visible object and visible object is not taken for a 'thing' or a person but is known as only a kind of rūpa appearing through the eyes, the eye-door is guarded. At that moment there is no attachment to visible object, no aversion towards it, no ignorance about it. Later on we may become absorbed in what we see and we may cling to it, but at the moment of mindfulness the doorways are guarded and there is restraint of the senses. Thus, mindfulness of nāma and rūpa, which is a form of bhāvanā (mental development), can also be considered as sīla.

Kusala kamma which is *bhāvanā* comprises studying and teaching Dhamma, samatha, tranquil meditation, and vipassanā, the development of right understanding of realities. The development of right understanding is the highest form of kusala kamma because it leads to the eradication of ignorance. When ignorance has been eradicated there are no more conditions for rebirth in a next life, one is freed from the cycle of birth and death.

We have accumulated different degrees of kusala kamma and akusala kamma and they are capable of producing their appropriate results when there is opportunity for it. We may be inclined to think that the term "accumulation" only pertains

[6] The Visuddhimagga I, 17 and following, describes many aspects of sīla.

to kamma, but not only kamma is accumulated, also tendencies to kusala and akusala are accumulated. When one steals, akusala kamma is accumulated which is capable of producing vipāka later on. However vipāka is not the only effect of this unwholesome deed. Also the tendency to stealing is accumulated and thus there are conditions that one steals again. We have the potential in us for all kinds of bad deeds and when there is an opportunity akusala cetanā can motivate a bad deed through body, speech and mind.

We should distinguish the condition for vipākacitta from the condition for kusala citta or for akusala citta. Accumulated kamma which produces vipāka is one type of condition. The accumulated tendencies to good and evil due to which kusala citta and akusala citta arise are another type of condition. Thus, there are different types of condition which play their part in our life.

Tendencies to all kinds of defilements are accumulated. When, for example, lobha-mūla-citta arises, the tendency to lobha is accumulated and thus there are conditions for the arising again of lobha-mūla-citta. We are bound to be attached because we have accumulated such an amount of lobha. Not only unwholesome tendencies, but also wholesome tendencies can be accumulated. When there is a moment of right mindfulness of the reality which appears now, it is a condition for the arising of mindfulness again, later on. We tend to be attached rather than to be mindful, but when mindfulness has been accumulated more it will be less difficult to be mindful. Whatever tendency is accumulated now will bear on our life in the future[7].

In the *Jātakas* (Birth Stories, Khuddaka Nikāya) we find many examples of people who committed the same deeds again and again in successive lives. For example, Devadatta who tried to kill the Buddha had tried to kill him before, in many former lives when the Buddha was still a Bodhisatta. We read in the 'Dhammaddhaja Jātaka' (220) that the Buddha said:

> "This is not the first time Devadatta has tried to murder me and has not even frightened me. He did the same before."

We read in the 'Dūta Jātaka' (260) about a monk who was very greedy. Also in former lives he had been greedy. The Buddha said to him:

> "You were greedy before, monk, as you are now; and in olden days for your greed you had your head cleft with a sword."

The Buddha related a story of one of his past lives: he had such a craving for the dainty food of a king that he took a piece of rice from the king's dish and this nearly cost him his life. After the Buddha had told this story he explained the four noble Truths and the greedy monk became an anāgāmī (the noble person who has attained the third stage of enlightenment). While he listened to the Buddha he must have been mindful of nāma and rūpa and his paññā developed to the degree that all clinging to sensuous objects could be eradicated.

In the 'Tila-Muṭṭhi Jātaka (252) we read about a monk who fell easily into a rage and spoke roughly. The Buddha said:

---

[7] See also Abhidhamma Studies V, 3, by Ven. Nyanaponika, B.P.S. Kandy 1976.

"This is not the first time, monks, that this man has been passionate. He was just the same before."

He then related a story of one of his past lives. After the discourse the Buddha explained the four noble Truths and the passionate monk became an anāgāmī. He eradicated anger completely. Even though one has strong inclinations to greed and anger, accumulated for many lives, the paññā of the eightfold Path can eventually eradicate defilements. The greedy monk and the angry monk in the above mentioned Jātakas could attain enlightenment because they had also accumulated sati and paññā. Listening to the Buddha was the right condition for them to attain the stage of the anāgāmī.

If we understand that our behaviour now is conditioned by accumulated inclinations we had in the past we will be less inclined to take it for 'my behaviour'. Each reality which arises is conditioned. Generosity which arises is conditioned by generosity in the past, it is not 'my generosity'. Anger which arises is conditioned by anger in the past, it is not 'my anger'. There is no self who can force citta to be kusala citta, but conditions can be cultivated so that kusala citta can arise more often. Important conditions for the arising of kusala citta with paññā are friendship with a person who has right understanding of the Dhamma and who can explain the Dhamma in the right way, listening to the teachings and studying them, and above all mindfulness of the reality which appears now.

We should consider why we want to perform kusala kamma. Is our aim kusala vipāka? Kusala kamma produces kusala vipāka because this is the natural course of things, but if we want to perform kusala kamma in order to have a pleasant result, such as a happy rebirth, there is clinging. The aim of the Buddha's teachings is the eradication of defilements. Wholesome deeds will be purer if we perform them because we see the benefit of eliminating defilements. Since human life is very short we should not lose any opportunity for dāna, sīla or bhāvanā. If we develop the eightfold Path there will eventually be purification of all defilements.

5.1.1 Questions

1. There is cetanā also when we are sound asleep. What is its function at such a moment?
2. When we observe sīla what is the function of cetanā?
3. Which cetasika is akusala kamma or kusala kamma?
4. How can a deed performed in the past produce a result later on?
5. What kind of result can be produced by akusala kamma patha (unwholesome course of action) which is completed?
6. What are the other forms of vipāka produced by kamma, apart from rebirth-consciousness?
7. What is the effect of the accumulation of tendencies to good and evil?
8. When we laugh is there akusala citta?
9. When we are daydreaming can there be akusala citta?
10. What are the conditions for kusala citta to arise more often?

6 Volition in the Cycle of Birth and Death

Cetanā, volition, is a cetasika which arises with every citta, as we have seen. Seeing, hearing or thinking which arise now are accompanied by cetanā. Every type of cetanā performs the function of coordinating the different tasks of the accompanying dhammas, no matter whether the citta is kusala citta, akusala citta, vipākacitta or kiriyacitta.

When cetanā accompanies kusala citta or akusala citta it performs, besides the function of coordinating, another function: it "wills" kusala or akusala and it can motivate a wholesome or an unwholesome deed through body, speech or mind. Kusala cetanā and akusala cetanā, which are actually *kusala kamma* and *akusala kamma*, are capable of producing the appropriate results of the deeds they motivated.

Kusala kamma and akusala kamma can produce results in the form of rebirth-consciousness in different planes of existence or in the form of vipākacittas which arise in the course of one's life, such as seeing, hearing, smelling, tasting or the experience of tangibles through the body-sense. We experience pleasant objects and unpleasant objects through the senses and it depends on kamma whether we have a pleasant experience or an unpleasant experience through these senses.

Cetanā or kamma which motivates a good deed or a bad deed falls away immediately together with the citta, but since each citta is succeeded by the next one, kamma is accumulated and thus it can produce its result later on, even in a next life. How do we know whether there is a next life? We will understand more about the next life if we understand our life right now. By the term 'human life' in conventional language we mean the duration of time we are in this human plane of existence. However, in order to know the truth we should know *realities*, not merely conventional terms. In fact, our life consists of innumerable moments of citta which arise and fall away, succeeding one another. There is birth and death of citta at each moment and thus life lasts as long as one moment of citta. When there is citta which sees, there is only that citta, there cannot be any other citta at the same time. At that moment our life is seeing. Seeing does not last, it falls away again. When there is citta which hears there is only that citta and our life is hearing. This citta also falls away and is succeeded by the next one. In this life we see and hear pleasant and unpleasant objects, we have pleasant feeling, unpleasant feeling or indifferent feeling. We are full of attachment, aversion and ignorance. Sometimes we perform wholesome deeds: we are generous, we abstain from killing and we develop right understanding. Our life actually consists of one moment of citta which experiences an object. The citta of a moment ago has fallen away completely, but right now another citta has arisen and this falls away again. When we understand that there are conditions for each citta to be succeeded by the next one, we will also understand that the last citta of this life, the dying-consciousness, will be succeeded by a next citta which is the rebirth-consciousness of the next life. So long as we are in the cycle of birth and death there are conditions for citta to arise and to be succeeded by a next one.

Rebirth-consciousness, the first citta of life, and its accompanying cetasikas are the mental result of kamma. In the planes where there are nāma and rūpa kamma also produces rūpas from the first moment of life. Also throughout life there are rūpas produced by kamma such as eyesense, earsense and the other senses which are the means for vipākacittas to experience pleasant or unpleasant objects. The rūpas produced by kamma are the physical results of kamma. The different rūpas of our body are not only produced by kamma, but also by citta, by temperature and by nutrition. Thus, there are four factors which each produce different rūpas of our body.

In this life we perform good deeds and bad deeds; we do not know which deed will produce the next rebirth-consciousness. Also a deed which was performed in a past life is capable of producing the next rebirth-consciousness. Since we are now in the human plane of existence, it was kusala kamma which produced the first citta of our life; birth in the human plane is a happy rebirth. If the kamma which will produce the rebirth-consciousness of the next life is akusala kamma, there will be an unhappy rebirth, and if it is kusala kamma there will be a happy rebirth. Nobody can choose his own rebirth, the rebirth-consciousness is a conditioned dhamma, it is saṅkhāra dhamma. This life consists of citta, cetasika and rūpa which are conditioned dhammas. Also in a next life there are bound to be citta, cetasika and rūpa, conditioned dhammas. There will be kusala cittas, akusala cittas, vipākacittas and kiriyacittas. If we are not born in an unhappy plane there can be again the development of right understanding.

Since kusala kamma and akusala kamma are capable of producing rebirth-consciousness, they are a link in the *'Dependant Origination'* (Paṭiccasamuppāda, the conditional origination of phenomena). The doctrine of the 'Dependant Origination' explains the conditions for the continuation of the cycle of birth and death by way of twelve links, starting from *ignorance* (avijjā). Ignorance is mentioned as the first link. It is because of not knowing realities as they are, that we have to be born and that we have to suffer old age, sickness and death. The eradication of ignorance is the end of the cycle and thus the end of dukkha.

Ignorance, the first link, conditions *saṅkhāra*, the second link. Saṅkhāra are the *kusala cetanās and akusala cetanās*, the *kammas*, which are capable of producing vipāka. Saṅkhāra conditions *viññāṇa* (consciousness). Viññāṇa, the third link, is vipākacitta which can be rebirth-consciousness or vipākacitta arising throughout life such as seeing or hearing. The Dependant Origination represents the conditions for our present life and our life in the future, thus, the conditions for the continuation of the cycle of birth and death.

Saṅkhāra, the second link in the Dependant Origination, is *cetanā* in its function of kamma which produces vipāka, so that the cycle of birth and death continues[1]. Under this aspect cetanā is also called *abhisaṅkhāra.* The prefix 'abhi' is sometimes used in the sense of preponderance. Cetanā which is kusala kamma or akusala kamma has preponderance in the conditioning of rebirth. Only cetanā

[1] Saṅkhāra is often translated as 'kamma-formation'.

which accompanies kusala citta or akusala citta can be 'abhisaṅkhāra'. Cetanā which accompanies vipākacitta and kiriyacitta cannot be abhisaṅkhāra.[2]

All abhisaṅkhāras or "kamma-formations" are a link in the Dependent Origination, they are conditioned by ignorance. Kusala kamma is still conditioned by ignorance, although at the moment of kusala citta there is no ignorance accompanying the citta. So long as there is ignorance we perform kamma which can produce vipāka; we will be reborn and thus the cycle continues. We read in the *Visuddhimagga* (XVII, 119) that the ignorant man is like a blind person:

```
As one born blind, who gropes along
Without assistance from a guide,
Chooses a road that may be right
At one time, at another wrong,
So while this foolish man pursues
The round of births without a guide,
Now to do merit he may choose
And now demerit in such plight.
But when the Dhamma he comes to know
And penetrates the Truths beside,
Then ignorance is put to flight
At last, and he in peace may go.
```

While we study the different aspects of cetanā we can see that cetanā is different as it arises with different cittas. Cetanā which accompanies kusala citta or akusala citta "wills" kusala or akusala and it is capable of producing vipāka; it is, except in the case of cetanā which accompanies magga-citta, abhisaṅkhāra or kamma-formation. The cetanās which accompany rūpāvacara citta and arūpāvacara citta can produce rebirth in higher planes of existence, in rūpa-brahma planes and arūpa-brahma planes, they are a link in the Dependant Origination. Cetanā which accompanies vipākacitta is vipāka, it is produced by akusala kamma or kusala kamma. This type of cetanā has only the function of coordinating the other dhammas it accompanies. The cetanā which accompanies kiriyacitta is not kusala or akusala, nor is it vipāka; it is of the jāti which is kiriya, inoperative. This type of cetanā has only the function of coordinating.

Cetanā which accompanies lokuttara citta is not a link in the Dependant Origination. The lokuttara citta which is 'magga-citta' (path-consciousness) produces vipāka (the phala-citta or fruit-consciousness) immediately; the phala-citta succeeds the magga-citta. Since the magga-citta eradicates defilements it will free one from the cycle of birth and death. The arahat is freed from rebirth. He does not perform kamma which can produce vipāka. The cetanā which accompanies the kiriyacittas of the arahat and the ahetuka kiriyacitta which is the hasituppāda-citta (smile-

[2] For details see Visuddhimagga XVII, 177-182.There are three kinds of formations, abhisaṅkhāra: the formation of merit, the formation of demerit and the formation of the imperturbable, aneñjābhisaṅkhāra, which is arúpāvacāra kusala citta

producing consciousness) of the arahat, is not abhisaṅkhāra, it is not a link in the Dependant Origination[3].

As we have seen, cetanā which is kusala kamma or akusala kamma can produce vipāka. Time and again there are pleasant or unpleasant experiences through the senses and these are vipākacittas: we see, hear, smell, taste or experience through the bodysense pleasant or unpleasant objects. We may know in theory that vipākacittas are cittas which are result, different from kusala cittas and akusala cittas, but theoretical knowledge is not enough. We should learn to distinguish different types of citta when they appear. Each situation in life consists of many different moments which arise because of different types of conditions. For example, when we hurt ourselves because of an accident, there is an unpleasant experience through the bodysense which is vipāka, but the moments of vipāka fall away immediately and very shortly afterwards aversion is bound to arise. It is difficult to distinguish the moment of vipāka from the moment of akusala citta; cittas succeed one another very rapidly. When we think: 'This is vipāka', the moments of vipāka have fallen away already, and the cittas which think are either kusala or akusala. There are different types of conditions for the cittas which arise. The akusala cittas and kusala cittas are conditioned by the accumulated tendencies to kusala and akusala, whereas the experience of a pleasant or unpleasant object through one of the senses such as seeing or hearing is vipāka, which is conditioned by kamma.

Cetanā is *saṅkhāra dhamma*, a conditioned dhamma. It is conditioned by the citta and the other cetasikas it accompanies. The word saṅkhāra has different meanings, depending on the context in which it is used. The word "saṅkhāra" used in the context of the Dependant Origination, means "kamma-formation". Cetanā as a link in the Dependant Origination is kamma-formation, kamma which is capable of producing vipāka so that the cycle of birth and death continues.

At this moment we are in the cycle of birth and death and we cling to life, we want to go on living. We think that life is desirable because we do not know what life really is: only nāma and rūpa which do not stay. We cling to the self, we want to be liked and admired by others, we want to be successful in our work. However, we have many frustrations in life; when we do not get what we want we are disappointed. So long as there are defilements there is no end to the cycle of birth and death, but there can be an end to the cycle if we begin to know this moment of seeing, visible object, hearing, sound or thinking as it is, as only conditioned realities which do not stay. We are forgetful of realities very often, but reminders to be aware are right at hand. We can be reminded to be aware when we notice our own as well as other people's clinging to all objects and the sorrow caused by clinging.

In the *Kindred Sayings* (III, First Fifty, Chapter 3, par23, Understanding) we read that the five khandhas, that is all conditioned realities which appear in our life, have to be understood as they are. We read that the Buddha, while he was at Sāvatthī, said to the monks:

---

[3] The arahat has no kusala cittas nor akusala cittas, cittas which are cause, which can motivate kamma which produces result. Instead he has kiriya cittas, inoperative cittas, which do not produce result.

Monks, I will show you things that are to be understood, likewise understanding. Do you listen to it.
And what, monks, are the things to be understood? Body, monks, is a thing to be understood; feeling is a thing to be understood; perception, the activities (saṅkhārakkhandha) and consciousness also. These, monks, are 'the things that are to be understood.'
And what, monks, is 'understanding?'
The destruction of lust, the destruction of hatred, the destruction of illusion; that, monks, is called 'understanding'.
If there is awareness and understanding right now of seeing, hearing or any other reality which appears, there will eventually be an end to rebirth.

6.0.1 Questions

1. How can we know that there is a next life?
2. Which kinds of cetanā are a link in the Dependant Origination?
3. Why is cetanā which accompanies magga-citta not kamma-formation?
4. Kusala kamma is capable of producing vipāka and thus it is a link in the Dependant Origination. Why does it still make sense to perform kusala kamma?

7 Concentration

7.1 Concentration (ekaggatā)

Ekaggatā, concentration or one-pointedness, is another cetasika among the seven 'universals' which arises with every citta: with kusala citta, akusala citta, vipākacitta and kiriyacitta. It arises with all cittas of all planes of consciousness, but, as we will see, its quality is different as it arises with different cittas.

The characteristic of citta is cognizing an object and thus, every citta which arises must have an object. There is no citta without an object and each citta can know only one object at a time. *Ekaggatā* is the cetasika which has as function to focus on that one object. Seeing-consciousness, for example, can only know visible object, it cannot know any other object and ekaggatā focuses on visible object. Hearing-consciousness can only know sound, it cannot know visible object or any other object and ekaggatā focuses on sound.

The word 'object' (ārammaṇa) as it is used in the Abhidhamma does not have the same meaning as the word 'object' or 'thing' we use in common language. In common language we may call a thing such as a vase an object. We may think that we can see a vase, touch it and know that it is a vase all at the same time. In reality there are different cittas which know different 'objects' (ārammaṇas) through their appropriate doorways. These cittas arise one at a time and know only one object at a time. The citta which sees knows only visible object, it cannot know tactile object or a concept. Visible object is that which is experienced through the eyes. What is seen cannot be touched. We may understand this in theory, but the truth should be verified by being mindful of different objects which appear one at a time.

When we speak about an ārammaṇa, an object, we have to specify *which kind of ārammaṇa.* There is *visible object* which is known through the eye-door. There is *sound* which is known through the ear-door. *Smell, taste* and *tactile object* are known through their appropriate sense-doors. Through the mind-door all these objects can be known as well. Everything which is real and also concepts and ideas, which are not real in the absolute sense, can be known through the mind-door. Thus we see that the word 'object' in the Abhidhamma has a very precise meaning.

Ekaggatā which has as function to focus on an object is translated as 'one-pointedness' or concentration. When we hear the word concentration we may believe that ekaggatā only occurs in samatha, tranquil meditation, but this is not so. It is true that when calm is developed ekaggatā also develops, but ekaggatā does not only occur in samatha. Ekaggatā accompanies *every citta,* although its quality is different as it arises with different cittas. Even when we are, as we call it in common language, 'distracted', there is ekaggatā arising with the akusala citta since it arises with every citta. It focuses on the object which is cognized at that moment. For example, when there is moha-mūla-citta (citta rooted in ignorance) accompanied by uddhacca (restlessness), there is also ekaggatā cetasika accompanying that citta. There is ekaggatā arising with all types of akusala citta. When we enjoy a beautiful sight or pleasant music there is ekaggatā cetasika with the lobha-mūla-citta. At that moment we are absorbed in the pleasant object and enslaved to it. There is concentration when one performs ill deeds.

Ekaggatā which accompanies akusala citta is also called 'micchā-samādhi', wrong concentration. Ekaggatā which accompanies kusala citta is also called 'sammā-samādhi', right concentration. *Samādhi* is another word for ekaggatā cetasika. Although wrong concentration and right concentration are both ekaggatā cetasika their qualities are different. Sammā-samādhi focuses on the object in the right way, the wholesome way. There are many levels of right concentration.

The *Atthasālinī* (1, Part IV, Chapter 1. 118, 119) states about ekaggatā, and here it deals actually with sammā-samādhi[1] :

> This concentration, known as one-pointedness of mind, has non-scattering (of itself) or non-distraction (of associated states) as characteristic, the welding together of the coexistent states as function, as water kneads bath-powder into a paste, and peace of mind or knowledge as manifestation. For it has been said: 'He who is concentrated knows, sees according to the truth.' It is distinguished by having ease (sukha) (usually) as proximate cause[2]. Like the steadiness of a lamp in the absence of wind, so should steadfastness of mind be understood.

The *Visuddhimagga* (XIV, 139) gives a similar definition, except that it mentions only peace of mind as manifestation, not knowledge.

Sammā-samādhi is one of the jhāna-factors which are developed in samatha in order to suppress the hindrances and attain jhāna[3] . The jhāna factors of applied thought (vitakka), sustained thought (vicāra), enthusiasm (pīti), happy feeling (sukha) and samādhi have to be developed together in order to attain jhāna. All the jhāna-factors assist the citta to attain tranquillity by means of a meditation subject.

Some people take wrong concentration for right concentration of samatha. They want to try to concentrate on one point with the desire to become relaxed. Then there is akusala citta with clinging to relaxation. The aim of samatha is not what we mean by the word 'relaxation' in common language, but it is the temporary elimination of defilements. In order to develop samatha in the right way, right understanding of its development is indispensable. Right understanding should know precisely when the citta is kusala citta and when akusala citta and it should know the characteristic of calm so that it can be developed. There are different stages of calm and as calm becomes stronger, samādhi also develops[4]. Ekaggatā cetasika

---

1 See also Dhammasangaṇi par11.

2 Pleasant feeling, sukha, is a jhāna-factor arising only in four stages of rūpa-jhāna. It supports samādhi in focusing on the meditation subject. In the highest stage of rūpa-jhāna pleasant feeling is abandoned and indifferent feeling accompanies the jhāna-citta instead.

3 See Abhidhamma in Daily Life Chapter 22.

4 In the beginning stage of calm there is still preparatory concentration (parikamma-samādhi) (Vis. IV, 31-33). When calm has reached the degree that it is approaching jhāna there is access-concentration (upacāra-samādhi). When jhāna has been attained there is at that moment samādhi which is attainment-concentration (appanā-samādhi).

which accompanies rūpāvacara citta (rūpa-jhānacitta) is altogether different from ekaggatā arising with kāmāvacara citta, citta of the sense-sphere. In each of the higher stages of jhāna there is a higher degree of calm and thus ekaggatā becomes more refined. Ekaggatā which accompanies arūpāvacara citta is different again: it is more tranquil and more refined than ekaggatā arising with rūpāvacara citta.

There is also sammā-samādhi of vipassanā. As we have seen, the second manifestation of ekaggatā cetasika or samādhi mentioned by the *Atthasālinī* is knowledge or wisdom. When paññā knows a nāma or a rūpa as it is, there is at that moment also right concentration performing its function. Sammā-samādhi is one of the factors of the eightfold Path. When paññā knows, for example, the visible object which presents itself as only a rūpa appearing through the eyes or the seeing which presents itself as only a nāma which experiences visible object, there is also right concentration at that moment: sammā samādhi focuses on the object in the right way. When sammā-samādhi accompanies lokuttara citta, sammā-samādhi is also lokuttara and it focuses on nibbāna. Then sammā-samādhi is a factor of the supramundane eightfold Path (lokuttara magga).

Some people believe that in the development of vipassanā they should try to focus on particular nāmas and rūpas in order to know them as they are. If concentration accompanies a citta with desire for result it is wrong concentration. So long as one has not become a sotāpanna (the person who has attained the first stage of enlightenment) the inclination to wrong practice has not been eradicated. We may still be led by desire and then we are on the wrong way. When a nāma or rūpa appears through one of the six doors there can be mindfulness of it and then, at that moment, right understanding of that reality can be developed. Right understanding is accompanied by right concentration which has arisen because of the appropriate conditions and which performs its function without the need to think of focusing on a particular object. Mindfulness, right understanding and right concentration are realities which arise because of their own conditions, they are anattā. There is no self who can direct the arising of any citta or who can regulate the experiencing of a particular object. But the conditions for right mindfulness and right understanding can be cultivated; they are: studying the realities the Buddha taught and considering them when they appear in daily life.

In the *Gradual Sayings* (Book of the Fours, Chapter V, par1, Concentration) we read about four ways of developing concentration. As to the first way, the Buddha explained that this is the development of the four stages of jhāna which leads to 'happy living' in this life. As to the second kind, this is the concentration on 'consciousness of light' which is a meditation subject of samatha. This leads to 'knowledge and insight' which means in this context, according to the commentary (Manorathapūraṇī), clairvoyance.

As regards the third way of developing concentration, this leads, if developed and made much of, to 'mindfulness and well-awareness'. We read:

> Herein, monks, the feelings which arise in a monk are evident to him, the feelings which abide with him are evident to him, the feelings which come to an end in him are evident to him. The perceptions which arise in him. . .the trains of thought which arise in him, which abide with him,

> which come to an end in him are evident to him. This monks, is called 'the making-concentration-to-become which conduces to mindfulness and well-awareness'.

As regard the fourth way of developing concentration, this leads to the destruction of the 'āsavas' (defilements). We read:

> And what sort of making-concentration-to-become, if developed and made much of, conduces to the destruction of the āsavas?
>
> Herein a monk dwells observing the rise and fall in the five khandhas of grasping, thus: Such is rūpa, such is the arising of rūpa, such its vanishing. Such is feeling ...such is perception ...such are the activities ...Such is consciousness, such is the arising of consciousness, such the vanishing of consciousness. This, monks, is called 'the making-concentration-to-become which conduces to the destruction of the āsavas'. These are the four forms of it. Moreover, in this connection I thus spoke in 'The Chapter on the Goal' in (the sutta called) 'The Questions of Puṇṇaka':

```
By searching in the world things high and low,
He who has naught to stir him in the world,
Calm and unclouded, cheerful, freed of longing,
He has crossed over birth and old age, I say.
```

When there is right mindfulness of a nāma or rūpa which appears, without trying to focus on a particular object, there is also right concentration which arises at that moment because of the appropriate conditions and performs its function. When right understanding develops it penetrates the arising and ceasing of the five khandhas and eventually there will be the destruction of the āsavas at the attainment of arahatship.

7.1.1 Questions

1. Are ekaggatā and samādhi the same cetasika?
2. Can there be samādhi with akusala citta?
3. What is the difference between sammā-samādhi in samatha and sammā-samādhi in vipassanā?
4. If we try to concentrate on sound is that the way to know sound as it is?

8 Vitality and Attention

8.1 Vitality (jīvitindriya)

Jīvitindriya (life-faculty or vitality) and *manasikāra* (attention) are two other cetasikas among the seven universals which arise with every citta. As regards *jīvitindriya*,[1] this cetasika sustains the life of the citta and cetasikas it accompanies. According to the *Atthasālinī* (part IV, Chapter I, 123, 124)[2] the characteristic of jīvitindriya is "ceaseless watching", its function is to maintain the life of the accompanying dhammas, its manifestation the establishment of them, and the proximate cause are the dhammas which have to be sustained.

The function of jīvitindriya is to maintain the life of citta and its accompanying cetasikas. It keeps them going until they fall away. Since jīvitindriya arises and falls away together with the citta, it performs its function only for a very short while. Each moment of citta consists actually of three extremely short periods:

- the arising moment (uppāda khaṇa)
- the moment of its presence, or static moment (tiṭṭhi khaṇa)
- the dissolution moment (bhaṅga khaṇa)

Jīvitindriya arises with the citta at the arising moment and it maintains the life of citta and the accompanying cetasikas, but it cannot make them stay beyond the dissolution moment; then jīvitindriya has to fall away together with the citta and the accompanying cetasikas.

The Atthasālinī states concerning jīvitindriya:

> ...it watches over those states (the accompanying dhammas) only in the moment of (their and its) existence, as water over lotuses, etc. And although it watches over them, arisen as its own property, as a nurse over the infant, life goes on only by being bound up with these states (accompanying dhammas) that have gone on, as the pilot on the boat. Beyond the dissolution moment it does not go on, owing to the non-being both of itself and of the states which should have been kept going. At the dissolution moment it does not maintain them, owing to its own destruction, as the spent oil in the wick cannot maintain the flame of the lamp. Its effective power is as its duration.

Citta and cetasikas cannot arise without jīvitindriya which maintains their lives and jīvitindriya cannot arise without citta and the accompanying cetasikas. When, for example, seeing arises, jīvitindriya must accompany seeing. Seeing needs jīvitindriya in order to subsist during the very short period of its life. When seeing falls away jīvitindriya also falls away. Then another citta arises and this citta is accompanied by another jīvitindriya which sustains citta and the accompanying cetasikas during that very short moment of their existence. Jīvitindriya has to arise with every citta in order to vitalize citta and its accompanying cetasikas.

---

[1] Jīvitaṃ means "life", and indriya means "controlling faculty".

[2] See also Dhammasangaṇi par19.

The cetasika jīvitindriya which vitalizes the accompanying nāma-dhammas is nāma. There is also jīvitindriya which is rūpa.[3] Rūpa-jīvitindriya is a kind of rūpa produced by kamma and it maintains the life of the other rūpas it arises together with. Rūpas of the body arise and fall away in groups, some of which are produced by kamma, some by citta, some by nutrition and some by temperature. Jīvitindriya is part only of the groups or rūpa which are produced by kamma. It maintains the life of the rūpas it accompanies and then it falls away together with them.

We used to take life for something which lasts. We cling to life and we take it for 'mine' and 'self'. However, there is no physical life nor mental life which lasts. Life-faculty is saṅkhāra dhamma, conditioned dhamma, which does not stay and which is not self. The study of the reality of jīvitindriya can remind us that life lasts only for a moment and then falls away to be succeeded by a next moment.

8.2 Attention (manasikāra)

Manasikāra, attention, is another cetasika among the universals which arises with every citta.[4] The *Atthasālinī* (I, Part IV, Chapter 1, 133) which defines manasikāra in the same wording as the *Visuddhimagga* (XIV, 152) states concerning the cetasika which is manasikāra:

> ...It has the characteristic of driving associated states towards the object, the function of joining (yoking) associated states to the object, the manifestation of facing the object. It is included in the saṅkhārakkhandha, and should be regarded as the charioteer of associated states because it regulates the object.

The *Visuddhimagga* (XIV, 152) adds that the proximate cause of manasikāra is an object.

The cetasika manasikāra which can be translated as attention is the 'controller of the object' because it turns the citta towards the object. However, also at the moments we are, as we call it in conventional language, 'distracted' and we think that we are without attention, there is still manasikāra with the citta since it accompanies every citta. Also when there is moha-mūla-citta accompanied by uddhacca (restlessness), citta cognizes an object; manasikāra accompanies the citta and 'joins' citta and the other cetasikas to that object. Every citta needs manasikāra in order to cognize an object.

There is citta at this moment and thus there must also be manasikāra. Manasikāra is different from phassa which contacts the object so that citta can expe-

---

[3] See Visuddhimagga XIV, 59

[4] There are also two kinds of citta which are called manasikāra (Atthasālinī 133 and Visuddhimagga XIV, 152). One kind of citta which is manasikāra is the pañca-dvārāvajjana-citta (five-sense-door adverting-consciousness), the first citta of the sense-door process, which adverts to the object; it is called 'controller of the sense-door process'. The other kind of citta which is manasikāra is the mano-dvārāvajjana-citta (mind-door adverting-consciousness) which in the sense-door process fulfills the function of votthapana, determining, and which in the mind-door process adverts to the object through the mind-door. It is succeeded by the javana cittas and it is called 'controller of the javanas'.

rience it, and it is different from ekaggatā cetasika which focuses on one object. Manasikāra has its own task while it assists the citta in cognizing the object. Manasikāra has attention to whatever object presents itself through one of the six doors and it 'joins' citta and the accompanying cetasikas to that object.

Manasikāra is different according as it arises with different types of citta. When, for example, seeing arises, it is accompanied by manasikāra which joins seeing and the accompanying cetasikas to visible object. Seeing is vipāka and thus manasikāra is also vipāka. Shortly after the seeing there can be attention to the shape and form of something and then the object is not visible object but a concept. At that moment there is another type of citta accompanied by another manasikāra. At each moment manasikāra is different. When there is lobha-mūla-citta, akusala citta rooted in attachment, manasikāra which accompanies lobha-mūla-citta is also akusala. When there is kusala citta the manasikāra which accompanies the kusala citta is also kusala.

When manasikāra accompanies a citta which cultivates samatha, it 'joins' citta and the other cetasikas to the meditation subject, such as a corpse or the Buddha's virtues. When the citta is rūpāvacara kusala citta, the accompanying manasikāra is also rūpāvacara; it is different from manasikāra which is kāmāvacara (belonging to the sense sphere). Rūpāvacara citta experiences the meditation subject with absorption and the accompanying manasikāra 'joins' citta and the accompanying cetasikas to that object. The manasikāra which accompanies arūpāvacara citta is still more tranquil and more refined than the manasikāra which accompanies rūpāvacara citta. When manasikāra accompanies the citta which develops vipassanā, right understanding of nāma and rūpa, there is attention towards the nāma or rūpa which is the object of mindfulness at that moment; manasikāra assists the citta and joins it to that nāma or rūpa. When manasikāra accompanies lokuttara citta, manasikāra is also lokuttara and it joins citta and the accompanying cetasikas to the object which is nibbāna.

We are likely to have a concept of self which has attention to this or that object, but attention, manasikāra, is a *conditioned dhamma,* it is conditioned by the citta and the cetasikas it accompanies, it arises and falls away together with them. At each moment there is a different citta and thus also a different manasikāra.

The *seven universals* have each their own specific characteristic, function, manifestation and proximate cause and they have different qualities as they arise with cittas of different jātis and of different planes of consciousness. Summarizing the seven 'universals', they are:

- phassa (contact)
- vedanā (feeling)
- saññā (remembrance)
- cetanā (volition)
- ekaggatā (concentration or one-pointedness)
- jīvitindriya (life faculty)
- manasikāra (attention)

All the 'universals' arise with every citta and they share the same object with the citta. They are all of the same jāti as the citta they accompany and of the same plane of consciousness. In the planes of existence where there are both nāma and rūpa, cetasikas arise at the same 'base', vatthu, as the citta they accompany and thus, they may arise at the eye-base, ear-base nose-base, tongue-base, body-base or heart-base.

Cetasikas never arise by themselves, they always accompany citta and other cetasikas. Therefore, when we study cetasikas, we should also study the different cittas they accompany.

There are other cetasikas besides the 'universals' which can arise with the citta, but there have to be at least the seven 'universals' with every citta.

There are ten types of cittas which are accompanied only by the 'universals', not by other cetasikas. These are the 'five pairs' (dvi-pañcaviññāṇa) which are: seeing-consciousness, hearing-consciousness, smelling-consciousness, tasting-consciousness and body-consciousness. These cittas are ahetuka (rootless) vipākacittas which can be either kusala vipāka or akusala vipāka and therefore, they are "five pairs".

When seeing-consciousness arises, each of the 'universals' which accompanies it performs its own function. Phassa which accompanies seeing-consciousness is eye-contact (cakkhu-samphassa). It contacts visible object. When there is eye-contact there is the coinciding of eye-base, visible object and seeing-consciousness. Vedanā, which is in this case indifferent feeling, experiences the 'taste' of visible object. Saññā 'marks' and remembers visible object. Cetanā coordinates the tasks of the accompanying dhammas. Since seeing-consciousness is vipākacitta, cetanā merely coordinates, it does not 'will' kusala or akusala. Ekaggatā performs its function of focusing on visible object; it does not focus on any other object. Jīvitindriya sustains citta and the accompanying cetasikas until they fall away. Manasikāra 'drives' citta and the accompanying cetasikas towards visible object. Seeing-consciousness needs the accompanying 'universals' in order to cognize visible object; it could not arise and cognize its object without the assistance of the accompanying cetasikas.

As we have seen, only the dvi-pañcaviññāṇas (the five pairs of sense-cognitions) are not accompanied by other cetasikas besides the 'universals'. All the other cittas which arise in the sense-door process and in the mind-door process and also the paṭisandhi-citta, rebirth-consciousness, the bhavanga-citta, life-continuum, and the cuti-citta, dying-consciousness, are accompanied by other cetasikas besides the 'universals'.

The 'universals' have different qualities as they arise with different cittas. For example, when kusala citta arises all the accompanying cetasikas, the 'universals' included, are kusala as well. Vedanā, feeling, which accompanies kusala citta can be pleasant feeling or indifferent feeling. Cetanā, volition, which accompanies kusala citta has a double function: it coordinates the tasks of the accompanying dhammas and it 'wills' kusala. If it motivates wholesome deeds it is capable of producing the appropriate result when it is the right time for it. Thus, kusala cetanā is different from cetanā which accompanies vipākacitta.

When the citta is akusala, all the accompanying cetasikas are akusala as well. Vedanā which accompanies akusala citta can be pleasant feeling (in the case of lobha-mūla-citta), unpleasant feeling (in the case of dosa-mūla-citta), or indifferent feeling (in the case of lobha-mūla-citta and moha-mūla-citta). As regards cetanā which accompanies akusala citta, this has a double function: it coordinates the accompanying dhammas on the object and it 'wills' akusala. If it motivates unwholesome deeds it is capable of producing the appropriate result when it is the right time. Ekaggatā, concentration or one-pointedness, which accompanies akusala citta is different from ekaggatā which accompanies kusala citta. Thus we see that mental phenomena which arise together condition one another. If we have more understanding of the many different conditions for the phenomena which arise, it will help us to see them as elements, not as a person, a self.

8.2.1 Questions

1. Does manasikāra, attention, arise when we are sound asleep?
2. Can manasikāra be lokuttara?
3. Do nāma-jīvitindriya and rūpa-jīvitindriya have different functions?
4. Which types of citta are accompanied only by the seven 'universals' and not by other cetasikas?
5. Each of the 'universals' has its specific characteristic, function, manifestation and proximate cause. Why can each one of them still have different qualities at different moments?
6. Through how many doors can the 'universals' experience an object?
7. Can the 'universals' experience a concept?
8. When the citta is akusala citta, it is accompanied by akusala cetasikas. Are the accompanying 'universals' akusala as well?

PART II: The Particulars

9 Applied thinking and Sustained thinking

9.1 The Particulars (pakiṇṇakā)

Seven cetasikas, the *universals* (sabbacitta-sādhāranā), arise with every citta. Besides these seven cetasikas there are *six cetasikas*, the *particulars* (pakiṇṇakā), which accompany *cittas of the four jātis but not every citta.* Both the "universals" and the "particulars" are of the same jāti as the citta they accompany. Thus, they can be kusala, akusala, vipāka or kiriya. In addition to the "universals" and the "particulars" there are also akusala cetasikas which arise only with akusala cittas and sobhana (beautiful) cetasikas which arise only with sobhana cittas.

9.2 Applied thinking (vitakka)

Vitakka, applied thinking or initial thinking, and *vicāra,* sustained thinking or sustained application, are two cetasikas among the "particulars"[1] . We believe that we know what thinking is. We think of what we have seen, heard, smelt, tasted or experienced through the bodysense, or we think of ideas and concepts. We build up long stories of what we experienced and we cling to thinking. In order to know the realities of vitakka and vicāra we should not be misled by the conventional term "thinking". Through the study of the Abhidhamma and the commentaries we can acquire a more precise knowledge of realities.

The *Visuddhimagga* (IV, 88) defines vitakka as follows:

> ...Herein, applied thinking (vitakkama) is applied thought (vitakka); hitting upon, is what is meant. It has the characteristic of directing the mind onto an object (mounting the mind on its object). Its function is to strike at and thresh—for the meditator[2] is said, in virtue of it, to have the object touched and struck at by applied thought. It is manifested as the leading of the mind onto an object...

The *Atthasālinī* (Book I, Part IV, Chapter I, 114) gives a similar definition. This commentary uses a simile of someone who wants to "ascend" the king's palace and depends on a relative or friend dear to the king to achieve this. In the same way the citta which is accompanied by vitakka depends on the latter in order to "ascend" to the object, to be directed to the object. Vitakka leads the citta to the object so that citta can cognize it.

In order to know more about vitakka, we should learn which cittas are accompanied by vitakka. We may think that vitakka accompanies only cittas arising in a mind-door process, but this is not so. Vitakka arises in sense-door processes as well as in mind-door processes. Vitakka accompanies all kāmāvacara cittas (cittas of the sense-sphere), except the dvi-pañcaviññāṇas (the five pairs which are seeing, hearing, etc.).

---

[1] See also Dhammasangaṇi par7 and 8.

[2] The Visuddhimagga deals with vitakka in the section on samatha. The meditator is someone who cultivates samatha.

We may wonder why vitakka does not arise with the dvi-pañcaviññāṇas. When seeing arises it performs the function of seeing, it sees visible object and it does not need vitakka in order to see. The other cittas of the eye-door process need vitakka in order to experience visible object, they do not see. The eye-door adverting-consciousness does not see, it adverts to visible object and it needs vitakka which directs it to visible object. It is the same with the other cittas of that process. As regards the other sense-door processes, the dvi-pañcaviññāṇas do not need vitakka in order to experience the object, but all the other cittas of these processes have to be accompanied by vitakka. All cittas of the mind-door process are accompanied by vitakka.

Vitakka accompanies not only cittas arising in processes, it also accompanies cittas which do not arise in processes: the paṭisandhi-citta (rebirth-consciousness), the bhavanga-citta (life-continuum) and the cuti-citta (dying-consciousness).

When vitakka accompanies kusala citta, vitakka is also kusala, and when it accompanies akusala citta it is also akusala. When we are not applying ourselves to kusala, we act, speak or think with akusala citta and thus the accompanying vitakka is also akusala. It is not often that we are performing acts of generosity, that we apply ourselves to sīla (good moral conduct) or to bhāvanā (mental development). There are many more akusala cittas in our life than kusala cittas and thus akusala vitakka is bound to arise very often. When we are attached to a pleasant object there is akusala vitakka which "touches" that object. Or when there is even a slight feeling of annoyance when things are not the way we want them to be, there is sure to be dosa-mūla-citta and this is accompanied by akusala vitakka which performs its function.

There are three kinds of *akusala vitakka* which are mentioned in particular in the suttas. They are

- thought of sense-pleasures (kāma-vitakka)
- thought of malevolence (vyāpāda-vitakka)
- thought of harming (vihiṁsā-vitakka)

We read in the "Discourse on the Twofold Thought" (Middle Length Sayings I, no. 19) that the Buddha, while he was still a Bodhisatta, considered both akusala vitakka and kusala vitakka. We read that when the thought of sense-pleasures arose, he comprehended thus:

> . . . "This thought of sense-pleasures has arisen in me, but it conduces to self-hurt and it conduces to the hurt of others and it conduces to the hurt of both, it is destructive of intuitive wisdom, associated with distress, not conducive to nibbāna." But while I was reflecting, "It conduces to self-hurt", it subsided; and while I was reflecting, "It conduces to the hurt of others", it subsided; and while I was reflecting, "It is destructive of intuitive wisdom, it is associated with distress, it is not conducive to nibbāna", it subsided. So I, monks, kept on getting rid of the thought of sense-pleasures as it constantly arose, I kept on driving it out, I kept on making an end of it. . .

The same is said about the thought of malevolence and the thought of harming. We then read:

> ...Monks, according to whatever a monk ponders and reflects on much, his mind in consequence gets a bias that way. Monks, if a monk ponder and reflect much on thought of sense-pleasures he ejects thought of renunciation; if he makes much of the thought of sense-pleasures, his mind inclines to the thought of sense-pleasures. Monks, if a monk ponder and reflect much on the thought of malevolence...he ejects the thought of non-malevolence... his mind inclines to the thought of malevolence. Monks, if a monk ponder and reflect much on the thought of harming, he ejects the thought of non-harming; if he makes much of the thought of harming, his mind inclines to the thought of harming...

It is useful to know on what we reflect most of the time. We have a bias towards akusala, since we have accumulated so much akusala. We are more inclined to unwholesome thoughts and therefore it is difficult to have wholesome thoughts. When there is a pleasant object the thought of sense-pleasures arises almost immediately. When there is an unpleasant object there is bound to be a thought of annoyance or malice, or there can even be a thought of harming. When someone else receives praise and honour, we may be inclined to jealousy and then there is akusala vitakka accompanying the dosa-mūla-citta with jealousy. It is difficult to cultivate kusala vitakka but the Buddha showed that it can be done. Further on in the sutta we read about three kinds of kusala vitakka which are the opposites of the three kinds of akusala vitakka. They are:

- the thought of renunciation (nekkhamma)
- the thought of non-malevolence (avyāpāda)
- the thought of non-harming (avihiṁsa)

The Bodhisatta realized that these lead neither to self-hurt, nor to the hurt of others, nor to the hurt of both, but that they are for "growth in intuitive wisdom", that they are "not associated with distress", "conducive to nibbāna". We read about kusala vitakka:

> ...Monks, if a monk ponder and reflect much on the thought of renunciation he ejects the thought of sense-pleasures; if he makes much of the thought of renunciation, his mind inclines to the thought of renunciation. Monks, if a monk ponder and reflect much on the thought of non-malevolence he ejects the thought of malevolence... Monks, if a monk ponder and reflect much on the thought of non-harming, he ejects the thought of harming; if he makes much of the thought of non-harming his mind inclines to the thought of non-harming...

One may wonder whether nekkhamma, renunciation, is the same as retirement from worldly life and whether it therefore pertains in particular to monks. Although a monk's life should be a life of contentment with little, he may not be cultivating nekkhamma. Whoever has not eradicated attachment to sense objects has still conditions for "thought of sense-pleasures", no matter whether he is a monk or a layman. When a monk receives delicious almsfood, is attachment not likely to arise?

There are many degrees of nekkhamma and not only monks should cultivate it, but laypeople as well. Actually, *all kusala dhammas are nekkhamma*[3]. When we perform dāna, observe sīla or apply ourselves to mental development, we are at such moments not absorbed in sense-pleasures, there is renunciation. We can experience that when there is loving kindness or compassion we do not think of ourselves; thus, there is a degree of detachment. If we see the disadvantages of being selfish, of thinking of our own pleasure and comfort, there are more conditions for being attentive to others. Detachment from the concept of self is still a higher degree of renunciation which can be achieved through the development of right understanding of realities. Both monks and laypeople should cultivate this kind of renunciation. When the concept of self has been eradicated, stinginess has been eradicated as well, and thus, there are more conditions for generosity. Moreover, sīla will be purer, there will be no more conditions for transgressing the five precepts.

9.3 Sustained Thinking (vicāra)

Vicāra can be translated as sustained thinking, discursive thinking or sustained application. We read in the *Visuddhimagga* (IV, 88) the following definition:

> ...Sustained thinking (vicaraṇa) is sustained thought (vicāra); continued sustenance (anusañcaraṇa), is what is meant. It has the characteristic of continued pressure on (occupation with) the object. Its function is to keep conascent (mental) states (occupied) with that. It is manifested as keeping consciousness anchored (on that object).

The *Atthasālinī* (Book One, Part IV, Chapter I, 114) defines vicāra in a similar way.

Vicāra is not the same reality as vitakka. Vitakka directs the citta to the object and vicāra keeps the citta occupied with the object, "anchored" on it. However, we should remember that both vitakka and vicāra perform their functions only for the duration of one citta and then fall away immediately, together with the citta. Both the *Visuddhimagga* and the *Atthasālinī* use similes in order to explain the difference between vitakka and vicāra. Vitakka is gross and vicāra is more subtle. We read in the *Visuddhimagga* (IV, 89):

> ...Applied thought (vitakka) is the first compact of the mind in the sense that it is both gross and inceptive, like the striking of a bell. Sustained thought (vicāra) is the act of keeping the mind anchored, in the sense that it is subtle with the individual essence of continued pressure, like the ringing of the bell...

Several more similes are used in order to explain the difference between vitakka and vicāra. Vitakka is like the bird's spreading out its wings when about to soar into the air, and vicāra is quiet, like the bird's planing with outspread wings. When we read this simile we may think that vitakka has to come first and that then vicāra follows. However, this simile is used in order to show that vitakka and vicāra have different characteristics.

---

[3] Vibhaṅga, Book of Analysis, 3, Analysis of the Elements, par182.

Another simile the *Visuddhimagga* and the *Atthasālinī* use is the following : vitakka is like the bee's diving towards a lotus and vicāra is like the bee's gyrating around the lotus after it has dived towards it.

Like vitakka, vicāra arises with all kāmāvacara cittas, cittas of the sense-sphere, except the dvi-pañcaviññāṇas (the sense-cognitions of seeing, hearing, etc.). When seeing-consciousness, for example, arises, it does not need vitakka nor does it need vicāra, because seeing-consciousness just sees. The other cittas of the eye-door process need vitakka which directs them to visible object and they need vicāra which keeps them occupied with visible object. It is the same in the case of the other sense-door processes. Vitakka and vicāra arise in sense-door processes as well as in mind-door processes, and they also accompany cittas which do not arise in processes[4] .

Vitakka and vicāra are conditioned dhammas, *saṅkhāra dhammas,* which arise and fall away together with the citta they accompany. They perform their functions only during an extremely short moment, namely the duration of one citta. Their object can be a paramattha dhamma or a concept. We may wonder how vitakka and vicāra perform their functions while we are engaged with the thinking of "stories". It seems that thinking can last for a while, but in reality there are many cittas accompanied by vitakka and vicāra and other cetasikas, which arise and fall away, succeeding one another. It is because of saññā, remembrance, that we can remember the previous thought and that different thoughts can be connected.

Both *vitakka* and *vicāra* are *jhāna-factors* which can be developed in samatha, tranquil meditation. The jhāna-factors are sobhana (beautiful) cetasikas which are developed in order to inhibit the "hindrances", defilements which obstruct the attainment of jhāna, absorption. Vitakka which is developed in samatha "thinks" of the meditation subject and it inhibits the hindrances which are *sloth* and *torpor* (thīna and middha). The *Visuddhimagga* states in the definition of vitakka (IV, 88) :

"...for the meditator is said, in virtue of it, to have the object struck at by applied thought, threshed by applied thought..."

Thus, in samatha vitakka "touches" the meditation subject again and again until calm has developed to the degree that jhāna can be attained.

As regards the jhāna-factor vicāra which is developed in samatha, this keeps the citta "anchored on" the meditation subject and inhibits the hindrance which is *doubt.* As we have seen, in the case of kāmāvacara cittas, both vitakka and vicāra arise together when they accompany the citta. In the case of jhānacittas however, a distinction has to be made. In the first stage of jhāna both vitakka and vicāra are needed in order to experience the meditation subject with absorption. Thus, both vitakka and vicāra accompany the rūpāvacara kusala citta, the rūpāvacara vipākacitta and the rūpāvacara kiriyacitta of the first stage of jhāna[5]. In the second stage of jhāna one has acquired more skill in jhāna and vitakka is no longer needed

---

[4] For details about the cittas accompanied by vitakka and vicāra, see par Appendix 3.

[5] Abhidhamma in Daily Life, Chapter 22. The rūpāvacara vipākacitta is the result of the rūpāvacara kusala citta. The rūpāvacara kiriyacitta is the citta of the arahat who attains jhāna.

in order to experience the meditation subject with absorption. At that stage vitakka has been abandoned, but vicāra still arises. In the subsequent stage of jhāna, which is more tranquil and more refined, also vicāra has been abandoned; it is no longer needed in order to experience the meditation subject with absorption. Some people have abandoned both vitakka and vicāra in the second stage of jhāna and thus for them there are only four stages of rūpa-jhāna instead of five. That is why the stages of jhāna can be counted in accordance with the *four-fold system* or the *five-fold system.*

When we consider the jhāna-factors vitakka and vicāra we may be able to understand that vitakka is more gross than vicāra. Vitakka is needed in the first stage of jhāna but it is abandoned in the second stage of jhāna which is more tranquil and more refined. Vicāra which is more subtle than vitakka still accompanies the jhānacitta of the second stage of jhāna. The person who has accumulated conditions to attain jhāna must be able to distinguish between different jhāna-factors such as vitakka and vicāra and this is most intricate. This shows us how difficult it is to develop calm to the degree of jhāna.

The more we study the realities which are taught in the Abhidhamma, the more we see that there are many different phenomena which each have their own characteristic. They appear one at a time, but when we try to name them there is thinking of a concept instead of mindfulness of a characteristic. Sometimes a reality which thinks may appear and then we may doubt whether it is vitakka or vicāra. It is useless to try to find out which reality appears because at such a moment there is no awareness. Thinking has a characteristic which can be realized when it appears and then there is no need to name it vitakka or vicāra.

There is yet another aspect of vitakka. Vitakka is one of the *factors of the eightfold Path* and as such it is called: *sammā-saṅkappa*, right thinking. Sammā-saṅkappa has to arise together with sammā-diṭṭhi, right understanding, in order to be a factor of the eightfold Path[6]. When there is right understanding of a nāma or rūpa which appears, there are both vitakka and vicāra accompanying the citta, but vicāra is not a factor of the eightfold Path. Sammā-saṅkappa has its specific function as path-factor. Sammā-saṅkappa "touches" the nāma or rūpa which appears so that sammā-diṭṭhi can investigate its characteristic in order to understand it as it is. Thus, sammā-diṭṭhi needs the assistance of sammā-saṅkappa

---

[6] The factors of the eightfold Path are: right understanding (see Chapter 34), right thinking, right speech, right action and right livelihood (for the last three see Chapter 32), right effort (see Chapter 10), right mindfulness (see Chapter 26) and right concentration (see Chapter 6). These factors perform each their specific function so that the goal can be attained: the eradication of defilements. The reader will also come across the terms insight or vipassanā and satipaṭṭhāna. The development of vipassanā, the development of satipaṭṭhāna or the development of the eightfold Path, it all amounts to the development of right understanding of nāma and rūpa, of ultimate realities. When a reality appears through one of the six doors there can be a moment of investigation of its characteristic: it can be seen as a nāma or a rūpa, not a person, not a thing. That is the beginning of understanding of its true nature of non-self. At such a moment there is also mindfulness, non-forgetfulness of the reality appearing at the present moment.

in order to develop. In the beginning, when paññā has not been developed, there cannot yet be clear understanding of the difference between the characteristic of nāma and of rūpa. When, for example, sound appears, there is also hearing, the reality which experiences sound, but it is difficult to know the difference between the characteristic of sound and the characteristic of hearing, between rūpa and nāma. Only one reality at a time can be object of mindfulness and when they seem to "appear" together it is evident that there is not right mindfulness. Only when there is right mindfulness of one reality at a time right understanding can develop. At that moment sammā-saṅkappa performs its function of "touching" the object of mindfulness.

When there is sammā-saṅkappa there is no akusala vitakka, wrong thinking; there is no "thought of sense-pleasures", no "thought of malice", no "thought of harming". When the eightfold Path is being developed the four noble Truths will be known and "unprofitable thoughts" will eventually be eradicated. We read in the "Kindred Sayings" (V, Mahā-vagga, Book XII, Chapter I, par7, thoughts) that the Buddha, while he was at Sāvatthī, said to the monks:

> Monks, think not evil, unprofitable thoughts, such as: thoughts of lust, thoughts of hatred, thoughts of delusion. Why do I say so?
>
> Because, monks, these thoughts are not concerned with profit, they are not the rudiments of the holy life, they conduce not to revulsion, to dispassion, to cessation, to tranquillity, to full understanding, to the perfect wisdom, they conduce not to nibbāna.
>
> When you do think, monks, you should think thus: This is dukkha. This is the arising of dukkha. This is the ceasing of dukkha. This is the practice that leads to the ceasing of dukkha. Why do I say this?
>
> Because, monks, these thoughts are concerned with profit, they are rudiments of the holy life...they conduce to nibbāna.
>
> Wherefore an effort must be made to realize: This is dukkha. This is the arising of dukkha. This is the ceasing of dukkha. This is the practice that leads to the ceasing of dukkha.

The "thinking" referred to in this sutta is not thinking about the four noble Truths. It refers to the direct realization of the four noble Truths which are: dukkha, which is suffering, its origin, which is craving, its cessation, which is nibbāna, and the way leading to its cessation, which is the eightfold Path. When there is right mindfulness of a reality which appears, sammā-saṅkappa "touches" it and then paññā can investigate its characteristic in order to know it as it is. This is the way to eventually realize the four noble Truths. At the moment of enlightenment the four noble Truths are penetrated. When the citta is lokuttara citta, sammā-saṅkappa is also lokuttara. It "touches" nibbāna.

9.3.1 Questions

1. Through how many doors can vitakka and vicāra experience an object?
2. Can vitakka and vicāra think of paramattha dhammas?
3. What is the difference between vitakka and vicāra?

4. Do vitakka and vicāra always arise together?
5. Can vitakka and vicāra arise in a sense-door process?
6. Which types of kāmāvacara cittas (cittas of the sense-sphere) are not accompanied by vitakka and vicāra?
7. In which stages of jhāna does vitakka arise?
8. Why is vitakka abandoned in the higher stages of jhāna?
9. In which stages of jhāna does vicāra arise?
10. Both vitakka and vicāra accompany the citta which is mindful of nāma and rūpa. Are both vitakka and vicāra factors of the eightfold Path?

10 Determination and Energy

10.1 Determination (adhimokkha)

Adhimokkha, determination or resolution, is another cetasika among the six "particulars" which arises with cittas of the four jātis but not with every citta.

The *Visuddhimagga* (XIV, 151) gives the following definition of adhimokkha:

The act of resolving is resolution. It has the characteristic of conviction. Its function is not to grope. It is manifested as decisiveness. Its proximate cause is a thing to be convinced about. It should be regarded as like a boundary-post owing to its immovableness with regard to the object.

The "Paramattha Mañjūsā" (489), the commentary to the *Visuddhimagga*, states that:

> " the act of resolving should be understood as the act of being convinced about an object".

The *Atthasālinī* (I, Part IV, Chapter I, 133) gives a definition similar to the one of the *Visuddhimagga*[1]

Adhimokkha is not the same as what we usually mean by the words "determination" and "decision" in conventional language. In order to understand the characteristic of adhimokkha we should know which types of citta it accompanies.

Since adhimokkha is one of the "particulars" it accompanies cittas of the four jātis and thus it can be kusala, akusala, vipāka or kiriya. As we have seen, the "particulars" do not arise with every citta. Adhimokkha does not accompany the dvi-pañcaviññāṇas (sense-cognitions) which are accompanied only by the "universals", not by other types of cetasikas. Seeing-consciousness, for example, arises at the eye-base and sees visible object. It does not need, apart from the seven "universals", adhimokkha or any other cetasika in order to see visible object.

Adhimokkha does not arise either with the type of moha-mūla-citta (citta rooted in ignorance) which is *accompanied by doubt (vicikicchā).* When there is doubt there cannot be at the same time the cetasika adhimokkha which "does not grope" and is "convinced" about the object.

Adhimokkha accompanies all cittas other than the afore-mentioned cittas. It arises in the sense-door process as well as in the mind-door process. Adhimokkha is one among the cetasikas which assist citta in cognizing its object. Adhimokkha also accompanies the cittas which do not arise in a process: the paṭisandhi-citta, the bhavanga-citta and the cuti-citta. It is "convinced" about the object these cittas experience.

---

[1] The Dhammasangaṇi does not mention adhimokkha in its list of dhammas, but it adds: "or whatever other factors there are" (par1). The Atthasālinī and the Visuddhimagga classify adhimokkha among the nine "whatsoevers" (ye vā panaka). Manasikāra is also classified among the "whatsoevers". Manasikāra and adhimokkha are mentioned in the "Discourse on the Uninterrupted" (Middle Length Sayings III, no. 111). See Abhidhamma Studies by Ven. Nyanaponika, in Chapter 4, p. 49, and in his Appendix. B.P.S. Kandy, 1976.

When we hear the word "decision" or "determination", we usually associate this word with a decision we have to consider carefully. We may not have expected adhimokkha to arise in a sense-door process, but, as we have seen, it arises in sense-door processes as well as in mind-door processes and it assists the citta in cognizing the object.

Adhimokkha which accompanies akusala citta is determination which is akusala. When one, for example, speaks harshly or hits someone else, there is akusala adhimokkha which is convinced about the object of aversion. Adhimokkha which accompanies kusala citta is determination which is kusala. When one, for example, decides with kusala citta to study the Dhamma, kusala adhimokkha accompanies the kusala citta. However, at such a moment there are also many other wholesome cetasikas accompanying the kusala citta and adhimokkha is only one of them. It is difficult to know exactly what adhimokkha is. There is, for example, kusala cetanā which "wills" kusala, there is non-attachment, alobha, and there are many other cetasikas which each have their own task in assisting the citta to perform its function. They all take part in " deciding" to study the Dhamma.

When one develops calm there is adhimokkha which is determined, sure about the object, which is in this case an object of samatha. When jhāna is attained adhimokkha accompanies the jhāna-citta and it performs its function of being determined as to the object of absorption.

When one develops right understanding of nāma and rūpa, there is adhimokkha accompanying the kusala citta. We may believe that *we* can decide to make sati arise, but there is *no self* who can decide this. When there are the appropriate conditions for sati and paññā they arise and then there is also adhimokkha which performs its function while it accompanies the kusala citta. When one begins to develop right understanding of nāma and rūpa, there will be doubt as to their different characteristics. When there is doubt adhimokkha does not arise. When there is right mindfulness of the nāma or rūpa which appears, adhimokkha performs its function of being "convinced", sure about the object.

Adhimokkha which accompanies lokuttara citta is "convinced", sure about the object which is nibbāna.

Adhimokkha is not self; it is saṅkhāra dhamma, a conditioned dhamma which arises and falls away with the citta it accompanies. It performs its function only while it is accompanying the citta and then it falls away together with the citta. If the next citta is accompanied by adhimokkha it is another adhimokkha and this falls away again.

Since adhimokkha arises with all cittas except the ten pañca-viññāṇas and the type of moha-mūla-citta which is accompanied by doubt, it arises with seventy-eight cittas in all[2].

[2] When cittas are counted as 89. Cittas can be counted as 89 or 121. When they are counted as 121 the lokuttara jhānacittas accompanied by jhāna-factors of the five stages of jhāna are included.

10.2 Energy (viriya)

Viriya, energy or effort, is another cetasika among the "particulars" which arises with cittas of the four jātis but not with every citta. The *Visuddhimagga* (XIV, 137) states concerning viriya:

Energy (viriya) is the state of one who is vigorous (vīra). Its characteristic is marshalling (driving). Its function is to consolidate conascent states (the accompanying citta and cetasikas). It is manifested as non-collapse. Because of the words "Bestirred, he strives wisely" (*Gradual Sayings* II, 115), its proximate cause is a sense of urgency; or its proximate cause is grounds for the initiation of energy. When rightly initiated, it should be regarded as the root of all attainments.

Viriya which is the root of all attainments is right effort, viriya accompanying kusala citta. Since viriya accompanies cittas of the four jātis, there is also akusala viriya, viriya accompanying vipākacitta and viriya accompanying kiriyacitta.

The *Atthasālinī* (I, Part IV, Chapter I, 120,121) gives a definition of viriya which is similar to the one given by the *Visuddhimagga*. Apart from this definition it gives first another one and here it deals with viriya under the aspect of "controlling faculty" or *indriya*. The Pāli term "indriya" means "governing or ruling principle". When kusala viriya has been developed it becomes a "controlling faculty". The controlling faculty of viriya "controls" or inhibits laziness, a defilement opposed to energy[3]. We read in the *Atthasālinī*:

> From its overcoming idleness it is a controlling faculty in the sense of predominance . . . Its characteristic is strengthening, and grasp or support. As an old house stands when strengthened by new pillars, so the aspirant (meditator), when strengthened by energy, does not fall off or deteriorate as to moral states. Thus should the characteristic of strengthening be understood. . .

The *Atthasālinī* then uses a simile of a small army which, if it goes to battle, might be repulsed. However, when they are supported by a strong reinforcement sent by the king, they can defeat the hostile army. We read:

> . . . thus energy does not allow associated states to recede, to retreat; it uplifts, supports them. Hence it has been said that energy has the characteristic of supporting.

The word "energy" as it is used in conventional language does not render the precise meaning of viriya. When we for example say that we are full of energy, what do we mean? Energy for what? Is it energy accompanying akusala citta or energy accompanying kusala citta? Besides, there are also vipākacittas and kiriyacittas which are accompanied by viriya. We are inclined to take energy for self, but energy is saṅkhāra dhamma, a conditioned dhamma. Energy is conditioned by the

---

[3] See Dhammasangaṇi par13, and for its explanation: Atthasālinī I, Part IV, Chapter 2, 146. There are five indriyas which should be developed together. They are the "spiritual faculties" which are the following wholesome qualities: saddhā (confidence), viriya, sati, samādhi (concentration) and paññā. These faculties control or overcome the defilements which are their opposites. When indriyas have been developed to the degree that they are "unshakable", they are "powers" or "strengths", balas. Powers cannot be shaken by the defilements which are their opposites.

citta and the other cetasikas it accompanies and thus there is a different kind of energy with different cittas. In order to have more understanding about viriya we should study which types of cittas it accompanies.

Viriya accompanies all akusala cittas and all sobhana cittas[4] (including jhānacittas and lokuttara cittas), but it does not arise with all vipākacittas and with all kiriyacittas. Viriya does not accompany the dvi-pañca-viññāṇas, the sense-cognitions. Seeing or hearing do not need viriya in order to experience their objects. The mind-door adverting-consciousness, *mano-dvārāvajjana-citta* and the *hasituppāda-citta* which causes smiling in the case of arahats are the only ahetuka cittas (rootless cittas) which are accompanied by viriya[5].

We read in the *Visuddhimagga* that the *function of viriya* is *to consolidate conascent states.* Viriya strengthens, supports the citta and the other cetasikas it accompanies so that they can carry out their work and do not "collapse".

Viriya accompanies every kusala citta and it supports the citta and accompanying cetasikas so that they can carry out their work in a wholesome way. When there is loving kindness, it is strengthened and supported by kusala viriya. If there were no viriya accompanying the kusala citta, no kusala could be performed. Also when the citta is akusala citta, viriya accompanies the citta and the cetasikas so that they can carry out their work in the unwholesome way. Viriya accompanies every akusala citta. When there is anger, dosa, it is strengthened and supported by viriya. Viriya which accompanies akusala citta is wrong effort and viriya which accompanies kusala citta is right effort.

Kusala viriya can be energy for dāna, for sīla, for samatha or for vipassanā. It depends on conditions which type of kusala arises at a particular moment. If one wants, for example, to subdue defilements through the development of calm and one knows how to develop calm, there is energy and perseverance with the development of calm. If one's goal is knowing realities as they are there are conditions for energy for vipassanā. This kind of energy or effort arises together with the citta which is mindful of a nāma or rūpa appearing now, at this moment. Right effort arises because of its own conditions; there is no self who can exert himself. When we have a notion of self who has to make an effort to be aware, there is wrong effort instead of right effort. Right effort is a conditioned dhamma, saṅkhāra dhamma, which arises because of its own conditions. It does not last, it falls away immediately with the citta it accompanies and then wrong effort may arise.

As we read in the definition of the *Visuddhimagga*, the proximate cause of viriya is "a sense of urgency or grounds for the initiation of energy". Birth, old age and death can remind us of the urgency to develop right understanding which eventually will lead to freedom from the cycle of birth and death. When we are "urged" to be

---

[4] Sobhana cittas, beautiful cittas, are cittas accompanied by sobhana cetasikas. They include not only kusala cittas but also vipākacittas accompanied by sobhana cetasikas and kiriyacittas (of the arahat) accompanied by sobhana cetasikas. The sobhana cittas of the sense-sphere, kāmāvacara sobhana cittas, are: mahā-kusala cittas, mahā-vipākacittas and mahā-kiriyacittas. "Mahā" means: "great". Sobhana cittas also include jhānacittas and lokuttara cittas.

[5] For details see Appendix 4.

mindful of realities, there is no self who makes an effort to be mindful. Right effort which is a reality arising because of its own conditions strengthens and supports the citta with mindfulness. There is energy, courage and perseverance to develop the eightfold Path since this is the only way leading to the end of dukkha.

The *Visuddhimagga* and the *Atthasālinī*, when they mention that the proximate cause of viriya is a sense of urgency, quote the words, "bestirred, he strives wisely", from a sutta of the *Gradual Sayings* (Book of the Fours, Chapter XII, par3, The Goad). In this sutta we read about four kinds of horses. One horse is already stirred to activity when he sees the shadow of the goadstick, whereas another one is not stirred by that, but is only stirred when his coat is pricked by the goad. Another one is stirred only when his flesh is pierced by the goad. We read about the fourth kind of horse:

Once more, monks, we may have a goodly thorough-bred steed, which is stirred, feels agitation neither at the sight of the goadstick nor when his coat is pricked, nor yet when his flesh is pierced with the goadstick; but when he is pierced to the very bone he is stirred...

We then read about four kinds of people who are compared to these horses:

> In this case, monks, here we may have a certain goodly thorough-bred man who hears it said that in such and such a village or township is a woman or a man afflicted or dead. Thereat he is stirred, he feels agitation. Thus agitated he strictly applies himself. Thus applied he both realizes in his own person the supreme truth, and sees it by penetrating it with wisdom...
>
> Again, monks, here we may have a goodly thoroughbred man who does not hear it said that in such or such a village or township is a woman or a man afflicted or dead, but with his own eyes sees it. Thereupon he is stirred...
>
> Then again, monks, here we may have a certain goodly thorough-bred man who does not hear it said...nor yet with his own eyes sees a woman or man afflicted or dead, but his own kinsman or blood-relation is afflicted or dead. Thereupon he is stirred...
>
> Once more, monks, here we may have a goodly thoroughbred man who neither hears it said...nor yet with his own eyes sees... nor is his own kinsman or blood-relation afflicted or dead, but he himself is stricken with painful bodily feelings, grievous, sharp, racking, distracting, discomforting, that drain the life away. Thereat he is stirred, he feels agitation. Being so stirred he strictly applies himself. Thus applied he both realizes with his own person the supreme truth and sees it by penetrating it with wisdom...

Sickness, old age and death are realities of daily life which can remind us of the urgency to develop right understanding, they are like a "goadstick" which can "stir" us. They are the proximate cause of right effort, which is energy for mindfulness of the reality appearing at the present moment.

Viriya is the "root of all attainments", as we read in the definition by the *Visuddhimagga*. Right effort is an *indriya*, controlling faculty, which has to be developed together with the other indriyas for the attainment of jhāna and the attainment of enlightenment. As the *Atthasālinī* states, viriya is the indriya which "controls" or inhibits laziness. Laziness is an obstruction to jhāna and to enlightenment. Right effort can also be seen under the aspect of *path-factor* and as such it is called *sammā-vāyāma of the eightfold Path.* Right effort has to accompany right understanding, sammā-diṭṭhi, of the eightfold Path in order to be a path-factor. Right effort of the eightfold Path develops through mahā-satipaṭṭhāna, the "four applications of mindfulness". When there is mindfulness of the reality which appears at the present moment there is also right effort.

Viriya is one of the *factors of enlightenment, bojjhangas.* The factors of enlightenment are: mindfulness (sati), investigation of the Dhamma (dhammavicaya, which is paññā), viriya, enthusiasm (pīti), calm (passaddhi), concentration (samādhi) and equanimity (upekkhā). When the enlightenment factors have been developed they lead to the realization of the four noble Truths. The enlightenment factors reach completion through the development of mahā-satipaṭṭhāna[6].

Thus we see that there are different aspects to right effort. We read in the scriptures about " four right endeavours" and these are aspects of right effort. We read for example in the *Middle Length Sayings* (III, 141, the Analysis of the Truths) that Sāriputta explained to the monks the four noble Truths. He spoke about dukkha, its origination, its cessation and the way leading to its cessation , the eightfold Path. He explained about right effort, one of the factors of the eightfold Path, and he pointed out that there are four right endeavours:

> And what, your reverences, is right endeavour? As to this, your reverences, a monk generates desire, endeavours, stirs up energy, exerts his mind and strives for the non-arising of evil unskilled states that have not arisen. . . for the getting rid of evil unskilled states that have arisen. . . for the arising of skilled states that have not arisen. . . for the maintenance, preservation, increase, maturity, development and completion of skilled states that have arisen. This, your reverences, is called right endeavour.

When there is mindfulness of visible object which appears now, seeing which appears now, sound which appears now, hearing which appears now, or any other reality which appears now, right understanding of the eightfold Path is being developed. This is the most effective way to avoid akusala, to overcome it, to make kusala arise and to maintain kusala and bring it to perfection. At the moment of right mindfulness right effort performs its task of strengthening the kusala citta so that there is perseverance with the development of the eightfold Path.

10.2.1 Questions

1. Which cittas are not accompanied by adhimokkha?
2. Can adhimokkha arise in a sense-door process?
3. Can viriya be akusala?

---

[6] Kindred Sayings V, Mahā-vagga, Kindred Sayings on the Limbs of Wisdom, Chapter I, par6.

4. Viriya is saṅkhāra dhamma. Why did the Buddha exhort people to strive for wisdom although there is no self who can put forth energy?
5. What is right effort of the eightfold Path?
6. Which are the proximate causes for right effort?
7. How can right effort of the eightfold Path be developed?
8. At which moment is right effort of the eightfold Path developed?
9. What is the object which right effort of the eightfold Path experiences?

11 Right Effort of the eightfold Path

As we have seen in chapter 9, there are several aspects to kusala viriya, right effort. It is a *factor of the eightfold Path* when it accompanies right understanding and right mindfulness of the eightfold Path and as such it is called *sammā-vāyāma*. This type of effort or energy is not energy for mindfulness in the future, but energy for mindfulness right now. When there is right mindfulness of any characteristic which appears right now, there is also right effort accompanying the citta at that moment.

We may find that mindfulness does not arise very often. It seems that we lack a true "sense of urgency", which is according to the *Atthasālinī* and the *Visuddhimagga* the proximate cause of right effort.

The *Visuddhimagga* (IV, 63) explains how there can be a greater sense of urgency and how the mind should be encouraged. We read:

How does he encourage the mind on an occasion when it should be encouraged? When his mind is listless owing to sluggishness in the exercise of understanding or to failure to attain the bliss of peace, then he should stimulate it by reviewing the eight grounds for a sense of urgency. These are the four, namely, birth, ageing, sickness and death, with the suffering of the states of loss as the fifth, and also the suffering in the past rooted in the round (of rebirth), the suffering in the future rooted in the round (of rebirth), and the suffering in the present rooted in the search for nutriment. And he creates confidence by recollecting the special qualities of the Buddha, the Dhamma and the Sangha. This is how he encourages the mind on an occasion when it should be encouraged.

The "states of loss" mentioned by the *Visuddhimagga* are the rebirths which are "removed from the happy destiny" (XIX, 92, 93), they are rebirth in the animal world, in the "ghost world", in the world of demons (asuras) or in hell planes.

Mindfulness right now can eventually lead to freedom from the danger of rebirth. We may think with fear of unhappy rebirth and then there is akusala citta with dosa, not mindfulness. However, we should remember that even fear can be object of mindfulness. Shortly after the dosa-mūla-citta has fallen away sati may arise and it can be aware of whatever characteristic appears at that moment, no matter it is an unpleasant object or akusala citta. When there is mindfulness there is also right effort.

We may think time and again of the urgency of mindfulness, but in spite of that we can notice that sati very seldom arises. We are impatient and we find it difficult to persevere with the development of satipaṭṭhāna. The suttas mention several factors which hinder "exertion, application, striving". We read in the *Gradual Sayings* (Book of the Tens, Chapter II, par4, Obstruction) about five mental obstructions which cause wholesome qualities to decline:

> Herein a monk has doubts and waverings about the Teacher. He is not drawn to him, he is not sure about him...
>
> Again, monks, a monk has doubts about the Dhamma, about the Sangha (the Order of monks), about the training...he is vexed with his comrades in the brahma-life, displeased, troubled in mind, come to a stop. In a

> monk who is thus, his mind inclines not to exertion, to application, to perseverance, to striving. . .

We may doubt whether there can be an "ariyan Sangha", people who have developed the eightfold Path and attained enlightenment. We may have doubts about the usefulness of sati right now, of mindfulness of visible object, sound or any other reality which appears. At the moment of doubt there cannot be right effort.

There will be less doubt and more confidence if we listen to the Dhamma as it is explained by the right person, if we read the scriptures, if we consider what we learnt and test the meaning of it ourselves. We can prove the truth of what we learnt by the application of the Dhamma in daily life.

The above-quoted sutta also mentions five "bondages of the heart" which hinder the development of good qualities:

> . . . Herein a monk is not dispassionate in things sensual; desire, affections, thirsting, distress and craving have not gone from him. . .
>
> Again in body a monk is not dispassionate; he is not dispassionate in the matter of material shapes; having eaten his bellyful he lives given to the pleasure of lying down on back or side, a prey to torpor; or he leads the brahma-life with a view to join some order of devas, with the thought: By virtue of this way of life or practice or austerity or brahma-life I shall become some deva or other. Whatsoever monk . . . has such an object in view, his mind inclines not to exertion, to application, to perseverance and striving. . .

We are infatuated by all the pleasant things of life. At such moments we forget to develop satipaṭṭhāna. We read in the same sutta that in the monk who has abandoned the mental obstructions and the "bondages of the heart", "growth, not decline, in good states may be looked for." However, we should realize that not all obstructions can be overcome at once. Even the sotāpanna who has eradicated doubt and who has an unshakable confidence in the Triple Gem is still attached to sense-pleasures. But he has no wrong view, he does not take attachment or any other reality for self. He has developed right understanding of all realities, also of akusala dhammas, by being aware of them when they appear. The sotāpanna cannot deviate from the eightfold Path anymore. Since he has realized the truth that all conditioned realities are impermanent and dukkha, his urgency to be freed from dukkha does not stem from theoretical understanding of the truth of dukkha, but from the direct realization of the truth of dukkha. He has a true sense of urgency which makes him persevere with the development of the eightfold Path.

When one has just started to develop satipaṭṭhāna, sati does not often arise. One may wonder how many years it will take before there can be any progress. When we think of the goal with desire or when we are afraid of failure there is akusala citta. We may not notice that there is any progress, but even if there is sometimes one moment of mindfulness of a reality appearing through one of the six doors, right understanding can develop little by little. Sati which arises falls away, but it is never lost, it conditions the arising again of sati later on. Instead of having desire for enlightenment we should see the value of right understanding at this moment.

When sati arises it is accompanied by kusala viriya, right effort, which performs its function of strengthening and supporting citta and the accompanying cetasikas, and in that way there can be perseverance to develop right understanding. It takes great patience and courage, even heroic fortitude, to persevere with mindfulness of all kinds of realities which appear, also of akusala dhammas we would rather shun as object of mindfulness.

Right understanding cannot be developed within a short time. The Buddha, when he was still a Bodhisatta, had to develop wisdom for aeons. He developed satipaṭṭhāna with great patience and an unshakable energy. Energy was one of the "perfections" he developed together with satipaṭṭhāna. He was willing to struggle and strive for an extremely long time, without becoming disenchanted with all the hardship and suffering he had to endure, all for the sake of the welfare of other beings.

The *Dhammasangaṇi* (par13), in its description of the "faculty (indriya) of energy", speaks about "zeal and ardour, vigour and fortitude, the state of unfaltering effort", "the state of unflinching endurance and solid grip of the burden." The Bodhisatta, when he in his last life was sitting under the Bodhi-tree, had unflinching endurance, he did not let go of the task he had to fulfil. His vigour and fortitude were unsurpassed. We read in the *Gradual Sayings* (Book of the Twos, Chapter I, par5) that the Buddha said to the monks that he did not shrink back from the struggle and struggled on thus:

> "Gladly would I have my skin and sinews and bones wither and my body's flesh and blood dry up, if only I may hold out until I win what may be won by human strength, by human energy, by human striving". By my earnest endeavour, monks, I won enlightenment, I won the unrivalled freedom from the bond.

Many of the Buddha's disciples developed the eightfold Path and attained enlightenment as well. However, they also had to accumulate right understanding during countless lives in order to attain enlightenment. When we read about the lives of the Buddha's disciples in the *Thera-therī-ġāthā* (Psalms of the Brothers and Sisters) we see that they also, like we, had periods of slackness with regard to the development of satipaṭṭhāna. However, ordinary events in their daily life could stir them and remind them of the urgency to develop right understanding.

We read that the Thera Uttiya (Thera-gāthā 30) had no purity of sīla and could not attain enlightenment. The Buddha taught him in brief the purification of sīla and the purification of view[1] . Uttiya developed insight and then he became ill. The Commentary to the "Thera-gāthā" (the Paramatthadīpanī) relates: "In his anxiety he put forth every effort and attained arahatship". He spoke the following verse with reference to the event which stirred him to continue to develop insight until he had reached the goal:

```
Since sickness has befallen me, O now
Let there arise in me true mindfulness.
```

[1] See Kindred Sayings V, Kindred Sayings on the Applications of Mindfulness, Chapter I, par3,5,6.

```
Sickness has now befallen me--'t is time
For me no more to dally or delay.
```

Sickness can remind us that we are not master of our body. What we take for "our body" and for "our mind" are only conditioned rūpas and nāmas which are beyond control. If we merely *think* of nāma and rūpa we will not know them as they are. Mindfulness of the reality which appears now is the only way to eventually know the true nature of realities.

The Buddha knew the accumulations of beings and, thus, whenever he preached to someone he could remind him in the way which was most suitable for him. He often reminded people of the foulness of "this short-lived body", in order to stir them to develop satipaṭṭhāna. The Thera Kimbila (Thera-gāthā 118) was stirred when the Buddha, by his supernatural power, conjured up the image of a beautiful woman and showed her passing to old age. The Commentary relates that he was greatly shaken by this image. He spoke this verse:

```
As bidden by some power age over her falls.
Her shape is as another, yet the same.
Now this myself, who never has left myself,
Seems other than the self I recollect.
```

Kimbila realized that what he took for self are ever-changing phenomena. Although what we call in conventional terms the "present personality" which has developed from the "past personality", there isn't any reality which is self. The phenomena of the present moment fall away immediately as soon as they have arisen and are completely gone. The commentary relates that Kimbila, while he considered the truth of impermanence, was yet more strongly agitated. He listened to the Buddha, became a monk and attained arahatship.

There are time and again signs of foulness and decay in our body. Our body is susceptible to decay, and death can come at any moment. We do not know when the last citta of our life, the dying-consciousness, will arise. For those who have accumulated conditions for sati the thought of death can remind them to be aware.

We read that the Buddha's disciples, when they were stirred by an event in their life, "put forth energy and strove with passionate ardour". We read, for example, in the "Therīgāthā (29) that Sāmā could not find peace of mind during the twenty five years she was a nun. In her old age she heard a sermon of the Buddha which stirred her, and she attained arahatship. We read that she said: "To free my path from all that causes dukkha, I strove with passionate ardour, and I won!" When we read these words we may misunderstand them. We are so used to thinking of effort as effort exerted by a self that we can hardly imagine how there can be effort arising because of its own conditions. Realities appear already through the five senses and through the mind-door. Visible object, for example, appears time and again. We could begin to investigate its characteristic until it is realized as *just visible object appearing through eyesense, not something or somebody.* There can be striving without the concept of self who strives.

Even though we are only starting to develop the Path events in our life can remind us to be aware now, just as they reminded the Buddha's disciples. At times we may have doubts about the benefit of sati, or it may happen that we are absorbed by our work or our circle of friends, or we may be infatuated by all the pleasant things of life, without mindfulness of such moments. Although we know in theory that any reality can be object of mindfulness, there may be a long period of sluggishness in our life. However, a painful event such as the loss of someone who is dear to us may remind us of the true nature of reality; this can become our "goad" which stirs us. If we truly see that even one moment of right understanding is beneficial we will have courage to continue with the development of satipaṭṭhāna and then there is right effort which arises because of its own conditions. We can come to understand that life without the development of right understanding is utterly meaningless.

11.0.1 Questions

1. What can obstruct right effort?
2. When we are thinking of the goal with discouragement, what can be done to persevere?
3. How can signs of foulness and decay in the body be reminders of awareness of the present reality?
4. Why is listening to the Dhamma as it is explained by the right person helpful for the arising of sati?

12 Enthusiasm

12.1 Enthusiasm (pīti)

Pīti, translated as enthusiasm, zest or rapture, is another cetasika among the six "particulars" which arise with cittas of the four jātis but not with every citta. Pīti can be kusala, akusala, vipāka or kiriya.

When we think of enthusiasm we presume that it is always kusala. We praise people who are enthusiastic. However, when we study the Abhidhamma we learn that enthusiasm is not always kusala, that it arises also with akusala cittas. There are many more akusala cittas in our life than kusala cittas and thus, when there is enthusiasm it is more often akusala than kusala. Don't we often take for kusala what is in fact akusala ? Through the study of the Abhidhamma we will have more understanding of kusala and akusala and of the different conditions for their arising.

The *Visuddhimagga* (IV, 94) gives the following definition of pīti:

> ...It refreshes (pīṇayati, gladdens, satisfies), thus it is happiness (pīti)[1]. It has the characteristic of satisfaction[2] (sampiyāna). Its function is to refresh the body and the mind; or its function is to pervade (thrill with rapture). It is manifested as elation...

The *Atthasālinī* (I, Part IV, Chapter 1, 115) gives a similar definition of pīti[3] .

> Pīti takes an interest in the object which citta cognizes and which is also experienced by the accompanying cetasikas. It is satisfied, delighted with the object and it "refreshes" citta and the accompanying cetasikas.

In the case of the kāmāvacara cittas (cittas of the sense-sphere) pīti arises with the cittas which are *accompanied by pleasant feeling* (somanassa). Thus, whenever there is somanassa, there is also pīti. Pīti is not the same as pleasant feeling, its characteristic and function are different. Pīti is not feeling, vedanākkhandha, but *saṅkhārakkhandha* (the khandha which includes all cetasikas except vedanā and saññā).

Pleasant feeling experiences the flavour of the object, its function is to exploit in one way or other the desirable aspect of the object (Vis. XIV, 128). Pīti does not feel, its characteristic is, as we have seen, satisfaction and its function is refreshing or invigorating body and mind, or to pervade them with rapture. Pīti takes an interest in the object and is delighted with it, it has its own specific function while it assists the citta; its function is different from the function of feeling.

The *Visuddhimagga* (IV, 100) explains in the section on the first jhāna the difference between pleasant feeling (sukha, translated here as "bliss") and pīti (translated here as "happiness") which are both jhāna-factors. We read:

> And whenever the two are associated, happiness (pīti) is the contentedness at getting a desirable object, and bliss (sukha) is the actual experience of it when got. Where there is happiness there is bliss; but where there

---

[1] Pīṇayati is the causative of pīṇeti which means: to gladden, please, satisfy or invigorate.

[2] The English translation uses here: endearment.

[3] See also Dhammasangaṇi par9.

> is bliss there is not necessarily happiness[4]. Happiness is included in the saṅkhārakkhandha; bliss is included in the vedanākkhandha. If a man exhausted in a desert saw or heard about a pond on the edge of a wood, he would have happiness; if he went into the wood's shade and used the water, he would have bliss. . .

The different words which are used to describe pleasant feeling and enthusiasm and also the above-quoted simile can help us to have theoretical knowledge of these two realities. If there is mindfulness of realities when they appear, a more precise understanding of their characteristics can be developed. However, we should not try to "catch" particular realities, it depends on conditions of which reality sati is aware.

As we have seen, in the case of the kāmāvacara cittas, pīti arises with the cittas which are accompanied by pleasant feeling. Whenever there is interest in the object and delight with it there is also pleasant feeling; in such cases there cannot be indifferent feeling or unpleasant feeling.

In the case of akusala cittas, pīti arises with the types of lobha-mūla-cittas which are accompanied by pleasant feeling[5]. When the lobha-mūla-citta is accompanied by pleasant feeling, the lobha is more intense than when it is accompanied by indifferent feeling. Pīti which arises together with lobha-mūla-citta accompanied by pleasant feeling takes an interest in the desirable object, it is delighted, thrilled with it. For example, when we have thoroughly enjoyed listening to beautiful music we may applaud with great enthusiasm. When we admire a musician, a painter or a famous sportsman, there may be many moments of lobha-mūla-citta with pīti. Whenever we are attached to an object with pleasant feeling, there is also pīti. The object may be a pleasant sight, a beautiful sound, a fragrant odour, a delicious flavour, a pleasant tangible object or an agreeable object experienced through the mind-door. There are many moments of akusala pīti we are not aware of.

Pīti does not arise with dosa-mūla-citta. When dosa-mūla-citta arises, the citta dislikes the object and then there cannot be at the same time a pleasurable interest. Pīti does not arise either with moha-mūla-citta; at the moment of moha-mūla-citta there is no enthusiasm.

As regards ahetuka cittas[6], only the two types which are accompanied by pleasant feeling arise with pīti: one type of santīraṇa-citta which is kusala vipāka and investigates an extraordinarily pleasant object[7] and the hasituppāda-citta, the smile-producing consciousness of the arahat[8].

---

[4] This is in the case of the rūpāvacara cittas of the fourth stage of jhāna (of the five-fold system), which are accompanied by happy feeling, sukha, but not by pīti.

[5] See Abhidhamma in Daily Life, Chapter 4.

[6] See Abhidhamma in Daily Life, Chapter 8 and 9. There are eighteen types of ahetuka cittas, cittas without akusala hetus or sobhana hetus, "roots". They are the sense-door-adverting-consciousness, the "five pairs" of sense-cognitions (seeing, hearing, etc.), two types of receiving-consciousness, three types of investigating-consciousness, the mind-door-adverting-consciousness and the smile-producing consciousness of the arahat.

[7] Abhidhamma in Daily Life, Chapter 13.

[8] Abhidhamma in Daily Life, Chapter 9.

When there is seeing, which is one of the dvi-pañcaviññāṇas (sense-cognitions), there is no delight or enthusiasm about visible object, seeing merely sees it. If visible object is an extraordinarily pleasant object, the santīraṇa-citta in that process which investigates visible object is accompanied by pleasant feeling and pīti. As regards the *kāmāvacara sobhana cittas* (beautiful cittas of the sense-sphere), only the types of citta which are accompanied by pleasant feeling arise with pīti. When we, with generosity and full of joy, help someone else, the kusala citta is accompanied by pleasant feeling and also by pīti which invigorates body and mind. Even if there was tiredness before, it is gone; one is refreshed. The same may happen when one reads a sutta with kusala citta accompanied by joy and enthusiasm. At such a moment one is not bored or tired, there is pīti which takes a pleasurable interest in the object.

Sometimes we are full of joy and enthusiasm while we help others, while we give something away or while we are performing other ways of kusala, but it is not always possible to have joy and enthusiasm at such moments. There are also moments of kusala citta accompanied by indifferent feeling, upekkhā, and then there is no pīti. It depends on conditions whether pīti arises or not. When one has great confidence in kusala and sees the benefit of it there are conditions for the arising of joy and enthusiasm while applying oneself to it. When kusala citta with pleasant feeling arises the accompanying pīti invigorates the citta and the other cetasikas. Viriya, for example, is intensified by pīti. We may be able to notice that, when there is joy and enthusiasm for kusala, we also have more energy to perform it.

There is another aspect of pīti: it can become an *enlightenment factor*. The other enlightenment factors are, as we have seen, mindfulness, investigation of the Dhamma (dhamma vicaya), energy (viriya), calm (passaddhi), concentration (samādhi) and equanimity (upekkhā)[9] . When the enlightenment factors have been developed through satipaṭṭhāna, they lead to the realization of the four noble Truths. When we have just started to be mindful of nāma and rūpa, we cannot expect the enlightenment factors to be developed yet. They will develop through satipaṭṭhāna.

The *Atthasālinī* (75) mentions the following factors which are conducive to the arising of the enlightenment factor of pīti:

> . . . recollection of the Buddha, the Dhamma and the Sangha, of sīla, of generosity, of devas, of peace (nibbāna), avoidance of rough (i.e. ill-tempered persons), serving meek persons, reflection on a Suttanta which instills confidence and a tendency to all this.

When we read a sutta, ponder over it and test the meaning by being mindful of the realities the Buddha taught time and again, we can prove the truth of his teachings. Thus our confidence in the Buddha, the Dhamma and the Sangha can grow and we will be inspired to continue to develop the eightfold Path. There can be conditions for the arising of enthusiasm which invigorates citta and the accompanying cetasikas. Also pīti can be object of mindfulness so that paññā can see it as it is, as not self. We should remember that without the development

---

[9] See Chapter 9, Viriya.

of satipaṭṭhāna the enlightenment factor of pīti and also the other enlightenment factors cannot develop.

We read in the "Mahānāma-sutta" (*Gradual Sayings*, Book of the Sixes, Chapter I, par10) that the Buddha recommended Mahānāma to recollect the Buddha, the Dhamma, the Sangha, sīla, generosity and devas (their good qualities). According to the *Visuddhimagga* Mahānāma was a sotāpanna, thus, he had right understanding of nāma and rūpa and he did not take any reality for self. We read:

> . . . Mahānāma, what time the ariyan disciple minds the Tathāgata, his heart is never overwhelmed by passion, never overwhelmed by hatred, never overwhelmed by delusion; then, verily, is the way of his heart made straight because of the Tathāgata. And with his heart's ways straightened, Mahānāma, the ariyan disciple becomes zealous of the goal, zealous of Dhamma, wins the joy that is linked to Dhamma; and of his joy zest (pīti) is born; when his mind is rapt in zest, his whole being becomes calm; calm in being, he experiences ease; and of him who dwells at ease the heart is composed.
>
> Mahānāma, of this ariyan disciple it is said: Among uneven folk he lives evenly; among troubled folk he lives untroubled; with the ear for Dhamma won, he makes become the ever minding of the Buddha.

The same is said with regard to the other recollections. According to the *Visuddhimagga* (VII, 121) only the ariyan disciple can cultivate the above mentioned subjects with success, since the non-ariyan cannot really fathom the meaning of these subjects. If one has not attained enlightenment, how could one know what it means to be enlightened and how could one clearly understand the meaning of "Buddha"? Nevertheless, also the non-ariyan can think of the Buddha with confidence and then pīti may arise as well.

We cannot induce the arising of kusala pīti, it can only arise because of its own conditions. Shortly after kusala pīti has arisen and fallen away, attachment is bound to arise. We may feel very satisfied about "our kusala" and we may find it very important to have pīti. We may think that it can last, but in reality it falls away immediately. It is essential to realize the difference between kusala citta and akusala citta; thus we will see that there are not kusala cittas all the time, even when we think that we are performing kusala. We may expect pleasant things from other people, we like to be praised by them, we want to show others our good qualities and our knowledge, or we are attached to the company of people. Defilements are so deeply rooted and they arise whenever there is an opportunity for their arising. There are many objects which can condition lobha and lobha can be accompanied by somanassa and pīti. Enthusiasm which is unwholesome can arise very shortly after enthusiasm which is wholesome and it is hard to know their difference. We may find it discouraging to discover that there are many more akusala cittas than kusala cittas, but at the moment of knowing akusala citta as it is there is right understanding. At such a moment the citta is kusala citta and there is no aversion nor feeling of discouragement.

Not only mahā-kusala cittas, kusala cittas of the sense-sphere, which are accompanied by somanassa arise with pīti, but also the mahā-vipākacittas and the mahā-kiriyacittas which are accompanied by somanassa arise with pīti. As regards mahā-vipākacittas, these are produced by kamma, and thus it depends on the kamma which produces the mahā-vipākacitta whether it is accompanied by somanassa and pīti or not. Among those who are reborn with mahā-vipākacitta, some are born with somanassa and pīti, others with upekkhā and in that case there is no pīti. If one is born with somanassa and pīti, all bhavanga-cittas of that life and also the cuti-citta (dying-consciousness) are accompanied by somanassa and pīti as well[10].

Pīti has many intensities. The *Visuddhimagga* (IV, 94) and the *Atthasālinī* (I, Part IV, Chapter 1, 115,116) explain that there are *five kinds of pīti.* We read in the *Visuddhimagga*:

> ...But it is of five kinds as minor happiness, momentary happiness, showering happiness, uplifting happiness, and pervading (rapturous) happiness.
>
> Herein, minor happiness is only able to raise the hairs on the body. Momentary happiness is like flashes of lightning at different moments. Showering happiness breaks over the body again and again like waves on the sea shore.
>
> Uplifting happiness can be powerful enough to levitate the body and make it spring into the air...
>
> But when pervading (rapturous happiness) arises, the whole body is completely pervaded, like a filled bladder, like a rock cavern invaded by a huge inundation (IV, 98).

Pīti is able to condition bodily phenomena. The "uplifting happiness" which is the fourth kind of pīti can even levitate the body. One example given by the *Visuddhimagga* and the *Atthasālinī* is the case of a young woman whose parents did not allow her to go to the monastery to listen to the Dhamma. She looked at the shrine which was lit by moonlight, saw people worshipping and circumambulating the shrine and heard the chanting. Then "uplifting happiness" made her jump into the air and arrive at the monastery before her parents.

In the case of kāmāvacara cittas, pīti always arises together with somanassa. In the case of the jhāna-cittas, this is not always so. Pīti is one of the *jhāna-factors* which are developed in samatha in order to inhibit the hindrances[11]. Pīti inhibits the hindrance which is ill-will (vyāpāda). When there is delight in a meditation subject there is no ill-will or boredom. As we just read, there are five kinds of pīti with different intensities. The fifth kind of pīti, the "pervading happiness", which has the greatest intensity, is the "root of absorption" and "comes by growth into association with absorption" (Vis. IV, 99).

At the first stage of rūpa-jhāna all five jhāna-factors arise with the jhānacitta. At each of the higher stages of jhāna the jhānacitta becomes more refined and more tranquil, and the jhāna-factors are successively abandoned. At the second stage

---

[10] Abhidhamma in Daily Life, Chapter 11. If the function of paṭisandhi is performed by an ahetuka vipākacitta (santīraṇa-citta accompanied by upekkhā which can be kusala vipāka or akusala vipāka), pīti does not accompany the citta.

[11] The other jhāna-factors are: vitakka, vicāra, sukha (happy feeling) and samādhi.

(of the five-fold system) vitakka is abandoned and at the third stage vicāra. At that stage there are three jhāna-factors remaining: pīti, happy feeling (sukha) and concentration (samādhi). At the fourth stage pīti has been abandoned but happy feeling still arises. In the case of the kāmāvacara cittas, pīti arises whenever there is pleasant feeling, but this is not so in the case of the jhāna-citta of the fourth stage of jhāna. The jhānacitta without pīti is more tranquil, more refined. The kind of pīti which has been abandoned at this stage is the "pervading happiness" which is of the highest intensity. The person who has experienced this kind of pīti and is able to forego it is worthy of praise as stated by the *Atthasālinī* (I, Part V, Chapters 111, 175).

At the highest stage of rūpa-jhāna (the fourth of the four-fold system and the fifth of the five-fold system) the jhāna-factor of sukha has been abandoned and pīti does not arise either at this stage. As regards arūpāvacara cittas, they are of the same type as the rūpāvacara cittas of the highest stage of rūpa-jhāna, and thus they are not accompanied by pīti. As regards lokuttara cittas, they are not always accompanied by pīti, this depends on different conditions[12] .

There are many different kinds of pīti as it accompanies different types of citta. The pīti which accompanies lobha-mūla-citta is entirely different from the pīti which accompanies kusala citta. The pīti which accompanies jhānacitta is again very different. As we have seen, the "pervading happiness", the fifth kind of pīti which is of the highest degree, is the "root of absorption". Pīti which is an enlightenment factor and which develops through mindfulness of nāma and rūpa is different again from all other kinds. We read in the *Kindred Sayings (IV*, Saḷāyatana-vagga, Part II, Kindred Sayings about Feeling, Chapter III, par29, Purified and free from carnal taint) about "zest", pīti, that is carnal, pīti that is not carnal and pīti that is still less carnal:

> And what, monks, is the zest that is carnal?
>
> There are five sensual elements, monks. What five? Objects cognizable by the eye, objects desirable, pleasant, delightful and dear, passion-fraught, inciting to lust. . . There are objects cognizable by the ear. . . the nose. . . the tongue. . . There are things cognizable by the body, tangibles, desirable, pleasant. . . These, monks, are the five sensual elements. Whatsoever zest, monks, arises owing to these five, that is called "zest that is carnal".

We then read about the " zest that is not carnal", which is pīti accompanying the jhānacitta. At the moment of jhānacitta carnal zest is temporarily subdued, one is not infatuated with the five "sensual elements". We read about the "zest that is still less carnal" than the other kinds:

> . . . And what monks, is the zest that is still less carnal than the other?
>
> That zest which arises in a monk who has destroyed the āsavas[13], who can look upon his heart as released from lust—that zest, monks, is called "the zest that is still less carnal than the other".

---

[12] See Atthasālinī II, Part VIII, Chapter I, 228, and Vis. XXI, 112. For details on cittas accompanied by pīti, see Appendix 5.

[13] āsavas or "cankers" are a group into which defilements are classified.

The same is said about pleasure, indifference and "release", which can be carnal, not carnal and still less carnal. The term "still less carnal" refers to the arahat who has eradicated all forms of attachment so that it never arises again. This sutta reminds us again to be aware of the realities appearing through the different doorways, one at a time. We are usually so absorbed in people and things that we forget that they are not realities, only concepts. It is not a person which is experienced through the eyes, but only a kind of rūpa which is visible object and does not last. We are infatuated with the objects we experience and we do not realize when there is "pīti which is carnal". Pīti which is carnal can arise on account of all the objects we experience through the six doors. The sutta illustrates how different pīti is when it arises with different types of citta. Pīti is conditioned by the accompanying dhammas and, in its turn, it conditions the accompanying dhammas. Pīti is saṅkhāra dhamma, not self. We may find it difficult to know when enthusiasm is wholesome and when it is unwholesome, but through mindfulness of it when it appears its characteristic can be known more precisely.

12.1.1 Questions

1. When we give a gift to someone and there is somanassa (pleasant feeling), is there pīti as well?
2. What is the function of pīti which arises with kusala citta?
3. When we are helping someone with pleasant feeling and enthusiasm, is there kusala pīti all the time?
4. How can we know the difference between kusala pīti and akusala pīti?
5. Does pīti arise with each kusala citta?
6. With how many types of lobha-mūla-citta does pīti arise?
7. Which types of vipākacitta are accompanied by pīti?
8. Does pīti always arise together with pleasant feeling, no matter of what plane of consciousness the citta is which pīti accompanies?
9. Pīti can be an enlightenment factor. How can we cultivate the enlightenment factor of pīti?
10. Which factors can condition kusala citta with pīti and somanassa?
11. Can recollections on the Buddha, the Dhamma and the Sangha be helpful even to those who are not ariyans and can therefore not really understand the meaning of Buddha, Dhamma and Sangha? In what way can they be helpful?

13 Zeal

13.1 Zeal (chanda)

Chanda, which is usually translated as zeal, desire or wish-to-do, is another cetasika among the six "particulars" which arises with cittas of the four jātis–but not with every citta. When we hear the word "desire", we may think that chanda is the same as lobha. However, chanda can be kusala, akusala, vipāka or kiriya. The cetasika chanda which is classified as one of the "particulars" is not the same as lobha, it has its own characteristic and function[1].

The *Visuddhimagga* (XIV, 150) defines chanda as follows:

> Zeal (chanda) is a term for desire to act. So, that zeal has the characteristic of desire to act. Its function is scanning for an object. It is manifested as need for an object. That same (object) is its proximate cause. It should be regarded as the extending of the mental hand in the apprehending of an object.

The *Atthasālinī* (I, Part IV, Chapter I, 132) gives a similar definition. Chanda searches, looks for the object which citta cognizes. Chanda needs that object which is also its proximate cause.

Chanda arises with the *eight types of lobha-mūla-citta*. When chanda arises with lobha-mūla-citta it searches for the desirable object, it needs that object. Although chanda is different from lobha which can only be of the jāti which is akusala, when they arise together it is hard to distinguish between them. When we like to obtain a pleasant object, lobha is attached and it is chanda which can accomplish the obtaining of that desired object. Lobha could not accomplish anything by itself. However, also when we do not need to obtain an object we are attached to, there is chanda accompanying the lobha-mūla-citta.

Chanda arises also with the *two types of dosa-mūla-citta*. Chanda "searches" the object the dosa-mūla-citta dislikes. Here we see more clearly that chanda is quite different from lobha which is attached to an object and which can never accompany dosa-mūla-citta.

Chanda does not accompany the two types of moha-mūla-citta. One type of moha-mūla-citta is accompanied by doubt (vicikicchā). Doubt has "wavering" as function, it is not sure about the object, and thus there cannot be at the same time chanda which searches for the object it needs. As we have seen, this type of moha-mūla-citta also lacks "decision" (adhimokkha), which is sure about the object. As to the second type of moha-mūla-citta, which is accompanied by restlessness or distraction (uddhacca-sampayutta), this type cannot be accompanied by chanda either.

As regards ahetuka cittas, "rootless" cittas, chanda does not accompany these types of cittas. Seeing-consciousness, an ahetuka vipākacitta which sees visible object, does not need chanda in order to perform its function of seeing. Sampaṭicchana-

[1] Sometimes the word chanda is used in a composite word such as kāmacchanda, sensuous desire, which is one of the five hindrances. This is a form of lobha.

citta which merely "receives" the object which was seen by seeing-consciousness does not need chanda in order to perform its function of receiving. It is the same with santīraṇa-citta and the other ahetuka cittas, they do not need chanda in order to perform their functions.

If the functions of paṭisandhi (rebirth), bhavanga (life-continuum) and cuti (dying) are performed by ahetuka citta[2], the citta is not accompanied by chanda.

As regards the *kāmāvacara sobhana cittas*, they are always accompanied by chanda. Whenever we perform kusala, the kusala citta is accompanied by chanda which is zeal for kusala, which desires to act in a wholesome way. It searches for the object the kusala citta cognizes and it assists the kusala citta in carrying out its task.

One may wonder what the difference is between kusala chanda and kusala cetanā which "wills" kusala. Kusala cetanā is the wholesome intention, kamma, which can motivate a wholesome action and which is able to produce its result later on. Moreover, kusala cetanā directs the accompanying dhammas in carrying out their functions in a wholesome way. Thus, its characteristic and function is different from the characteristic and function of chanda.

Chanda is a necessary factor for all kinds of kusala, for dāna, for sīla and for bhāvanā. When we, for example, visit a sick person, when we want to console someone who is in trouble or when we try to save an insect from drowning, there has to be kusala chanda which assists the kusala citta. If there were no wholesome zeal, "wish to act", we could not perform such acts of mettā (loving kindness) and karuṇā (compassion).

Chanda is also a necessary factor for the development of calm. The *Atthasālinī* (I, Part V, Chapter 13, 194) states in the section on the development of the meditation subjects which are the "divine abidings" (brahma vihāras) of mettā, karuṇā, muditā (sympathetic joy) and upekkhā (equanimity) :

> ...the wish-to-do (chanda) is the beginning; the discarding of the hindrances is the middle; absorption is the end...

In order to develop a meditation subject the wish-to-do is necessary. Without this wholesome desire one could not develop it. When calm has been developed more the hindrances can be temporarily eliminated and jhāna can be attained. Also at the moment of jhānacitta there is chanda.

Chanda accompanies all types of sobhana cittas. Chanda accompanies the *rūpāvacara cittas* and the *arūpāvacara cittas.* The chanda which accompanies these types of cittas is not kāmāvacara (of the sense-sphere), but rūpāvacara or arūpāvacara. Chanda is different as it accompanies different types of citta of different planes of consciousness. Chanda which accompanies jhānacitta "searches for" the meditation subject which the jhānacitta experiences with absorption.

The lokuttara cittas are accompanied by chanda which "searches for" nibbāna. This kind of chanda is lokuttara, it is different from longing for nibbāna. It assists

[2] See Abhidhamma in Daily Life, Chapter 11.

the lokuttara citta to carry out its function. The lokuttara citta and thus also the accompanying chanda directly experience nibbāna[3].

How do we know when chanda is kusala and when it is akusala? For instance, when we have desire for sati, is this kusala chanda or attachment? We have accumulated a great deal of attachment and thus there is likely to be more often attachment than kusala chanda. We are attached to a concept of sati and we believe that we can cause its arising. Wanting to have sati is different from the moment sati arises. There are many moments of forgetfulness but sometimes there may be a moment of mindfulness of only one object at a time appearing through one of the six doors. When sati arises it is accompanied by kusala chanda which performs its function.

Kusala chanda is a necessary factor for the development of the eightfold Path. If there is no wish-to-do one does not develop it. However, we do not have to try to have chanda, it arises because of its own conditions together with the citta which develops the eightfold Path.

We read in the *Kindred Sayings* (V, Mahā-vagga, XLV, Kindred Sayings on the Way, Chapter IV, II, Restraint of Passion, par3) that chanda is one of the factors which are "forerunners" of the arising of the ariyan eightfold Path:

> Just as, monks, the dawn is the forerunner, the harbinger of the arising of the sun, so possession of desire (chanda) is the forerunner, the harbinger of the arising of the ariyan eightfold way.
>
> Of a monk who is possessed of desire, monks, it may be expected that he will cultivate the ariyan eightfold way, that he will make much of the ariyan eightfold way. . .

When we develop kusala, chanda may be predominant; it may have predominance over the accompanying dhammas. There are four factors which can be predominant, but only one at a time can be predominant. The four predominant factors (adhipatis) are: chanda, viriya, citta (particular types of citta) and "investigation" or "reflection" (vīmaṃsā, which is paññā cetasika)[4]. When these factors have been developed they become the four "Roads to Success" (iddhipādas) leading to the attainment of the "supernormal powers" (abhiññās). There are five "supernormal powers" which are developed through jhāna (Vis. Chapter XII). The sixth power, which is the extinction of all defilements, is developed through vipassanā. Chanda or one of the three other "Roads to Success" can be predominant in the development of vipassanā[5] .

---

[3] For details about the cittas which are accompanied by chanda, see Appendix 6.

[4] See Dhammasangaṇi par269, and Atthasālinī I, Part VII, 212,213. Citta can be a predominant factor, but not all cittas; only the cittas which are accompanied by at least two hetus and perform the function of javana can be predominant. For example, lobha-mūla-citta and kusala citta can be predominant, since they are rooted in more than one hetu, but moha-mūla-citta cannot, since it is rooted only in moha. In the field of kusala, when chanda, viriya or vīmaṃsā are not predominant, there can be firmness of kusala citta which is predominant.

[5] The four "Roads to Success" are among the thirty seven factors pertaining to enlightenment, bodhipakkhiya dhammas, Visuddhimagga XXII, 33.

Thus we see that there are many kinds and degrees of chanda. Chanda is conditioned by the citta and other cetasikas it accompanies. Chanda is *saṅkhāra dhamma,* conditioned dhamma. Different kinds of chanda arise due to different conditions.

It is hard to distinguish the different kinds of cetasikas from each other since there are several cetasikas at a time which accompany citta and assist it in carrying out its function. As we have seen, the "universals" arise with each citta. Summarizing them, they are:

- contact (phassa)
- feeling (vedanā)
- remembrance or "perception" (saññā)
- volition (cetanā)
- concentration (ekaggatā)
- life-faculty (jīvitindriya)
- attention (manasikāra)

As regards the six "particulars", they do not arise with every citta but they arise with cittas of the four jātis. Summarizing them, they are:

- applied thinking (vitakka)
- sustained thinking (vicāra)
- determination (adhimokkha)
- energy or effort (viriya)
- enthusiasm or rapture (pīti)
- zeal or wish-to-do (chanda)

The "universals" and the "particulars" arise with cittas of the four jātis and these thirteen cetasikas are classified as one group: the *aññasamānā cetasikas"*[6]. The aññasamānā cetasikas are different from the akusala cetasikas which only arise with akusala cittas and different from sobhana cetasikas which only arise with sobhana cittas. However, this does not mean that the "universals" and the "particulars" cannot be akusala or sobhana. When the aññasamānā cetasikas arise with akusala citta they all are akusala; they assist the akusala citta to carry out its function in an unwholesome way. When they accompany kusala citta they all are kusala; they assist the kusala citta in carrying out its function in a wholesome way. Cetasikas are conditioned by the citta and the other cetasikas they accompany and they are of an entirely different quality as they accompany akusala citta, kusala citta, vipākacitta or kiriyacitta.

When akusala citta arises, it is accompanied by the "universals" and by the "particulars" which are vitakka, vicāra, adhimokkha (except in the case of moha-mūla-citta accompanied by vicikicchā, doubt), viriya and chanda (except in the

[6] Añña means "other" and samānā means "common", the same. The aññasamānās which arise together are of the same jāti as the citta they accompany and they all change, become "other", as they accompany a citta of a different jāti. Akusala is "other" than kusala and kusala is "other" than akusala.

case of the two types of moha-mūla-citta which are not accompanied by chanda). It is accompanied by pīti only when the feeling is pleasant feeling. It is also accompanied by cetasikas which arise only with akusala citta. The "universals" and the "particulars" are all akusala in this case. Cetanā, for example, "wills" akusala; vitakka "thinks" of the object in an unwholesome way; adhimokkha, if it arises, is convinced about the object which is the object of akusala citta; viriya supports the citta and accompanying cetasikas; pīti, if it arises, takes an interest in the object; chanda, if it arises, needs the object, searches for it.

When mahā-kusala citta (kāmāvacara kusala citta or kusala citta of the sense-sphere) arises, it is accompanied by the "universals" and by the "particulars" which are vitakka, vicāra, adhimokkha, viriya and chanda. It is accompanied by pīti only when the feeling is pleasant feeling. It is also accompanied by sobhana cetasikas which arise only with sobhana citta. The "universals" and the "particulars" are all kusala in this case. Cetanā, for example, "wills" kusala; vitakka "thinks" of the object in the wholesome way; adhimokkha is convinced about the object which is the object of kusala citta; viriya supports the citta and the accompanying cetasikas; pīti, if it arises, takes an interest in the object and "refreshes" citta and the accompanying cetasikas; chanda searches for the object in a wholesome way, it assists the citta in the accomplishment of kusala.

As we have seen, the same type of cetasika is very different as it accompanies different cittas. If we realize that cetasikas fall away immediately together with the citta and that the next moment another citta arises accompanied by other cetasikas, we will be less inclined to think that we own such qualities as energy, determination or enthusiasm. The more we study, the more will we understand, at least on the theoretical level, that all phenomena which arise are conditioned phenomena, saṅkhāra dhammas. We still act and think as if there were a self, but as our confidence in the Buddha's teachings grows, we will be inclined to develop the Path in order to directly experience that all phenomena which arise are saṅkhāra dhammas, not self.

13.1.1 Questions

1. What is the difference between chanda and lobha?
2. How can one know the difference between kusala chanda and lobha?
3. Does kusala chanda always arise when we perform wholesome deeds?
4. Akusala cetasikas arise only with akusala cittas and sobhana cetasikas arise only with sobhana cittas. The aññasamānā cetasikas arise with cittas of the four jātis. Is it correct to say that the latter types are neither wholesome nor unwholesome?
5. Why is it helpful to know that cetasikas such as viriya or pīti can be at one moment kusala and shortly afterwards akusala and thus entirely different?
6. Can the study of the different cetasikas help us with the development of the Path? In what way?

PART III: Akusala Cetasikas

14 Introduction to Akusala Cittas

Akusala citta and akusala cetasika are akusala dhammas, dhammas which are unskilful, unprofitable, unclean, impure. Do we realize when there is akusala citta? Whenever the citta is not intent on wholesomeness, we act, speak or think with akusala citta. We may not have unkind thoughts or thoughts of coarse desire, but the cittas which think can still be akusala cittas; they are akusala cittas whenever we do not think wholesome thoughts. We think time and again of people, of things which have happened or will happen, and we should find out for ourselves when thinking is kusala and when akusala. When we are "daydreaming", do we think wholesome thoughts? If that is not so, then the cittas are akusala cittas.

By akusala one harms oneself, other people or both oneself and other people. We may find it difficult to see that even when we do not harm or hurt others, the citta can still be akusala. For example, when we like nature, there is a degree of attachment and attachment is not kusala, it is different from unselfishness. We may see the danger of akusala which is coarse, but it is difficult to see the danger of akusala which is more subtle. However, through the study of the Dhamma we can acquire more understanding of akusala dhammas and then we may begin to see the danger of all degrees of akusala.

When the citta is kusala, there is confidence in wholesomeness. Kusala citta is pure and it is capable of producing a pleasant result. Whereas akusala citta is impure and it leads to sorrow. At the moment of akusala citta there is no confidence in wholesomeness, one does not see that akusala citta is impure and harmful. For example, when we see a pleasant sight, akusala cittas with attachment tend to arise. At such a moment there is "unwise attention" to the object which is experienced; we are enslaved to that object and do not see the danger of akusala. Thus we go on accumulating more and more akusala.

If one has not listened to the Dhamma, one does not know exactly what is kusala and what is akusala and thus there are many conditions for unwise attention to the objects which are experienced through the five sense-doors and through the mind-door. Foolish friends are also a condition for akusala cittas. The person who is inclined to akusala will associate with friends who have similar inclinations. Thus he accumulates more and more vices and then it is very difficult to turn to kusala and develop virtues.

Akusala citta is bound to arise more often than kusala citta because there have been countless akusala cittas in the past and thus the conditions for akusala have been accumulated. If there is no development of right understanding akusala cannot be eradicated and we will continue to accumulate more akusala.

The Buddha reminded people of the ill effects of akusala. Akusala kamma is capable of producing an unpleasant result in the form of rebirth or in the form of unpleasant experiences through the senses in the course of our life. Through the doing of evil deeds one acquires a bad name and one loses one's friends. Moreover, the person who commits evil is not calm when he faces death. We read in the *Gradual Sayings* (Book of the Fours, the Fourth Fifty, Chapter XIX, par4, Fearless) that the brāhmin Jāṇussoni said to the Buddha that he believed that everyone was afraid of death. The Buddha thereupon spoke to Jāṇussoni about four kinds of people who are afraid of death and four who are not. We read that the Buddha said:

> ...In this case, brāhmin, a certain one is not freed from passions, not freed from lusts, not freed from desire, affection, from thirst and fever, not freed from craving. Then a grievous sickness afflicts such an one. Thus afflicted by grievous sickness it occurs to him: Alas! The passions that I love will leave me, or I shall leave the passions that I love. Thereupon he grieves and wails, laments and beats the breast and falls into utter bewilderment. This one, brāhmin, being subject to death, is afraid, he falls a-trembling at the thought of death.
>
> Again, brāhmin, here a certain one who as regards body is not freed from lusts...is not freed from craving. Then a grievous sickness afflicts him. Thus afflicted it occurs to him: Alas! The body that I love will leave me, or I shall leave the body that I love. Thereupon he grieves...and falls into utter bewilderment. This one, brāhmin, being subject to death, is afraid, he falls a-trembling at the thought of death...

The same is said about the person who has omitted good deeds and committed evil, and about the person who is full of doubts as to "true Dhamma". The opposite is true of the people who do not have these vices. When a grievous sickness afflicts them they are not afraid of death.

We make ourselves unhappy through unwholesome deeds, speech and thoughts, and then we have no peace of mind. Akusala is a mental disease and this is more grave than bodily disease.

Right understanding of the danger and ill effects of akusala can condition kusala citta. But shortly after the kusala cittas have fallen away, akusala cittas tend to arise again and at such moments we have no confidence in wholesomeness. We may, for example, speak harsh words to someone else and when the moments of anger have fallen away, we cannot understand that we behaved in such a bad way. We may wonder how we can be such a different person at different moments. In reality there is no self who is at one moment kusala and at another moment akusala. There are different types of citta which arise because of their own conditions. Sometimes kusala citta arises but more often akusala citta arises. There is no self who can prevent the arising of akusala citta.

Because of ignorance we take the satisfaction in pleasant experiences through the senses for true happiness. Do we consider the enjoyment of pleasant things the goal of our life? We tend to forget that pleasant things do not last, that our body declines and that we are susceptible to sickness and death. There is ignorance with each akusala citta. At such a moment we do not know the danger of the accumulation of akusala.

If we do not develop right understanding of realities we live with our dreams and illusions. We want happiness for ourselves and we are ignorant of what is kusala and what is akusala. Thus there is bound to be decline in good qualities. We read in the *Gradual Sayings* (Book of the Sixes, Chapter VIII, par10, Day and Night):

> ...Monks, if a monk follow six things, come day come night, just a falling away in right things may be expected, not a growth. What six?

> Herein, monks, a monk desires much, is fretful, discontented with this and that requisite: robe, alms, lodging, medicaments—is without faith or virtue, is indolent, forgetful in mindfulness and lacks insight.
>
> Monks, if a monk follow these six, come day come night, just a falling away in right things may be expected, not a growth.
>
> (But the opposite is true for a monk who is not like that.)

This sutta can remind both monks and laypeople that if there is no mindfulness of the reality appearing at this moment, no development of insight, there will be decline in good qualities.

The Buddha, when he was still a Bodhisatta, considered the satisfaction in life, the misery and also the escape therefrom. We read in the *Gradual Sayings* (Book of the Threes, Chapter XI, par101, Before):

Before my enlightenment, monks, when I was yet but a Bodhisat, this occurred to me: What, I wonder, is the satisfaction in the world, what is the misery in the world, what is the escape therefrom?

Then, monks, this occurred to me: That condition in the world owing to which pleasure arises, owing to which arises happiness,—that is the satisfaction in the world. That impermanence, that suffering, that changeability in the world,—that is the misery in the world. That restraint, that riddance of desire and passion in the world,—that is the escape therefrom...

The "escape" can be realized through the development of insight. Right understanding of realities eventually leads to freedom from all akusala, to the end of all sorrow.

The Abhidhamma teaches us in detail about all akusala dhammas. They are not listed just to be read and memorized, they are *realities* of daily life and they can be known as they are by being mindful of them. If we consider akusala dhammas when they appear and begin to be mindful of them, we will come to know also defilements which are more subtle. We will learn that behaviour and speech we thought to be agreeable and pleasant are often motivated by selfishness; this happens for example when we want to endear ourselves to others in the expectation of some gain or favour from them. Our actions and speech are more often motivated by akusala cittas than by kusala cittas. Through the study of the Abhidhamma we learn about many types of defilements which arise time and again in our daily life. We learn about our tendencies and inclinations to akusala which we did not know before.

Among the cetasikas which can accompany akusala cittas, there are three which are unwholesome roots, akusala hetus[1]. These hetus are the foundation of the akusala citta. They are:

- attachment or greed, in Pāli: lobha
- aversion or anger, in Pāli: dosa
- ignorance, in Pāli: moha

---

[1] There are three akusala hetus and three sobhana (beautiful) hetus which are the opposites of the akusala hetus. A root or hetu is the foundation of the akusala citta or the sobhana citta, just as the roots are the foundation of a tree.

Besides these roots there are other akusala cetasikas which can accompany akusala citta, and each of these has its own characteristic and function. There are *twelve types of akusala cittas* and they are classified according to their roots. They are:

- 8 types of citta rooted in attachment, lobha-mūla-citta
- 2 types of citta rooted in aversion, dosa-mūla-citta
- 2 types of citta rooted in ignorance, moha-mūla-citta[2]

The cittas rooted in attachment have ignorance, moha, and attachment, lobha, as their roots; the cittas rooted in aversion have moha and aversion, dosa, as their roots; the cittas rooted in moha have moha as their only root. There is ignorance with each akusala citta.

Akusala cittas are accompanied by the "universals" and by the "particulars", but not all particulars accompany every akusala citta. When the universals and the particulars accompany akusala citta they are also akusala. There are *fourteen akusala cetasikas* which can accompany only akusala citta, but not all akusala cetasikas accompany each akusala citta. Some akusala cetasikas accompany only certain types of akusala cittas. There are twelve types of akusala citta, but there are many more varieties of them since they are, at one time or other, accompanied by different cetasikas. Moreover, akusala cittas can have many different degrees of akusala. Akusala citta may or may not have the intensity to motivate an unwholesome deed, akusala kamma patha.

There are *four types of akusala cetasikas* which have to arise *with every akusala citta.* These cetasikas are:

- ignorance, moha
- shamelessness, ahirika
- recklessness, anottappa
- restlessness, uddhacca

One of these, ignorance, is root, the other three are not roots. These four types have to assist each akusala citta in performing its function. So long as these types have not been eradicated akusala citta will arise. Only the arahat has eradicated these four types. For him there are no more conditions for the arising of akusala.

---

[2] See Abhidhamma in Daily Life, Chapter 4, 6 and 7.

15 Ignorance, Shamelessness, Recklessness and Restlessness

15.1 Moha

Moha, ignorance, is one of the four akusala cetasikas which are always present when there is akusala citta. We read in the *Dhammasangaṇi* (A Buddhist Manual of Psychological Ethics, par390) about moha, here translated as dullness:

> What on that occasion is dullness?
> The lack of knowledge, of vision, which is there on that occasion; the lack of coordination, of judgement, of enlightenment[1], of penetration[2]; the inability to comprehend, to grasp thoroughly; the inability to compare, to consider, to demonstrate; the folly, the childishness, the lack of intelligence; the dullness that is vagueness, obfuscation, ignorance, the Flood (ogha) of ignorance, the Bond (yoga) of ignorance, the bias[3] of ignorance, the obsession of ignorance, the barrier of ignorance; the dullness that is the root of badness—this is the dullness that there then is.

Ignorance is firmly fixed, it always lies latent and it is hard to eradicate. The *Atthasālinī* (II, Part IX, Chapter I, 249) gives the following definition of moha:

> "Delusion" has the characteristic of blindness or opposition to knowledge; the essence of non-penetration, or the function of covering the intrinsic nature of the object; the manifestation of being opposed to right practice[4] or causing blindness; the proximate cause of unwise attention; and should be regarded as the root of all immoralities.

The *Visuddhimagga* (XIV, 163) gives a similar definition.

Moha is not the same as lack of worldly knowledge such as science or history, but it is ignorance of ultimate realities. There are many degrees of moha. Moha does not know the true nature of the object which is experienced and therefore its essence is, as stated by the *Atthasālinī,* non-penetration and its function "covering up" the intrinsic nature of the object. Moha does not know nāma and rūpa as impermanent, dukkha and non-self, anattā. Moha is the root of all that is unwholesome. Every akusala citta is rooted in moha; not only the two types of moha-mūla-citta, but also the types of lobha-mūla-citta and dosa-mūla-citta have moha as root.

Moha is a "folly", it is "blindness", because whenever there is moha, there is "unwise attention" to the object which is experienced. For example, when we eat delicious food, attachment is bound to arise and then there is also moha. We are at that moment enslaved to the object which is experienced and we do not know that there is unwise attention. Moha does not know akusala as akusala and kusala as

---

[1] The Atthasālinī (II, 254), in its explanation of this passage of the Dhammasangaṇi, states about lack of enlightenment that it is: "not connecting them (things) with impermanence, dukkha and anattā", and "perceiving in an unreal, distorted way".

[2] No penetration of the four noble Truths.

[3] ignorance is a bias, it continually lies latent, in the sense of being firmly fixed.

[4] In Pāli: paìipatti. The English text translates here as: right conduct.

kusala and it does not know the conditions for their arising. If one has not studied the Dhamma one does not know that whether or not akusala citta arises depends on the manner of attention to the object and not on the pleasant or unpleasant objects themselves. Thus, the citta is the source of kusala or akusala, not the objects which are experienced, not the outward circumstances. We desire pleasant objects and when the object is unpleasant we are disappointed and sad. If one has not studied the Dhamma there is ignorance of kamma and vipāka. When one suffers pain one does not realize that the unpleasant experience through the bodysense is vipāka, that it is the result of a bad deed which has been committed.

If we study the Buddha's teachings we become less ignorant of realities, we begin to have more understanding of kamma and vipāka, of kusala and akusala, of ultimate realities. However, moha cannot be eradicated merely by thinking about realities. It can eventually be eradicated by the wisdom which knows the true nature of realities. Although we have learnt what is kusala and what is akusala, there are more often akusala cittas than kusala cittas. When we eat delicious food, how often is there wise attention to the object? We read in the *Gradual Sayings* (Book of the Threes, Chapter XIII, par121) that the Buddha spoke about two kinds of monks who receive almsfood. We read about a certain monk who has eaten the almsfood:

> Now it occurs to him: A good thing in sooth for me to be thus served by a housefather or a housefather's son! Then he thinks: I should indeed be glad to have this housefather or housefather's son serve me in like manner in the future. Thus he enjoys that almsgiving and is attracted by it, infatuated with it, attached to it. He sees not danger therein. He is blind to the escape therefrom. The result is that his train of thought is sensual, malevolent and harmful to others. Now, monks, I declare that what is given to such a monk has no great fruit. Why so? Because the monk lives amiss.

We then read about a certain monk who is not attached to his almsfood. What is given to him is of great fruit because he is vigilant. If there is mindfulness of the reality which appears, also while eating, right understanding can be developed.

Moha is the root of all that is unprofitable, of akusala which is coarse and of akusala which is more subtle. When one commits akusala kamma through body, speech or mind there is moha. There is ignorance of the danger of akusala kamma which is capable of producing an unpleasant result, even in the form of an unhappy rebirth. As we have seen, moha accompanies each akusala citta. When there are akusala cittas with avarice, jealousy or conceit, there is also moha. When one takes realities for self there is wrong view, diṭṭhi, and at that moment there is also moha. Moha conditions diṭṭhi but they are different realities. Moha is ignorant of the true nature of realities and diṭṭhi has wrong view about them.

There is much ignorance about the processes of cittas which experience objects through the six doors. Do we realize whether there is at this moment seeing, hearing or thinking, or does it seem that these experiences occur all at the same time? In reality only one object can be experienced at a time through the appropriate doorway. When there is hearing only sound is experienced through the ears and when we think of the meaning of the words which are spoken there is not hearing but thinking of concepts. Thinking arises in another process of cittas, it arises in a mind-door process and this is different from the ear-door process. Does it seem that hearing can stay for a while? In reality this is not so, it falls away immediately. But when right understanding has not been developed the arising and falling away of cittas cannot be realized.

Moha is ignorant of the true nature of realities, it does not know nāma and rūpa as they are. Moha is lack of knowledge about the four noble Truths: about dukkha, the origination of dukkha, the ceasing of dukkha and the way leading to the ceasing of dukkha[5]. So long as ignorance has not been eradicated we have to continue to be in the cycle of birth and death, we have to be born again and again. The Pāli term *avijjā* is used for ignorance in connection with the "Dependent Origination", the conditional arising of phenomena in the cycle of birth and death. Avijjā is the first link in the chain of conditions for the continuation of this cycle. At the attainment of arahatship ignorance is eradicated and then there are no more conditions for rebirth.

We read in the *Kindred Sayings* (III, Khandha-vagga, Kindred Sayings on Elements, III, Last Fifty, Chapter 3, par129, Satisfaction) that in the Deerpark at Isipatana Mahā-Koṭṭhita said to Sāriputta:

> "'Ignorance! Ignorance!' is the saying, friend Sāriputta. Pray, friend, what is ignorance, and how far is one ignorant?"
>
> "Herein, friend, the untaught manyfolk know not as it really is the satisfaction in, the misery of, the escape from body. So with feeling, perception, the activities. . . they know not the satisfaction in, the misery of, the escape from consciousness.
>
> This, friend, is ignorance, and thus far is one ignorant."

In the next sutta (par130) it is said that wisdom is knowing as it really is the satisfaction in, the misery of and the escape from the five khandhas.

If there is no development of right understanding one does not see that conditioned realities which arise and then have to fall away again are dukkha, and thus there cannot be escape from dukkha.

It is hard to know the characteristic of moha. The Buddha taught us to be mindful of the realities which appear, but we have many moments of dullness. We should learn to see the difference between awareness and forgetfulness of realities. When there is forgetfulness of realities the citta is akusala. Even when there is no attachment or aversion, there can be akusala citta; there can be the type of moha-mūla-citta which is accompanied by restlessness (uddhacca)[6]. This type is bound to arise very often in between the other types of akusala citta, but we do not realize it. Ignorance is dangerous and extremely hard to eradicate. The sotāpanna sees realities as they are, he has no more wrong view about them, but he has not eradicated ignorance. Ignorance is eradicated stage by stage and only the arahat has eradicated ignorance completely.

---

[5] Dhammasangaṇi, par1061.

[6] There are two types of moha-mūla-citta: one is accompanied by doubt (vicikicchā-sampayutta) and one is accompanied by restlessness (uddhacca-sampayutta).

15.2 Shamelessness and Recklessness

Ahirika, shamelessness or consciencelessness, and anottappa, recklessness or disregard of blame, are two other akusala cetasikas which arise with every akusala citta. In the *Visuddhimagga* (XIV, 160) ahirika is translated as consciencelessness and anottappa as shamelessness. They are defined as follows:

Herein, it has no conscientious scruples, thus it is consciencelessness. It is unashamed, thus it is shamelessness (anottappa). Of these, ahirika has the characteristic of absence of disgust at bodily misconduct, etc., or it has the characteristic of immodesty. Anottappa has the characteristic of absence of dread on their account, or it has the characteristic of absence of anxiety about them...

The *Atthasālinī* (II, Part IX, Chapter I, 248) gives a similar definition. The *Visuddhimagga* and the *Atthasālinī* do not give the function, manifestation and proximate cause of shamelessness and recklessness. The *Paramattha Mañjūsā* (Mahā-Tīka), a commentary to the *Visuddhimagga*, deals with these aspects[7].

According to the *Paramattha Mañjūsā*, the function of shamelessness is doing evil without being ashamed of it, and the function of recklessness is doing evil without dreading it. Their manifestation is not to shrink or draw back from evil.

The two cetasikas shamelessness and recklessness seem to be very close in meaning, but they have different characteristics. Shamelessness does not shrink from evil because it is not ashamed of it and does not abhor it. The "Paramattha Mañjūsā" compares it to a domestic pig which does not abhor filth. Defilements are like filth, they are unclean, impure. Shamelessness does not abhor defilements, be it attachment, aversion, ignorance, avarice, jealousy, conceit or any other kind of unwholesomeness.

As to recklessness, it does not abhor, draw back from evil because it does not see the danger of akusala and it does not fear its consequences such as an unhappy rebirth. The "Paramattha Mañjūsā" compares recklessness to a moth which is attracted to the fire, although this is dangerous for it. Are we enslaved by pleasant experiences? We may even commit evil through body, speech or mind on account of them. Then recklessness does not fear the danger of akusala, it does not care about the consequences of akusala.

The proximate cause of shamelessness is lack of respect for oneself and the proximate cause of recklessness is lack of respect for someone else. In order to have more understanding of this, we should first study their opposites: moral shame, hiri, and moral fear of blame, ottappa. Shame has a subjective origin, it is influenced by oneself; its proximate cause is self-respect. Fear of blame has an external cause, it is influenced by the world; its proximate cause is respect for someone else.

The *Atthasālinī* (I, Part IV, Chapter I, 125) states that shame, which has a subjective origin, arises from consideration of one's birth, one's age, heroism (courage and strength) and wide experience. In the case of shamelessness there is lack of such considerations. For example, when we give in to anger or when we are jealous of someone else who receives praise or other pleasant things, there is no consid-

---

[7] I have used the Thai translation, given by Ms. Sujin Boriharnwanaket, in her Abhidhamma lectures at the Saket Temple in Bangkok.

eration of our education or upbringing in morality. At such moments we have no moral strength, we behave like a weakling or a fool, in a childish way. Thus, at the moment of akusala citta there is lack of respect for ourselves, we are forgetful of all we have learnt from the Buddha's teachings.

As regards the origin of recklessness, anottappa, we should study first what is said about the origin of its opposite, ottappa or fear of blame. We refrain from evil owing to fear of blame from without, from the "world". Thus, fear of blame has an external origin. In the case of recklessness, anottappa, there is lack of fear of blame or punishment from the "world". When someone, for example, steals, he may acquire a bad name, he may be punished for this crime, but at the moment of akusala citta there is no consideration of such factors and there is lack of respect for others.

When there are conditions for the arising of akusala citta, shamelessness is not ashamed of akusala and recklessness does not fear its consequences. We may think that we are ashamed of and abhor killing or stealing and that we will never do such things. However, when the situation becomes difficult good intentions are forgotten and then we have no shame or fear of doing evil deeds. For example, generally we may not lie, but out of consideration for our relatives or friends we may not be ashamed of lying.

Akusala cittas arise time and again and these are always accompanied by shamelessness and recklessness. Also when the akusala citta does not have the intensity to motivate evil deeds, for example, when we are thinking with ignorance and forgetfulness of realities, there are shamelessness and recklessness performing their functions. It may seem that forgetfulness of realities is not so dangerous, since we do not harm other people by it. However, all kinds and degrees of akusala are dangerous. If right understanding is not developed defilements cannot be eradicated and we have to be subject to birth, old age, sickness and death, again and again. After there have been many moments of forgetfulness, mindfulness may arise again and then we are ashamed of our ignorance and forgetfulness of realities, and we see its danger.

We read in *As it was said* (Itivuttaka, The Twos, Chapter II, par3, Khuddaka Nikāya):

> This was said by the Exalted One...
>
> "Monks, ignorance leads the way to the attainment of unprofitable things; shamelessness and disregard of blame follow after. But, monks, knowledge leads the way to the attainment of profitable things, shrinking and fear of blame follow after."

This is the meaning...

```
What so be these ill-bourns in this world and the next,
All rooted are in ignorance, of lust compounded.
And since the wicked man is void of shame, and has
No reverence, therefore he works wickedness,
And through that wickedness he to the Downfall goes.
Wherefore forsaking longing, lust and ignorance
```

```
And causing knowledge to arise in him, a monk
Should give up, leave behind, the ill-bourns one and all...
```

When we see that all akusala dhammas are ugly and impure, we do not neglect mindfulness of realities, such as hardness, seeing or sound which appear at this moment. This is the only way to develop the wisdom which can eradicate defilements. For the arahat there are no conditions for akusala and thus shamelessness and recklessness do not arise.

15.3 Restlessness

Uddhacca, translated as restlessness, agitation, excitement or confusion, is another akusala cetasika which arises with each akusala citta. The *Atthasālinī* (II, Part IX, Chapter I, 250) gives the following definition of uddhacca:

> ...It has mental excitement as characteristic like wind-tossed water; wavering as function, like a flag waving in the wind; whirling as manifestation like scattered ashes struck by a stone; unsystematic thought owing to mental excitement as proximate cause; and it should be regarded as mental distraction over an object of excitement.

The *Visuddhimagga* (XIV, 165) gives a similar definition[8]. The commentaries illustrate with similes that when there is uddhacca, there is no steadiness, there is not the stable condition, the calm of kusala. When there is uddhacca there is forgetfulness of kusala, whereas when there is mindfulness, sati, there is watchfulness, non-forgetfulness of kusala, be it generosity, morality, the development of calm or insight. Mindfulness is watchful so that the opportunity for kusala is not wasted.

Uddhacca is not the same as what we mean by "restlessness" or "agitation", used in conventional language. When we use the word restlessness we usually think of aversion and unpleasant feeling. However, uddhacca arises with each akusala citta, not only with citta rooted in aversion, dosa-mūla-citta, but also with citta rooted in attachment, lobha-mūla-citta, and citta rooted in ignorance, moha-mūla-citta. When there is uddhacca we are forgetful as to kusala, we are unable to apply ourselves to any kind of kusala. Even when there is pleasant feeling, for example, when we are attached to a quiet place, there is restlessness, uddhacca, which arises together with lobha-mūla-citta. We may think that we are calm at such a moment, but we have actually "mental excitement".

It is difficult to know exactly when the citta is kusala and when it is akusala. We may take for calm what is actually akusala. If someone wants to develop samatha, the calm which is wholesome, he has to know very precisely when the citta is kusala and when it is akusala. Thus, samatha cannot be developed without right understanding. Understanding knows when the citta is peaceful in the wholesome way and when the citta is clinging to quietness and thus akusala.

As we have seen, uddhacca accompanies each akusala citta, it accompanies lobha-mūla-citta, dosa-mūla-citta and moha-mūla-citta. There are two types of moha-mūla-citta, one is associated with doubt and one is associated with restless-

---

[8] See also Dhammasaṅgaṇi par429.

ness. The fact that one type of moha-mūla-citta is called "associated with restlessness", uddhacca-sampayutta, does not mean that restlessness does not arise with the type of moha-mūla-citta which is associated with doubt. The second type of moha-mūla-citta is called "associated with restlessness" in order to differentiate it from the first type of moha-mūla-citta which is associated with doubt.

Restlessness arises very often, but we do not notice it. It is one of the "five hindrances"[9] and as such it is mentioned as a pair with regret (kukkucca). Restlessness prevents the citta from applying itself to kusala, thus it is a hindrance. We often waste opportunities for kusala. Time and again we are thinking with akusala citta, for example, we think with worry of the tasks which lie ahead of us. However, even while we are thinking there is an opportunity for kusala, namely the development of right understanding. There are realities all the time which have different characteristics, and these can be known when there is non-forgetfulness of them. Also thinking is a reality with its own characteristic and this can be known when it appears. When there is mindfulness there is no restlessness.

Only the arahat has eradicated restlessness. So long as there are still conditions for the arising of akusala citta, it has to be accompanied by moha, ignorance, which is ignorant of realities, by ahirika, shamelessness, which does not abhor akusala, by anottappa, recklessness, which does not fear the consequences of akusala, and by uddhacca, restlessness, which is restless as to kusala. No matter whether the akusala citta is coarse or more subtle, these four akusala cetasikas have to accompany the akusala citta and assist it in performing its function.

15.3.1 Questions

1. How many akusala cittas are accompanied by ignorance?
2. Why is the manifestation of ignorance "causing blindness"?
3. Of what is moha ignorant?
4. Can ignorance experience an object?
5. What is the difference between hiri, shamelessness and
6. anottappa, recklessness?
7. Why does one not see, at the moment of akusala citta, that
8. akusala is impure and why does one not fear its danger?
9. When we enjoy nature is there restlessness?
10. Why is understanding a necessary factor not only for the
11. development of insight but also for the development of samatha?
12. Can restlessness experience an object?

[9] Defilements are classified into different groups and one of these are the "hindrances", which are the following: sensuous desire, ill-will, sloth and torpor, restlessness and regret, and doubt.

16 Attachment

16.1 Attachment (lobha)

Akusala dhammas are altogether different from kusala dhammas. Akusala dhammas are impure, they are dangerous and they lead to sorrow. As we have seen, there are four akusala cetasikas which arise with every akusala citta: moha (ignorance), ahirika (shamelessness), anottappa (recklessness) and uddhacca (restlessness). Apart from these four akusala cetasikas there are several other akusala cetasikas which can accompany akusala citta.

Lobha, attachment or greed, is another akusala cetasika. Lobha does not arise with every akusala citta, it can arise only with eight types of citta, the eight types of lobha-mūla-citta[1]. Lobha is a "root", hetu. The lobha-mūla-cittas have both moha and lobha as their roots.

The *Dhammasangaṇi* (par1059), in the section where it deals with lobha as hetu, gives a long list of different names for lobha in order to illustrate its different shades and aspects. Lobha is compared to a creeper, it strangles its victim such as a creeper strangles a tree. It is like the ocean, it is insatiable. Lobha can be coarse or it can be more subtle such as hoping or expecting. It is a "bondage" because it binds beings in the round of births. It is a depravity because it corrupts the mind[2].

The *Visuddhimagga* (XIV, 162) gives the following definition of lobha: ...greed has the characteristic of grasping an object like "monkey lime". Its function is sticking, like meat put in a hot pan. It is manifested as not giving up, like the dye of lamp-black. Its proximate cause is seeing enjoyment in things that lead to bondage. Swelling with the current of craving, it should be regarded as taking (beings) with it to states of loss, as a swift-flowing river does to the great ocean.

The *Atthasālinī* (II, Part IX, Chapter I, 249) gives a similar definition[3].

Greed has the characteristic of grasping like monkey lime. Monkey lime was used by hunters in order to catch monkeys. We read in the *Kindred Sayings* (V, Mahā-vagga, Book III, Chapter I, par7, The monkey) that a hunter sets a trap of lime for monkeys. Monkeys who are free from "folly and greed" do not get trapped. We read:

> ...But a greedy, foolish monkey comes up to the pitch and handles it with one paw, and his paw sticks fast in it. Then, thinking: I'll free my paw, he seizes it with the other paw, but that too sticks fast. To free both paws he seizes them with one foot, and that too sticks fast. To free both paws and the one foot, he lays hold of them with the other foot, but that too sticks fast. To free both paws and both feet he lays hold of them with his muzzle: but that too sticks fast.
>
> So that monkey thus trapped in five ways lies down and howls, thus fallen on misfortune...

---

[1] See my Abhidhamma in Daily Life, Chapter IV.

[2] See the Atthasālinī II, Book II, Chapter II, 362-367.

[3] See also Dhammasangaṇi par389.

In this way the hunter can catch him and roast him over the fire. The Buddha explained to the monks that the monk who is not mindful gets trapped by the "five sensual elements": visible object, sound, scent, savour and tangible object. When one is taken in by these objects, "Māra gets access"[4]. Clinging is dangerous, it leads to one's own destruction. Are we at this moment taken in by one of the "five sensual elements"? Then we are in fact "trapped". At the moment of lobha we enjoy the object of clinging and we do not see that lobha makes us enslaved, we do not see the danger of lobha. Therefore it is said that the proximate cause of lobha is seeing enjoyment in things that lead to bondage. Growing into a river of craving, lobha takes us to the "states of loss". Lobha can motivate unwholesome deeds which are capable of producing an unhappy rebirth. So long as lobha has not been eradicated we are subject to birth, old age, sickness and death.

Lobha is attached to many different kinds of objects and it has many degrees. Different names can denote the cetasika which is lobha. Rāga (greed), abhijjā (covetousness) and taṇhā (craving) are other names for lobha. When lobha is coarse it motivates akusala kamma patha (unwholesome course of action) through body, speech or mind. Because of lobha one may commit many kinds of bad deeds in order to obtain what one desires. If the degree of akusala is such that it motivates an evil deed, the result of it may be an unhappy rebirth or unpleasant experiences through the senses in the course of life. Lobha can motivate akusala kamma pathas through the body, which are stealing and sexual misbehaviour, and akusala kamma pathas through speech which are lying, slandering and idle talk. Lobha can motivate *covetousness* or *abhijjā,* the desire to take away someone else's property, which is akusala kamma patha through the mind. Moreover, when it is accompanied by diṭṭhi, it can motivate certain kinds of wrong view which are akusala kamma patha through the mind[5]. As regards covetousness, the *Atthasālinī* (II, Part IX, Chapter I, 249) states that it should be regarded as the outstretched hand of the mind (reaching) for others' prosperity. If one merely wishes to have someone else's property but does not plan to take it away, greed is not akusala kamma patha. There are many degrees of greed and only when one really plans to take away someone else's property it is akusala kamma patha through the mind[6].

We may not have the intention to steal, but our wish to obtain something for ourselves can condition behaviour and speech which is not sincere. The *Book of Analysis* (Vibhaṅga, Chapter 17, par851) speaks about people who have "evil wishes", that is, who pretend to have qualities they do not possess; they may pretend to be virtuous, wise and even without defilements. The monk may behave in a hypocritical way in order to obtain requisites. The *Vibhaṅga* (par861, 862) gives us striking examples of "guile" and "insinuating talk":

Therein, what is "guile"? In one who depends on gain, honour and fame, who has evil wishes, who is troubled by wishes: by the so called using of the requisites, by

---

[4] Māra is that which is evil, akusala, and in a wider sense: everything which is bound up with dukkha.

[5] Certain kinds of wrong view, not every kind, are akusala kamma patha through the mind. I shall deal with these in Chapter 16.

[6] Atthasālinī I, Part III, Chapter V, 101.

talking allusively, by the setting up or by the arranging or by the proper arranging of the posture: there is knitting the brows, act of knitting the brows, guile, being guileful, state of being guileful. This is called guile.

Therein, what is "insinuating talk"? In one who depends on gain, honour and fame, who has evil wishes, who is troubled by wishes: that which to others is welcoming talk, insinuating talk, entertaining talk, laudatory talk, flattering talk, inferential talk, repeated inferential talk, coaxing talk, repeated coaxing talk, constant pleasant talk, servility (in talking), beansoupery (in talking), dandling (behaviour). This is called insinuating talk.

"Beansoupery" is talk of which only a little is true, the rest being false, just as in beansoup, only a few beans do not get cooked, and the greater part gets cooked[7].

These passages are also excellent reminders for laypeople: one may have lovely manners but in reality one may be full of hypocrisy and pretence. Pleasant speech can easily have selfish motives. Don't we want to be popular, to be liked by others? In order to endear ourselves to others we may even tell lies or slander. When there is mindfulness of the present reality we can find out whether our nice way of speaking is in reality flattering and coaxing talk or not. Through mindfulness we can become more sincere in our behaviour.

There is lobha, not only when we want to obtain things, but also when we enjoy pleasant sights, sounds, smells, flavours, tangible objects and mental objects. Don't we like softness while we are sitting or lying down? When we sit on a hard floor we have aversion, and when we sit in a comfortable chair we find it agreeable and then there is lobha. Are we not attached to temperature, to the temperature which is just right for us: not too hot, not too cold? When we drink coffee or tea we want it to be of the temperature we like. When eating and drinking we are attached not only to flavour, but also to temperature. And don't we like the smell of our food, the sight of it and the softness or hardness of it? There is bound to be attachment through each of the six doors, time and again.

Lobha may be accompanied by pleasant feeling or by indifferent feeling. When it is accompanied by pleasant feeling there is enthusiasm (pīti) as well. When there is pleasant feeling we are delighted with it and then pleasant feeling becomes another object of attachment. When there is attachment there is also ignorance, shamelessness, recklessness and restlessness (uddhacca). Ignorance does not see the true nature of the object of clinging, it does not see that it is only a conditioned reality which does not stay. Shamelessness is not ashamed of akusala and recklessness does not see its danger. Restlessness is instability due to akusala, it prevents the citta from applying itself to kusala.

Lobha can be accompanied by indifferent feeling and then it is not as intense as when it is accompanied by pleasant feeling. When we want to go somewhere or want to do something, lobha is likely to arise, but it may not always be accompanied by pleasant feeling, there may be indifferent feeling instead. Lobha-mūla-citta with indifferent feeling is likely to arise countless times, but we are so ignorant, we do not notice it.

---

[7] Visuddhimagga I, 75.

All degrees of lobha are dangerous, even the more subtle forms of lobha. When we do evil deeds which harm others it is evident that lobha is dangerous. But when lobha is only enjoyment of a pleasant sight or sound and we do not harm other people, we find it harder to see the danger of lobha. Lobha, be it gross or more subtle, makes us enslaved. When there is lobha we cling to the object which is experienced at that moment and we take it for happiness. The next moment the pleasant object is gone and then we are likely to have aversion. The Buddha reminded people of the futility of sense-pleasures. We read in the *Dhammapada* (verses 146-149):

```
What is laughter, what is joy, when the world is ever burning?
Shrouded by darkness, do you not seek a light?
Behold this beautiful body, a mass of sores, a heaped-up (lump),
diseased, much thought of, in which nothing lasts,
        nothing persists.
Thoroughly worn out is this body, a nest of diseases, perishable;
This putrid mass breaks up; truly life ends in death.
```

Lobha is extremely hard to eradicate because it has been accumulated, also in past lives; it is deeply rooted. Even when we have studied the Dhamma and we have heard about the dangers of lobha we still want pleasant things for ourselves. We want possessions and we are attached to people. At the moment of attachment we do not realize that all the things we desire are susceptible to change, that they cannot last.

We read in the *Middle Length Sayings* (I, no. 26), in the "Discourse on the Ariyan Quest", that the Buddha spoke to the monks about the ariyan quest and the unariyan quest. The unariyan quest is the seeking of all the things which are impermanent. The Buddha spoke about things which are "liable to birth". Birth is followed by decay and death. Whatever is born, what has arisen because of conditions, has to fall away, it cannot be true happiness. We read:

> ...And what monks, is the unariyan quest? As to this, monks, someone, liable to birth because of self, seeks what is likewise liable to birth; being liable to ageing because of self, seeks what is likewise liable to ageing; being liable to decay because of self...being liable to dying because of self...being liable to sorrow because of self...being liable to stain because of self, seeks what is likewise liable to stain. And what, monks, would you say is liable to birth? Sons and wife, monks, are liable to birth, women-slaves and men-slaves are liable to birth, goats and sheep are liable to birth, cocks and swine are liable to birth, elephants, cows, horses and mares are liable to birth, gold and silver are liable to birth. These attachments, monks, are liable to birth; yet this (man), enslaved, infatuated, addicted, being liable to birth because of self, seeks what is likewise liable to birth...

It is then explained that all the things which are mentioned as being liable to birth are also liable to ageing, disease, dying, sorrow and stain. We are attached to family, possessions, gold and silver, to everything we believe can give us pleasure. We long for what is pleasant and we have aversion when we do not get what we want. Our attachment is a source of endless frustrations. Further on in the sutta we read that the person who sees the peril of all the things which are impermanent seeks "the unborn, uttermost security from the bonds- nibbāna". This is the ariyan quest. We may understand the disadvantage of lobha, but lobha cannot be eradicated immediately. This sutta can remind us to develop right understanding of realities, since this can eventually lead to the eradication of lobha.

The Buddha taught people to be mindful of whatever reality appears. When akusala dhamma appears it can be object of awareness and right understanding. Some people may feel guilty when there is attachment to pleasant things and they may be inclined to think that they should not be mindful of lobha. If we have accumulations for arts such as painting or music should we give these up in order to develop vipassanā? That would not be the right practice. We should know the realities of our daily life. One person has accumulations for art, another is skilful in cooking or writing, we all have different accumulations. A layman does not live the monk's life, he could not force himself to live as a monk. We should develop understanding in our daily life, because then we will see that whatever arises, does so because of its own conditions.

The characteristic of lobha can be known only when it appears. When we help someone else there are likely to be many moments of attachment in between the moments of true generosity. Are we pleased to be in the company of the person we help, are we attached to him? Are we pleased with "our own" kusala and do we expect something in return for our kindness? Mindfulness of realities is the only way to know the different moments of wholesomeness and unwholesomeness more clearly. Mindfulness will prevent us from deluding ourselves.

There may be attachment even to kusala, to calm or to mindfulness, sati. We want to have a great deal of sati and we want it to last, but wanting to have sati is not sati, it is clinging. We should not avoid being aware of such clinging when it appears, because only if we know it as it is can it be eradicated.

There are time and again experiences through the different doorways. There is seeing, hearing, the experience of tangible object or thinking. It seems that all these experiences arise immediately one after the other. However, they arise in different processes and in these processes there are "javana-cittas"[8] which are either kusala cittas or akusala cittas. For example, shortly after hearing, which is vipākacitta (result of kamma), has arisen and fallen away, there may be attachment to sound, and then there are lobha-mūla-cittas, performing the function of javana. Even during the sense-door process, before the object is experienced through the mind-door, lobha can arise. The javana-cittas which arise in the different processes of cittas, experiencing objects through the six doors, are more often akusala cittas then kusala cittas, but we are ignorant of them. After a sense-object such as sound is experienced through the ear-door, it is experienced by cittas arising in a mind-door process. The cittas arising in the mind-door process which follows upon the

[8] See my Abhidhamma in Daily Life, Chapter 14. There are usually seven cittas in a process performing the function of javana, "running through the object".

sense-door process, in this case the ear-door process, merely experience the sound, they do not think about it, and they do not know what kind of sound it is. After that process there can be other mind-door processes of cittas which think of the source of the sound, of the meaning of it, of concepts. The thinking of concepts after the seeing, hearing or the experiences through the other sense-doors, is usually done with lobha, even if we do not feel particularly glad. When we, for example, after hearing a sound, know that it is the sound of a bird, this is not hearing but thinking, and this is usually done with lobha. We want to know the meaning of what we hear. We want to know the meaning of all we have experienced through the senses. When we pay attention to the shape and form of things, after the seeing, there is thinking of concepts, which is usually done with clinging. We *like* to notice all the familiar things around us, we would not like to miss noticing them. Thus, we have many moments of clinging arising in sense-door processes and mind-door processes; we have many more moments of lobha than we ever thought and it is beneficial to realize this. It can remind us to be aware of the different realities which appear in order to know them as they are.

The Buddha reminded people of the many forms of lobha in order to help them to develop right understanding. This is the aim of the many classifications of realities we find in the scriptures. *Taṇhā*, for example, is another word which denotes lobha. Taṇhā is usually translated as craving. Taṇhā can be classified in the following way[9]:

- kāma-taṇhā or sensuous craving
- bhava-taṇhā or craving for existence
- vibhava-taṇhā or craving for non-existence

Kāma-taṇhā is craving for the sense-objects which are experienced through the six doors as well as craving for kāmāvacara cittas (cittas of the sense-sphere) and the accompanying cetasikas. We cling not only to visible object or sound but also to seeing and hearing. We want to see and hear, we want to go on experiencing objects through the senses. Kāma-taṇhā may be accompanied by wrong view or it may be unaccompanied by wrong view.

Bhāva-taṇhā is craving for becoming. This kind of clinging may be accompanied by wrong view or not. The kind of bhava-taṇhā which is accompanied by wrong view, diṭṭhi, is "eternity view", the belief that realities last. Because of eternity view one believes that there is a self who will continue to exist forever.

There may also be clinging to rebirth without the wrong view of self who continues to exist. Clinging to the result of rūpa-jhāna (fine-material jhāna), which is rebirth in a rūpa-brahma plane, and clinging to the result of arūpa-jhāna (immaterial jhāna), which is rebirth in an arūpa-brahma plane, are forms of clinging which are included in bhava-taṇhā.

Vibhava-taṇhā, craving for non-becoming, is annihilation-belief which is a kind of wrong view. This is the belief that there is a self who will be annihilated after death. People who have this view do not see that so long as there are conditions

[9] Book of Analysis, Vibhaṅga, Chapter 17, Analysis of Small Items, par916.

for the arising of nāma and rūpa, they will arise again and again. Since they do not understand this they believe that there is no rebirth.

There are different ways of classifying taṇhā. The *Visuddhimagga* (XVII, 234-236) deals with *hundred-and-eight kinds of craving. There* are six kinds of craving for the objects experienced through the six doors, and each of these six kinds can be reckoned as threefold according to its mode of occurrence as craving for sense-objects, craving for becoming and craving for non-becoming. As regards craving for becoming, the eternity view can arise in connection with what is experienced through each of the six doors: there is the belief that these objects last. As regards the craving for non-becoming, the annihilation view can arise in connection with what is experienced through each of the six doors. In this way one can count eighteen kinds of craving. Moreover, there can be craving for "one's own" colour or for colour outside oneself and even so with regard to the other objects, including the objects of craving for becoming and craving for non-becoming. In this way one can count thirty six kinds of craving. If one takes into account craving in the past, craving in the present and craving in the future, there are one hundred-and-eight kinds of craving. The different classifications of taṇhā remind us of the fact that there are many kinds of clinging to different objects.

The sotāpanna (the streamwinner, who has attained the first stage of enlightenment) has eradicated clinging which is accompanied by wrong view, but the other forms of clinging may still arise. The anāgāmī (the non-returner, who has attained the third stage of enlightenment) has eradicated all forms of sensuous clinging, but he still clings to birth. He may cling to rūpa-jhāna and its result and to arūpa-jhāna and its result. He has no "eternity view" because he is without wrong view. The arahat has eradicated all kinds of clinging, he does not cling to any kind of rebirth. For him there are no longer conditions for rebirth.

When there is mindfulness of the present object more often, we will see more clearly how deep-rooted our clinging is. We can prove in this way that the Abhidhamma teaches about realities. We will learn that there is clinging to all the objects which are experienced through the six doors.

So long as there is clinging there will be birth, old age, sickness and death. Desire is the second noble Truth, the origin of dukkha. We read in the *Middle Length Sayings* (III, no. 141, the Analysis of the Truths) that Sāriputta said to the monks about the second noble Truth:

And what, your reverences, is the ariyan truth of the arising of dukkha? Whatever craving is connected with again-becoming, accompanied by delight and attachment, finding delight in this and that, namely the craving for sense-pleasures, the craving for becoming, the craving for annihilation— this, your reverences, is called the ariyan truth of the arising of dukkha.

Craving is one of the links in the "Dependent Origination". Ignorance and craving are the roots of the "wheel of becoming", the cycle of birth and death (*Visuddhimagga* XVII, 285).

In the *Thera-gāthā* (57, Kuṭivihārin 2) the kamma which produces rebirth is symbolised by the building of a dwelling place, a hut. Who still has desire to "build" will be reborn. A Thera did his studies in an old hut. He thought: "This old hut is now rotten; I ought to make another". So he turned his mind to new action (kamma). A spirit who was seeking salvation said to him:

```
This was an ancient hut, you say? To build
Another hut, a new one, is your wish?
O cast away the longing for a hut!
New hut will bring new pain, monk, to you.
```

When the Thera heard these words he was agitated, developed insight and attained arahatship. For him there were no more conditions for rebirth, since he was free from clinging.

16.1.1 Questions

1. Why is lobha-mūla-citta dangerous, even when it does not have the intensity to motivate bad deeds?
2. Visible object is what appears through the eyes, it is not a "thing". Can attachment to visible object arise during the eye-door process?
3. Even the sotāpanna who has realized that phenomena are impermanent and non-self has attachment to pleasant things. How is that possible?
4. Is bhava-taṇhā, craving for becoming, always accompanied by wrong view?
5. Who has eradicated all forms of bhava-taṇhā?
6. Can the sotāpanna (streamwinner) have vibhava-taṇhā, clinging to non-existence?
7. Can the anāgāmī (non-returner) have clinging to seeing?
8. Can the anāgāmī have attachment to jhāna?
9. Is it possible to have attachment when we help someone else?
10. Can attachment to sati be a hindrance to the development of the eightfold Path?
11. Attachment to music is akusala. Monks are not allowed to apply themselves to music. Should even laypeople give up music in order to develop vipassanā?
12. Can attachment be the object of mindfulness?

17 Wrong View

17.1 Wrong View (diṭṭhi)

The Buddha taught the truth about all realities which appear in daily life: seeing, hearing, attachment, hardness, softness, heat, cold and all the other phenomena which can be experienced. However, we are ignorant of the realities in and around ourselves and we have wrong view about them.

What is wrong view? It is a distorted view of realities, a misinterpretation of them. Do we, for example, know hearing as only an element which hears or do we still cling to an idea of self who hears? Do we know sound as it is, as only a reality which can be heard, or do we take what is heard for a "person" or a "thing" such as a voice or a car? Person, voice or car are concepts we can think of but which cannot be heard. Hearing and thinking occur at different moments and these realities experience different objects. Only one object can be experienced at a time through the appropriate doorway, but we still have many misunderstandings about reality. Through the study of the Dhamma we may have acquired theoretical understanding of realities as being impermanent and non-self, but wrong view cannot be eradicated through theoretical understanding. It can only be eradicated through the practice, through the development of the eightfold Path.

The *Atthasālinī* (II, Part IX, Chapter I, 248) gives the following definition of wrong view, diṭṭhi: ...It has unwise conviction as characteristic; perversion as function; wrong conviction as manifestation; the desire not to see the ariyans as proximate cause. It should be regarded as the highest fault.

The *Visuddhimagga* (XIV, 164) gives a similar definition of diṭṭhi. The *Dhammasangaṇi* (par38) calls diṭṭhi a "wrong road" and the *Atthasālinī* (II, Part IX, Chapter II, 253) explains: ...From being not the right path, it is a "wrong path". For just as one who is gone astray, although he holds that this is the path to such a village, does not arrive at a village, so a man of false opinions, although he holds that this is the path to a happy destiny, cannot get there; hence from being not the right path it is a wrong path...

Diṭṭhi has unwise conviction[1] as characteristic. When there is diṭṭhi one clings to a false view of reality. Its function is "perversion"[2]: because of diṭṭhi one takes for permanent what is impermanent, one takes for self what is not self. Ignorance covers up the true nature of realities and wrong view sees them wrongly, in a distorted way. Diṭṭhi is a factor of the wrong Path. If one follows the wrong Path defilements cannot be eradicated and thus there will be no end to the cycle of birth and death. Because of diṭṭhi someone may believe that his wrong practice can lead to purification of defilements. In the scriptures we read about people in the Buddha's time who followed different ways of wrong practice; they behaved like a dog or like a cow, because they thought that such practices would lead to

[1] In Pāli: ayoniso abhinivesa, unwise inclination, unwise adhering.

[2] In Pāli: parāmasa, derived from parāmasati, to touch, to hold on to, to be attached or fall a victim to.

purification[3]. So long as diṭṭhi has not been eradicated there are conditions for deviating from the right Path, even though one may have theoretical understanding of the right Path. The Buddha taught that all realities which appear through the six doors can be object of mindfulness. One may be inclined to think that it is not possible to know nāma and rūpa which appear now, in daily life. Some people believe that they have to follow certain rules with regard to the development of satipaṭṭhāna, such as, for example, refraining from reading or talking. They think that they have to go to a quiet place where there is no noise, in order to have less akusala cittas. In the beginning we all may be inclined to believe that we should not be aware of akusala dhammas, but also akusala dhammas have characteristics which can be known and understood. If they are not known as they are, as nāmas which arise because of their own conditions, they cannot be eradicated. Even dullness or forgetfulness of nāma and rūpa is a reality of daily life and it has a characteristic which can be known. It is important to know the difference between the moments of awareness and the moments of forgetfulness. There is forgetfulness of realities very often but sometimes mindfulness may arise and then we can learn the difference.

The proximate cause of diṭṭhi is "the desire not to see the ariyans"[4], being without regard for them. If one does not listen to the Dhamma as it is explained by the "good friend in Dhamma" and does not put it into practice, there are no conditions for the development of right understanding. Instead of listening to the right friend one may associate with the wrong person. We read in the *Book of Analysis* (Chapter 17, par901) about evil friendship:

> Therein, what is "having evil friends"? There are those persons who are without confidence[5], of wrong morality, without learning, mean, of no wisdom. That which is dependence on, strong dependence on, complete dependence on, approaching, approaching intimately, devotion to, complete devotion to, entanglement with them. This is called having evil friends.

Those who have accumulations for the development of right understanding have conditions to meet the right friend in the Dhamma and those who have tendencies to wrong view are bound to associate with people who have wrong view and thus they accumulate more and more wrong view.

Wrong view should be regarded as the "highest fault". Wrong view is dangerous because it can lead to many kinds of evil. We read in the *Gradual Sayings* (Book of the Ones, Chapter XVII):

---

[3] This is "clinging to rules and ritual", sīlabbatupādāna. See Dialogues of the Buddha III, no. 24, Mystic Wonders, I, 7.

[4] See "The Mūlapariyāya Sutta and its Commentarial Exegesis", translated by Ven. Bhikkhu Bodhi, BPS. Kandy, 1980. In the commentary to this sutta ("The Root of Existence", Middle Length Sayings I, no. 1), in the "Papañcasūdani", it is explained that "the desire not to see the ariyans", or being without regard for the ariyans, means that one does not realize the three characteristics of impermanence, dukkha and anattā; that one does not attain the Dhamma attained by the ariyans.

[5] Confidence in what is wholesome.

Monks, I know not of any other single thing so apt to cause the arising of evil states not yet arisen, or if arisen, to cause their more-becoming and increase, as perverted view...

Monks, in one of perverted view evil states not yet arisen do arise, and if arisen, are apt to grow and grow...

Monks, I know not of any other single thing so apt to cause the non-arising of good states not yet arisen, or, if arisen, to cause their waning, as perverted view...

Monks, in one of perverted view good states not yet arisen arise not, or, if arisen, waste away...

Monks, I know not of any other single thing so apt to cause the arising of perverted view, if not yet arisen, or the increase of perverted view, if already arisen, as unsystematic attention[6].

In him who gives not systematic attention perverted view, if not arisen, does arise, or, if already arisen, does increase...

Monks, I know not of any other single thing so apt, when body breaks up after death, to cause the rebirth of beings in the Waste, the Way of Woe, the Downfall, in Hell, as perverted view...

We read of each case that the opposite is true for right view. Further on, in the same chapter, we read that wrong view is compared to a nimbseed, the seed of a creeper or of a cucumber:

> ...Whatsoever essence it derives from earth or water, all that conduces to its bitterness, its acridity, its unpleasantness. What is the cause of that? The ill nature of the seed. Just so, monks, in a man of perverted view, all deeds whatsoever...conduce to Ill. What is the cause of that? Monks, it is perverted view.

Right view is compared to a seed of sugar-cane, paddy or grape: "whatsoever essence it derives from earth or water, all that conduces to its sweetness, pleasantness and delicious flavour." Even so in a man who has right view, all deeds conduce to happiness.

In order to have more understanding of the implications of this sutta we should consider the difference between the life of the non-ariyan and the life of the sotāpanna. The non-ariyan who has not eradicated wrong view has conditions to commit akusala kamma patha which can lead to an unhappy rebirth and thus he is in a dangerous situation. The sotāpanna, who has eradicated wrong view, has no conditions anymore to transgress the five precepts, he has no conditions anymore to commit akusala kamma patha which can cause an unhappy rebirth. He has eradicated stinginess and jealousy, he is full of generosity. When one does not cling anymore to the concept of self and sees realities as they are, this will bear on one's actions, speech and thoughts.

Diṭṭhi does not arise with every type of citta. Diṭṭhi is connected with clinging, it arises only with *lobha-mūla-citta*. There are four types of lobha-mūla-citta which are accompanied by diṭṭhi (diṭṭhigata-sampayutta), and of these types two are accompanied by pleasant feeling (somanassa) and two by indifferent feeling (up-

---

6 Ayoniso manasikāra, unwise attention.

ekkhā). They can be "unprompted" (asaṅkhārika, not induced by someone else or oneself) or they can be "prompted" (sasaṅkhārika, induced by someone else or by oneself)[7]. Diṭṭhi which arises with lobha-mūla-citta always stands for wrong view, micchā-diṭṭhi.

There are many kinds of wrong views and they are of different degrees. Three kinds of wrong view are unwholesome courses of action, akusala kamma patha, through the mind, and these are capable of causing an unhappy rebirth. They are the following three views:

1. There is no result of kamma (natthika-diṭṭhi)
2. There are no causes (in happening, ahetuka-diṭṭhi)
3. There is no such thing as kamma (akiriya-diṭṭhi)

As regards the first view, this was taught by Ajita Kesakambali[8]. He also taught that there is annihilation at death.

The second view was taught by Makkhalī. He taught that there is no cause for the depravity or purity of beings, that there is no human effort and that all living creatures are "bent by fate, chance and nature"[9] .

The third view was taught by Pūraṇa Kassapa[10]. He denied that there is akusala kamma and kusala kamma. The tormenting of others is not an evil deed according to him.

Although these three views are distinct from each other, they are nevertheless related. When one does not see kamma as cause one does not see its result either, and when one does not see the result of kamma, one does not see kamma as cause either[11].

The above-mentioned three wrong views are akusala kamma patha through the mind if one is firmly convinced about them. These three views in particular are very dangerous, they can give rise to many evil deeds.

There are many other kinds of wrong views and, although they are not akusala kamma patha, they are still dangerous. The scriptures often refer to the *eternalistic view* and to the *annihilationistic view*. Eternalism is the belief that there is a "self" who is permanent. Annihilationism is the belief that there is a "self" who will be annihilated after death. There is also a "semi-eternalistic view": one holds that some phenomena are eternal while others are not. One may sometimes cling to the eternalistic view and sometimes to the annihilistic view.

In the *Brahma-jāla sutta* ("The All-Embracing Net of Views"[12], The Dialogues of the Buddha I, no. 1) sixtytwo kinds of wrong view are mentioned. Of these there

---

[7] See Abhidhamma in Daily Life, Chapter 4.

[8] Middle Length Sayings II, no. 60, On the Sure, 401.

[9] Ibidem, 407, and see also Dialogues of the Buddha I, no. 2, "The Fruits of the Life of a Recluse", 54.

[10] Middle Length Sayings II, no. 60, 404.

[11] See also Kindred Sayings III, Khandha-vagga, Kindred Sayings on Views, I, par5-7, and Dialogues of the Buddha I, no. 2, 52-56, and Atthasālinī I, Part III, Chapter V, 101.

[12] Translated with its commentary by Ven. Bodhi, BPS. Kandy, 1978.

are eighteen speculative theories concerning the past, and forty-four concerning the future. There are speculative theories about the world being finite or infinite, about the origin of the "soul" or the world. There are speculations about good and evil and about nibbāna.

People of all times have been inclined to speculative theories and also today we can see that such views still persist. When we speculate about past lives and future lives we may cling to a "self" who "travels" from one life to another. We are so used to thinking in terms of self. As regards annihilationism, those who believe that there is a soul or self who will be annihilated after death do not realize that the dying-consciousness which falls away is succeeded by the rebirth-consciousness of the next life so long as there are conditions for rebirth. Annihilationism is different from the wisdom which sees the impermanence, the arising and falling away, of nāma and rūpa. For the arahat there are no conditions for rebirth, his dying-consciousness is not succeeded by rebirth-consciousness. This is not annihilation, it is freedom from the cycle of birth and death. The arahat has cultivated the right conditions for the attainment to this freedom.

When the wrong view of self has been eradicated one will not cling to speculative theories anymore. But so long as one still believes in a self, one is bound to cling to speculative theories. We all have accumulated "personality-belief" or "sakkaya-diṭṭhi". We read in the *Kindred Sayings* (IV, Saḷāyatana-vagga, Kindred Sayings about Citta, par3, Isidatta) that the monk Isidatta said to Citta, the housefather:

> Herein, housefather, the untaught manyfolk, who discern not those who are ariyans, who are unskilled in the ariyan doctrine, who are untrained in the ariyan doctrine. . . they regard body as the self, they regard the self as having body, body as being in the self, the self as being in the body. . .

Thus, there are four kinds of the wrong view of personality-belief with regard to "body", rūpa-kkhandha. The same is said about the wrong views with regard to the four nāma-kkhandhas of feeling, perception, the "formations" or "activities" and consciousness. Since there are four kinds of the wrong view of personality-belief, sakkāya-diṭṭhi, concerning each of the five khandhas, there are twenty kinds of this wrong view in all[13]. One may cling with wrong view to the idea of "I see", "my body", "my will". But they are only khandhas, conditioned elements which arise and fall away.

There is wrong view with regard to nāmas such as seeing, hearing or thinking, and also with regard to rūpas, such as hardness or visible object. One may take a nāma such as seeing for self, and one may also take visible object for a person or a thing which exists. When we take things for self we do not see them as elements which can, one at a time, be experienced through the appropriate doorway. Visible object is only a kind of rūpa which can be experienced through the eyesense, it is not a person or a thing, it falls away again. Sound is only a kind of rūpa which can be experienced through the earsense, it is not a person or a thing. Each citta which arises experiences one object at a time through the appropriate doorway and then falls away, it is quite different from the preceding citta. Seeing only sees, it does

---

[13] Dhammasangaṇi, par1003.

not hear, it does not think. We read in the *Book of Analysis* (Chapter 16, Analysis of Knowledge, par763):

> "Do not experience each other's object" means: Ear-consciousness does not experience the object of eye-consciousness; eye-consciousness does not experience the object of ear-consciousness either. Nose-consciousness does not experience the object of eye-consciousness; eye-consciousness does not experience the object of nose-consciousness either. Tongue-consciousness does not experience the object of eye-consciousness; eye-consciousness does not experience the object of tongue-consciousness either. Body-consciousness does not experience the object of eye-consciousness; eye-consciousness does not experience the object of body-consciousness either...

One tends to cling to an idea of self who coordinates all the different experiences. Someone may think that he can look at someone else and listen to his words at the same time. The lists and classifications which we find in the Abhidhamma are not meant to be used only for theoretical understanding, they are meant to be used for the practice. They are reminders to be aware of the reality which appears now so that wrong view can be eradicated. When hearing appears there can be awareness of its characteristic so that right understanding can know it as it is: as only a type of nāma, not a self, who hears. We may have doubts about the difference between the characteristic of hearing and of the paying of attention to the meaning of the sound. We are inclined to confuse all the six doorways. But hearing does not experience the object of thinking. Intellectual understanding of realities can condition the arising of mindfulness but we are usually infatuated with pleasant objects and we reject unpleasant objects, we forget to be mindful. For example, when we feel hot, we have aversion and then we are forgetful of realities such as heat, feeling or aversion.

So long as wrong view has not been eradicated it can still arise when there are conditions for its arising. Only through mindfulness will we be able to know when it arises. When we think of concepts such as people and things there is not necessarily wrong view. We can think of a person with kusala citta, for example, when we have compassion for him. Or we can think of a person with lobha-mūla-citta without wrong view or with dosa-mūla-citta.

Wrong view has to be eradicated first before other defilements can be eradicated. As we have seen, the non-ariyan, who has not eradicated wrong view, still has conditions to neglect the five precepts; he still has conditions for killing, stealing, sexual misbehaviour, lying and the taking of intoxicants, including alcoholic drinks. When we understand that the clinging to the concept of self causes us many problems in life, that it leads to what is unprofitable, we may see the benefit of the development of right understanding. If we really see the danger of wrong view, it can condition the arising of mindfulness and thus right understanding can develop. Right understanding can only develop if there is mindfulness now, not if we merely think of ways how to have more mindfulness later on.

17.1.1 Questions

1. What is an example of wrong practice which people may follow today?

2. Why is the proximate cause of wrong view "not to see ariyans"?
3. What is the difference between annihilationism, the view that a self will be annihilated after death, and the seeing of the impermanence of conditioned phenomena?
4. In which way can one think of past lives with wrong view?
5. Personality view can be eradicated through mindfulness of nāma and rūpa. Why is that so?
6. Why does one not cling to speculative theories anymore when personality belief has been eradicated?
7. When there is no awareness is there wrong view all the time?
8. What is the difference between ignorance and wrong view?
9. Why are the three kinds of wrong view which are akusala kamma patha particularly dangerous?
10. Why is it wrong to believe that we can see and hear at the same time?
11. Does the fact that wrong view has not been eradicated have any influence on our morality (sīla)?

18 Conceit

18.1 Conceit (māna)

Conceit, māna, is another akusala cetasika. There is conceit or pride when we consider ourselves important. Because of conceit we may compare ourselves with others. There can be conceit when we think ourselves better, equal or less than someone else. We may believe that there can be conceit only when we think ourselves better than someone else, but this is not so. There can be a kind of upholding of ourselves, of making ourselves important, while we compare ourselves with someone else, no matter in what way, and that is conceit.

We read in the *Dhammasangaṇi* (par1116):

> What is the Fetter of conceit?
> Conceit at the thought "I am the better man"; conceit at the thought "I am as good (as they)"; conceit at the thought "I am lowly"- all such sort of conceit, overweening conceitedness, loftiness, haughtiness, flaunting a flag, assumption, desire of the heart for self-advertisement—this is called conceit.

The three ways of comparing oneself with others may occur in someone who is actually superior, in someone who is actually equal and in someone who is actually inferior. Under this aspect there are nine kinds of conceit[1].

There is no need for comparing, no matter whether we are in fact superior, equal or inferior. We accumulate more akusala whenever we make ourselves important in comparing ourselves with others, no matter under what aspect.

Even when we do not compare ourselves with someone else we may find ourselves important and then there is conceit. Conceit always goes together with attachment, with clinging. It can arise with the four types of lobha-mūla-citta which are not accompanied by wrong view. Conceit and wrong view are different realities which do not arise at the same time. When one takes a reality for permanent or for self there is wrong view and there cannot be at the same time conceit, which is pride or self-assertion. This does not mean that there is conceit every time lobha-mūla-citta without wrong view arises. Lobha-mūla-citta without wrong view may sometimes be accompanied by conceit, sometimes not.

The *Atthasālinī* (II, Part IX, Chapter III, 256) gives the following definition of conceit: . . . Herein conceit is fancying (deeming, vain imagining). It has haughtiness as characteristic, self-praise as function, desire to (advertise self like) a banner as manifestation, greed dissociated from opinionatedness as proximate cause, and should be regarded as (a form of) lunacy.

Attachment is the proximate cause of conceit, but it is attachment which is dissociated from wrong view (diṭṭhigata-vippayutta). As we have seen, conceit does not arise together with wrong view; it arises with lobha-mūla-citta which is dissociated from wrong view.

---

[1] Book of Analysis par962 and Atthasālinī II, Book II, Part II, Summary, par Chapter II, 372.

The *Visuddhimagga* (XIV, 168) gives a similar definition, but it mentions as manifestation of conceit "vaingloriousness" and it does not mention the desire to advertise oneself like a banner[2].

In the definition of the *Atthasālinī* conceit as desire for self-advertisement is compared to the desire for a banner. A banner is hoisted into the air so that everyone can see it. We tend to find ourselves important, to uphold ourselves.

Conceit is like a lunacy or madness. Although there is no need for self-advertisement or for comparing ourselves with others we still do so, because conceit has been accumulated. The study of akusala dhammas is most helpful. If we do not know what conceit is and in which cases it can arise, we will accumulate more and more conceit without realizing it.

So long as conceit has not been eradicated there are many opportunities for its arising. It arises more often than we would think. The *Book of Analysis* (Vibhaṅga, Chapter 17, par832) gives a very revealing list of the objects on account of which pride and conceit can arise[3]:

Pride of birth; pride of clan; pride of health; pride of youth; pride of life; pride of gain; pride of being honoured; pride of being respected; pride of prominence; pride of having adherents; pride of wealth; pride of appearance; pride of erudition; pride of intelligence; pride of being a knowledgeable authority; pride of being (a regular) alms collector; pride of being not despised; pride of posture (bearing); pride of accomplishment; pride of popularity; pride of being moral; pride of jhāna; pride of dexterity; pride of being tall; pride of (bodily) proportion; pride of form; pride of (bodily) perfection...

All these objects can be a source of intoxication and conceit and we should consider them in daily life, that is why they are enumerated. Conceit can arise on account of each of the objects which are experienced through the senses. When we experience a pleasant object through one of the senses we may have conceit because of that; we may think ourselves superior in comparison with someone else who did not receive such a pleasant object. At that moment we forget that the experience of pleasant objects through the senses is only vipāka, conditioned by kamma. Thus, there is no reason to be proud of a pleasant experience. But ignorance covers up the truth, it conditions the arising of all sorts of akusala dhammas. Conceit can arise not only on account of the objects experienced through the senses, but also on account of the senses themselves. When we see someone who is blind there may be pride on account of our eyesense.

One may be proud because of one's birth, because of the family into which one is born. Or conceit may arise on account of the race one belongs to, on account of one's nationality or the colour of one's skin. Some people may find the colour of their skin better than the colour of someone else's skin. That is conceit. Conceit may also arise because of beauty, possessions, rank or work. Or because of one's

---

[2] Compare also Dhammasangaṇi par1116, and the explanation of it in the Atthasālinī, Book II, Summary, Chapter II, 372.

[3] Pride is the translation of "mada", which literally means intoxication. In par843, 844, the same list of objects is mentioned as being objects for pride (māna) and conceit. In par845 pride is defined in the same way as conceit.

skills, knowledge, education or wisdom. There may be the wish to "advertise" oneself because of these things. We like to be honoured and praised and the worst thing which can happen to us is to be forgotten, to be overlooked. We think of ourselves as "somebody" and we do not want to be treated as a "nobody". Our actions, speech and thoughts are often motivated by an idea of competition; we may not want other people to be better than we are, even with regard to kusala and right understanding.

The "Book of Analysis" classifies conceit in many different ways in order to show different aspects. We read, for example, about "self-disrespect conceit" (omāna, par881). When someone has self-disdain or self-contempt he still upholds himself and finds himself important. There is also "over-estimating conceit". Someone may erroneously think that he has attained jhāna or realized stages of wisdom and have conceit about it. We read in the *Book of Analysis* (Chapter 17, par882) about over-estimating conceit (adhimāna):

> Therein, what is "over-estimating conceit"? In not having reached, there is perception of having reached; in not having done, there is perception of having done; in not having attained, there is perception of having attained; in not having realized, there is perception of having realized; that which is similar, conceit, being conceited, the state of being conceited, loftiness, haughtiness, (flaunting a) flag, assumption, desire of consciousness for a banner. This is called over-estimating conceit.

There are many forms of conceit. Conceit has been accumulated for so long and it is bound to arise time and again. When we are dissatisfied with the way other people treat us there are bound to be moments of aversion, but there may also be moments of conceit. We find ourselves important and then we suffer again from desire for self-advertisement; we want to be esteemed. We may be conceited about erudition, about "being a knowledgeable authority", as the "Book of Analysis" expressed it so accurately. We may want to prove our value to others in the field of knowledge about Dhamma. Then we let the banner fly again.

We tend to have prejudices about certain people, even about our relatives, we may look down on them. We should find out whether we have conceit when we are together with other people. If we understand the disadvantage of all akusala dhammas, also of conceit, there are conditions for the arising of wholesome qualities such as loving kindness or compassion. We believe that it is mostly our anger and aversion which are unpleasant for others, but when there is conceit there is also lack of kindness and consideration for other people. When there is loving kindness there is no opportunity for conceit.

There are many moments of forgetfulness and then we do not notice when there is conceit. A moment of conceit, of upholding ourselves, can arise so easily. For example, when we hear about the salary someone else is earning, there may be a moment of comparing, of upholding ourselves. Or, when one is driving the car and sees others waiting for the bus, there may be a notion of "I have a car, I am lucky", a short moment of comparing, instead of cultivating loving kindness and compassion. We find such thoughts ugly and we do not like to admit that we have them, but they arise because there are conditions for their arising; conceit is a conditioned dhamma (saṅkhāra dhamma). We should be sincere and investigate the realities which arise, including akusala dhammas. This is the only way to see that they are non-self.

When one is young, one may compare oneself with someone who is old. When we see someone who is sick or who is about to die, we may be glad that we are healthy and alive and there may be conceit about our health. We are subject to old age, sickness and death at this very moment. There is no need for comparing. Instead of conceit there could be right understanding of the impermanence of all conditioned realities.

Conceit is like a "lunacy", we are foolish when we have conceit. Conceit is akusala dhamma, it is impure. When there is conceit there is also ignorance which does not know the true nature of realities. There is shamelessness, ahirika, which is not ashamed of akusala, there is recklessness, anottappa, which does not see the danger of akusala, and there is restlessness, uddhacca, which is confused and prevents the citta from being stable in kusala.

Conceit is eradicated only when arahatship has been attained. The sotāpanna (who has attained the first stage of enlightenment), the sakadāgāmī (who has attained the second stage of enlightenment) and the anāgāmī (who has attained the third stage of enlightenment) still have conceit. Even those who have eradicated the wrong view of self and who have realized that what is called a "person" are only nāmas and rūpas which arise and fall away, may still cling to nāma and rūpa with conceit. Conceit has been accumulated for so long. One may think "one's own" nāmas and rūpas better, equal or less than someone else's, even though one has realized that there is no self.

All those who are not arahats, even the ariyans who have not attained arahatship, have to develop satipaṭṭhāna until all akusala dhammas have been eradicated. This reminds us to be aware of what appears now, even if it is conceit. The akusala dhammas which arise can remind us of the need to continue to be mindful even though we do not see much progress. We should be grateful to the Buddha who taught us all dhammas. If he had not taught about conceit we would not have known that there are many opportunities for its arising. It is beneficial to come to realize one's akusala dhammas.

18.1.1 Questions

1. Conceit arises with lobha-mūla-citta without wrong view. Is there conceit every time such a type of lobha-mūla-citta arises?
2. Why is there conceit when one thinks oneself inferior to someone else?
3. The sotāpanna has eradicated the wrong view of self. Why can he still have conceit?

19 Aversion

19.1 Aversion (dosa)

Dosa, aversion, is another akusala cetasika. When the citta dislikes the object it experiences there is dosa, aversion. When there is dosa, the feeling which accompanies the citta is always unpleasant feeling. We do not like to feel unhappy and we want to suppress our unpleasant feeling. However, dosa-mūla-citta arises when there are conditions for its arising. We may try to suppress unpleasant feeling because we cling to pleasant feeling; we are ignorant of the real cause of unpleasant feeling and of the disadvantages of akusala.

We should study the factors which condition dosa-mūla-citta. The scriptures and the commentaries show us many aspects of dosa and if we study these aspects we will have more understanding of the disadvantages and the danger of dosa. Right understanding sees the danger of akusala and conditions kusala. It is more beneficial to have right understanding of dosa than just trying to suppress it without any understanding of it.

There always seem to be numerous causes for dosa and they invariably seem to be outside ourselves: other people's actions or unhappy events which occur. However, the real cause is within ourselves. Dosa has been accumulated and it can always find an object. We are attached to pleasant objects and when we do not experience pleasant objects there is bound to be dosa. When dosa arises it shows that the attachment which conditions it must be very strong.

The *Atthasālinī* (II, Book I, Part IX, Chapter III, 257) defines dosa as follows:

...It has flying into anger or churlishness as characteristic, like a smitten snake; spreading of itself or writhing as when poison takes effect, as function; or, burning that on which it depends[1] as function, like jungle-fire; offending or injuring as manifestation, like a foe who has got his chance; having the grounds of vexation as proximate cause, like urine mixed with poison.

The *Visuddhimagga* (XIV, 171) gives a similar definition of dosa[2].

We read that the characteristic of dosa is flying into anger like a smitten snake. When a snake has been hit he is likely to become fierce and attack. Dosa is aggressive, just like a snake which has been hit. The function of dosa is spreading of itself or writhing as when poison takes effect. When poison has been taken it affects the whole body and it causes suffering. Dosa has likewise an ill effect, it is harmful. The function of dosa is also compared to a jungle-fire which burns that on which it depends. Dosa is destructive like a jungle-fire which consumes the forest. The proximate cause of dosa are "grounds for annoyance, like urine mixed with poison". Urine mixed with poison is not liked by anybody, although urine was taken as a medicine in India. It is useful to study the proximate cause of dosa, the "grounds

---

[1] Namely, its physical base, which is the heart-base. The rūpa which is the physical base of all cittas other than the sense-cognitions of seeing, hearing, etc., is called the heart-base. See Abhidhamma in Daily Life, Chapter 17.

[2] Compare also Dhammasangaṇi par418.

for annoyance". Dosa often arises on account of what others are doing or saying to us or to someone else. Even a good deed done to someone else can be a reason for annoyance if we dislike that person. We read in the *Book of Analysis* (Chapter 17, par960) about nine reasons for dosa:

> Therein what are "nine bases of vexation"? "He has done me harm", thus vexation arises; "He is doing me harm", thus vexation arises; "He will do me harm", thus vexation arises; "He has done harm, . . . he is doing harm, . . . he will do harm to one dear and pleasant to me", thus vexation arises; "He has done good, . . . he is doing good, . . . he will do good to one not dear and not pleasant to me", thus vexation arises. These are nine bases of vexation.

Dosa arises with two types of citta, of which one is "unprompted" (asaṅkhārika) and one "prompted" (sasaṅkhārika)[3]. There are many degrees of dosa. It may be a slight aversion or it may be stronger, appearing as moodiness, bad temper, anger or hate. When dosa is strong one may speak harsh words or throw things about the house. One may feel desperate and commit suicide, one may hit others and even commit murder. When we hear about crimes other people have committed with dosa, we wonder how it could happen. When strong dosa arises it can lead to the committing of akusala kamma which we may not have thought ourselves capable of. Strong dosa can even motivate "heinous crimes" (anantarika kamma) which produce an unhappy rebirth immediately after the life during which one committed the crime has ended. We read about five heinous crimes in the *Gradual Sayings* (Book of the Fives, Chapter 13, par9, Festering):

> Monks, five are lost in hell who lie festering, incurable. What five?
>
> (By him) has his mother been deprived of life; his father; an arahat; (by him), with evil thought, has the Tathāgata's blood been drawn; (by him) has the Order been embroiled.
>
> Verily, monks, these are the five lost in hell who lie festering, incurable.

We should remember that all degrees of dosa are dangerous, even the lesser degrees. If we do not develop right understanding we accumulate more and more dosa without realizing it. Therefore, it is helpful to study the different aspects of dosa.

Dosa can motivate akusala kamma patha (unwholesome courses of action) through body, speech and mind. The akusala kamma patha through body which is killing is motivated by dosa. As to stealing, this can be motivated by lobha or by dosa. It is motivated by dosa when one wants to harm another person. Three of the four akusala kamma pathas through speech, namely lying, slandering and idle talk, can be motivated by lobha or by dosa. They are motivated by dosa when one wants to harm someone else. The akusala kamma patha which is rude speech is motivated by dosa. The akusala kamma patha through the mind which is ill-will is motivated by dosa. This is the intention to hurt or harm someone else. Akusala kamma brings sorrow both in this life and the next. The person who has committed akusala kamma may become afraid of the result it will bring and he has no peace

---

[3] See Abhidhamma in Daily Life, Chapter 6.

of mind. Dosa is harmful for mind and body. Because of dosa our appearance becomes ugly: we may become red in the face, our features become unpleasant and the corners of our mouth droop. If we remember that it is not considerate to show others an unpleasant face it can condition patience instead of dosa. There are many ill effects of dosa. It causes sleeplessness, the loss of friends, the loss of one's good name, of prosperity and wealth. And after this life has ended one may have an unhappy rebirth because of dosa.

We may not have dosa of the intensity to motivate the committing of akusala kamma patha, but even dosa which is of a lesser degree can condition unpleasant behaviour and speech. We can easily, before we realize it, utter harsh speech to someone else. When there is dosa, even if it is a slight annoyance, there is no loving kindness, no consideration for other people's feelings. When, for example, unexpected visitors arrive at a time we do not want to be disturbed, we may be annoyed. At such a moment there is mental rigidity, we are unable to adapt ourselves to a new situation with kindness and hospitality. The *Book of Analysis* (Chapter 17, par833) gives us a short but very effective reminder in a section in which pairs of realities are summed up (Twofold Summary): . . . Absence of softness and inhospitality.

This statement is meant as a reminder to be aware of realities of daily life. How true it is that inhospitality goes together with absence of softness, with mental rigidity. However, although there may be aversion at first when we are, for example, disturbed by unexpected visitors, right understanding can change our attitude. We may see the disadvantage of being inconsiderate to others and of absence of softness, of gentleness. Then we can receive our guests with kindness and we can see for ourselves that there is no longer mental rigidity and harshness, but pliancy of mind.

Dosa can also appear as fear. When there is fear one dislikes the object which is experienced. Fear is harmful for mind and body. One may have fear of people, of situations, of sickness, old age and death. So long as dosa has not been eradicated it will always find an object.

People have different accumulations: some people may have aversion at certain occasions while others do not. Dosa does not only arise because of what other people do or don't do, it can arise on account of any object experienced through one of the six doors. One may even be cross with the rain, the sun or the wind. We read in the *Atthasālinī* (II, Book II, Part II, Summary, Chapter II, 367):

> . . . "Or when vexation (springs up) groundlessly" means anger without reason; for example, someone gets angry saying "it rains too much", "it does not rain", "the sun shines too much", "it does not shine"; gets angry when the wind blows, when it does not blow, gets angry at being unable to sweep away the Bodhi leaves, at being unable to put on his robe; he gets angry with the wind, in slipping he gets angry with a tree-stump. . .

The Buddha compares someone who gets angry very easily with an open sore. An open sore hurts at the slightest touch, it is foul and unpleasant to look at. We read in the *Gradual Sayings* (Book of the Threes, Chapter III, par25, The open sore):

> ...of what sort, monks, is the one whose mind is like an open sore? Herein a certain person is irritable and turbulent. When anything, no matter how trifling, is said to him, he becomes enraged, he gets angry and quarrelsome: he resents it and displays anger, hatred and sulkiness. Just as, for instance, when a festering sore, if struck by a stick or shard, discharges matter all the more, even so, monks, a certain person...displays anger, hatred and sulkiness. This one is called "He whose mind is like an open sore"...

The Buddha then spoke about the "lightning-minded", the person who has realized the four noble Truths but who is not yet arahat, and about the "diamond-minded", the arahat. Just as a diamond can cut everything, even a gem or a rock, even so has the arahat cut off, destroyed, the "āsavas"[4].

So long as we cling to the pleasant "worldly conditions" (loka-dhammas) of gain, fame, praise and well-being, we are bound to have aversion when they change. They change all the time but we forget that they are impermanent. When we lose possessions, when we do not receive honour, when we are blamed or when we suffer pain, we have aversion and sadness. Right understanding of realities, of kamma and vipāka, can help us to be more even-minded about pleasant and unpleasant things which happen to us. When we experience unpleasant objects through the senses, it is caused by akusala kamma, by unwholesome deeds which have been committed already, and nobody can avoid akusala vipāka when it is the right time for its arising. When we understand that aversion about akusala vipāka is not helpful, there can be "wise attention" instead of "unwise attention" to the objects which are experienced. There may be intellectual understanding of realities but this understanding cannot eradicate dosa and the other defilements. Only right understanding developed in vipassanā can eradicate them.

Dosa can be temporarily eliminated by the development of calm. When one sees the disadvantages of clinging to sensuous objects and one has accumulations for the development of calm to the degree of jhāna, one can be temporarily free from sense-impressions. Rūpāvacara kusala cittas (of "fine material jhāna") can produce result in the form of rebirth in rūpa-brahma planes and arūpāvacara kusala cittas (of immaterial jhāna) can produce results in the form of rebirth in arūpa-brahma planes. Although lobha and moha can arise in these planes[5], there are no conditions for dosa. However, dosa arises again when there is rebirth in one of the sensuous planes. As we have seen, clinging to sense objects conditions dosa. Only when the stage of the anāgāmī has been attained dosa has been eradicated. The anāgāmī does not cling to sense objects and thus he has no conditions for dosa.

Dosa can eventually be eradicated only if we develop right understanding of realities. Right understanding sees dosa as it really is: as saṅkhāra dhamma, conditioned dhamma, non-self. Through mindfulness of dosa its characteristic can be known. We believe that it is easy to recognize dosa, but we usually think of the concept "dosa" or "aversion", and then its characteristic will not be known. We

---

[4] "Intoxicants", a group of defilements.

[5] Except in the rūpa- brahma plane which is the asañña-satta plane, the plane of "unconscious beings", where there is only rūpa.

will still take it for "my dosa", instead of realizing that it is only a kind of nāma which arises because of conditions.

It may happen that we have so much aversion about our aversion and about the unpleasant feeling which accompanies it, that we believe that we cannot be mindful of the reality of the present moment. In theory we know that there can be mindfulness of any reality which appears now, but what about the practice? When we see the benefit of right understanding of whatever reality appears, there are conditions for the arising of mindfulness, even when it seems that we are not "in the mood" for it.

It seems that we do not have hatred or anger, but this does not mean that dosa has been eradicated. So long as there is still the latent tendency of dosa, it can arise any time. We read in the *Middle Length Sayings* (I, no. 21, The Parable of the Saw) about Videhikā who was calm so long as there was no opportunity for dosa. It seemed that she had no dosa at all. She had an excellent reputation, she appeared to be gentle, meek and calm. Her servant Kāḷiī wanted to test her and she came to work later every day. Because of this Videhikā lost her temper: she hit Kāḷiī on her head with the pin used for securing the door bolt. Because of that she acquired an evil reputation. We read that the Buddha said to the monks:

> Even so, monks, some monk here is very gentle, very meek, very tranquil so long as disagreeable ways of speech do not assail him. But when disagreeable ways of speech assail the monk it is then that he is to be called gentle, is to be called meek, is to be called tranquil...

The Buddha exhorted the monks to have a "mind of friendliness", even if others spoke to them in a disagreeable way, even if low-down thieves would carve them limb by limb with a double-handled saw.

Those who have eradicated dosa, the anāgāmī and the arahat, never have anger nor the slightest displeasure, even in circumstances which are very difficult to bear, even when they have to endure sickness or pain.

We tend to have aversion when we have pain or when we are sick. When an unpleasant object impinges on the bodysense, body-consciousness accompanied by painful feeling experiences that object. Body-consciousness is vipākacitta, it is in this case the result of akusala kamma. Shortly afterwards in that process of cittas dosa-mūla-cittas are likely to arise which experience that object with aversion. It seems almost inevitable that aversion arises after the body-consciousness which experiences an unpleasant object. In order to have right understanding of the different phenomena which occur, it is necessary to develop mindfulness of nāma and rūpa. There are many different types of nāma and rūpa when we have pain and when we have aversion about pain, and they can be objects of awareness one at a time. Right understanding of nāma and rūpa will help us to bear great pains and to be patient in case of sickness. If we begin to develop right understanding of realities at this moment we accumulate conditions for its arising when we are sick or when we are about to die.

19.1.1 Questions

1. Is the suppression of unpleasant feeling always done with kusala citta?

2. What are the proximate causes for dosa?
3. When there are unpleasant “worldly conditions” we are likely to have dosa. How can right understanding of kamma and vipāka help us to have kusala citta instead of dosa?
4. Why is there no dosa in the rūpa-brahma planes and in the arūpa-brahma planes?
5. Why can dosa not be eradicated without developing right understanding of nāma and rūpa? Why can it not be eradicated by just developing loving kindness?
6. When we suffer from sickness and when we are about to die what is the most beneficial thing that can be done in order not to be overcome by dosa? What should be done if dosa arises in such circumstances?

20 Envy, Stinginess, Regret

20.1 Introduction

There are three akusala dhammas which can arise only with dosa-mūla-citta, citta rooted in aversion, namely: *envy* (issā), *stinginess* (macchariya) and *regret* (kukkucca). Aversion tends to arise often, both in sense-door processes and in mind-door processes, because we have accumulated so much aversion. Dosa-mūla-citta is always accompanied by unpleasant feeling. We may notice that we have aversion and unpleasant feeling, but we should also come to know other defilements which can arise with dosa-mūla-citta, namely: envy, stinginess and regret. These akusala cetasikas can, one at a time, accompany dosa-mūla-citta. This does not mean that dosa-mūla-citta is always accompanied by one of these three akusala cetasikas. Sometimes dosa-mūla-citta is accompanied by one of these three and sometimes it is not accompanied by any of them. I shall now deal with these three akusala cetasikas.

20.2 Envy (issā)

As regards envy or jealousy, this can arise when someone else receives a pleasant object. At such a moment we may wonder why he receives a pleasant object and why we don't. Envy is always accompanied by unpleasant feeling, because it can only arise with dosa-mūla-citta, with the citta which dislikes the object which is experienced. We dislike unpleasant feeling, but merely disliking it does not help us to have kusala citta instead of akusala citta. We should know the different types of defilements which can arise with akusala citta. It is useful to study their characteristics, functions, manifestations and proximate causes. When we see how ugly defilements are and when we understand their danger, we are reminded to develop satipaṭṭhāna which is the only way to eradicate them. There is no other way.

The *Atthasālinī* (II, Book I, Part IX, Chapter III, 257) gives the following definition of envy: ...It has the characteristic of envying, of not enduring the prosperity of others, the function of taking no delight in such prosperity, the manifestation of turning one's face from such prosperity, the proximate cause being such prosperity; and it should be regarded as a fetter.

The *Visuddhimagga* (XIV, 172) gives a similar definition[1].

The proximate cause of envy is someone else's prosperity. When there is jealousy one cannot stand it that others receive pleasant objects. At that moment there cannot be "sympathetic joy" (muditā). We may be jealous when someone else receives a gift, when he receives honour or praise because of his good qualities or his wisdom. When there is jealousy we do not want someone else to be happy and we may even wish that he will lose the pleasant objects or the good qualities he possesses.

---

[1] Compare also Dhammasangaṇi, par1121, and Vibhaṅga par893.

Envy is dangerous. When it is strong it can motivate akusala kamma patha (unwholesome course of action) and this is capable of producing an unhappy rebirth. One may, because of jealousy, even kill someone else.

We all have accumulated jealousy and thus it is bound to arise. It is useful to notice the moments of jealousy, also when it is of a slight degree. We may be jealous when someone else is praised. We want to be praised ourselves and we do not want to be overlooked, we find ourselves important. In reality there is no self, only nāma and rūpa which arise because of their own conditions. The sotāpanna has right understanding of realities, he knows that there is no person who can receive or possess pleasant objects. He realizes that all experiences are only conditioned realities which do not stay and do not belong to a self. He has no more conditions for jealousy, he has eradicated it.

When we see the disadvantages of envy we will cultivate conditions for having it less often. Sympathetic joy, muditā, is the opposite of envy. Muditā is sympathetic joy in someone else's prosperity and happiness. The Buddha taught us different ways of developing wholesomeness and the development of sympathetic joy is one of them. At first it may be difficult to rejoice in other people's happiness, but when we appreciate the value of sympathetic joy there are conditions for its arising. It can gradually become our nature to rejoice in other people's happiness. When there is sympathetic joy, the citta is kusala citta. Each kusala citta is accompanied by non-attachment, alobha, non-hate, adosa, and it may be accompanied by right understanding or without it. Envy cannot be eradicated by sympathetic joy, even if we have many moments of it. Only right understanding of nāma and rūpa can eventually eradicate envy.

20.3 Stinginess (macchariya)

Stinginess or avarice, macchariya, is another akusala cetasika which can arise with dosa-mūla-citta. It does not arise with every dosa-mūla-citta, but when it arises it accompanies dosa-mūla-citta. When there is stinginess there is also aversion towards the object which is experienced at that moment and the feeling is unpleasant feeling. Stinginess cannot arise with lobha-mūla-citta or with moha-mūla-citta.

The *Atthasālinī* (II, Book I, Part IX, Chapter II, 257) gives the following definition of avarice (meanness):

It has, as characteristic, the concealing of one's property, either attained or about to be attained; the not enduring the sharing of one's property in common with others, as function; the shrinking from such sharing or niggardliness or sour feeling as manifestation; one's own property as proximate cause; and it should be regarded as mental ugliness.

The *Visuddhimagga* (XIV, 173) gives a similar definition.

When there is stinginess there is a cramped state of mind, one cannot stretch out one's hand in order to give a gift. The proximate cause of avarice is one's own property, whereas, as we have seen, the proximate cause of envy is someone else's prosperity. When there is avarice one is unable to share what one has (or will acquire) with someone else.

There are five kinds of objects on account of which stinginess can arise. We read in the *Dhammasangaṇi* (par1122) in its definition of the fetter of meanness:

> The five meannesses, (to wit) meanness as regards dwelling, families, gifts, reputation, dhamma—all this sort of meanness, grudging, mean spirit, avarice and ignobleness, niggardliness and want of generosity of heart—this is called the fetter of meanness.

The *Atthasālinī* (II, Book II, Part II, Chapter II, 376), in its explanation of the words of the *Dhammasangaṇi*, states that the mean person also hinders someone else from giving. Stinginess can motivate one to try to persuade someone else, for example one's husband or wife, to give less or not to give at all. We read in the *Atthasālinī* :

```
...and this also has been said,
Malicious, miserly, ignoble, wrong...
Such men hinder the feeding of the poor...
```

> A "niggardly" person seeing mendicants causes his mind to shrink as by sourness. His state is "niggardliness". Another way (of definition):- "niggardliness is a "spoon-feeding". For when the pot is full to the brim, one takes food from it by a spoon with the edge bent on all sides; it is not possible to get a spoonful; so is the mind of a mean person bent in. When it is bent in, the body also is bent in, recedes, is not diffused—thus stinginess is said to be niggardliness.
>
> "Lack of generosity of heart" is the state of a mind which is shut and gripped, so that it is not stretched out in the mode of making gifts, etc., in doing service to others. But because the mean person wishes not to give to others what belongs to himself, and wishes to take what belongs to others, therefore this meanness should be understood to have the characteristic of hiding or seizing one's own property, occurring thus: "May it be for me and not for another"...

As regards the five kinds of objects one can be stingy about[2], the *Atthasālinī* (II, Book II, Part II, Chapter II, 373-375) explains about these five kinds and mentions that there is no stinginess if one does not want to share these things with a person who will use them in the wrong way or with a bhikkhu who will disgrace the Sangha.

As regards stinginess about dwelling, the "dwelling" can be a monastery, a single room or any place where one stays, no matter whether it is big or small. We can be stingy with regard to any place where we are comfortable, such as a corner in a room or a seat.

As regards stinginess about "family", this can be a family of servitors to a monastery or one's relatives. A bhikkhu who is stingy does not want another bhikkhu to approach a family he usually visits, because he does not want to share with someone else the goods he receives. We may be stingy not only with regard to things, but also with regard to words of praise. For example, when we, together with others, have accomplished a work of charity, we may only want to be praised

---

[2] Compare also Vibhaṅga, Chapter 17, par893, for these five kinds of objects.

ourselves; we may not want to share honour and praise with others, although they deserve to be praised as well. We should scrutinize ourselves as to this form of stinginess; we should find out whether it is easy for us to praise others. If we understand that praising someone's virtues is an act of generosity, we will more often remember to do this when the opportunity arises. When we praise someone else there is no room for stinginess. There are many different ways of kusala and in our daily life there are opportunities right at hand for one kind of kusala or other, no matter whether we are alone or with other people.

Someone may be stingy as to Dhamma. He may not want to share Dhamma with others because he is afraid that they will acquire the same amount of knowledge as he himself or even more. The sotāpanna who has realized the four noble Truths, has eradicated all forms of stinginess. He wishes everyone to know and realize the Dhamma he has realized himself. Those who are non-ariyans may have stinginess as to Dhamma. However, there may be good reasons for not teaching Dhamma. One should not teach Dhamma to someone who is bound to abuse the Dhamma and to interpret it wrongly, or to someone who will erroneously take himself for an arahat because of his knowledge. There is no stinginess if one does not teach Dhamma to such persons, because one acts then out of consideration for the Dhamma or out of consideration for people.

In the ultimate sense there are no things we can possess, there are only nāma and rūpa. If we remember this we can see that it is foolish to think that realities which arise and fall away belong to us and that we can keep them. Why are we stingy about what does not belong to us? We cannot take our possessions, our money with us when we die. Human life is so short and we waste many opportunities for kusala because of our stinginess. In the absolute sense there is no self, no person who can possess anything. Our life consists of nāma and rūpa which arise and fall away. Life is actually one moment of experiencing an object; this moment falls away and is succeeded by a next moment which is different again. We cannot possess visible object or hardness. They are only rūpas which do not stay and do not belong to us. When understanding has been developed more there will be less stinginess. The sotāpanna who sees nāma and rūpa as they are, as impermanent and not self, has no more conditions for stinginess.

We should find out why we are stingy. We do not want to give things away because we fear that our possessions will decrease, but then we are likely to suffer from the very things we are afraid of. The experience of objects through the senses is vipāka, the result of kamma. We read in the *Kindred Sayings* (I, Sagāthā-vagga, Chapter I, The Devas, Part 4, par2, Avarice) that devas of the Satullapa group came to see the Buddha and spoke to him about avarice and generosity. One among them said:

```
...That which the miser dreads, and hence gives not,
To him not giving just that danger it is:
Hunger and thirst---for this the thing he dreads---
Just this the doom that does befall the fool
In this and also in some other world.
```

```
Hence should he avarice suppress, and make
Offerings of charity, mastering the taint.
Sure platform in some other future world
Rewards of virtue on good beings wait.
```

The five kinds of avarice can motivate akusala kamma which is capable of producing an unhappy rebirth or akusala vipāka in the course of one's life: one may have to endure hardship, poverty, disease and dishonour. The *Atthasālinī*, in the section about meanness (375) speaks about the unpleasant results produced by the five kinds of stinginess and states about the results of stinginess with regard to praise and to Dhamma:

> ...one who extols his own praises and not those of others; who mentions this and that fault of anyone saying, "What praise does he deserve?" and does not impart any doctrine of learning to him, becomes ugly, or has a mouth dripping with saliva...

The person who has a mouth dripping with saliva cannot speak in a pleasant way and is ugly to look at, therefore people do not like to listen to him. Further on the *Atthasālinī* states that the result of stinginess with regard to praise can also be that one is born without beauty or reputation. Owing to stinginess with regard to Dhamma one may also be reborn in one of the hell planes, the "hot-ash hell".

So long as one has not become a sotāpanna there are opportunities for the arising of stinginess. Some people have stinginess more often than others, or someone may have stinginess as to certain objects, such as money, but not as to other objects, such as praise or Dhamma; it all depends on people's accumulations. But even if someone is very stingy by nature, his attitude can be changed. Through right understanding one can learn to develop generosity.

We read in the commentary to the *Sudhābhojana-Jātaka* (Jātakas, Book V, no. 535) about a monk in the Buddha's time who practised the utmost generosity. He gave away his food and even if he received something to drink which was merely sufficient to fill the hollow of his hand, he would, free from greed, still give it away. But formerly he used to be so stingy that "he would not give so much as a drop of oil on the tip of a blade of grass". The Buddha spoke about one of this monk's former lives when he was the miser Kosiya and this is the story of the "Sudhābhojana Jātaka".

Kosiya did not keep up the tradition of almsgiving of his ancestors and lived as a miser. One day he had craving for rice-porridge. When his wife suggested that she would cook rice-porridge not only for him but also for all the inhabitants of Vārānasi, he felt "just as if he had been struck on the head with a stick". As we have read in the definition of avarice in the *Atthasālinī*, its manifestation is "the shrinking from such sharing, or niggardliness or sour feeling..." When there is avarice there is always unpleasant feeling, there cannot be any happiness.

We then read in the Jātaka that Kosiya's wife subsequently offered to cook for a single street, for the attendants in his house, for the family, for the two of them, but he turned down all her offers. He wanted to cook porridge only for himself, in the forest, so that nobody else could see it. We should remember that the characteristic of stinginess is the concealing of one's property. One wants to hide it because one does not want to share it.

We then read in the Jātaka that the Bodhisatta who was at that time the god Sakka wanted to convert him and came to him with four attendants disguised as brahmins. One by one they approached the miser and begged for some of his porridge. Sakka spoke the following stanza, praising generosity (387):

```
From little one should little give, from moderate means likewise,
From much give much: of giving nought no question can arise.
This then I tell thee, Kosiya, give alms of that is thine:
Eat not alone, no bliss is his that by himself shall dine,
By charity thou mayst ascend the noble path divine.
```

Kosiya reluctantly offered some porridge to them. Then one of the brahmins changed himself into a dog. The dog made water and a drop of it fell on Kosiya's hand. Kosiya went to the river to wash and then the dog made water in Kosiya's cooking pot. When Kosiya threatened him he changed into a "blood horse" and pursued Kosiya. Then Sakka and his attendants stood in the air and Sakka preached to Kosiya out of compassion and warned him of an unhappy rebirth. Kosiya came to understand the danger of stinginess. He gave away all his possessions and became an ascetic.

At the end of the Jātaka the Buddha said: "Not now only, monks, but of old also I converted this niggardly fellow who was a confirmed miser".

Right understanding sees the danger of akusala and it conditions the development of kusala. When we still cling so much to our possessions and are stingy with regard to them it will be all the more difficult to become detached from the self. We should develop generosity in giving away useful things and also in praising those who deserve praise. We should see the value of all kinds of kusala. When the citta is kusala citta there is no stinginess, but stinginess can only be eradicated by the development of right understanding of any reality which appears.

20.4 Regret (kukkucca)

Regret or *worry,* kukkucca, is another akusala cetasika which can arise with dosa-mūla-citta. It does not arise with every dosa-mūla-citta, but when it arises, it arises only with dosa-mūla-citta. It cannot arise with lobha-mūla-citta or with moha-mūla-citta. When there is regret there is also aversion towards the object which is experienced at that moment. Therefore, the feeling which accompanies kukkucca is always unpleasant feeling.

The *Atthasālinī* (II, Book II, Part IX, Chapter III, 258) gives the following definition of kukkucca:

> ...It has repentance as characteristic, sorrow at deeds of commission and omission as function, regret as manifestation, deeds of commission and omission as proximate cause, and it should be regarded as a state of bondage.

The *Visuddhimagga* (XIV, 174) gives a similar definition.

The characteristic of kukkucca is repentance. Repentance is generally considered a virtue, but the reality of kukkucca is not wholesome, it arises with dosa-mūla-citta. Kukkucca which "regrets" the commission of evil and the omission of kusala is different from wholesome thinking about the disadvantages of akusala and the value of kusala. The conventional term "worry" which is also used as translation of kukkucca may not be clear either. When we say that we worry, it may not be the reality of kukkucca but it may be thinking with aversion about an unpleasant object without there being kukkucca. For example, we may worry about the way how to solve a problem in the future; this kind of worry is not the reality of kukkucca.

If we take note of the proximate cause of kukkucca we will better understand what kukkucca is. The proximate cause of kukkucca is akusala kamma through body, speech and mind which has been committed and also kusala kamma through body, speech and mind which has been omitted. We read in the *Dhammasangaṇi* (par1304 and 1305):

> Which are the states that conduce to remorse?:
>
> Misconduct in act, word and thought. Besides, all bad states conduce to remorse.
>
> Which are the states that do not conduce to remorse?
>
> Good conduct in act, word and thought. Besides, no good states (absence of good states) conduce to remorse.

The *Atthasālinī* (II, Book II, Part II, Chapter II, 389, 390) explains this passage of the *Dhammasangaṇi*:

> In the exposition of the couplet of what "conduces to remorse" (*Dhammasangaṇi*, par1304), "remorse" arises from what has been done and what has been left undone. Acts of misconduct burn from commission, acts of good conduct burn from omission. Thus a person feels remorse (literally: burns) at the thought, "I have misconducted myself", "I have left undone the right act"; "I have spoken amiss", . . . I have left undone the right thoughts". Similarly with what does not "conduce to remorse". Thus a person doing good does not feel remorse over acts of commission or omission.

When we have slandered or spoken harsh words there may be remorse about it afterwards. There can also be remorse about our neglectfulness of kusala, we often waste opportunities for kusala. We may be stingy when there is an opportunity for giving or for praising someone who deserves praise. Or we are neglectful as to the development of right understanding of realities. As a consequence of our omission of kusala regret may arise.

We read in the *Middle Length Sayings* (III, 129, Discourse on Fools and the Wise) about the anguishes which may be experienced by a fool who has done wrong deeds through body, speech and mind. He experiences anguish because other people talk about his akusala, and thus he acquires a bad name. He fears punishment for his evil deeds and therefore he experiences anguish. Moreover, he has remorse because of his evil deeds and his neglectfulness as to kusala. We read:

> And again, monks, while a fool is on a chair or bed or lying on the ground, at such a time those evil deeds that he has formerly wrongly done by body, speech and thought rest on him, lie on him, settle on him. Monks, as at eventide the shadows

of the great mountain peaks rest, lie and settle on earth, so, monks, do these evil deeds that the fool has formerly wrongly done by body, speech and thought rest, lie and settle on him as he is on a chair or bed or lying on the ground. Thereupon, monks, it occurs thus to the fool: "Indeed what is lovely has not been done by me, what is skilled has not been done, no refuge against fearful (consequences) has been made, evil has been done, cruelty has been done, violence has been done. Insofar as there is a bourn for those who have not done what is lovely, have not done what is skilled, have not made a refuge against fearful (consequences), who have done evil, cruelty and violence, to that bourn I am going hereafter". He grieves, mourns, laments, beats his breast, wails and falls into disillusionment. . .

The committing of akusala kamma and the omitting of kusala kamma is a condition for remorse and because of this remorse one is unhappy, one does not have peace of mind. Akusala kamma can produce an unhappy rebirth and also unpleasant experiences through the senses in the course of life.

Regret is one of the "hindrances" (nīvaraṇas) and as such it forms a pair with restlessness, uddhacca. The "hindrances" are akusala cetasikas which hinder the performing of kusala. When regret arises there cannot be kusala at that moment.

We read in the definition of regret that it should be regarded as a state of bondage. The citta with regret is not free, it is enslaved. At such a moment there is no peacefulness, no happiness.

If one has not studied the Dhamma and if one does not know about the different types of citta which arise there are less conditions for the cultivation of kusala. If kusala is not developed there are more akusala cittas and thus also more opportunities for the arising of remorse.

The monk who has to observe the rules of the Vinaya may have worry with regard to his observance of these rules. He may have scruples and he may even wrongly assume that he transgresses a rule or that he observes a rule. Worry and doubt may arise because of this. We read in the *Dhammasangaṇi* (Chapter IX, par1161):

> What is worry (kukkucca)?
>
> Consciousness of what is lawful in something that is unlawful; consciousness of what is unlawful in something that is lawful[3] ; consciousness of what is immoral in something that is moral; consciousness of what is moral in something that is immoral—all this sort of worry, fidgeting, overscrupulousness, remorse of conscience, mental scarifying- this is what is called worry.

It is hard to eradicate regret. Even the sotāpanna may still have regret, although he has no conditions for regret on account of akusala kamma which is of the intensity to produce an unhappy rebirth; he has eradicated the tendencies to such evil deeds. The sotāpanna still has lobha-mūla-citta, dosa-mūla-citta and moha-mūla-citta. He does not have dosa-mūla-citta with envy or stinginess, but dosa-mūla-citta still arises, and sometimes it may be accompanied by regret. He may speak harshly, or he may have laziness as to the performing of kusala, and on account of this regret

[3] Referring to rules pertaining to things such as kinds of food or the hour of the meal.

can arise. The sotāpanna is bound to have regret less often than those who are non-ariyans. When one has not attained enlightenment one may be often inclined to brood over the past. The sotāpanna has developed the four "Applications of Mindfulness", and thus he has less conditions than the non-ariyan to worry about the past. When regret arises he realizes that it is only a conditioned dhamma, saṅkhāra dhamma, and he does not take it for self.

We still consider regret as "my regret". We regret our akusala and our lack of mindfulness. If we realize that thinking with worry is not helpful it may be a condition to cultivate kusala. When there is forgetfulness of realities we should remember that it is a conditioned reality, not self. We should know the characteristics of akusala dhammas which arise as not self. Then there will be less regret.

According to the *Visuddhimagga* (XXII, 71) the anāgāmī has eradicated regret completely[4]. For him dosa-mūla-citta does not arise anymore and thus regret cannot arise either.

We should not only know the characteristic of dosa, but also the characteristics of other akusala cetasikas which can arise with dosa-mūla-citta: envy, stinginess and regret. As we have seen, dosa-mūla-citta can be accompanied by only one of these three akusala cetasikas at a time; they cannot arise simultaneously. They may or may not arise when dosa-mūla-citta arises. Sometimes there is dosa-mūla-citta without any of these three akusala cetasikas, sometimes there is dosa-mūla-citta accompanied by one of these three. We will come to know the characteristics of the different defilements more clearly by being mindful of them.

20.4.1 Questions

1. Why can envy arise only with dosa-mūla-citta?
2. Why is it helpful to cultivate the wholesome quality of sympathetic joy (muditā)?
3. Who has eradicated envy?
4. Can suffering from hunger and thirst be a result of stinginess?
5. Can those who are very stingy by nature learn to become less stingy? In what way?
6. Who has eradicated stinginess?
7. What is the proximate cause of regret?
8. In what way can akusala kamma cause sorrow both in this world and the next?
9. Who has eradicated regret completely?

---

[4] According to the Atthasālinī (Book II, Part II, Chapter II, 384) the sotāpanna has eradicated regret. The sotāpanna has eradicated regret pertaining to coarse defilements, whereas the anāgāmī has eradicated regret which also pertains to subtle defilements.

21 Sloth, Torpor and Doubt

21.1 Sloth (thīna), Torpor (middha)

Thīna and middha are two akusala cetasikas which always arise together, they form a pair. Thīna can be translated as sloth or stolidity and middha as torpor or languor. When there are sloth and torpor one has no energy for kusala. In order to have more understanding of sloth and torpor we should study their characteristics, functions, manifestations and their proximate cause, and we should know which types of citta they can accompany.

The *Atthasālinī* (II, Book I, Part IX, Chapter II, 255) states about sloth and torpor: "Absence of striving, difficulty through inability, is the meaning." We then read the following definitions of sloth and torpor:

> The compound "sloth-torpor" is sloth plus torpor; of which sloth has absence of, or opposition to striving as characteristic, destruction of energy as function, sinking of associated states as manifestation; torpor has unwieldiness as characteristic, closing the doors of consciousness as function, shrinking in taking the object, or drowsiness as manifestation; and both have unsystematic thought, in not arousing oneself from discontent and laziness (or indulgence), as proximate cause.

The *Visuddhimagga* (XIV, 167) gives a similar definition. The *Dhammasangaṇi* calls sloth (thīna) indisposition and unwieldiness of mind (par1156) and torpor (middha) indisposition and unwieldiness of cetasikas (par1157)[1]. When there are sloth and torpor there is no wieldiness of mind which is necessary for the performing of kusala. Instead there are mental stiffness and rigidity, mental sickness and laziness.

As we have seen, the *Atthasālinī* states that the characteristic of sloth is opposition to "striving", to energy. Also akusala citta is accompanied by energy (viriya), but this is wrong effort; it is different from right effort which accompanies kusala citta. When there are sloth and torpor there is no energy, no vigour to perform dāna, to observe sīla, to listen to Dhamma, to study the Dhamma or to develop calm, no energy to be mindful of the reality which appears now. This does not mean that whenever there is lack of mindfulness sloth and torpor arise. As we will see, they do not arise with all types of akusala citta.

As regards torpor, its characteristic is unwieldiness and its function is closing the doors of consciousness. It obstructs the performing of kusala, it "oppresses..., it injures by means of unwieldiness", the *Atthasālinī* (378) explains. The manifestation of sloth is "sinking of associated states", it causes the citta and cetasikas it accompanies to decline. The manifestation of torpor is "shrinking in taking the object" or drowsiness. The *Dhammasangaṇi* (par1157) calls torpor (middha) "drowsiness, sleep, slumbering, somnolence". The *Atthasālinī* (378) adds to drowsiness: "Drowsiness makes blinking of the eyelashes, etc." The arahat has eradicated

---

[1] See Vibhaṅga par547 and Atthasālinī II, Book II, Part II, Chapter II, 377.

sloth and torpor. He can still have bodily tiredness and he may sleep, but he has no sloth and torpor[2].

We may be inclined to think that sloth and torpor arise only when there is sleepiness, but when we study the types of citta which can be accompanied by sloth and torpor we will see that there can be many moments of them, also when we do not feel sleepy.

As we have seen, the proximate cause of sloth and torpor is "unsystematic thought, in not arousing oneself from discontent and laziness". When there are sloth and torpor there is "unsystematic thought", that is, unwise attention (ayoniso manasikāra) to the object which is experienced. At such moments we do not realize that life is short and that it is urgent to develop all kinds of kusala and in particular right understanding of realities. We all have moments that there is no energy to read the scriptures or to consider the Dhamma. We may be overcome by boredom, we are not interested to study and to consider the Dhamma, or we make ourselves believe that we are too busy. Sometimes, however, we may realize that even the reading of a few lines of the scriptures can be most beneficial, that it can remind us to be aware of realities which appear. We should remember that when there are sloth and torpor we are not merely standing still as to the development of kusala, but we are "sinking", we are going "downhill", since there is opportunity for the accumulation of more akusala. If we realize that the opportunity to develop right understanding of the present moment is only at the present moment, not at some moment in the future, there can be conditions for mindfulness and then there is "wise attention" instead of "unwise attention".

Sloth and torpor can arise only with akusala cittas which are "prompted", *sasaṅkhārika*. Some types of cittas are "unprompted" or not induced (asaṅkhārika) and some types are "prompted", instigated or induced. The inducement can be done by someone else or by oneself. The cittas which are prompted are, according to the *Visuddhimagga* (XIV, 91) "sluggish and urged on". Thus, sloth and torpor which are lazy and sluggish with regard to the performing of kusala arise only with the akusala cittas which are prompted[3]. They can arise with the *four types of lobha-mūla-citta* which are *sasaṅkhārika* and with *one type of dosa-mūla-citta*, the type which is *sasaṅkhārika*[4]. This does not mean that they arise every time the akusala citta is "prompted"; they may or may not arise with these five types of akusala citta. The two types of moha-mūla-citta are not "prompted", they cannot be accompanied by sloth and torpor.

Sloth and torpor can arise together with *wrong view*, *diṭṭhi*, and in this case they accompany lobha-mūla-citta which is associated with wrong view and prompted. Sloth and torpor can arise together with conceit, māna, and in this case they ac-

---

2 Atthasālinī II, Book II, Part II, Chapter II, 378.

3 In A Manual of Abhidhamma, in a footnote to akusala cetasikas, Ven. Narada explains that since sloth and torpor lack urge they cannot arise with cittas which are unprompted, cittas which are "keen and active".

4 There are eight types of lobha-mūla-citta, of which four are unprompted and four prompted; there are two types of dosa-mūla-citta, of which one is prompted and one unprompted. See Abhidhamma in Daily Life Chapter 4 and 6.

company lobha-mūla-citta which is without wrong view and prompted[5]. Sloth and torpor which arise with lobha-mūla-citta may be accompanied by pleasant feeling or by indifferent feeling.

Sloth and torpor can arise together with envy (issā), stinginess (macchariya) or regret (kukkucca) which, one at a time, can accompany dosa-mūla-citta, and in that case the dosa-mūla-citta is prompted. The accompanying feeling is unpleasant feeling.

Sloth and torpor are hard to eradicate. Even the sotāpanna, the sakadāgāmī and the anāgāmī still have sloth and torpor. Only the arahat has eradicated them completely. We are likely to have many moments of sloth and torpor, but it is not easy to know when they occur. We should remember that, when there are defilements such as wrong view, conceit, envy, stinginess or regret, sloth and torpor can arise as well if the citta they accompany is prompted. Sloth and torpor cause mental unwieldiness and mental indisposition or sickness, so that there is no vigour, no energy for kusala. Sloth and torpor are harmful, they are among the "hindrances" which prevent us from performing dāna, observing sīla or applying ourselves to mental development.

The Buddha told the monks to be moderate in eating and warned them not to be attached to the "ease of bed", because such attachments give rise to sloth and torpor which are mental sickness and which destroy energy for kusala. We read in the *Middle Length Sayings* (I, no. 16, Discourse on Mental Barrenness) that the Buddha, when he was staying near Sāvatthī, in the Jeta Grove, spoke about ways of mental barrenness and mental bondages. One of the mental bondages is attachment to food and sleep. We read that the Buddha said:

And again, monks, a monk having eaten as much as his belly will hold, lives intent on the ease of bed, on the ease of lying down, on the ease of slumber. Whatever monk, having eaten as much as his belly will hold, lives intent on the ease of bed, on the ease of lying down, on the ease of slumber, his mind does not incline to ardour, to continual application, to perseverance, to striving...

It is helpful, not only for monks, but also for laymen, to be reminded of conditions for laziness as to kusala.

We read in the *Gradual Sayings* (Book of the Fives, Chapter VI, par6, The preceptor) about a monk who complained to his preceptor concerning his lack of energy for kusala:

> Now a certain monk approached his preceptor and said:
>
> "My body, sir, is as it were drugged; the quarters are not seen by me; things[6] are not clear to me; sloth and torpor compass my heart about and stay; joyless, I live the holy life; and doubt about things are ever with me."

---

[5] Four of the eight types of lobha-mūla-citta are associated with wrong view, diṭṭhi, and four are without wrong view. Conceit can accompany lobha-mūla-citta without wrong view, but this is not always so.

[6] Dhammas. The commentary, the "Manorathapūraṇī", explains: samatha and vipassanā do not appear to that monk.

Such complaints may sound familiar to us, we may feel at times as though "drugged". Doubts about realities cannot be solved unless right understanding is being developed. There are nāma and rūpa all the time, there is seeing, visible object, hearing, sound, anger or attachment; the objects of which right understanding is to be developed are right at hand but often there is no awareness of them. We read that the preceptor went with this monk to the Buddha who exhorted him thus:

> "Monk, it is ever thus! When one dwells with doors of the senses unguarded, with no moderation in eating, not bent on vigilance, not looking for righteous things, nor day in day out practise the practice of making become things that are wings to enlightenment; then is the body as though drugged, the quarters are not seen, things are not clear, sloth and torpor compass the heart and stay; joyless, one lives the divine life; and doubts about things are ever with one".

We then read that the Buddha told that monk to guard the doors of the senses, to be moderate in eating, to be vigilant and to cultivate the factors leading to enlightenment. The monk followed the Buddha's advice. The Buddha's words were the right condition for him to develop insight, even to the degree that he could attain arahatship. Thus he was no longer subject to sloth and torpor.

Sloth and torpor destruct energy for kusala. When there is right effort there are no sloth and torpor. However, there is no self who can put forth energy for kusala, for the study of the Dhamma or for the development of right understanding. We can prove this when there is listlessness and no energy for kusala. At such a moment we cannot force ourselves to take an interest in kusala. Right effort is only a conditioned dhamma, not self. There can be a long period of indolence, but at times there can be conditions for remembering words of the teachings which can encourage us to develop right understanding. Also sad events which happen in life can serve as a reminder of the impermanence of conditioned realities and then we may be urged to be vigilant, to "guard the sense-doors", that is, to be mindful of the realities appearing through the different doorways. In this life we are in the human plane where there is opportunity for all kinds of kusala, for the study of the Dhamma and the development of right understanding. The goal has been reached only when all defilements have been eradicated, when arahatship has been attained. When we realize the task which lies ahead of us we are reminded not to waste time with akusala. When there is a true sense of urgency to develop right understanding there will be less opportunity for sloth and torpor. In the following sutta we are reminded of what we fail to win when there is indolence and what can be won when there is right energy. We read in the *Kindred Sayings* (II, Nidāna-vagga, Kindred Sayings on Cause, 3, par22) that the Buddha encouraged the monks to apply energy in order to attain the goal. He said:

> Sadly, monks, lives the man of sloth, involved in bad, wicked things. Great is the salvation which he fails to win. But he of stirred up energy lives happily, aloof from bad, wicked things. Great is the salvation that he makes perfect.

21.2 Vicikicchā

Vicikicchā or doubt is another akusala cetasika and this can accompany only one type of citta, namely the type of moha-mūla-citta which is called: moha-mūla-citta vicikicchā sampayutta (rooted in ignorance, accompanied by doubt).

The reality of vicikicchā is not the same as what we mean by doubt in conventional language. Vicikicchā is not doubt about someone's name or about the weather. Vicikicchā is doubt about *realities*, about nāma and rūpa, about cause and result, about the four noble Truths, about the "Dependant Origination".

The *Atthasālinī* (II, Part IX, Chapter III, 259) defines vicikicchā as follows:

> . . . It has shifting about as characteristic, mental wavering as function, indecision or uncertainty in grasp as manifestation, unsystematic thought (unwise attention) as proximate cause, and it should be regarded as a danger to attainment.

The *Visuddhimagga* (XIV, 177) gives a similar definition.

When there is doubt one "wavers", one is not sure about realities. The *Dhammasangaṇi* (par425) describes doubt in different ways and states among others that it is "uncertainty of grasp", "stiffness of mind". The *Atthasālinī* (II, 259, 260) in its explanation of this paragraph of the *Dhammasangaṇi* states:

> . . . "Fluctuation" is the inability to establish anything in one mode, thus, "Is this state permanent, or is it impermanent?" Because of the inability to "comprehend" there is "uncertainty of grasp". . . .

As to "stiffness", the *Atthasālinī* remarks that "mental rigidity" is the inability to come to a decision as to the object. We read: "Stiffness is the meaning. For perplexity having arisen makes the mind stiff. . . ."

When there is doubt one wonders about realities: "Is it such or is it such?" One wonders, for example, whether a reality is permanent or impermanent, or whether the reality which appears now is nāma or rūpa. When there is doubt there is mental rigidity, there is not the wieldiness of mind which is necessary for the understanding of realities. Doubt is to be considered as a "danger for attainment"; when there is doubt it is impossible to apply oneself to mental development.

Doubt is different from ignorance, moha, which does not know realities. But when there is doubt there is also moha which accompanies all akusala dhammas. When doubt accompanies the akusala citta, there cannot be determination (adhimokkha) which is "sure about the object", neither can there be "wish-to-do" (chanda) which "searches for the object" and wants it[7].

The proximate cause of doubt is "unwise attention" to the object which is experienced at that moment. We read in the *Gradual Sayings* (Book of the Ones, Chapter II, par5) that the Buddha said to the monks:

> Monks, I know not of any other single thing of such power to cause the arising of doubt and wavering, if not already arisen; or, if arisen, to cause its more-becoming and increase, as unsystematic attention.
>
> In him who gives not systematic attention arises doubt and wavering, if not already arisen; or, if arisen, it is liable to more-becoming and increase.

[7] See Chapter 9 and Chapter 12.

When one performs dāna, observes sīla, studies Dhamma or is mindful of nāma and rūpa, there is no opportunity for doubt, because during such moments there is "wise attention".

We read in the *Middle Length Sayings* (I, no. 2, All the cankers) that the Buddha, when he was near Sāvatthī, in the Jeta Grove, spoke to the monks on the means of controlling all the cankers. He spoke about unwise attention and about various kinds of doubt, pertaining to the past, the future or the present, which may arise when there is no wise attention. We read about doubt:

> In these ways he is not wisely attending: if he thinks, "Now, was I in a past period? Now, was I not in a past period? Now, what was I in a past period? Now, how was I in a past period? Now, having been what, what did I become in a past period?. . . .

We read the same about doubt pertaining to the future and doubt pertaining to the present.

When doubt is accumulated there can be doubt about many different subjects. We read in the *Dhammasangaṇi* (par1004) that there can be doubt about the Buddha, the Dhamma and the Sangha, the Discipline, the past or the future or both, the "Dependant Origination"[8].

The *Atthasālinī* (II, Book II, Part II, Chapter I, 354, 355) explains as to doubts about the Buddha, the Dhamma and the Sangha, that one may doubt about the qualities of the Buddha or about the characteristic marks of his body[9], that one may doubt whether there is attainment of enlightenment, whether there is nibbāna, or whether there are people who can attain enlightenment. As to doubt about the past and the future, this doubt can concern the "khandhas", the "dhātus" (elements) and "āyatanas" (twelve bases) in the past and in the future.

Do we have doubt about rebirth? One may not be sure whether it is true that the last citta in this life will be succeeded by the first citta of the next life. One may have theoretical understanding of the fact that each citta which falls away is succeeded by a next one, but there may still be moments of doubt. We may at times also doubt whether it is possible to develop right understanding and whether this is the way leading to enlightenment. Doubt can never be eradicated by thinking. When we begin to develop understanding of nāma and rūpa there may be doubt whether the reality appearing at the present moment is nāma or rūpa. Their characteristics are quite different but we are confused about them. There can only be less doubt if we continue to be mindful of them when they appear one at a time. Only in this way can we learn, for example, that hardness is different from the experience of hardness and that visible object is different from the experience of visible object. It is useful to know that doubt is akusala, that it is a hindrance to the performing of dāna, the observance of sīla and to mental development. However, doubt can be object of mindfulness; when there is mindfulness of its characteristic right understanding can know it as it is.

[8] Book of Analysis, Chapter 17, par915.

[9] A Buddha has 32 bodily marks. See Dialogues of the Buddha III, no. 30.

Those who are not ariyans have not realized the four noble Truths and they may still have doubt about realities. The sotāpanna sees realities as they are, he has eradicated doubt completely. We read in the suttas that the sotāpanna has "crossed over doubt". We read, for example, in the *Middle Length Sayings* (II, no. 91, Brahmāyusutta) about Brahmāyu:

> ...Having seen dhamma, attained dhamma, known dhamma, plunged into dhamma, having crossed over doubt, put away uncertainty and attained without another's help to full confidence in the Teacher's instruction...

The sotāpanna still has to continue to develop satipaṭṭhāna, but he is sure to be eventually liberated from the cycle of birth and death. He is full of confidence in the Buddha, the Dhamma and the Sangha. His confidence is unshakable and thus he has no more doubts about the Buddha, the Dhamma and the Sangha. Those who have not attained enlightenment need to listen often to the Dhamma and to be reminded to be aware of realities in order to eradicate doubt.

It is useful to study the different types of akusala citta and their accompanying cetasikas[10]. The study will help us to see that akusala dhammas arise because of their appropriate conditions, that citta and cetasikas which arise together condition one another. We are reminded by the study of realities that akusala dhamma is not a person, that it does not belong to a self. However, we should not be contented with merely theoretical knowledge of the truth. We should continue to develop right understanding of realities which appear through the six doors. Akusala dhammas cannot be eradicated immediately. We should first learn to see them as they are: as conditioned nāmas, not self. Through right understanding of realities doubt, wrong view and all the other akusala dhammas can be eradicated.

21.2.1 Questions

1. Why are sloth and torpor mental sickness?
2. Why is it said that sloth is opposition to energy?
3. Can there be sloth and torpor when there is conceit?
4. Can they arise when there is wrong view?
5. What is the meaning of "prompted", sasaṅkhārika?
6. Why did the Buddha warn the monks not to be attached to the ease of bed or to food?
7. The anāgāmī is not attached to the ease of bed or to food. Can he still have sloth and torpor?
8. What is the best cure for sloth and torpor?
9. Which kinds of feeling can accompany sloth and torpor?
10. Vicikicchā is doubt about realities. Which are the realities one may have doubts about?
11. Who has eradicated doubt?

---

[10] For a summary of them see Appendix 7.

22 Different Groups of Defilements Part I

We are inclined to think that our suffering in life are due to causes outside ourselves, to unpleasant events or to other people's behaviour. However, the real cause of sorrow is within ourselves. Our defilements lead to sorrow. The goal of the Buddha's teachings is the eradication of defilements and this cannot be achieved unless right understanding of realities has been developed. All three parts of the Tipiṭaka, the Vinaya, the Suttanta and the Abhidhamma, have been taught in order to encourage people to develop the way which leads to the end of defilements. If we do not forget this goal, no matter which part of the scriptures we are reading, we can profit to the full from our study.

In the Abhidhamma realities are classified in numerous ways. In the Third Book of the *Dhammasangaṇi* akusala dhammas have been classified in different groups. The study of these different classifications can help us to see the danger of akusala. However, in order to really know our defilements we should be aware of them when they appear. For example, we know in theory that there is clinging to visible object, sound, odour, flavour, tangible object and to mental objects, but when there is mindfulness we learn that even now, after a moment of seeing or a moment of hearing, attachment can arise and that it is bound to arise again and again. Defilements are not merely abstract categories, they are realities which can appear at any time and there are many more moments of them than we ever thought.

The fourteen akusala cetasikas which arise with the akusala cittas in various combinations can be classified in different groups. Each of these classifications shows a particular aspect and function of the akusala cetasikas. Some cetasikas occur in several of these groups, and each time a different aspect is shown. Attachment occurs in all of these groups and this reminds us of the many ways of clinging to different kinds of objects.

One of the groups of defilements is the *āsavas*. Āsava can be translated as canker, poison or intoxicant. There are four āsavas (*Dhammasangaṇi* par1096-1100):

1. the canker of sensuous desire, kāmāsava
2. the canker of becoming, bhavāsava
3. the canker of wrong view, diṭṭhāsava
4. the canker of ignorance, avijjāsava

The *Atthasālinī* (I, Part I, Chapter II, 48) explains that āsavas flow from the senses and the mind. In all planes where there is nāma arising āsavas occur, even in the highest plane of existence which is the fourth arūpa-brahma plane. The āsavas are like liquor which has fermented for a long time, the *Atthasālinī* explains. The āsavas are like poisonous drugs or intoxicants. The *Visuddhimagga* (XXII, 56) states that the āsavas are exuding "from unguarded sense-doors like water from cracks in a pot, in the sense of constant trickling". The āsavas keep on flowing from birth to death, they are also flowing at this moment. Are we not attached to what we see? Then there is the canker of sensuous desire, kāmāvara. Seeing experiences visible object, and shortly after seeing has fallen away there are most of the time akusala cittas rooted in attachment, aversion or ignorance. When the object is pleasant there is likely to be attachment to the object because we have accumulated such a great deal of attachment. We are attached to visible object, sound, odour, flavour and tangible object. We are infatuated with the objects we experience through the senses and we want to go on experiencing them. Because of our foolish attachment to what is actually impermanent we have to continue to be in the cycle of birth and death. We have to be reborn again and again until the cankers have been extinguished. The arahat has eradicated the cankers, he does not have to be reborn again.

We may not understand that birth is sorrowful, but when right understanding has been developed we will see that all that is impermanent is sorrowful. We cling to all we experience through the senses, we cling to life. Clinging is deeply accumulated; even the first javana-cittas of our life were lobha-mūla-cittas, cittas rooted in attachment, and this is the case for every living being.

The canker of desire for rebirth, bhavāsava, is another one of the āsavas. Even the anāgāmī who has eradicated all clinging to sensuous objects, can still have clinging to becoming or rebirth. So long as there is attachment to any kind of rebirth one has to continue to be in the cycle of birth and death.

The canker of wrong view, diṭṭhāsava, comprises, according to the *Dhammasangaṇi* (par1099) the conceiving of all speculative theories such as eternalism, annihilationism, theories about the world, the soul and the body. So long as one has not attained enlightenment one tends to cling to the concept of self and this is so deeply rooted that it is extremely hard to eradicate it.

The canker of ignorance, avijjāsava, is moha cetasika. It is ignorance of the four noble Truths, of the past, the future or both, and of the "Dependant Origination" (*Dhammasangaṇi*, par1100). We have innumerable moments of ignorance. Ignorance is dangerous, at the moment it arises we do not realize that there is ignorance.

We are time and again overcome by the āsavas. It is hard for us to see their danger. We cannot help being attached to the objects we experience through the senses. How could we prevent ourselves from liking pleasant objects? The Buddha warned people of the danger of sense-pleasures. We read in the *Middle Length Sayings* (I, no. 22, The Parable of the Water-snake) that the Buddha explained about the things which are "stumbling blocks" to the monk Ariṭṭha who had wrong understanding of the Dhamma. The Buddha stated about sense-pleasures:

> . . . Sense-pleasures are said by me to be of little satisfaction, of much pain, of much tribulation, wherein is more peril. Sense-pleasures are likened by me to a skeleton. . . to a lump of meat. . . to a torch of dry grass. . . to a pit of glowing embers. . . to a dream. . . to something borrowed. . . to the fruits of a tree. . . to a slaughter-house. . . to an impaling stake. . . sense-pleasures are likened by me to a snake's head, of much pain, of much tribulation, wherein is more peril. . . .

When one is still infatuated with sense-pleasures such words are hard to grasp. We may not like to hear that sense-pleasures are as sorrowful and dangerous as the things the Buddha compares them to. At the moment of attachment the object which is experienced seems to be so pleasant and we fail to see that we are lured by attachment. It is wisdom, paññā, which sees the danger of sense-pleasures.

The anāgāmī and the arahat fully understand the danger of sense-pleasures; they have no conditions for the arising of the canker of sensuous desire, kāmāsava, because it has been eradicated. When understanding of realities begins to develop it cannot yet achieve detachment from sense-pleasures. Some people are inclined to think that they must first of all become detached, before they can begin to develop right understanding of nāma and rūpa. However, this is not the right way of practice. Right understanding of whatever reality appears, even if it is attachment, should be developed. Only paññā which knows nāma and rūpa as they are can eventually bring about detachment.

The *Visuddhimagga* states about the āsavas that they "exude from unguarded sense-doors". The sense-doors are "guarded" through the development of satipaṭṭhāna. We read in the *Gradual Sayings* (Book of the Threes, Chapter II, par16, The Sure Course) that a monk who possesses three qualities is "proficient in the practice leading to the Sure Course" and "has strong grounds for the destruction of the āsavas". These three qualities are moderation in eating, the guarding of the six doors and vigilance. We read concerning the guarding of the six doors:

> And how does he keep watch over the door of his sense faculties?
>
> Herein, a monk, seeing an object with the eye, does not grasp at the general features or at the details thereof. Since coveting and dejection, evil, unprofitable states might overwhelm one who dwells with the faculty of the eye uncontrolled, he applies himself to such control, sets a guard over the faculty of the eye, attains control thereof. . . .

The same is said about the other doorways. The six doorways should be guarded. How does one, when seeing an object with the eye, not "grasp at the general features or at the details thereof"? In being mindful of the reality which appears. This is the way to see realities as they are, to see them as impermanent, dukkha and non-self. However, even the sotāpanna who has eradicated the "canker of wrong view", diṭṭhāsava, still clings to sensuous objects. Even someone who has realized the arising and falling away of visible object which appears, of sound which appears, may still cling to them. Clinging has been accumulated from life to life, how then could one become detached at once?

There are four stages of enlightenment, and at each stage defilements are progressively eradicated. Paññā has to grow keener and keener in order to be able to eradicate them. The lokuttara magga-citta (supramundane path-consciousness) which, at the first stage of enlightenment (the stage of the sotāpanna), experiences nibbāna for the first time, eradicates only the canker of wrong view. The sotāpanna still has the canker of sensuous desire, the canker of desire for rebirth and the canker of ignorance. He still has desire, but it has become less gross than the desire of the non-ariyan, the "worldling" (puthujjana). The magga-citta of the sakadāgāmī (who has attained the second stage of enlightenment) does not eradicate desire, but desire has become attenuated more. The magga-citta of the anāgāmī (who has attained the third stage of enlightenment) eradicates the canker of sensuous desire, but he still has the canker of desire for rebirth and the canker of ignorance. The magga-citta of the arahat eradicates the canker of desire for rebirth and the canker of ignorance. The arahat is "canker-freed".

Another group of defilements is the group of the *Floods* or *Oghas* (*Dhammasangaṇi* par1151). There are four floods which are the same defilements as the cankers, but the classification as floods shows a different aspect. The floods are:

- the flood of sensuous desire (kāmogha)
- the flood of desire for rebirth (bhavogha)
- the flood of wrong view (diṭṭhogha)
- the flood of ignorance (avijjogha)

We read in the *Atthasālinī* (I, Part I, Chapter II, 49) that the "floods" submerge a person again and again in the cycle of birth and death.

The *Visuddhimagga* (XXII, 56) states:

> ...The Floods are so called in the sense of sweeping away into the ocean of becoming, and in the sense of being hard to cross....

The classification of defilements under the aspect of floods reminds us of their danger. A flood is dangerous, it can drown us.

In the suttas the cycle of birth and death has been compared to a dangerous ocean, which has to be crossed. We read in the *Kindred Sayings* (IV, Saḷāyatana-vagga, Fourth Fifty, Chapter 3, par187, Ocean):

> "The ocean! The ocean!" monks, says the ignorant worldling. But that, monks, is not the ocean in the discipline of the ariyan. That ocean (of the worldling), monks, is a heap of water, a great flood of water.
> The eye of a man, monks, is the ocean. Its impulse is made of objects. Who so endures that object-made impulse,- of him, monks, it is said, "he has crossed over. That ocean of the eye, with its waves and whirlpools, its sharks and demons, the brahmin has crossed and gone beyond. He stands on dry ground"....

When there is no more clinging to the eye and objects, or to all the other realities, one has "crossed over". Further on we read that the Buddha spoke the verse:

```
Who so has crossed this monster-teeming sea,
With its devils and fearsome waves impassable,
''Versed in the lore'', ''living the holy life'',
''Gone to world's end'', and ''gone beyond'' he is called.
```

The arahat has crossed the sea of the cycle of birth and death (saṁsāra), he has gone to the world's end, he has "gone beyond".

The danger of being drowned is real. We are infatuated with visible object, sound, smell, and all the other objects which can be experienced through the six doors. Every time we like one of the sense objects we are in the flood of sensuous desire, we fail to see the danger of this flood, we are forgetful. Many times we are forgetful and we do not even want to be mindful. The Buddha reminded people that pleasant objects do not last and that we all have to suffer old age, sickness and death. If we listen to the Buddha's words without developing understanding we cannot grasp their real meaning. If we develop right understanding of all realities which appear we will know more clearly when there is clinging to the objects we experience and we will come to see the danger of clinging. The floods are eradicated at the different stages of enlightenment, at the same stages as the corresponding cankers.

The *Yokes* or *Yogas* are another group of defilements. This group consists again of the same defilements as the cankers and the floods. We read in the *Atthasālinī* (I, Part I, Chapter II, 49) that the "yokes" tie a person to the cycle of birth and death.

The *Visuddhimagga* (XXII, 56) states about the yoghas (here translated as bonds):

> The Bonds are so called because they do not allow disengagement from an object and disengagement from suffering (dukkha).

The four yoghas are:

1. the yoke of sensuous desire, kāmayogha
2. the yoke of desire for rebirth, bhavayogha
3. the yoke of wrong view, diṭṭhiyogha
4. the yoke of ignorance, avijjāyogha

Thus, the yokes are the same defilements as the cankers and the floods, but the classification by way of yokes reminds us that we are tied to the round of rebirths. The different yokes are eradicated at the same stages of enlightenment as the corresponding cankers and floods

22.0.1 Questions

1. What is the use of classifying the same cetasikas as cankers, floods and yokes?
2. Do we have to be detached first before we develop wisdom?
3. We may agree that sense-pleasures are dangerous, but attachment to them still arises. How can one really see their danger?

23 Different Groups of Defilements Part II

The akusala cetasikas which are attachment, wrong view and ignorance are classified in different groups: as four cankers, four floods and four yokes. Each of these groups consists of the same defilements, but different aspects are shown by these classifications. The cankers flow or "exude", or they are like intoxicants. The floods are dangerous, they can drown us, they sweep us away into the ocean of rebirths. The yokes tie us to the cycle of birth and death.

There are still other groups of defilements and by their classifications again different aspects are shown. One of these groups is the *ties* or *knots*, *ganthas*. Instead of gantha the term *kāyagantha, bodily tie,* is used as well. Kāya which means body refers to the physical body as well as to the "mental body" (Vis. XXII, 54). The ganthas tie us to the round of rebirths. We read in the *Atthasālinī* (I, Part I, Chapter II, 49):

In the knot-group, states which knot or tie in repeated rounds of birth by way of birth and decease the person in whom they exist are termed "knots".

There are four kāyaganthas, "bodily ties" (*Dhammasangaṇi*, par1135-1140):

1. the bodily tie of covetousness (abhijjhā kāyagantha)
2. the bodily tie of ill-will (vyāpāda kāyagantha)
3. the bodily tie of clinging to rules and rituals or wrong practice (sīlabbata parāmāsa kāyagantha)
4. the bodily tie of dogmatism (idaṃ-saccābhinivesa kāyagantha)

The first tie comprises all kinds of covetousness, all degrees of lobha, be they gross or subtle. We should know that there can also be lobha in the form of hopes and expectations: we hope for good health, we hope that other people will like us, we hope for honour and praise, for success in our undertakings. All degrees and shades of lobha are a tie which binds us to the cycle of birth and death.

The tie of ill-will is dosa. All degrees of dosa such as irritation, ill-temper, ill-will or hostility are a tie which binds us to the round of rebirths.

The tie of clinging to rules and rituals is wrong practice and this is a form of wrong view. People are entangled by this tie when they erroneously believe that, in order to develop the way leading to enlightenment, they have to follow certain rules such as abstaining from particular kinds of food or refraining from reading or talking. So long as wrong view has not been eradicated one may have many moments of wrong practice, and one may mistake the wrong practice for the right practice. People may cling to particular places or situations as being favourable for the development of satipaṭṭhāna. They believe that mindfulness can only arise in such places or situations. Then there is bound to be wrong practice. If we know when there is wrong practice we can be cured of it.

The tie of dogmatism (idaṃ-saccābhinivesa, the belief: this alone is truth) comprises all forms of wrong view, except wrong practice which is the third tie, as we have seen. People are entangled by the fourth tie when they have a wrong interpretation of reality and when they believe that only their interpretation is the truth. When someone, for example, believes that there is no kamma and no result of kamma, he is entangled by the fourth tie. The view that there is no kamma and no result of kamma is very dangerous, it can condition unwholesome deeds. One may believe that, after death, one will be annihilated, that there is no rebirth. Then one is entangled by the fourth tie.

As we have seen, wrong view, diṭṭhi, has been classified as canker, as flood, as yoke and as (bodily) tie. Under the aspect of tie diṭṭhi has been classified as twofold: as wrong practice and as false view.

The magga-citta of the sotāpanna eradicates the third and the fourth ties. The sotāpanna knows the right Path and he cannot deviate from it anymore, he has no conditions for wrong practice. He has no wrong view of realities. He still has the first tie, covetousness, and the second tie, ill-will, but they are not of the degree that they lead to an unhappy rebirth.

The magga-citta of the anāgāmī eradicates the second tie, ill-will. As regards the first tie, the anāgāmī does not cling to sensuous objects, but he has not eradicated the more subtle forms of clinging, which is clinging to rebirth in rūpa-brahma planes and arūpa-brahma planes. Thus, he still clings to rebirth. He has not eradicated the first tie.

The magga-citta of the arahat eradicates the first tie. He has no more clinging, no clinging to rebirth; he is no longer entangled by any of the four ties.

Another group of defilements is the *ways of clinging* or *upādāna.* There are four ways of clinging (*Dhammasangaṇi*, par1213-1217):

1. sensuous clinging (kāmupādāna)
2. clinging to wrong view (diṭṭhupādāna)
3. clinging to "rules and rituals" (sīlabbatupādāna)
4. clinging to personality belief (attavādupādāna)

The first way of clinging, sensuous clinging, comprises clinging to all the objects which can be experienced through the senses (*Visuddhimagga*, XVII, 243). We should scrutinize ourselves whether there is clinging at this moment. We may not notice that there is clinging very often, after seeing, hearing, smelling, tasting, touching or on account of the experience of an object through the mind-door. When we sit on a soft chair there is likely to be clinging already to softness, but we do not notice it. We look at birds, dogs and cats and we do not notice that we tend to cling already before we define what it is that is seen. At the moment of clinging we create a new condition for life to go on in the cycle of birth and death. Clinging is one of the links in the "Dependant Origination" (Paṭiccasamuppāda), the conditional arising of phenomena in the round of rebirths. Because of craving (taṇhā) there is clinging or firm grasping (upādāna). So long as there is any form of clinging we have to continue to be in the cycle of birth and death.

We read in the *Kindred Sayings* (II, Kindred Sayings on Cause, Chapter 5, par52, Grasping, Upādāna):

> While staying at Sāvatthī the Exalted One said:–
>
> In him, monks, who contemplates the enjoyment that there is in all that makes for grasping, craving grows. Grasping is conditioned by craving. Becoming is conditioned by grasping. Birth is conditioned by becoming.

> Decay-and-death is conditioned by birth. Grief, lamentation, suffering, sorrow, despair come to pass. Such is the uprising of this entire mass of ill.

The Buddha then uses a simile of a bonfire which keeps on burning so long as it is supplied with fuel. If there is no fuel the fire will become extinct. We read further on:

> Even so in him who contemplates the misery that there is in all that makes for grasping, craving ceases, and hence grasping ceases, becoming, birth, decay-and-death, and sorrow cease. Such is the ceasing of this entire mass of ill.

We want to go on living and experiencing objects through the senses, this is beyond control. However, the Buddha's words about the impermanence of all conditioned things, about decay and death, can remind us of what life really is: only fleeting phenomena.

The other three ways of clinging are forms of wrong view. As regards clinging to wrong view (diṭṭhupādāna), this comprises clinging to false views about kamma and the result of kamma, and to other speculative theories. As regards clinging to wrong practice, when someone takes the wrong practice for the right practice there are no conditions for the development of right understanding of realities and thus wrong view cannot be eradicated. Wrong practice is also one of the "ties", as we have seen.

Clinging to personality belief is a form of wrong view which arises when one firmly believes that the five khandhas are "self". We can think of concepts such as "body" or "mind" but there may not necessarily be wrong view. However, the latent tendency of wrong view has not been eradicated so long as one has not become a sotāpanna. We all have accumulated personality belief and when there are conditions it can arise. Someone may cling with wrong view to the rūpa-kkhandha, he may take the body for self. When one becomes older and suffers from sickness, it is obvious that the body changes, but there may still be clinging to an idea of the body which belongs to a "self". What is taken for "my body" consists of different rūpas which arise and fall away. When we are walking, standing, sitting or lying down, it is not "my body" which can be directly experienced, there are only different elements, rūpas, such as hardness, softness, heat or cold, and these can be experienced one at a time. When mindfulness arises it can be aware of one reality at a time and in this way right understanding can develop and the wrong view of self can eventually be eradicated.

Someone may take the khandha of feeling for self, but feeling changes all the time. Feeling which arises now is not the same as feeling a moment ago. The khandha of perception or remembrance (saññā) is different each moment, but one may be inclined to take it for self. When we recognize or remember something, it is not self who does so, but saññā. Saṅkhārakkhandha, the khandha of "formations" or "activities" (all cetasikas other than feeling and saññā), changes all the time; sometimes akusala cetasikas arise, sometimes kusala cetasikas, but one may still be inclined to take cetasikas for self. Viññāṇakkhandha, consciousness, changes all the time; there are seeing, hearing and thinking of concepts at different moments, but there can be a deep-rooted belief of "I see", "I hear", "I think". In reality the seeing sees, the hearing hears, and another citta again thinks of concepts, they are all different cittas which are not self. There are different cittas which arise and fall away, one at a time, and each of them experiences just one object. There may be theoretical understanding of the truth, but wrong view is deeply rooted; it cannot be eradicated by thinking. Wrong view can be eradicated only by developing right understanding of the reality which appears at the present moment.

Among the ways of clinging, clinging to wrong view has been classified as threefold: as clinging to wrong view (speculative theories), as clinging to wrong practice and as clinging to personality belief. Each of these three classifications shows a different aspect of wrong view.

The magga-citta of the sotāpanna eradicates the three ways of clinging which are clinging to wrong view. He still has the first way of clinging, sensuous clinging. Even the sakadāgāmī and the anāgāmī have the first way of clinging. The anāgāmī has no more clinging to sensuous objects, but he still has clinging to rebirth which is the result of jhāna, and this form of clinging is in this classification included in the first way of clinging. The magga-citta of the arahat eradicates the first way of clinging (Visuddhimagga, XVII, 245).

The *Hindrances* or *Nīvaraṇas* are another group of defilements. In the *Dhammasangaṇi* (par1152-1163) the hindrances are classified as sixfold:

1. sensuous desire (kāmacchanda)
2. ill will (vyāpāda)
3. sloth and torpor (thīna-middha)
4. restlessness and regret (uddhacca-kukkucca)
5. doubt (vicikicchā)
6. ignorance (avijjā)[1]

In the suttas and in the *Visuddhimagga* (IV, 104, 105) the hindrances are classified as fivefold; ignorance is not among them. However, this should not be seen as a discrepancy. Classifications are not rigid, their aim is to remind us of reality.

The hindrances are obstructions, overwhelming the mind, weakening insight[2]. The hindrances obstruct the development of what is wholesome. When we are attached to pleasant sights and sounds, to people or to particular places, there is the hindrance of *sensuous desire*. At the moment of attachment we do not realize that it obstructs the arising of kusala citta, but we should know that at such a moment there cannot be generosity or loving kindness.

Ill will is another akusala dhamma which is one of the hindrances. The hindrance of ill will is dosa cetasika and it comprises all shades and degrees of aversion. Even a moment of slight annoyance is a hindrance, it obstructs kusala. When there is ill-will there is no loving-kindness, no compassion, no understanding of nāma and

[1] For sensuous desire see Chapter, 15, for ill will Chapter 18, for sloth and torpor Chapter 20, for restlessness Chapter 14, for regret Chapter 19, for doubt Chapter 20 and for ignorance Chapter 14.

[2] Atthasālinī, II, Book II, Part II, Chapter II, 382.

rūpa. However, some moments later mindfulness can arise and be aware of any reality which appears, even of annoyance.

Sloth and *torpor* are two akusala cetasikas which are classified as a pair among the hindrances. When they arise there is mental indisposition and unwieldiness. They have the same proximate cause, namely, unwise attention. When there are sloth and torpor there is no energy, no vigour for kusala, and thus they obstruct kusala. When there are sloth and torpor one has no confidence in the development of right understanding.

Restlessness and *regret* (uddhacca-kukkucca) is another pair among the hindrances. When there is restlessness and regret the citta is not peaceful. As we have seen, restlessness accompanies each akusala citta and regret accompanies only dosa-mūla-citta. The omission of kusala and the commission of akusala are the objects of regret. Restlessness and regret obstruct the performing of kusala, and at such moments there cannot be mindfulness of nāma and rūpa.

Doubt (vicikicchā) is another akusala dhamma which is a hindrance. Doubt about the Buddha, the Dhamma and the Sangha, doubt about realities, all these kinds of doubt are a hindrance to the development of kusala, a hindrance to the development of right understanding. We need courage to continue to develop satipaṭṭhāna, so that doubt can eventually be eradicated. Doubt is a reality and thus it can be the object of sati. The citta which is accompanied by mindfulness is kusala citta, but mindfulness can have as its object any reality which appears, even akusala dhamma.

Ignorance (avijjā) can, as we have seen, also be classified as a hindrance. There is ignorance with each akusala citta, ignorance is the root of all evil. Ignorance blinds us, it is a hindrance to kusala and to right understanding. We may see the danger of lobha and of dosa, but we may not see the danger of ignorance. If we see its danger we will develop right understanding so that ignorance can eventually be eradicated.

In samatha the hindrances can be temporarily subdued by the jhāna-factors which accompany the jhāna-cittas of the different stages of jhāna, but they cannot be eradicated. They can be eradicated only by the right understanding which is developed in vipassanā.

We read in the *Kindred Sayings* (V, Mahā-vagga, Book II, Kindred Sayings on the Limbs of Wisdom, Chapter IV, par5) about the condition for the arising of the hindrances:

> Monks, in him who practises unsystematic attention, sensual desire, if not already arisen, arises; and, if already arisen, sensual desire conduces to the more-becoming and growth thereof.
>
> So also malevolence, sloth and torpor, excitement and flurry, doubt and wavering, if not yet arisen, do arise; and, if arisen, conduce to the more-becoming and growth thereof.

In the following sutta we read that systematic attention (wise attention) conditions the arising of the "limbs of wisdom" which, if they have arisen, by cultivation go to fulfilment. The "limbs of wisdom", which are also called the "factors of enlightenment" (bojjhangas), are: mindfulness, investigation of Dhamma (dhamma-vicaya), energy, rapture, tranquillity, concentration and equanimity.

Further on, in the same section (par8), we read again about the hindrances which weaken insight and about the "limbs of wisdom" which conduce to realizing the fruits of liberation by knowledge. We read:

> Now, monks, at the time when the ariyan disciple makes the Dhamma his object, gives attention to it, with all his mind considers it, with ready ear listens to the Dhamma,—at such a time these five hindrances do not exist in him; at such a time the seven limbs of wisdom by cultivation go to fulfilment.

This sutta reminds us of the great value of listening to the Dhamma and carefully and thoroughly considering it, in order to be able to apply it.

The hindrances are eradicated at different stages of enlightenment. The magga-citta of the sotāpanna eradicates doubt. Since the sotāpanna has no more wrong view and sees realities as they are, there cannot be any doubt about them. The magga-citta of the anāgāmī eradicates sensuous desire, ill will and regret. The magga-citta of the arahat eradicates sloth and torpor, restlessness and ignorance. The arahat is free of all the hindrances. Defilements can only be eradicated stage by stage because they are so deeply rooted.

In order to eradicate defilements we should have patience to develop understanding gradually. It is essential to know the difference between the moments we are absorbed in thinking of concepts, such as people and possessions, situations or events of life, and the moments of mindfulness which is aware of only one reality at a time as it presents itself through one of the six doors. We should not try to suppress thinking, it is real; it arises because it is conditioned. Thinking can be object of mindfulness, it can be known as a type of nāma, arising because of its own conditions, not self. There is not only thinking, there are also seeing, visible object, hearing or sound, but we are mostly forgetful of these realities. We are used to paying attention only to concepts, but gradually we can learn to be mindful of realities. We cannot expect to have full understanding of realities at once. If we are intent only on what appears at the present moment we do not worry about the fact that understanding will have to be developed for a long time, even for many lives. There is no self who has understanding, it is understanding, paññā cetasika, which can develop and see things as they really are. We tend to forget that paññā is a conditioned nāma.

We read in the *Kindred Sayings* (II, Niddāna-vagga, Chapter XXI, Kindred Sayings about Brethren, par6, 11, 12) about different monks who attained arahatship. They had to develop right understanding life after life. The Buddha repeatedly said that it was "no easy matter" to attain the goal. We read for example about Kappina (par11) that the Buddha said:

> ... That monk is highly gifted, of wondrous power. No easy matter is it to win that which he formerly had not won, even that for the sake of which clansmen rightly leave the home for the homeless, even that uttermost goal of the divine living which he has attained, wherein he abides, having

come just here and now to know it thoroughly for himself and to realize it.

23.0.1 Questions

1. When does the "bodily tie of dogmatism" arise?
2. Is it a discrepancy that the hindrances are sometimes classified as fivefold, ignorance being excluded, and sometimes as sixfold?
3. Why is even a slight annoyance a hindrance to kusala?
4. Why can wrong view about seeing, hearing or thinking only be eliminated by paññā as they appear in daily life?

24 Different Groups of Defilements Part III

Defilements can be classified in many different ways and each classification reminds us of the danger of akusala. There is another group of defilements which is again completely different, namely the group of the *latent tendencies* or *anusayas*.

In the *Dhammasangaṇi* the latent tendencies have not been classified as a group. Only lobha as "latent bias", anusaya, has been specifically mentioned among the many aspects of lobha (par1059). The *Atthasālinī* (II, Part II, Chapter II, 366) comments: "As latent bias greed lies chronically in us as a strong (tendency)". There is not only the latent tendency of lobha, there are seven akusala dhammas which can be classified as latent tendencies and these lie dormant in us as strong leanings. We read in the *Book of Analysis* (Vibhaṅga, Chapter 17, par949) that there are seven anusayas[1]:

1. the latent tendency of lust for sense pleasure (kāmarāgānusaya)
2. the latent tendency of aversion (paṭighānusaya)
3. the latent tendency of conceit (mānānusaya)
4. the latent tendency of wrong view (diṭṭhānusaya)
5. the latent tendency of doubt (vicikicchānusaya)
6. the latent tendency of lust for becoming (bhava-rāgānusaya)
7. the latent tendency of ignorance (avijjānusaya)

The classification of akusala dhammas by way of latent tendencies reminds us of their stubbornness, their pertinaciousness. The latent tendencies are like microbes investing the body. They are latent but they may become active at any moment, when conditions are favourable[2]. Latent tendencies are hard to get rid of.

We read in the *Visuddhimagga* (XXII, 60) about the stubbornness of the latent tendencies:

> ...For it is owing to their inveteracy that they are called inherent tendencies (anusaya) since they inhere (anusenti) as cause for the arising of greed for sense desires, etc. , again and again.

The latent tendencies are "inveterate", that is, they are firmly established, for a long time, obstinate, hard to eradicate.

One may wonder why not all akusala dhammas have been classified as latent tendencies. Have we not accumulated all akusala dhammas from life to life? We should note that the seven akusala dhammas which have been classified as latent tendencies are particularly obstinate and condition the arising of the other defilements.

So long as latent tendencies have not been eradicated, defilements arise again and again. For example, when someone is reborn in one of the brahma-planes, there are

---

[1] See also Visuddhimagga XXII, 60, and Yamaka, the sixth Book of the Abhidhamma, Part VII (translation: Guide through the Abhidhamma Piṭaka, Ven. Nyanatiloka, BPS. Kandy, 1971).

[2] Ven. Nyanaponika, Abhidhamma Studies V, The Problem of Time, 3, the Concept of the Present in the Abhidhamma. BPS. Kandy, 1976.

no conditions for aversion in that plane. However, so long as the latent tendency of aversion has not been eradicated, aversion is bound to arise again when that person is reborn in one of the sensuous planes, after his lifespan in the brahma-plane has been terminated.

Latent tendencies are eradicated at different stages of enlightenment[3]. The magga-citta of the sotāpanna eradicates the latent tendency of wrong view and of doubt and thus these akusala dhammas can never arise again. The magga-citta of the sakadāgāmī does not completely eradicate any of the other latent tendencies, but, it "severs the gross latent bias of sense-desires and the gross latent bias of aversion", as the *Atthasālinī*[4] states.

As we have seen, there are many degrees of defilements, they can be gross or more subtle. The sakadāgāmī still has the latent tendencies of sensuous desire and aversion, but they have become attenuated. Therefore, in comparison with the sotāpanna these latent tendencies are less gross, they are more subtle. The group of latent tendencies as a whole can be called subtle defilements. They are subtle in so far as they are latent; they are subtle in comparison with akusala citta rooted in lobha, dosa or moha, which appears, and which can be called "medium defilement" and with akusala citta which has the intensity to motivate evil deeds through body, speech or mind, which can be called "gross defilement". However, the term subtle should not mislead us. The latent tendencies are dangerous, pertinacious, they are hard to eradicate. They condition the arising of akusala dhammas again and again.

The magga-citta of the anāgāmī eradicates completely the latent tendencies of sense-desire and aversion, these can never arise again. However, he has not eradicated all forms of clinging, he still has the latent tendency of lust for becoming, rebirth which is the result of jhāna. The magga-citta of the arahat eradicates the latent tendencies of lust for becoming, of conceit and of ignorance. When there is no more "soil" for defilements to grow in, the round of becoming comes to an end.

The *Fetters* or Saṃyojanas are another group of akusala dhammas. The saṃyojanas "fetter khandhas (in this life) to khandhas (of the next), or kamma to its fruit[5], or beings to suffering. . . (*Visuddhimagga* XXII, 48). Through the fetters we are tied to the cycle of birth and death[6]. In the *Dhammasangaṇi* (par1113) we find the following classification of ten fetters[7]:

1. sensuous desire (kāma-rāga)
2. ill will (vyāpāda)
3. conceit (māna)
4. wrong view (diṭṭhi)
5. doubt (vicikicchā)
6. clinging to rules and rituals (sīlabbata-parāmāsa)

---

[3] Atthasālinī II, Book I, Part VIII, Chapter I, 235-236.
[4] Ibidem.
[5] So long as kamma is performed there will be vipāka and, thus, life goes on.
[6] Atthasālinī (I, Book I, Part I, Chapter II, 48).
[7] The Book of Analysis, Vibhaṅga, Chapter 17, par969, has the same classification.

7. clinging to rebirth (bhava-rāga)
8. envy (issā)
9. stinginess (macchariya)
10. ignorance (avijjā)

In the classifications of the fetters as given above, diṭṭhi has been classified under two aspects: wrong view and wrong practice (clinging to rules and rituals). When there is no right practice, the wrong view of self and other defilements cannot be eradicated and thus we are fettered to the cycle of birth and death. When there is no mindfulness of one reality at a time, the nāma or rūpa appearing now, there is no right practice, one does not develop the eightfold Path. So long as one has not become a sotāpanna there may be wrong practice.

Envy and stinginess are akusala dhammas which have only been classified by way of fetters but not in the other groups of defilements. We should find out whether there is envy when someone else receives a token of honour we did not receive. Attachment to self conditions coarse akusala such as jealousy. The sotāpanna who has eradicated the wrong view of self has also eradicated jealousy as well as stinginess. If we develop understanding of nāma and rūpa in daily life, we may begin to see that life is actually one moment of experiencing an object. Sometimes the object is pleasant, sometimes it is unpleasant, this depends entirely on conditions. The experience of pleasant objects and unpleasant objects is conditioned by kamma, by deeds which have been done. If we see life as different phenomena which each arise because of their own conditions, there will be less opportunity for jealousy. When we see how we at times can be overpowered by jealousy and other akusala dhammas we can be reminded to develop right understanding of nāma and rūpa in order to eradicate akusala.

There is another way of classifying fetters and this shows us again that classifications are not rigid. We find for example in the *Book of Analysis* (Chapter 17, par940)[8] the following classification of the fetters which makes a distinction between "lower fetters" and "higher fetters". There are five lower fetters (orambhāgiya-saṃyojana) which tie beings to the sensuous planes and five higher fetters (uddhambhāgiya-saṃyojana) which tie beings to the higher planes, the rūpa-brahma planes and the arūpa-brahma planes.

The lower fetters are:

- personality belief (sakkāya-diṭṭhi)
- doubt (vicikicchā)
- clinging to rules and rituals (sīlabbata-parāmāsa)
- sensuous desire (kāma-rāga)
- ill will (vyāpāda)

The higher fetters are:

- lust for rebirth in rūpa-brahma planes (rūpa-rāga)

---

[8] See also Visuddhimagga XXII, 48. The same way of classification also occurs in the suttas, for example in the Dialogues of the Buddha III, no. 33, 234.

- lust for rebirth in arūpa-brahma planes (arūpa-rāga)
- conceit (māna)
- restlessness (uddhacca)
- ignorance (avijjā)

In this classification wrong view has been classified as twofold: under the aspect of personality belief and wrong practice. Clinging has been classified as threefold: as sensuous desire, as clinging to rebirth which is the result of rūpa-jhāna and as clinging to rebirth which is the result of arūpa-jhāna. Envy and stinginess do not occur in this classification.

The magga-citta of the sotāpanna eradicates the three lower fetters of personality belief, clinging to rules and rituals (wrong practice) and doubt. He has not eradicated sensuous desire and ill will, but for him these are not as gross as in the case of the non-ariyan; they cannot lead to an unhappy rebirth.

The magga-citta of the sakadāgāmī does not eradicate the fetters of sensuous desire and ill-will, but they have become attenuated. Paññā has to be developed to a high degree in order that desire and ill will can be eradicated. The anāgāmī eradicates both these fetters. He is no longer tied by the lower fetters, but he is still tied by the higher fetters. This shows how hard it is to eradicate these fetters. Only the magga-citta of the arahat can eradicate them. The arahat does not cling at all, he does not cling to the result of jhāna, he does not cling to rebirth in any plane of existence. He has no more conceit, restlessness and ignorance, he has eradicated all akusala dhammas. He has no akusala citta nor kusala citta, instead he has kiriyacitta which does not produce any result. The arahat is truly a perfected one, his task has been fulfilled. He is no longer fettered to the cycle of birth and death.

Another group of akusala dhammas are the *defilements, kilesas*. They are dirty, unclean, impure; they defile or torment the mind. The following ten akusala dhammas have been classified as defilements (*Dhammasangaṇi*, par1229)[9] :

1. greed (lobha)
2. hate (dosa)
3. ignorance (moha)
4. conceit (māna)
5. wrong view (diṭṭhi)
6. doubt (vicikicchā)
7. sloth (thīna)
8. restlessness (uddhacca)
9. shamelessness (ahirika)
10. recklessness (anottappa)

We can use the word defilement or kilesa in a wider sense and then we mean all akusala dhammas. But when defilements are classified as a particular group only the above mentioned akusala dhammas are meant. Torpor (middha), stinginess

[9] See also the Book of Analysis, Vibhaṅga, Chapter 17, par966.

(macchariya), regret (kukkucca) and envy (issā) have not been classified in this group. The *Visuddhimagga* (XXII, 49) states about defilements: "They are so called because they are themselves defiled and they defile the states associated with them."

Shamelessness and recklessness which have not been classified in one of the other groups are classified among the defilements. Shamelessness has no shame of akusala and recklessness does not fear its consequences. They arise with each akusala citta, they defile citta and the accompanying cetasikas. There are many degrees of shamelessness and recklessness. Some people are ashamed of gross defilements and they fear their consequences, but they are not ashamed of akusala citta which is not of the intensity to motivate unwholesome deeds. For example, when we are at this moment forgetful of realities such as seeing or hearing it is evident that we have no shame of neglectfulness with regard to the development of right understanding.

Defilements are eradicated at the different stages of enlightenment. The magga-citta of the sotāpanna eradicates wrong view and doubt. The magga-citta of the anāgāmī eradicates hate. The anāgāmī does not cling to sensuous objects but he may still cling to rebirth which is the result of jhāna. Since this kind of clinging is, in this group of akusala dhammas, included in the defilement of greed, lobha, he has not eradicated this defilement. The magga-citta of the arahat eradicates the defilements of greed, ignorance, conceit, sloth, restlessness, shamelessness and recklessness. The arahat is free from all defilements.

Summarizing the different groups of akusala dhammas, they are:

1. cankers, āsavas
2. floods, oghas
3. yokes, yoghas
4. ties, ganthas
5. ways of clinging, upādānas
6. hindrances, nīvaraṇas
7. latent tendencies, anusayas
8. fetters, saṃyojanas
9. defilements, kilesas

Attachment, lobha, occurs in all of these groups and wrong view, diṭṭhi, in all groups except the group of the hindrances. This reminds us of our entanglement by lobha and diṭṭhi. Lobha and diṭṭhi occur sometimes within one group more than once, under different aspects. We should know what the object of lobha is in each classification, because sometimes lobha stands for sensuous clinging and sometimes clinging to the result of jhāna has been included as well.

Each of these groups can remind us of the dangers of akusala dhamma. For example, the classification by way of ties (ganthas) or of fetters (saṃyojanas) can remind us of the danger of being tied or chained to the cycle of birth and death. We are overcome by the cankers and by the floods, we are chained and fettered, but we may not realize it. The classification by ways of clinging (upādānas) shows us how we are in the grip of clinging to objects which are experienced through the senses and of clinging to the self. We forget that attachment cannot lead to happiness, that it leads to sorrow.

In the *Kindred Sayings* (II, Niddāna-vagga, Chapter XVII, Kindred Sayings on Gain and Favours) we read in fortythree suttas that the Buddha reminded the monks of the danger of attachment to gains, favours and flattery. We read for example in the first sutta of this section (par1, Dire) that the Buddha said to the monks:

> Dire, monks, are gains, favours and flattery, a bitter, harsh obstacle in the way of arriving at uttermost safety.
>
> Wherefore, monks, thus should you train yourselves:-
>
> "When gains, favour and flattery come to us, we will put them aside, nor when they come shall they take lasting hold on our hearts."

Why did the Buddha stress so repeatedly the danger of attachment to gains, favours and flattery? Because our happiness seems to depend entirely on the getting of the pleasant "worldly conditions". Don't they play an all-important role in our life? We want to be treated well by others, we consider ourselves very important and we forget that gain, loss, honour and dishonour are dependant on conditions, that they are beyond control. We cannot exert control over what will happen next: gain or loss, honour or dishonour. The Buddha explained that desire is the root of sorrow, but we may not fully understand this truth. Only right understanding which has been developed can see the truth of the Buddha's words.

Precise understanding of all the different phenomena of our life has to be developed. We usually pay attention only to pleasant or unpleasant sense objects, and we tend to overlook realities such as seeing or hearing. We should remember that when we experience praise or blame there are many different types of cittas. The cittas which see or hear pleasant or unpleasant objects are vipākacittas, conditioned by kamma which was committed already, and we cannot prevent them from arising. The moment of vipākacitta such as hearing which merely experiences sound is different from akusala citta which may arise shortly afterwards and which experiences sound in an unwholesome way, for example with attachment or aversion. Then there are other processes of cittas, cittas which may think in an unwholesome way about concepts. We may, for example, think for a long time about the wrongs other people committed towards us. If one is ignorant of vipāka one will be inclined to continually blame others for unpleasant objects which are received through the senses. We should know vipākacittas such as seeing and hearing as well as the other types of cittas. When we realize how ignorant we still are we will be reminded to go on developing right understanding. Through right understanding we will gradually learn to attach less importance to "self", and as a consequence we will be inclined to think more of other people's happiness instead of our own happiness.

In the *Kindred Sayings* (V, Mahā-vagga, Kindred Sayings on the Way, Book I, Chapter VIII) we read about groups of akusala dhammas and their eradication. We read, for example, about the floods:

> Monks, there are four floods. What four? The flood of sensual desire, the flood of becoming, the flood of view, the flood of nescience. These are the four. It is for the full comprehension, realization, wearing down

> and abandoning of these four floods that the ariyan eightfold way must be cultivated.

We read the same about other groups of defilements, such as the yokes, ties, latent tendencies, hindrances, the lower fetters and the higher fetters. We read at the end of this section, after the summing up of the higher fetters:

> ...It is for the full comprehension, the realization, wearing down and abandoning of these five fetters of the higher sort that the ariyan eightfold way must be cultivated. ...And how does a monk cultivate the ariyan eightfold way?
>
> Herein a monk cultivates right view, right thinking, right speech, right action, right livelihood, right effort, right mindfulness, right concentration, that ends in the restraint of lust, of hatred, of illusion; that plunges into the deathless, that has the deathless for its goal, that ends in the deathless; that flows to nibbāna, that slides to nibbāna, that tends to nibbāna.
>
> It is for the full comprehension, for the realization, for the wearing out and abandoning of these five fetters of the higher sort, monks, that this ariyan eightfold way must be cultivated.

Before there can be abandoning of akusala dhammas, there must be right understanding of all nāmas and rūpas of our daily life.

24.0.1 Questions

1. We have accumulated all kinds of akusala, from life to life. Why then are there only seven akusala dhammas which are classified as latent tendencies?
2. Who has eradicated the five lower fetters?
3. Who has eradicated the five higher fetters?

PART IV: Beautiful Cetasikas

25 Beautiful Cetasikas

25.1 Introduction

When we perform dāna, observe sīla, apply ourselves to the development of calm or the development of insight there is kusala citta. Kusala citta is accompanied by sobhana (beautiful) cetasikas and these assist the citta in performing its task. At the moment of kusala citta there is no attachment, aversion or ignorance, one is temporarily free from defilements. However, after the kusala cittas have fallen away there are bound to be akusala cittas. There are many more akusala cittas in our life than kusala cittas.

Kusala citta does not often arise since we have accumulated so many defilements. Each kusala citta is accompanied by non-attachment (alobha), but this quality seems to be against our nature. We are absorbed in and infatuated with the objects we experience through the six doors. We want pleasant objects for ourselves and it is our nature to think of ourselves in the first place. Akusala is deeply rooted and so long as latent tendencies have not been eradicated akusala citta is bound to arise time and again. Even if we try not to be stingy, jealous or proud, these defilements still arise. There is no self who has authority over the cittas which arise, cittas are not self. When we experience a beautiful object attachment tends to arise and when we experience an unpleasant object aversion tends to arise.

We read in the *Gradual Sayings* (Book of the Ones, Chapter II, par1-5):

> Monks, I know not of any other single thing of such power to cause the arising of sensual lust, if not already arisen, or, if arisen, to cause its more-becoming and increase, as the feature of beauty (in things).
>
> In him who pays not wise attention to the feature of beauty, sensual lust, if not already arisen, arises; or, if already arisen, is liable to more becoming and increase.
>
> Monks, I know not of any other single thing of such power to cause the arising of malevolence, if not already arisen, or, if arisen, to cause its more-becoming and increase, as the repulsive feature (of things).
>
> In him who pays not wise attention to the repulsive feature, malevolence, if not already arisen, arises; or, if arisen, it is liable to more-becoming and increase.

It may seem to us that a desirable object is the fundamental cause of attachment and an unpleasant object the fundamental cause of aversion[1]. However, the real cause of akusala is not in the object which is experienced. Whether akusala citta or kusala citta arises, depends on one's accumulations. There can be wise attention or unwise attention to the object, depending on conditions. When there is wise attention to the object we see the value of kusala and we have confidence in kusala. However, more often akusala citta arises and then there is unwise attention to the object. It is possible to change our habits and develop kusala. Gradually

[1] Atthasālinī I, Part II, Chapter I, 75.

our accumulations can be changed through the study of the Dhamma and the development of right understanding.

Through the study of the Dhamma we may begin to realize that conditioned realities do not last, that they are impermanent. We may remember more often that it is useless to cling to our possessions since our life is short and we cannot take our possessions with us when we die. The Buddha explained that it is difficult to be reborn in the human plane where there is an opportunity to hear the Dhamma and to develop right understanding of realities. We should therefore not, like fools, waste our life with akusala.

We read in the *Kindred Sayings* (I, Sagāthā-vagga, The Devas, Chapter IV, par 6, Faith):

```
...It is a fool's part heedless to waste his life:---
Such are the folk who will not understand.
He who is wise does foster earnestness
As he were watching over his chiefest wealth.
Give not yourselves to wastage in your lives,
Nor be familiar with delights of sense.
He who does strenuously meditate,
His shall it be to win the bliss supreme.
```

The person who with courage and perseverance develops right understanding will win "the bliss supreme", he will eventually attain arahatship. The Buddha pointed out the dangers and disadvantages of akusala, its ill effects both in this life and in the lives to come. It is right understanding which sees the disadvantage of akusala and the benefit of kusala. We can find out from our own experience that happiness connected with attachment makes us restless, since attachment can never be satisfied, and that generosity and consideration for others can condition peace of mind. We may be inclined to anger, but when we see the value of kusala we can develop loving kindness. We may be inclined to stinginess, but when we see the value of generosity there are conditions for generosity instead of stinginess. The kusala citta which arises falls away immediately but kusala is accumulated and thus there is a condition for the arising of kusala citta again later on. Mindfulness of nāma and rūpa is difficult so long as sati has not been accumulated. If we see that right understanding cannot grow without mindfulness of the reality appearing at the present moment, there are conditions for the arising of mindfulness more often. There is no other moment but the present moment in which we can develop right understanding. The Buddha used the simile of the well-trained horse, the "thorough-bred", in order to point out that right understanding should be developed. A horse does not become well-trained in one day, he has to practise certain things over and over again. In the same way we should not expect to attain enlightenment without developing right understanding.

We read in the *Gradual Sayings* (Book of the Sixes, Chapter I, par5, The thorough-bred):

> Monks, a rajah's goodly thorough-bred endowed with six points is fit for a rajah, is a rajah's asset, is reckoned a rajah's portion. What six?

> Herein, monks, the goodly thorough-bred endures forms, sounds, smells, tastes, touches and has beauty. . . Even so, monks, a monk with six qualities is worthy of offerings. . . the world's peerless field for merit. What six?
>
> Herein, monks, a monk endures forms, sounds, smells, tastes, touches and things of the mind.
>
> Verily, monks, a monk with these six qualities is worthy of offerings. . .

One will learn to "endure" the objects which present themselves through the six doors by the development of right understanding of realities. At the moment of mindfulness of the reality which appears paññā can investigate it so that it will be seen as it is: only a nāma or a rūpa, not self. Eventually one will no longer be absorbed in and infatuated with the objects which are experienced.

In order to be able to apply oneself to the development of kusala and in particular to the development of right understanding, there have to be the right conditions for it. The *Atthasālinī* (Part II, Chapter I, 75) mentions these right conditions: residence in a suitable place, dependence on good associates, hearing the "good Dhamma", merit performed in former existences. It is helpful to live in a country or place where one can hear the Dhamma and learn to develop the Path which leads to the eradication of defilements. In order to learn how to be mindful of nāma and rūpa one should associate with the good friend in Dhamma (kalyāṇa-mitta) who can explain the Dhamma in the right way.

What are the qualities the good friend in Dhamma should have? We read in the *Middle Length Sayings* (III, no. 110, Lesser Discourse at the time of a Full Moon) that the Buddha, while he was staying near Sāvatthī, in the palace of Migāra's mother, in the Eastern Monastery, spoke to the monks about the bad man (asappurisa) and the good man (sappurisa). We read about the good friends a good man consorts with: . . . And how, monks, does a good man consort with good men? As to this, monks, those recluses and brahmans who have faith (saddhā), shame, fear of blame, who have heard much, are of stirred up energy, whose mindfulness is aroused, who have wisdom—these are the friends and companions of that good man. It is thus, monks, that a good man consorts with good men. . .

The ariyan is endowed with the qualities of the good men, mentioned in the sutta. He has an unshakable confidence in the Buddha, the Dhamma and the Sangha, and in wholesomeness. How can we find out who is an ariyan? So long as we have not attained enlightenment ourselves we cannot know who is an ariyan. It depends on conditions whether or not someone will meet an ariyan. However, we can find out whether or not our friend in the Dhamma helps us to develop right understanding.

The Buddha taught that all realities are anattā, non-self, but it is extremely hard to become more detached from the self in the situations of daily life. We think of ourselves most of the time, we want to get pleasant things for ourselves. When we associate with the good friend in the Dhamma we can learn to develop right understanding and then there will eventually be less clinging to the concept of self. The person who has developed right understanding and encourages others through his example to be less selfish and more considerate for others is a true friend in the

Dhamma. He does not pay mere lip-service to the Dhamma, but he practises the Dhamma in his daily life.

"Hearing the good Dhamma" is also a necessary factor for the development of kusala. We should not listen passively; when we truly listen, we consider what we hear and apply it; otherwise the listening is not fruitful.

Another factor which conditions the development of kusala is "meritorious deeds done in the past". If someone has applied himself to dāna, sīla and bhāvanā in the past he has conditions for confidence in kusala today.

The consideration of the conditions for kusala can remind us of the fact that nothing arises without the appropriate conditions. Kusala citta does not belong to a self; there is no self who can direct the arising of kusala citta.

The *Atthasālinī* (I, Part II, Chapter I, 62) states about kusala:

> By kusala is meant (moral) "good" in the sense of destroying or disturbing contemptible states; or in the sense of wholesomeness, faultlessness, and accomplishment by skill...

The *Atthasālinī* explains that the word "kusala" can be used in the sense of healthy, not being sick in body. When the word kusala is used for mental phenomena, "it should be understood in the sense of 'health', i.e., absence of sickness, illness or disease through the 'corruptions'. Moreover, from the absence of the faultiness, hate, and torments of the 'corruptions', kusala has the sense of faultlessness."

The *Atthasālinī*, in the same section (63), defines kusala as follows:

> its characteristic is that it has faultless, happy results,
> its function is the destruction of immoralities,
> its manifestation is purity,
> its proximate cause is wise attention.

The *Atthasālinī* gives a second method of defining kusala:

> its characteristic is faultlessness by being opposed to fault,
> its function is purity,
> its manifestation is desirable results,
> its proximate cause is wise attention.

The *characteristic* of kusala, according to the first definition, is that it has pleasant results, whereas, according to the second definition, pleasant results are the *manifestation* of kusala. Classifications are not rigid and by means of different methods of classification different aspects are shown. Pleasant results can be experienced in daily life, they are a manifestation of the fact that good deeds have been performed. Whenever we see, hear, smell, taste or touch a pleasant object there is kusala vipākacitta, the result of a good deed. The moments of vipākacitta fall away immediately, they are only conditioned elements which do not last. When this truth has not been realized there is bound to be clinging to pleasant objects and sadness when these objects are gone.

The characteristic of kusala, according to the second definition, is faultlessness by being opposed to fault. At the moment of kusala citta there is no opportunity for akusala citta. When there is an opportunity for kusala it should not be neglected. There are opportunities for kusala right at hand, such as a kind word, a thought of appreciation of other people's good qualities, or a moment of mindfulness of realities such as hardness, softness, sound or hearing.

We should find out whether there is at this moment, on account of what is seen, kusala citta or akusala citta. We are usually absorbed in the details of the things around us, but sometimes there can be confidence in the value of awareness of the reality which appears now. Even if we are only beginners and there is not yet clear understanding of nāma and rūpa, there can be confidence in awareness of the present reality and then there are kusala cittas.

The function of kusala, according to the first definition, is the destruction of akusala. Akusala cannot be eradicated unless right understanding of realities has been developed, but this does not mean that dāna or sīla should be neglected. Through right understanding the wrong view of self can be eliminated, but, if there is no development of generosity and we keep on clinging to our possessions, how could there ever be detachment from the self? It is beneficial to develop all kinds of kusala for which we have accumulations, but when it is developed together with right understanding of realities akusala can eventually be eradicated.

Purity is the manifestation of kusala according to the first definition, whereas in the second definition purity is the function of kusala. When the citta is akusala, it is impure, unclean. When we are attached to an object we experience, we are enslaved and at such a moment the citta is not pure. Whereas when kusala citta arises, there is no enslavement, no selfishness; the citta is pure, free from defilements. If we know the difference between akusala citta and kusala citta we can understand that purity is a quality of kusala citta.

According to both definitions, the proximate cause of kusala is wise attention. When akusala citta arises there is unwise attention to the object and when kusala citta arises there is wise attention to the object. When there is wise attention, there is no infatuation with the object, there is no aversion, no ignorance. Seeing realities as they are conditions wise attention. The arahat has the highest degree of wise attention: for him defilements do not arise on account of any object he experiences, no matter it is pleasant or unpleasant.

Kusala citta does not arise alone, it is accompanied by cetasikas: by the *universals* (sabbacitta sādhāranā), the cetasikas which accompany each citta, by *particulars* (pakiṇṇakā), cetasikas which accompany cittas of the four classes (jātis) of kusala, akusala, vipāka and kiriya[2] , but which do not accompany every citta, and by *sobhana cetasikas*, beautiful cetasikas. Kusala citta cannot be accompanied by akusala cetasikas. One may wonder why the term "sobhana" and not the term "kusala" is used for cetasikas which accompany kusala citta. The reason is that sobhana cetasikas do not only accompany kusala cittas, but also cittas of the jātis which are vipāka and kiriya[3]. All the cittas which are accompanied by sobhana cetasikas are called sobhana cittas.

---

[2] See Introduction.

[3] There are also vipāka-cittas and kiriyacittas which are not sobhana cittas, namely ahetuka (rootless) vipākacittas and ahetuka kiriyacittas. See Abhidhamma in Daily Life, Chapter 19.

There are twentyfour sobhana cittas of the sense-sphere, kāma-sobhana cittas. They are:

- 8 mahā-kusala cittas[4]
- 8 mahā-vipākacittas
- 8 mahā-kiriyacittas[5]

Cittas of the sense-sphere can be sobhana cittas, cittas accompanied by sobhana cetasikas, or asobhana cittas, cittas which are not accompanied by sobhana cetasikas. Cittas of the planes of consciousness other than the sensuous plane are always sobhana cittas. Those who have developed calm to the stage of absorption, jhāna, have jhāna-cittas and these are sobhana cittas. There are rūpa-jhānacittas or rūpāvacara cittas and arūpa-jhānacittas or arūpāvacara cittas. Rūpa-jhāna can be translated as "fine-material" jhāna and arūpa-jhāna can be translated as "immaterial" jhāna. Arūpa-jhāna is more refined than rūpa-jhāna since the meditation subjects of arūpa-jhāna are not dependant on materiality.

The sobhana cittas which are rūpāvacara cittas, pertaining to five stages of rūpa-jhāna, are the following:

- 5 rūpāvacara kusala cittas
- 5 rūpāvacara vipākacittas
- 5 rūpāvacara kiriyacittas (of the arahat)

The sobhana cittas which are arūpāvacara cittas, pertaining to four stages of arūpa-jhāna, are the following:

- 4 arūpāvacara kusala cittas
- 4 arūpāvacara vipākacittas
- 4 arūpāvacara kiriyacittas

Apart from the sobhana cittas which are jhānacittas, there are sobhana cittas which are lokuttara cittas, supramundane cittas experiencing nibbāna. There are *eight lokuttara cittas*, but when one takes into account the lokuttara cittas which are accompanied by jhāna-factors of the different stages of jhāna, there are *forty lokuttara cittas*[6].

When cittas are counted as *eightynine* (not including lokuttara cittas accompanied by jhāna-factors of the different stages of jhāna), there are *fiftynine sobhana cittas*, and when cittas are counted as *hundred and twentyone* (including forty lokuttara cittas accompanied by jhāna-factors), there are *ninetyone sobhana cittas.*

Sobhana cittas are accompanied by the universals, by particulars and by sobhana cetasikas. There are *twentyfive sobhana cetasikas in all* which can accompany sobhana cittas. Not all twentyfive sobhana cetasikas accompany every sobhana citta, but *at least nineteen sobhana cetasikas* have to accompany each sobhana citta.

---

[4] Mahā means great. Here the term is used in the case of sobhana cittas of the sense-sphere.

[5] The arahat has, instead of mahā-kusala cittas, mahā-kiriyacittas.

[6] See Abhidhamma in Daily Life, Chapter 22.

Among the twentyfive sobhana cetasikas *three are sobhana hetus* (roots). These are:

- non-attachment, alobha
- non-aversion, adosa
- wisdom, amoha or paññā

Non-attachment and non-aversion have to accompany every sobhana citta, and wisdom or understanding may or may not accompany sobhana citta.

Every sobhana cetasika has its own specific characteristic, function, manifestation and proximate cause (immediate occasion). When we perform dāna, observe sīla, apply ourselves to the development of calm, samatha, or insight, vipassanā, sobhana cetasikas assist the kusala citta in carrying out its task of wholesomeness.

The sobhana vipākacittas are also accompanied by at least nineteen sobhana cetasikas. Vipākacittas do not perform deeds, they are results. Sobhana vipākacittas are results of deeds which are performed by kusala cittas accompanied by sobhana cetasikas. The rebirth-consciousness, for example, can be the result of a deed performed by kusala citta accompanied by sobhana hetus and other sobhana cetasikas. In that case it is sahetuka vipākacitta (with hetus).

The arahat does not perform kusala kamma, he is free from the cycle of birth and death. Thus, instead of kusala cittas he has kiriyacittas which are accompanied by sobhana hetus and other sobhana cetasikas. Sobhana kiriyacittas are accompanied by at least nineteen sobhana cetasikas.

26 Confidence

26.1 Confidence (saddhā)

Saddhā, confidence or faith, is one of the sobhana cetasikas which arises with every sobhana citta: with the sobhana cittas of the sense-sphere (kāma-sobhana cittas), with the rūpāvacara cittas, with the arūpāvacara cittas and with the lokuttara cittas. Saddhā is not blind faith in a person, it is confidence in wholesomeness. There is saddhā with dāna, with sīla and with bhāvanā. There cannot be any kind of wholesomeness without saddhā. Saddhā is called by the *Atthasālinī* the "forerunner" of wholesomeness.

The *Atthasālinī* (I, Part IV, Chapter I, 119) states about saddhā:

> ...It has purifying or aspiring as its characteristic. As the water-purifying gem of the universal monarch thrown into water causes solids, alluvia, waterweeds and mud to subside and makes the water clear, transparent and undisturbed, so faith arising discards the hindrances, causes the corruptions to subside, purifies the mind and makes it undisturbed; the mind being purified, the aspirant of noble family gives gifts, observes the precepts, performs the duties of "uposatha"[1] , and commences bhāvanā. Thus faith should be known to have purifying as its characteristic...

The *Atthasālinī* refers to a simile given in the *Questions of King Milinda* (35)[2] : a universal monarch crosses a small stream with his army. The water has been polluted by the army but his water-purifying gem purifies the water so that mud, sand and waterweeds subside and the water becomes clear and undisturbed. The water which is disturbed by pollution is like the mind which is disturbed by defilements. Faith purifies the mind so that it becomes clear, transparent and undisturbed.

As to the characteristic of "aspiring", the *Atthasālinī* uses another simile in order to explain this. A crowd standing on both banks of a great river full of crocodiles, monsters, sharks and ogres, is afraid to cross over. A hero crosses the river and repels the dangerous animals with his sword, and leads the crowd in crossing over. The *Atthasālinī* (120) states:

> ...So faith is the forerunner, the precursor to one who is giving gifts, observing the precepts, performing the duties of uposatha and commencing bhāvanā. Hence it has been said: Faith has purifying and aspiring as its characteristic.

The *Atthasālinī* also uses another method of defining saddhā:

---

[1] Uposatha days are days of fasting or vigil; uposatha is observed on the days of full-moon and new-moon, and sometimes also on the days of the first and last moon-quarter. In Buddhist countries there is a tradition for lay-followers to visit temples and to observe eight precepts on these days.

[2] Containing discussions on Dhamma between King Milinda and the arahat Nāgasena. This work which is not part of the Tipiṭaka must have been written before the time of Buddhaghosa, but its date is not known. It gives most valuable explanations of the Buddhist teachings and it often refers to the texts of the Tipiṭaka.

> ...Faith has confiding as its characteristic; purifying as its function, like the water-purifying gem, or aspiring faith as function, like the crossing of the floods; freedom from pollution or decision as its manifestation; an object worthy of faith or factors of "streamwinning" as its proximate cause.

The *Visuddhimagga* (XIV, 140) defines confidence in the same way as the *Atthasālinī* in the second method.

When akusala citta arises there is no confidence in kusala. For example, when we are attached to a pleasant sight or when we have aversion towards an ugly sight, there is forgetfulness of kusala, no aspiration for it. Whereas, when there is faith or confidence, there is aspiration for kusala. Only when people have confidence in the value of dāna, sīla or bhāvanā will they apply themselves to it. It depends on a person's accumulations which kind of kusala he is inclined to perform. Some people have confidence in dāna and sīla but they do not see the benefit of being aware right now of seeing or hearing, in order to know these realities as non-self.

As we have seen, purifying has been mentioned as a function of confidence and freedom from pollution as one of its manifestations. When the citta is accompanied by confidence, it is pure, free from the hindrances. But so long as latent tendencies have not been eradicated defilements are bound to arise, time and again. The purity of confidence is in the ariyan of a higher degree than in the non-ariyan. The sotāpanna does not cling to the concept of self, he has eradicated wrong view, and thus his good deeds are purer. His sīla is more purified than the sīla of the non-ariyan, he has no more conditions to transgress the five precepts.

Another manifestation of confidence is decision or resolution. When there is determination to accomplish kusala, it is evident that there is confidence in kusala. There is no self who decides for kusala, it depends on conditions whether or not kusala citta arises. When there are conditions for aversion and discouragement, there is no resolution for kusala. We may have no energy for any kind of kusala when we feel annoyed because of our shortcomings, or when we are disappointed about other people, when we feel lonely and depressed, when we find life useless and frustrating. When we are depressed we are self- centred. We want pleasant objects for ourselves and when we do not get these we feel dissatisfied with life. If there would be less clinging to the self there would be less conditions for feelings of frustration. Right understanding can eventually eradicate the clinging to the self, but it can only develop very gradually. If we are impatient because we do not notice any progress in the development of right understanding, we should remember the patience and determination of the Buddha in the lives when he was still a Bodhisatta. He was determined to develop right understanding life after life, without becoming discouraged, without coming to a halt halfway. Courage and patience are needed in order to develop understanding of the realities appearing in daily life. One has to have "aspiring confidence" like the hero who crosses the floods. It is useless to worry about the lack of mindfulness, or to think of ways to make it arise. When there is more understanding of what the object of mindfulness is, an ultimate reality, there are conditions for mindfulness now of whatever reality appears.

"An object worthy of faith" is a proximate cause of confidence. The Buddha, the Dhamma and the Sangha are objects worthy of confidence. This does not mean that someone who never heard of the Dhamma cannot have confidence. Confidence is an ultimate reality with its own characteristic, it is not specifically Buddhist. Each kusala citta is accompanied by confidence; kusala is kusala, no matter what nationality or race one is, no matter what faith one professes. Also those who never heard of the Dhamma can have confidence in ways of kusala such as generosity and true loving kindness. Also good deeds are objects worthy of confidence. If one listens to the Dhamma and develops right understanding there are conditions for the eradication of akusala and thus there will be more opportunity for the development of wholesomeness.

The "factors of streamwinning", that is the factors, necessary for attaining the first stage of enlightenment, the stage of the "streamwinner" or sotāpanna, are also a proximate cause for confidence. These factors are: association with the right friend, hearing the Dhamma, wise attention and practice in accordance with the Dhamma[3]. Confidence in the Buddha, the Dhamma and the Sangha starts with listening to the Dhamma as it is explained by the right friend. We read in many suttas that people first listened to the Buddha, considered what they heard and then took their refuge in the Buddha, the Dhamma and the Sangha. Their confidence was based on listening, inquiring and considering.

We read in the *Middle Length Sayings* (I, no. 4, Discourse on Fear and Dread) that the Buddha, while staying near Sāvatthī, in the Jeta Grove, spoke to the Brahman Jāṇussoṇi about his living in the forest without fear and dread, and his attainment to Buddhahood. Jāṇussoṇi, after he listened to the Buddha, took his refuge in the Buddha, the Dhamma and the Sangha with the following words:

> ...Excellent, good Gotama, excellent, good Gotama. It is as if one might set upright what had been upset, or might disclose what was covered, or show the way to one who had gone astray, or bring an oil-lamp into the darkness so that those with vision might see material shapes—even so in many a figure has dhamma been made clear by the reverend Gotama. Thus I am going to the reverend Gotama for refuge, to the Dhamma and to the Order of monks. May the reverend Gotama accept me as a layfollower going for refuge from today forth for as long as life lasts.

Some people have confidence to become a lay-disciple and others have confidence to become a monk, it depends on one's accumulated inclinations. There are also people who are inclined to listen, but who do not gain enough confidence to practise the teachings. It may not be the right time for them to begin with the development of the Path, but in a future life they may listen again and then gain enough confidence to practise the teachings. We should find out for ourselves whether our confidence is to the degree that we apply the Dhamma we have heard or not yet. If one has enough confidence one will continue to develop right understanding until enlightenment is attained and all doubt and wrong view are eradicated.

There is still another aspect to confidence, saddhā, and that is the aspect of indriya, controlling faculty. An indriya exercises leadership over the dhammas it

---

[3] Dialogues of the Buddha, III, 33, Saṅgīti Sutta, 227.

accompanies. There are five wholesome cetasikas, indriyas, called the "spiritual faculties", which should be developed. They are: confidence, energy, mindfulness, concentration and wisdom. These faculties overcome the defilements which are their opposites. Confidence governs the accompanying dhammas, citta and cetasikas, in its quality of purifying and of confiding in kusala. It overcomes lack of confidence in kusala. Without confidence kusala citta and its accompanying cetasikas could not arise. The *Atthasālinī* (I, Part IV, Chapter I, 119) states:

> "From the overcoming of lack of faith, faith is a controlling faculty in the sense of predominance, or in its characteristic of decision it exercises lordship (over associated states)."

When the "spiritual faculties" have been developed they become "powers" or "strengths" (balas). Then they have become firm and unshakable, they cannot be shaken by the defilements which are their opposites. The same cetasikas which can be considered under the aspect of indriya can also be considered under the aspect of power. We read in the *Dhammasangaṇi* about confidence as faculty, indriya, and as power, bala:

> The faith which on that occasion is a trusting in, the professing confidence in, the sense of assurance, faith, faith as a faculty and as a power—this is the faith that there then is.

The *Atthasālinī* (I, Part IV, Chapter II, 145) explains this passage and states that assurance is abundant assurance in the virtues of the Buddha. Such assurance is not based on mere theoretical understanding of the Buddha's teachings. There can only be abundant confidence in the Buddha's virtues when right understanding of realities has been developed.

Those who want to develop calm to the degree of jhāna have to develop the five "spiritual faculties". We read in the *Visuddhimagga* (IV, 45-49), in the section on the conditions necessary for the attainment of jhāna, that the faculties, indriyas, have to be "balanced". When any one of them is too strong and other faculties weak, they cannot perform their functions. The faculty of faith has to be balanced with the faculty of wisdom:

> ...For one strong in faith and weak in understanding has confidence uncritically and groundlessly. One strong in understanding and weak in faith errs on the side of cunning and is as hard to cure as one sick of a disease caused by medicine. With the balancing of the two a man has confidence only when there are grounds for it...

Further on we read that concentration and faith must be balanced: "One working on concentration needs strong faith, since it is with such faith and confidence that he reaches absorption..."

The "spiritual faculties" have to be developed also for the attainment of enlightenment and they must be balanced. How are the faculties balanced in vipassanā? One may have confidence in the Buddha's teachings but right understanding of realities may not have been developed and then confidence is not balanced with the other faculties. But when right understanding of the present moment has been developed, there is also confidence and this is balanced with understanding and the other faculties.

When we are forgetful of realities there is no confidence in awareness of the present moment. This may happen, for example, when we are listening to the stories other people tell us and we are quite absorbed in these stories. But sometimes there may be mindfulness of one reality at a time, for example of sound, and then this can be realized as only a rūpa, a reality which can be heard, not a voice or a person. At such a moment there is confidence which sees the value of right understanding. When we develop right understanding, we do not have to aim at confidence, it arises already. Confidence grows to the extent that right understanding develops. Through mindfulness of nāma and rūpa, thus, through the development of the four "Applications of Mindfulness" (satipaṭṭhāna) the five spiritual faculties develop together.

As we have seen, when the faculty of confidence has been more developed, it can become unshakable and firm, it can become a "power" or "strength" (bala). So long as one has not attained enlightenment confidence can still be shaken. One may have doubt about the value of the development of right understanding, doubt about the eightfold Path. The confidence of the sotāpanna cannot be shaken anymore; he has eradicated doubt. He has an unshakable confidence in the Buddha, the Dhamma and the Sangha. At each stage of enlightenment the faculties and thus also confidence have become more developed. At the moment of the attainment of arahatship they have reached completion.

As we have seen, one of the proximate causes of confidence is an object worthy of confidence. The Buddha, the Dhamma and the Sangha are objects worthy of confidence. So long as we are not ariyans we do not really understand what enlightenment means; we have only theoretical understanding about it and thus our knowledge is very limited. We take our refuge in the Buddha, but our confidence in his virtues cannot be as strong as the sotāpanna's confidence. The second Gem in which we take refuge is the Dhamma. The term "dhamma" has many meanings, it can stand for the teachings, or for paramattha dhamma, ultimate reality. Seeing and attachment are real, they are dhammas. We do not take our refuge in every dhamma. Nibbāna is lokuttara dhamma and this is the second Gem, the Dhamma we take our refuge in. Also the eight types of lokuttara cittas which experience nibbāna are included in the second Gem; thus there are "nine lokuttara dhammas" in which we take our refuge. Again, our understanding of the second Gem is limited so long as we have not attained enlightenment. Our confidence in the teachings which lead to enlightenment cannot be as strong as the sotāpanna's confidence; he knows from experience what enlightenment means. The ariyan Sangha is the third Gem in which we take our refuge. We do not really know what it means to be an ariyan so long as we are not ariyans ourselves and thus our confidence in the ariyan Sangha is still weak.

When we realize how weak our confidence still is, we should not become discouraged. When we think of all the virtues of the ariyan, his unshakable confidence in wholesomeness, his purity of sīla and his generosity, we should not forget that it all started with listening to the Dhamma, considering it and developing right understanding. We read in the *Middle Length Sayings* (II, no. 70, Kīṭāgiri sutta) that the Buddha, while he was in Kāsi, said that enlightenment could not be attained without diligence. He spoke to the monks about people with different accumulations who attained enlightenment, and then said:

> I, monks, do not say that the attainment of profound knowledge comes straightaway; nevertheless, monks, the attainment of profound knowledge comes by a gradual training, a gradual doing, a gradual course. And how, monks, does the attainment of profound knowledge come by means of a gradual training, a gradual doing, a gradual course? As to this, monks, one who has faith draws close; drawing close, he sits down near by; sitting down near by he lends ear; lending ear he hears dhamma; having heard dhamma he remembers it; he tests the meaning of the things he has borne in mind; while testing the meaning the things are approved of; there being approval of the things desire[4] is born; with desire born he makes an effort; having made the effort he weighs it up; having weighed it up he strives; being self-resolute he realizes himself the highest truth itself and, penetrating it by means of wisdom, he sees. . .

The ariyan is often described as a person who has heard much. He has listened to Dhamma and has applied what he has heard. If he had been a passive listener he could not have attained enlightenment. We may wish to reach the goal without cultivating the right cause which leads to the goal. If there is no beginning of the development of understanding at this moment how can we expect the arising of profound wisdom? Realities such as hardness, feeling or sound appear time and again. If one begins to be mindful of the reality which appears now, one cultivates the right conditions for the growth of right understanding. There should be confidence which is as courageous and determined as the hero who crosses the flood. Many moments of such courageous determination are needed in order to realize what one has not yet realized.

26.1.1 Questions

1. Which are objects worthy of confidence?
2. Can confidence arise with mahā-vipākacitta?
3. How do we know when there is confidence?
4. How can confidence grow?
5. What hinders confidence?
6. Why is the sotāpanna's confidence "unshakable"?
7. How is confidence "balanced" with the other spiritual faculties in vipassanā?
8. At which moment is there confidence in the development of the four Applications of Mindfulness?
9. People can take their refuge in the Triple Gem with confidence, but why is the confidence of the non-ariyan still weak in comparison with the confidence of the ariyan?

[4] kusalacchanda, "wish-to-do" which is kusala.

27 Mindfulness

27.1 Mindfulness (sati)

When we apply ourselves to generosity, dāna, to morality, sīla, or to mental development, bhāvanā, confidence, saddhā, arises with the kusala citta. Without confidence in the value of kusala we could not perform any kind of kusala. Kusala citta does not only need confidence in order to perform its task, it also needs mindfulness, sati, which is heedful, non-forgetful, of kusala. There are many opportunities for generosity, for morality and for mental development, but we are often forgetful of kusala and we waste such opportunities. When mindfulness arises there is heedfulness of kusala and then the opportunity for kusala which presents itself is not wasted. There has to be mindfulness with dāna, with sīla, with samatha and with the development of insight.

Mindfulness, sati, is one of the nineteen sobhana cetasikas which have to arise with every sobhana citta. The *Atthasālinī* (I, Part IV, Chapter I, 121) states that the characteristic of mindfulness is "not floating away". Mindfulness "does not allow the floating away of moral states", such as the four applications of mindfulness and the other factors leading to enlightenment. Another characteristic of mindfulness the *Atthasālinī* mentions is "acquiring" or "taking up"[1], that is, acquirement of what is useful and beneficial. Mindfulness, when it arises, "searches well the courses of states, advantageous and disadvantageous: —'these states are advantageous, those disadvantageous, these states are serviceable, those not serviceable'—and then removes the disadvantageous and takes up the advantageous."

The *Atthasālinī* then gives another definition of mindfulness:

> . . . Mindfulness has "not floating away" as its characteristic, unforgetfulness as its function, guarding, or the state of facing the object, as its manifestation, firm remembrance (saññā) or application in mindfulness as regards the body, etc. , as proximate cause. It should be regarded as a door-post from being firmly established in the object, and as a door-keeper from guarding the door of the senses.

The definition of mindfulness in the *Visuddhimagga* (XIV, 141) is similar to this definition.

Mindfulness is non-forgetful of what is kusala and it keeps us from akusala. Also those who do not know about the Dhamma are able to perform wholesome deeds, but it is through the Dhamma that one can know more precisely what is kusala and what is akusala. Association with the good friend in Dhamma, listening to the Dhamma and considering it are most helpful conditions for mindfulness in the field of dāna, sīla, samatha and insight, thus, for all levels of mindfulness. The generosity, the patience and all the other good qualities of the true friend in Dhamma can remind one to develop such qualities as well.

There are different ways of kusala and in order to be more heedful of what is wholesome, it is helpful to know more in detail about them. Dāna, generosity, for

---

[1] In Pali: upagaṇhanā.

example, is not only the giving away of useful things. There are also other ways of generosity included in dāna, such as expressing our appreciation of someone else's kusala (anumodana dāna). We may be stingy as to words of praise or we are lazy with regard to kusala and then we let opportunities for such a way of generosity go by. It is mindfulness which is non-forgetful of this way of generosity when the opportunity arises. Another form of generosity is to give someone else, no matter he lives in this world or in some other plane of existence, the opportunity to rejoice in our good deeds, so that he has kusala citta as well. It is mindfulness, not self, which is heedful of kusala. Without mindfulness it is impossible to perform any kind of kusala.

Abstaining from ill deeds is a way of kusala included in sīla. The Buddha explained in detail what is right and what is wrong. We should consider his words and test their meaning. Then we can verify ourselves the truth of his teachings. Before we studied the Dhamma we may not have known that also the killing of insects, for example, is akusala. Through the Dhamma we acquire more understanding of our different cittas, of kusala cittas and akusala cittas. We come to understand that killing is motivated by dosa and that the killing of any living being, insects included, is akusala kamma which can produce akusala vipāka. When we see the disadvantages of all kinds of akusala there are conditions for the arising of mindfulness which is heedful, non-forgetful of abstaining from akusala.

Through the Dhamma we learn about different ways of kusala. Before we studied the Dhamma we may not have known that politeness and respect are ways of kusala kamma. Politeness and respect which are expressed by gestures or words are forms of sīla. When there is an opportunity for such a way of kusala, mindfulness may arise and be non-forgetful of it, so that this opportunity is not wasted; that is the function of mindfulness.

There is not only mindfulness which is non-forgetful of dāna or of sīla, there is also mindfulness with mental development. The development of calm, samatha, is one way of mental development. There is mindfulness with the kusala citta which develops calm. There are many degrees of calm. Jhāna, absorption, is a high level of calm and it is extremely difficult to attain this level; one can only attain jhāna if one has accumulations for it and if there is right understanding of its way of development. One may have no accumulations for jhāna, but there can be moments of calm in daily life. For example, if there is right understanding of the characteristic of loving kindness, which is one of the meditation subjects of samatha, this quality can be developed in daily life and then there is calm conditioned by loving kindness. When there is calm, no matter of what degree, there is also mindfulness of the object of calm, be it loving kindness, compassion, the recollection of the Buddha or any other object of samatha.

The study of the Dhamma is included in mental development. When we study the Dhamma with the aim to have more understanding of realities there is mindfulness at that moment. When we study the Dhamma and consider it there is intellectual understanding of realities and this is different from direct understanding of the reality which appears at the present moment. Intellectual understanding is a necessary foundation for the development of direct understanding or insight, vipassanā.

In order to understand what mindfulness of vipassanā is, we should know what its object is. The object of mindfulness in the development of vipassanā is the nāma or rūpa which appears at the present moment. Nāma and rūpa are ultimate realities, different from "conventional realities" or concepts, such as person, mind, body, animal or tree. Concepts are objects we can think of but they are not real in the absolute sense.

We should know the difference between ultimate realities and concepts. If we only know concepts and not ultimate realities we believe that a person or self really exists. We tend to think of a "whole" of mind and body, of the human person. When we study the Dhamma we learn that what we call mind are different types of citta accompanied by different cetasikas, and that these change all the time. What we call body are different rūpas, some of which are produced by kamma, some by citta, some by temperature and some by nutrition. These rūpas arise and then fall away, they change all the time. Through the study of the Dhamma we learn about the different conditions for the cittas, cetasikas and rūpas which arise. For instance, people are born with different bodily features: some are beautiful, some are ugly, some are strong in body, some are weak. Such differences are caused by kamma. People have, as we say in conventional language, different characters, and through the Dhamma we acquire a more precise understanding of the conditions for their different characters. People had, in past lives, different abilities, different inclinations, and these have been accumulated from one moment of citta to the next moment of citta; therefore, they can condition the citta arising at the present moment. Kusala cittas and akusala cittas which arise are conditioned by accumulated inclinations to wholesomeness and unwholesomeness. We have pleasant experiences and unpleasant experiences through the senses and these are conditioned phenomena, they are vipākacittas produced by kamma. When we study the different conditions for the phenomena which arise we will understand more clearly that they are only fleeting phenomena, that there is no person or self who can exert control over the events of life.

We are used to paying attention only to concepts, but through the study of the Dhamma we learn to see the value of developing understanding of ultimate realities, of nāma and rūpa. We learn through the study of the Abhidhamma that the sense-objects are experienced through their appropriate doorway by cittas which arise in processes. Visible object is experienced through the eye-door by cittas arising in the eye-door process. Tangible object such as hardness is experienced through the body-door by cittas arising in the body-door process. Each object is experienced through its appropriate doorway; tangible object, for example, could not be experienced through the eye-door. Only one object can be experienced at a time, through one doorway; the different doorways should not be confused with each other. When we only pay attention to concepts we think, for example, that we can see and touch a flower. But in reality the seeing sees only what is visible, visible object, and the body-consciousness experiences tangible object such as hardness or softness. We can think of a "whole" such as a flower because of remembrance of different experiences through different doorways. The thinking is conditioned by seeing and other sense impressions.

Nāma and rūpa appear one at a time and each one of them has its own characteristic. These characteristics cannot be altered. Seeing, for example, has its own characteristic; we can give it another name, but its characteristic cannot be altered. Seeing is always seeing for everybody, no matter whether an animal or any other living being sees. Concepts are only objects of thinking, they are not realities with their own characteristics, and, thus, they are not objects of which right understanding is to be developed. Nāma and rūpa which are real in the absolute sense are the objects of which right understanding should be developed.

Only one reality at a time can be experienced by citta and thus also mindfulness which accompanies the kusala citta can experience only one object at a time. Since we are so used to paying attention to "wholes", to concepts such as people, cars or trees, we find it difficult to consider only one reality at a time. When we know the difference between the moments of thinking of concepts and the moments that only one reality at a time, such as sound or hardness appears, we will gradually have more understanding of what mindfulness is.

In order to remind people of the truth of conditioned realities the Buddha taught about six doors, the objects experienced through these doorways and the realities which experience these objects. We read, for example, in the *Middle Length Sayings* (III, no. 148, "Discourse on the Six Sixes") that the Buddha, while he was staying near Sāvatthī, in the Jeta Grove, explained to the monks:

> ...When it is said, "Six internal sense-fields are to be understood", in reference to what is it said? It is in reference to the sense-field of eye, the sense-field of ear, the sense-field of nose, the sense-field of tongue, the sense-field of body, the sense-field of mind. When it is said, "Six internal sense-fields are to be understood", it is said in reference to this. This is the first Six.
>
> When it is said, "Six external sense-fields are to be understood", in reference to what is it said? It is in reference to the sense-field of material shapes, the sense-field of sounds, the sense-field of smells, the sense-field of tastes, the sense-field of touches, the sense-field of mental states. When it is said, "Six external sense-fields are to be understood", it is said in reference to this. This is the second Six.
>
> When it is said, "Six classes of consciousness are to be understood", in reference to what is it said? It is in reference to the visual consciousness that arises because of eye and material shapes; the auditory consciousness that arises because of ear and sounds; the olfactory consciousness that arises because of nose and smells; the gustatory consciousness that arises because tongue and tastes; the bodily consciousness that arises because of body and touches; the mental consciousness that arises because of mind and mental states. When it is said, "Six classes of consciousness are to be understood", it is said in reference to this. This is the third Six...

We then read about the six classes of impingement (contact or phassa), about the six classes of feeling conditioned by those impingements and about the six classes of craving conditioned by the six classes of feeling. Direct understanding of all these realities which arise because of their own conditions can eradicate the wrong view of self and can eventually lead to "turning away", to detachment from realities.

This sutta reminds us that each reality which appears through one of the six doors should be known separately, we should not confuse different realities with each other. We are so used to the idea of seeing people. However, the only object which can be seen is visible object. If there is mindfulness of visible object when it appears we will understand that visible object is a reality which can be experienced through the eyesense, that it is not a person. We may find it difficult to grasp this truth and we may wonder whether we have to avoid thinking of concepts. We do not have to avoid this, then we could not live our daily life. The citta which thinks of concepts is a reality, it arises because of conditions and it can be known as only a kind of nāma, not self. We can live our daily life as usual, thinking of concepts and expressing ourselves by means of conventional language, in terms of "I", "self" or "person", but at the same time right understanding of nāma and rūpa can be developed. Even when we think of people and talk to them, there are nāma and rūpa which appear, and these can be objects of mindfulness.

The cetasika sati, mindfulness, is different from what is meant by mindfulness in conventional language. Someone may think that he is mindful when he directs his attention to what he is doing or to what is going on around him. That is not the characteristic of sati in the development of insight. Sati of vipassanā is, as we have seen, mindful of a nāma or a rūpa which appears, without a thought of self who makes a particular effort or who is directing the attention to an object. Also sati is only a type of nāma, not self.

When there is mindfulness of a nāma or rūpa which appears, direct understanding of that reality can at that moment be developed. When we learn a subject such as mathematics or history, we study books and try to understand the subject we study. In order to understand realities we have to investigate or "study" them, but that is not study through thinking, it is the development of direct understanding of realities. When a reality such as sound appears and there is mindfulness of it, its characteristic can be "studied" or investigated, just for an extremely short moment. In that way it can be known as it is: a conditioned reality which does not belong to anyone. The word "study" can remind us that there should be mindfulness of realities again and again, until they are known as they are. Full understanding cannot be achieved within a short time.

As we have seen in the definition of the *Atthasālinī*, "guarding" is a manifestation of mindfulness. Through mindfulness the six doors are guarded. When there is no mindfulness after having seen visible object through the eyes, there is bound to be attachment, aversion and ignorance on account of the object. We are absorbed in the objects which are experienced through the six doors. When mindfulness arises there is no akusala citta on account of the object which is experienced and, thus, the doorways are guarded. The *Atthasālinī* compares mindfulness with a doorkeeper.

In order to understand the function of mindfulness it is helpful to know the danger of the absence of mindfulness. The definition of "Heedlessness" in the *Book of Analysis* (Vibhaṅga, Chapter 17, Analysis of Small Items, par 846) reminds us of the danger of akusala and the value of mindfulness which guards the six doors. We read:

> Therein what is "heedlessness"? Wrong bodily action or wrong verbal action or wrong mental action or the succumbing and repeated succumbing of consciousness to the five strands of sense pleasures or not working carefully, not working constantly, working spasmodically, being stagnant, relinquishing wish (desire-to-do, chanda), relinquishing the task, non-pursuance, non-development, non-repetition, non-resolution, non-practising, heedlessness in the development of good states; that which is similar, heedlessness, being heedless, state of being heedless. This is called heedlessness.

When we are not mindful we succumb repeatedly to the "five strands of sense pleasures". The doors of the eye, ear, nose, tongue, bodysense and the mind-door are not guarded. We are working "spasmodically", or we are stagnant; we are lazy as to the development of right understanding. We cannot force the arising of mindfulness, but when we see the danger of akusala it can condition non-forgetfulness of the reality appearing at the present moment. When mindfulness arises there is no "relinquishing of the task", namely the task of the development of right understanding.

It may seem uninteresting to investigate realities such as visible object, seeing, sound or hearing, but we should remember that right understanding of realities bears directly on our daily life. It can eliminate wrong bodily action, wrong verbal action and wrong mental action. When wrong view has been eradicated completely we shall never again neglect the five precepts since there are no more conditions for neglecting them. Even when one has not yet become a sotāpanna, mindfulness can prevent akusala kamma. For instance, when there is an unpleasant sound, aversion may arise and it could motivate akusala kamma. Whereas when there is mindfulness of sound as only a kind of rūpa, not the voice of someone, not the sound of a radio, the doors are guarded. When mindfulness guards the six doors it is to the benefit of ourselves as well as of other people.

As we have seen, the *Atthasālinī* states that the proximate cause of mindfulness is firm remembrance (saññā) or the four applications of mindfulness (satipaṭṭhāna). There can be mindfulness of the nāma or rūpa which appears because of firm remembrance of all we learnt from the teachings about nāma and rūpa. Listening is mentioned in the scriptures as a most important condition for the attainment of enlightenment, because when we listen time and again, there can be firm remembrance of the Dhamma. Mindfulness is different from remembrance, saññā. Saññā accompanies every citta; it recognizes the object and "marks" it, so that it can be recognized again. Mindfulness, sati, is not forgetful of what is wholesome. It arises with sobhana cittas. But when there is sati which is non-forgetful of dāna, sīla, of the object of calm or, in the case of vipassanā, of the nāma and rūpa appearing at the present moment, there is also kusala saññā which remembers the object in the right way, in the wholesome way.

The other proximate cause of mindfulness is the four applications of mindfulness or satipaṭṭhāna[2]. All realities can be object of mindfulness in the development of insight and are thus included in the four applications of mindfulness which are rūpa, feeling, citta and dhamma. For those who have accumulations to develop calm to the degree of jhāna and to develop insight as well, also jhānacitta can be object of mindfulness in vipassanā, in order to see it as non-self. Right understanding of realities is developed through mindfulness of any nāma or rūpa which appears now, be it akusala citta, mahā-kusala citta, jhānacitta or any other reality. One should not try to direct mindfulness to a particular object; there is no self who can have power over any reality or who can direct sati. There is not any reality which is excluded from the four applications of mindfulness.

Mindfulness is one of the "five spiritual faculties" (indriyas) which should be developed. As we have seen, the other spiritual faculties are: confidence, energy, concentration and wisdom. We read in the *Dhammasangaṇi* (par 14) about the faculty of mindfulness:

> What on that occasion is the faculty of mindfulness?
>
> The mindfulness which on that occasion is recollecting, calling back to mind; the mindfulness which is remembering, bearing in mind, the opposite of superficiality and of obliviousness; mindfulness as faculty (indriya), mindfulness as power (bala), right mindfulness— this is the faculty of mindfulness that there then is.

The *Atthasālinī* (I, Part IV, Chapter II, 147), in its explanation of this passage, states about "non-superficiality":

> . . . "non-superficiality" (in the sense of diving or entering into the object) is the state of not letting the object float away. Not as pumpkins and pots, etc., which float on the water and do not sink therein, does mindfulness sink into the object. Hence it is said to be non-superficiality. . .

Mindfulness is an indriya, a "controlling faculty", a "leader" of the citta and accompanying cetasikas in its function of heedfulness, of non-forgetfulness of what is wholesome. We read in the *Atthasālinī*, in the same section:

> . . . It exercises government (over associated states) in the characteristic of presenting or illuminating the object—this is the faculty of mindfulness.

Mindfulness is non-forgetful of the object, and understanding (paññā) has the function of knowing it as it is. Mindfulness, when it is developed, becomes a power or strength (bala), and then it is unshakable by its opposite, by forgetfulness. We read in the same section of the *Atthasālinī* : . . . It does not fluctuate on account of negligence—this is "strength of mindfulness". "Right mindfulness" is irreversible, emancipating, moral mindfulness.

> The five wholesome controlling faculties, the "spiritual faculties", must be developed in samatha in order to attain jhāna and in vipassanā in order to attain enlightenment. It is our nature to be forgetful of the reality which appears now, but gradually mindfulness can be accumulated. It can even become a "power".

---

[2] Satipaṭṭhāna means mindfulness of vipassanā or the object of mindfulness of vipassanā.

Right mindfulness is one of the factors of the eightfold Path. It is "emancipating"; the factors of the eightfold Path lead to freedom from defilements. Mindfulness is also one of the enlightenment factors (bojjhangas). The other factors are: investigation of Dhamma (dhamma vicaya), energy, enthusiasm (pīti), tranquillity (passaddhi), concentration and equanimity.

One may wonder how, in the development of insight, the faculty of mindfulness, the power of mindfulness, the Path factor right mindfulness and the enlightenment factor of mindfulness can be developed. The answer is: through mindfulness of the nāma and rūpa which appears right now. There is no other way. Colours, sounds, scents, flavours and tangible objects are most of the time objects of attachment, aversion and ignorance. If mindfulness arises and right understanding of the object is being developed, one is at that moment not enslaved to the object nor disturbed by it. If we understand that mindfulness of realities can eventually have an immediate effect on our daily life, we will have more courage to develop it at this moment.

27.1.1 Questions

1. What is the object of mindfulness with dāna?
2. What is the object of mindfulness with sīla?
3. What is the object of mindfulness in samatha?
4. Why can the body as a whole not be the object of mindfulness in the development of insight?
5. How does one know when there is mindfulness of the level of samatha and when mindfulness of the level of insight?
6. In what way can the "study" of realities such as visible object, seeing, sound or hearing have a wholesome effect on our daily life?
7. Does the word "mindfulness" as we use it in daily life represent the reality of sati of vipassanā?

28 Moral Shame and Fear of Blame

28.1 Moral Shame (hiri) and Fear of Blame (ottappa)

When we apply ourselves to kusala there is confidence, there is mindfulness which is non-forgetful of kusala, and there are many other sobhana cetasikas which each have their own specific function while they accompany the kusala citta. Moral shame, hiri, and fear of blame, ottappa, are two other sobhana cetasikas which accompany every sobhana citta. Moral shame or conscientiousness has shame of akusala and fear of blame has fear of the consequences of akusala. Every akusala citta is accompanied by the opposites of moral shame and fear of blame, namely by shamelessness, ahirika, and by recklessness, anottappa. Whenever there is kusala citta there have to be moral shame and fear of blame.

There are many degrees of kusala and, thus, there are many degrees of moral shame and fear of blame. The more we see the impurity of akusala and realize its danger, the more moral shame and fear of blame will be developed; they will abhor even akusala which is more subtle.

The *Visuddhimagga* (XIV, 142) gives the following definition of hiri, moral shame (here translated as conscience), and ottappa, fear of blame (here translated as shame):

> It has conscientious scruples (hiriyati) about bodily misconduct, etc., thus it is conscience (hiri). This is a term for modesty. It is ashamed (ottappati) of those same things, thus it is shame (ottappa). This is a term for anxiety about evil. Herein, conscience has the characteristic of disgust at evil, while shame (ottappa) has the characteristic of dread of it. Conscience has the function of not doing evil and that in the mode of modesty, while shame has the function of not doing it and that in the mode of dread. They are manifested as shrinking from evil in the way already stated. Their proximate causes are self-respect and respect of others (respectively)...

The words shame, scruples, fear or anxiety do not, in this case, have the same meaning as in conventional language. When we think with aversion or worry about our akusala there are akusala cittas. Moral shame, hiri, and fear of blame, ottappa, do not arise with a citta accompanied by aversion and worry; they accompany kusala citta.

Moral shame and fear of blame always arise together but they are two different cetasikas with different characteristics. The *Atthasālinī* (I, Part IV, Chapter I, 125-127) gives a similar definition as the *Visuddhimagga* of moral shame and fear of blame and illustrates their difference. The *Atthasālinī* explains that moral shame (hiri) has a subjective origin, that its proximate cause is respect for oneself. Fear of blame (ottappa) has an external cause, it is influenced by the "world"; its proximate cause is respect for someone else[1].

---

[1] See also Chapter 14, where I deal with their opposites, shamelessness and recklessness.

Moral shame, as the *Atthasālinī* explains, can arise because of consideration of one's birth, one's age, heroism (courage and strength) and wide experience. Moral shame arises from consideration of one's birth when someone of a respectable family does not want to act as someone who has not had a proper education. Moral shame arises from consideration of one's age when someone who is an adult does not want to behave like a child. Moral shame arises from consideration of heroism when someone does not want to act like a weakling but feels that he should have courage and strength. Moral shame arises from consideration of wide experience when one does not want to act like a fool who has not learnt anything. It may happen that, although we have listened to the Dhamma and see the value of having less attachment to self, we are still selfish, disinclined to help others, or still easily inclined to anger. However, there may also be moments that we remember that the Dhamma we studied should be applied and that it is foolish to give in to selfishness and anger. At such moments moral shame arises because of consideration of what we have learnt, because of the understanding we have acquired from the study of the Dhamma.

As we have seen, fear of blame, ottappa, fears the consequences of evil. These consequences are manifold. There are many degrees of akusala kamma and these produce different degrees of result, vipāka. Some akusala kammas produce their results in the course of our life by way of unpleasant experiences through the senses; when we are blamed by others or receive punishment it is the result of kamma. There is also akusala kamma which produces result by way of an unhappy rebirth. When we consider the consequences of akusala we should not only think of the vipāka it produces, but we should also see the danger of accumulating more and more tendencies to akusala. Because of defilements we are unhappy, we have no peace of mind.

Even if one has not studied the Dhamma one can still have moral shame and fear of blame. One may not know very precisely what akusala is and what its consequences are, but one can still appreciate the value of kusala and see some of the disadvantages of akusala. There may be stinginess or laziness as to kusala, but at the moment the value is seen of kusala, moral shame and fear of blame which abhor akusala arise with the kusala citta.

Moral shame and fear of blame are the proximate cause of sīla, morality. We read in the *Visuddhimagga* (I, 22):

> . . . For when conscience (hiri) and shame (ottappa) are in existence, virtue arises and persists; and when they are not, it neither arises nor persists. . .

There are many degrees of sīla and thus it is evident that there are many degrees of shame and fear of blame as well. When there are no shame and fear of blame even as to gross defilements, one lives like an animal. We read in the *Gradual Sayings* (I, Book of the Twos, Chapter I, par 9) that if moral shame and fear of blame would not protect the world there would be promiscuity between people, even between relatives, as exists "among goats and sheep, fowls and swine, dogs and jackals". That is why moral shame and fear of blame are called the "guardians of the world".

There may be moral shame and fear of blame with regard to gross defilements but not with regard to defilements which are more subtle. One may not kill or steal, but one may have no shame and fear as regards gossiping or unkind thoughts. We may often mislead ourselves as to kusala and akusala. There are countless moments of clinging but we do not notice them. When the citta is akusala citta there is ignorance which does not know what is right and what is wrong, and there is also shamelessness, ahirika, which has no shame of akusala, and recklessness, anottappa, which does not fear its consequences. Through the Dhamma we will know more precisely when the citta is kusala citta and when akusala citta, and thus moral shame and fear of blame will develop.

Through the development of right understanding we come to see the danger of all kinds of akusala, be it gross or more subtle. One may know in theory that wrong view is dangerous, but there may still be the tendency to take realities for self. When there is still a notion of self who sees or hears, there is no shame and fear of akusala. When we consider the difference between the sotāpanna who has eradicated wrong view and the non-ariyan, it will help us to see the danger of wrong view. The sotāpanna has no more conditions to commit gross akusala kamma which can produce an unhappy rebirth whereas the non-ariyan still has conditions for the committing of gross akusala kamma. Because of clinging to "self" one becomes more and more enslaved to gain and loss, praise and blame and the other vicissitudes of life. So long as defilements have not been eradicated we have to continue to be in the cycle of birth and death. Even if one cannot see the danger of rebirth one may understand that it is sorrowful that defilements are bound to arise again and again.

We read in the *Gradual Sayings* (Book of the Fives, Chapter IX, par 4) about the factors which, if a monk possesses them, hinder the attainment of the goal of monkhood, and about the factors which lead to the goal:

> Monks, possessed of five qualities, an elder becomes not what he ought to become...
>
> He is without faith (saddhā), modesty (hiri), fear of blame (ottappa), he is lazy and lacks insight...
>
> Monks, possessed of five qualities an elder becomes what he ought to become...
>
> He has faith, modesty, fear of blame, he is diligent and develops insight...

This sutta can remind both monks and laypeople that if there is no development of understanding of the reality appearing at this moment, people will not become what they ought to become: a person who has eradicated defilements. If we remember the shortness of life there will be more often moral shame and fear of blame which abhor laziness as regards kusala. The Buddha reminded people not to be heedless, but to be earnest, mindful at this very moment.

To the extent that understanding develops, moral shame and fear of blame develop as well and they can become powers (balas). As we have seen, the five sobhana cetasikas which are classified as faculties, indriyas, are also classified as powers, namely: confidence, energy, mindfulness, concentration and wisdom. However, in addition to these five powers also moral shame and fear of blame can be classified as powers. We read in the *Dhammasangaṇi* (par 30) about the power of moral shame, hiri, here translated as conscientiousness:

The feeling of conscientious scruple which there is on that occasion when scruples ought to be felt, conscientious scruple at attaining to bad and evil states—this is the power of conscientiousness that there then is.

We read (in par 31) about the power of fear of blame:

> The sense of guilt which there is on that occasion, where a sense of guilt ought to be felt, a sense of guilt at attaining to bad and evil states—that is the fear of blame that there then is.

A power is unshakable by its opposite. The powers of moral shame and fear of blame cannot be shaken by their opposites shamelessness (ahirika) and recklessness (anottappa), which arise with each akusala citta.

The sotāpanna has moral shame and fear of blame which are unshakable by their opposites with regard to akusala kamma which can produce an unhappy rebirth. However, although he is on the way to eventually reach the state of perfection, he has not eradicated all defilements. He still clings to pleasant objects, he still has aversion. At the subsequent stages of enlightenment moral shame and fear of blame become more refined and at the moment of the attainment of arahatship they have reached perfection.

We will not understand the functions of moral shame and fear of blame merely by reading general definitions of them, but we have to consider the difference between kusala citta and akusala citta when they arise in our daily life. Then we will notice that, for example, the citta with avarice is completely different from the citta with generosity. When there is true generosity moral shame and fear of blame perform their functions. However, in between the moments of generosity there are bound to be moments of clinging and we may not notice these. We may be attached to the object we give or we may expect the receiver to be kind to us. Also such moments can be known. We should be grateful to the Buddha who taught us to develop right understanding so that the present moment can be known as it really is. Through right understanding we will have more confidence in kusala and we will see the dangers and disadvantages of akusala. Thus, moral shame and fear of blame will develop.

28.1.1 Questions

1. Why will moral shame and fear of blame develop to the extent that wisdom develops?
2. Why can moral shame and fear of blame be classified as powers?
3. What is the difference between moral shame and fear of blame of the sotāpanna and those of the non-ariyan?

29 Non-Attachment

29.1 Non-Attachment (alobha)

Non-attachment, alobha, is one of the three sobhana hetus, beautiful roots. A root (hetu or mūla) gives a firm support to the citta and cetasikas it arises together with. All sobhana cittas are rooted in non-attachment, alobha, and non-aversion, adosa, and they may or may not be rooted in wisdom, paññā. Thus, non-attachment has to accompany every sobhana citta.

We have many more moments with attachment than with non-attachment and we are so used to live with attachment that we hardly realize that it is akusala. A person who is leading the life of a layman takes it for granted to be attached to people and possessions. We may think that such kinds of attachment are not dangerous, provided we do not harm others, but all kinds of akusala lead to sorrow. There is attachment time and again and, thus, we accumulate it evermore. When we stand up, move around, reach for things, eat or go to sleep, we *want* most of the time something for ourselves and then there are cittas rooted in attachment. We are almost all the time thinking of ourselves, we try to acquire pleasant things for ourselves and we expect other people to be agreeable to us. Even when we think that we apply ourselves to kusala, for example, when we listen to the Dhamma or speak about the Dhamma, there are likely to be many moments of attachment arising after the kusala cittas. We may be attached to "our kusala", we tend to like the idea of ourselves being good and wise, we find ourselves important.

If we come to know more precisely the citta arising at the present moment we will be able to notice that the moments of clinging are entirely different from the moments of unselfishness or detachment. There is non-attachment with every kusala citta, but it does not last. There are many more akusala cittas in our life than kusala cittas.

Non-attachment, alobha, has many shades and degrees. It can be described as unselfishness, liberality or generosity. There is alobha when there are thoughts of sacrifice and sharing, when there is renunciation and dispassion[1].

The *Atthasālinī* (I, Book I, Part IV, Chapter I, 127) gives the following definition of alobha:

> . . . absence of greed (alobha) has the characteristic of the mind being free from cupidity for an object of thought, or of its being detached, like a drop of water on a lotus leaf. It has the function of not appropriating, like an emancipated monk, and the manifestation of detachment, like a man fallen into a foul place. . .

The *Visuddhimagga* (XIV, 143) gives a similar definition[2].

When there is a moment of non-attachment there cannot be attachment at the same time. Non-attachment has the characteristic of non-adherence like a water

[1] See The Roots of Good and Evil, p. 19, by Ven. Nyanaponika, The Wheel no. 251-253, B.P.S. Kandy.

[2] See also Dhammasangaṇi, par32.

drop on a lotus leaf. The lotus grows in the water but it is not wetted by the water, that is its nature. A drop of water glides off a lotus leaf without affecting it. So it is with non-attachment, alobha. It is not attached to the object which is experienced, it is unaffected by it. That is the nature of non-attachment. Sometimes there are conditions for non-attachment, but shortly afterwards we are affected again by objects. Through right understanding one will become less affected. We read in the *Sutta Nipāta* (Khuddaka Nikāya, The Group of Discourses, vs. 811-813,)[3] :

> ...Not being dependent upon anything, a sage holds nothing as being pleasant or unpleasant. Lamentation and avarice do not cling to him, as water does not cling to a (lotus-)leaf.
>
> Just as a drop of water does not cling to a (lotus-)leaf, as water does not cling to a lotus, so a sage does not cling to what is seen or heard or thought.
>
> Therefore a purified one does not think that purity is by means of what is seen, heard, or thought, nor does he wish for purity by anything else[4]. He is neither impassioned nor dispassioned.

The function of non-attachment is, as we have seen, "not appropriating, like an emancipated monk". A monk who has attained arahatship does not hold on to any object which presents itself; he is not enslaved but completely detached and thus free, emancipated.

The *Atthasālinī* states that non-attachment has the manifestation of detachment like someone who has fallen into a foul place. Someone who falls into a cesspool does not consider that a place of shelter where he could stay. He sees it as a danger, as something to be abhorred, and therefore, he would get out of it as soon as possible. It is the same with non-attachment, it does not take refuge in what is actually a danger. Attachment to the objects which are experienced is dangerous, because attachment leads to all kinds of evil deeds which can produce an unhappy rebirth. Any form of attachment, even if it is more subtle, is dangerous, because so long as attachment has not been eradicated we are subject to rebirth and, thus, also to old age, sickness and death.

It is difficult to know the characteristic of non-attachment, since the moments of non-attachment are rare. We are often too lazy to do something for someone else; we are attached to our own comfort or to quiet. Or we may find some excuses: the weather is too cold or too hot to exert ourselves for someone else. However, when there are conditions for non-attachment, we do not care about tiredness or discomfort, we do not think of ourselves but we see the usefulness of helping someone else. We can learn from experience that non-attachment is beneficial both for ourselves and for others. At the moment of non-attachment we renounce our own pleasure and then there is peace of mind. It may seem that at a particular moment a choice between kusala and akusala can be made, but there is no self who makes a choice; each moment of citta is conditioned by many factors. It is not self but the cetasika alobha which performs the function of detachment. We cannot force

---

[3] I am using the P.T.S. translation by K.R. Norman.

[4] By any other way than the Noble Eightfold Path, according to the commentary. See the Discourse Collection, Wheel Publication no. 82, B.P.S. Kandy.

ourselves to renounce sense-pleasures, but we can learn the difference between the characteristic of kusala and of akusala when they appear. Thus, we will gradually see that kusala is beneficial and that akusala is not beneficial but harmful.

Whenever kusala citta arises non-attachment accompanies the kusala citta. Non-attachment can arise in the sense-door processes of citta as well as in the mind-door process. In each of these processes there are javana-cittas (translated as "impulsion"), which are, in the case of non-arahats, kusala cittas or akusala cittas. When kusala citta arises there is "wise attention" to the object which is experienced, there are no attachment, aversion and ignorance. Non-attachment which accompanies the kusala citta may, for example, arise in the eye-door process of cittas which experience visible object. We usually cling to visible object but when there are conditions for kusala citta there is non-attachment to the object.

When we perform a good deed, there is non-attachment already, we do not have to try to be detached or to renounce something. When we perform dāna we give up our selfish inclination and we think of the benefit of someone else, at least for that moment. When we refrain from harsh speech we give up something, we renounce evil speech by which we harm both ourselves and others. When there is loving kindness, which is the cetasika non-aversion, adosa, there must be non-attachment as well which renounces selfishness. When there is selfish affection for other people there cannot be loving kindness at the same time. When we are attached to someone, our attachment does not do him any good, we only cling to our own pleasant feeling we derive from his or her company. It is essential to know our own different feelings. We should find out when pleasant feeling goes together with selfishness and when it is the joy which may accompany kusala citta. We are so attached to just having pleasant feeling that we do not notice when it is akusala and, thus, useless. At the moment loving kindness or compassion arises there is genuine concern for someone else and we forget for a few moments the "I" we often consider the centre of the world.

There are many degrees of non-attachment. Right understanding is the condition for higher degrees of non-attachment. If right understanding knows when there is akusala citta and when kusala citta, there can be the development of calm. Calm can be developed with meditation subjects such as loving kindness, the contemplation of the Buddha's virtues, the foulness of the body or other subjects. The citta with calm is accompanied by non-attachment. When calm has been developed to the degree of jhāna, defilements are temporarily subdued but they are not eradicated. Attachment to one's attainment of jhāna may arise. Only the development of insight can eventually lead to complete detachment from all objects.

The direct understanding of nāma and rūpa will lead to detachment from them. So long as there is still the wrong view of self, attachment cannot be eradicated. We are attached to persons, to "self", and we may not be ready to accept the truth that in the ultimate sense no "people" exist. If right understanding of realities is developed we will know that what we take for people are only citta, cetasika and rūpa which do not last.

In the beginning it is difficult to persevere being mindful of seeing, visible object and the other realities, because we do not notice an immediate result and we sometimes doubt whether it is really useful. Is helping someone else not more useful than being aware of visible object which appears now? All degrees of kusala are useful and we should not neglect any one of them. If we help someone else or listen to him with loving kindness and compassion, there are moments of giving up our selfishness. But shortly after the kusala cittas have fallen away there tend to be akusala cittas with clinging to "our kusala" or with attachment to people. Also while we help others there can be mindfulness of realities such as seeing or visible object. In this way we will become truly convinced that what is seen is not a person, only a reality which can be experienced through the eyes. There is already a degree of detachment, although it is still weak, when there is mindfulness of visible object and understanding of it as "only a reality", not a person. In the beginning understanding is weak, but we should have confidence that it can be developed through mindfulness of whatever reality appears through one of the six doors. Thus clinging to "self" or to beings can decrease.

The sotāpanna has eradicated all clinging to the concept of self, but he still clings to sensuous objects. The sakadāgāmī has less clinging to sensuous objects but he still has not eradicated it. The anāgāmī has eradicated clinging to sensuous objects but he still clings to rebirth and he still has cittas rooted in attachment which are accompanied by conceit. The arahat has eradicated all forms of clinging and this shows how hard it is to eradicate it. We may think that we cannot be happy without attachment, but complete detachment means the highest happiness, it is freedom from all sorrow.

We may have read in the scriptures that clinging is the root of sorrow, but we tend to forget this. We read, for example, in the *Middle Length Sayings* (II, no. 87, Discourse on "Born of Affection") that the Buddha explained to a householder who had lost his only son, that "grief, sorrow, suffering, lamentation and despair are born of affection, originate in affection". However, the householder did not accept this truth. We read that King Pasenadi spoke about this subject with Queen Mallikā. When the Queen said that she agreed with the Buddha's words, the King was displeased. Further on we read that the Queen tried to explain the truth of the Buddha's words to the King with examples from his daily life. She said :

> . . . "What do you think about this, sire? Is your daughter Vajīrī dear to you?"
>
> "Yes, Mallikā. My daughter Vajīrī is dear to me."
>
> "What do you think about this, sire? From an alteration and otherness in your daughter Vajīrī would there arise in you grief, sorrow, suffering, lamentation and despair?"
>
> "From an alteration and otherness, Mallikā, in my daughter Vajīrī there would be a change for me, even for life. How should there not arise in me grief, sorrow, suffering, lamentation and despair?"
>
> "It was in reference to this, sire, that it was said by the Lord, who knows, who sees, perfected one, fully Self-Awakened One: 'Grief, sorrow, suffering, lamentation and despair are born of affection, originate in affection.' . . ."

> The Queen then asked the same question with regard to the noble lady Vāsabhā, the King's consort, General Viḍūḍabha, the son of the King and Vāsabhā, and the peoples of Kāsi and Kosala. The King then understood the truth of the Buddha's words and he thereupon paid respect to the Buddha and uttered words of praise.

We often forget the truth that suffering is rooted in desire. There is most of the time clinging after seeing, hearing or the other experiences through the senses. We have to read and reread the scriptures many times and consider the Buddha's words. His teaching is like food for our mind. If we realize that clinging is the root of all sorrow and suffering we will develop right understanding at this moment so that, eventually, there will be detachment from all objects.

29.1.1 Questions

1. Are all kinds of kusala helpful in order to be less selfish?
2. Why can calm when it is developed in samatha not eradicate clinging?
3. Why is the development of insight the only way to become detached from all objects?
4. Why has only the arahat eradicated clinging completely?

30 Non-Aversion

30.1 Non-Aversion (adosa)

Non-aversion or non-hate, is one of the three sobhana hetus, beautiful roots. As we have seen, each sobhana citta is rooted in non-attachment and non-aversion, and it may or may not be rooted in wisdom. We may notice it when we have aversion, dosa, but we may not know the characteristic of non-aversion, adosa. We dislike having aversion because it is always accompanied by unpleasant feeling. When the aversion is gone we may think that there is non-aversion but is that so? At this moment there may not be aversion but can we be sure that there is non-aversion which accompanies kusala citta? There may be attachment to visible object and then there cannot be non-aversion at the same time. Whenever non-aversion arises there has to be non-attachment, alobha, as well and several other sobhana cetasikas which each perform their own function while they assist the kusala citta.

Adosa can be translated as non-aversion or non-hate, but there are many forms and degrees of it. Loving kindness, mettā, is a form of adosa which is directed towards living beings. Adosa can also be non-aversion with regard to an object which is not a being and then it can be described as patience. There can be non-aversion or patience with regard to heat, cold, bodily pain or other unpleasant objects.

The *Atthasālinī* (I, Book I, Part IV, Chapter I, 127) defines non-aversion, adosa, as follows:

> . . . Absence of hate has the characteristic of freedom from churlishness or resentment, like an agreeable friend; the function of destroying vexation, or dispelling distress, like sandalwood; the manifestation of being pleasing, like the full moon. . .

The *Visuddhimagga* (XIV, 143) gives a similar definition[1]. Non-aversion has the characteristic of freedom from savagery or violence, it is gentle like a good friend. We may see the difference between aversion and non-aversion when they appear in our daily life. We may be very annoyed about someone or something, but when we see the disadvantage of aversion there are conditions for patience. At that moment all the harshness which characterizes aversion has gone and there is gentleness instead. There is no self who is patient and gentle, but it is the cetasika non-aversion, adosa.

The function of non-aversion is the removing of annoyance or vexation and non-aversion is compared to sandalwood which has a very agreeable odour and is said to cure fever. When there is aversion we are vexed and annoyed; we burn with the fever of hate and we may become uncontrolled, we may not know what we are doing. Aversion is like a fire, it is hard to extinguish. However, when non-aversion arises we are cured of the fever of aversion, all annoyance has gone.

Both aversion and non-aversion influence our bodily disposition. We read in the *Atthasālinī* (I, Book I, Part IV, Chapter I, 129):

---

[1] See also Dhammasangaṇi par33.

> ...Absence of hate is the cause of youthfulness, for the man of no hate, not being burnt by the fire of hate, which brings wrinkles and grey hairs, remains young for a long time...

The *Atthasālinī* states that the manifestation of non-aversion is agreeableness like the full moon. Non-aversion is agreeable both for oneself and for others, it conduces to harmonious living among people. Through aversion or hate a person loses his friends, and through non-aversion he acquires friends. We read in the same section of the *Atthasālinī* (129):

> ...Absence of hate is the cause of the production of friends, for through love friends are obtained, not lost...

Non-aversion accompanies each kusala citta, it performs its function of destroying vexation while we apply ourselves to dāna, observe sīla, develop calm or insight. Dāna is an act of kindness. When we are giving a gift with kusala citta we show kindness. When there is non-aversion there must also be non-attachment which performs its function of detachment from the object.

When we observe sīla there is non-aversion accompanying the kusala citta. When we abstain from akusala kamma which harms both ourselves and others we show an act of kindness. The *Atthasālinī* (in the same section) states:

> Good-will is that which does not ruin one's own or another's bodily or mental happiness, worldly or future advantage and good report.

The Buddha reminded the monks to show acts of kindness to one another, both privately and in public and this is to be applied by laypeople as well. When there is true kindness it appears in our manners and speech. When someone else speaks harshly to us it is difficult not to have aversion and retort his speech with angry words. We are attached to pleasant objects and when there is an unpleasant object our attachment conditions aversion. When we see the ugliness of aversion and its disadvantages there are conditions to refrain from harsh speech. When we have aversion on account of what other people are doing or saying we forget to be mindful of our own cittas. When there is mindfulness it prevents us from wrong speech and then there is also non-aversion which removes vexation.

We read in the *Kindred Sayings* (I, Sagāthā-vagga, Chapter XI, Sakka Suttas, I, par 4) that Sakka, ruler of the gods, was reviled by Vepacitti, an Asura (a demon). Sakka explained to Mātali, the charioteer, that it was not because of weakness that he showed forbearance. He praised patience and forbearance and he said:

```
...Worse of the two is he who, when reviled,
Reviles again. Who does not, when reviled,
Revile again, a twofold victory wins.
Both of the other and himself he seeks
The good; for the other's angry mood
Does understand and grows calm and still.
He who of both is a physician, since
Himself he heals and the other too,
Folk deem him fool, they knowing not the Dhamma...
```

There are many opportunities for being impatient with people. We may be irritated about someone's faults and mistakes, about his way of speech or his appearance. We may be irritated because someone moves slowly and is in our way when we are in a hurry. Most of the time we are concerned about ourselves but not about someone else. When we find ourselves important aversion can arise very easily and then there is no kindness. Selfishness and lack of consideration for others stand in the way of kindness. When there are conditions for kindness and patience there is peace of mind and then we can see the difference between kindness and the harsh moments of aversion.

Kindness, mettā, is a form of adosa which is directed towards living beings. Patience, as we have seen, is another aspect of adosa. There can be patience with regard to beings and also with regard to objects which are not beings, thus with regard to all objects which can be experienced through the six doors. When there is aversion towards unpleasant objects there is no patience. When we have to endure hardship it may be difficult not to have aversion, but when non-aversion arises we can endure what is unpleasant. The Buddha exhorted the monks to endure unpleasant objects. We read in the *Middle Length Sayings* (I, no. 2, Discourse on All the Cankers) that the Buddha spoke about different ways of getting rid of the cankers and he explained that one of these ways is endurance. It is to be understood that the cankers cannot be eradicated unless right understanding is developed. We read:

> And what, monks, are the cankers to be got rid of by endurance? In this teaching, monks, a monk, wisely reflective, is one who bears cold, heat, hunger, thirst, the touch of gadfly, mosquito, wind and sun, creeping things, ways of speech that are irksome, unwelcome; he is of a character to bear bodily feelings which, arising, are painful, acute, sharp, shooting, disagreeable, miserable, deadly. Whereas, monks, if he lacked endurance, the cankers which are destructive and consuming might arise. But because he endures, therefore these cankers which are destructive and consuming are not. These, monks, are called the cankers to be got rid of by endurance.

When we feel sick or when we experience another unpleasant object through one of the senses we may feel sorry for ourselves and complain about it. We give in to aversion and we are apt to put off the development of kusala until we are in more favourable conditions. Then we overlook the opportunity for the development of kusala which is right at hand: when there are unpleasant objects there is an opportunity to cultivate patience. We all are bound to suffer from hunger and thirst, heat and cold; these things occur in our daily life time and again. The experience of an unpleasant object through one of the senses is vipāka, the result of kamma, and we cannot avoid vipāka. After the moments of vipāka have fallen away, there are kusala cittas or akusala cittas, depending on whether there is "wise attention" or "unwise attention" to the object. If we see the benefit of patience in all circumstances there are conditions for non-aversion instead of aversion.

One of the hardest things to endure is the separation from those who are dear to us. We read in the *Gradual Sayings* (IV, Book of the Sevens, Chapter V, par 10) about Nanda's mother, an anāgāmī, who had through the development of right understanding eradicated aversion. After she had offered dāna to the monks with Sāriputta and Moggallāna at their head she testified to Sāriputta about marvellous things which had happened to her. We read:

> "...Rajahs, for some reason, took by force and slew my only son, Nanda, who was dear and precious to me; yet when the boy was seized or being seized, bound or being bound, slain or being slain, I knew no disquietness of heart."
>
> "It is marvellous and wonderful, O mother of Nanda, that you should have so purged the surges of the heart."
>
> "Nor is that all, reverend sir...When my husband died, he rose among the yakkas[2] ; and he revealed himself to me in his old form; but I knew no disquietness of heart on that account."

Nanda's mother then spoke about her purity of sīla, her attainment of the different stages of jhāna, and she declared that she had eradicated the "five lower fetters". These fetters are eradicated at the attainment of the state of anāgāmī.

The anāgāmī or "non-returner", who has attained the third stage of enlightenment, has no more attachment to sensuous objects and thus, when there is an unpleasant object instead of a pleasant object, he has no conditions for aversion. Nanda's mother who was an anāgāmī, had no sadness, fear or anxiety, no matter what happened to her. If we understand that attachment to people can lead to utter distress when we lose them, we may see the danger of attachment, and then we can be reminded to develop right understanding which leads to the eradication of all defilements.

In the development of right understanding patience has to be applied. When there are many moments of akusala citta we should have patience to be mindful even of akusala citta. When there is aversion we may be annoyed about it, or we may take it for "my aversion". When there is mindfulness of aversion it can be known as only a type of nāma which has arisen because of its appropriate conditions. At the moment of mindfulness there is non-aversion, adosa, instead of aversion, dosa.

Loving kindness, mettā, is, as we have seen, a form of adosa which is in particular directed towards living beings. The *Visuddhimagga* (Chapter IX, 93) gives, apart from the definition of non-aversion, a definition of loving kindness or mettā:

As to characteristic, etc. , loving kindness is characterized here as promoting the aspect of welfare. Its function is to prefer welfare. It is manifested as the removal of annoyance. Its proximate cause is seeing lovableness in beings. It succeeds when it makes ill-will subside, and it fails when it produces (selfish) affection.

Loving kindness can arise with right understanding or without it. Someone may be kind to others because he has accumulated kindness, but there may not be right understanding. If there is right understanding of the characteristic of loving kindness it can be developed. It can be developed as a subject of samatha, but one cannot succeed if one does not practise it in daily life.

The "near enemy" of loving kindness is selfish affection, attachment. Attachment tends to arise very closely after moments of loving kindness but we may not notice

[2] Non-human being.

this. We should find out whether we want to be kind only to people we particularly like, or whether we are kind to whomever we meet, because we are truly concerned for his welfare. From our own experience we can learn to see the difference between loving kindness and selfish affection. If we are attached to someone we will miss him when he is no longer with us; attachment conditions aversion. When there is loving kindness we do not think of our own enjoyment in someone's company. When loving kindness arises, there is detachment, alobha, and also equanimity or impartiality (tatramajjhattatā).

When we are giving a gift to someone or when we are helping someone, there may be pleasant feeling. However, instead of pure loving kindness there can be attachment. We should remember that pleasant feeling can arise with kusala citta as well as with citta rooted in attachment. We find pleasant feeling very important and we tend to think that it is kusala all the time, but we can easily be misled by pleasant feeling.

When loving kindness arises there is not necessarily pleasant feeling all the time. Kusala citta can be accompanied by pleasant feeling or by indifferent feeling.

The *Visuddhimagga* (Chapter IX) gives advice for the application of loving kindness for someone who is inclined to give in to anger. He should review the danger in hate and the advantage of patience. A person harms himself when he is angry. When he is angry with someone he should not pay attention to the bad qualities of that person but only to his good qualities, and if he has none he should be compassionate instead of angry. That person's accumulation of akusala will bring him sorrow. We should remember that we all are "heirs" of our deeds, we will receive the results of our deeds.

We could also regard the person we are angry with as five khandhas (aggregates) or as elements which are impermanent. These arise and then fall away immediately and, thus, what is then the object we are angry with? The citta of the other person which motivated unpleasant speech or an unpleasant deed has fallen away already and, thus, it belongs to the past. Another way of overcoming anger is giving a gift. We can learn from experience that, when we give a gift, there are conditions for kusala citta both for the giver and the receiver. Giving and receiving mellows the heart and the relationship between people can be improved.

We could also, in order to have less anger and more loving kindness, reflect on the virtues the Bodhisatta accumulated. We read in the *Visuddhimagga* (IX, 26) about the way of reviewing these:

> ...is it not the fact that when your Master was a Bodhisatta before discovering full enlightenment, while he was still engaged in fulfilling the Perfections during the four incalculable ages and a hundred thousand aeons, he did not allow hate to corrupt his mind even when his enemies tried to murder him on various occasions? For example, in the Sīlavant Birth Story (Jātakas I, 261) when his friends rose to prevent his kingdom of three hundred leagues being seized by an enemy king who had been incited by a wicked minister in whose mind his own queen had sown hate for him, he did not allow them to lift a weapon. Again when he was buried, along with a thousand companions, up to the neck in a hole dug

in the earth in a charnel ground, he had no thought of hate. And when, after saving his life by a heroic effort helped by jackals scrapping away soil when they had come to devour the corpses, he went with the aid of a spirit to his own bedroom and saw his enemy lying on his own bed, he was not angry but treated him as a friend, undertaking mutual pledge, and he then exclaimed:

``‘The brave aspire, the wise will not lose heart;
I see myself as I had wished to be.’’ (Jātakas I, 267)``

However, only reflecting on loving-kindness is not enough, it should be practised. For example, when others talk to us we can listen to them with loving kindness. When there is more right understanding of realities there are more conditions for loving kindness in our relationship with others. When we cling to a concept of "people" we tend to be attached to an idea of having friends. We feel lonely when we are without friends. In the ultimate sense there are no friends who exist, there are only citta, cetasika and rūpa, and these arise and then fall away immediately. Actually, friendship or loving kindness can arise with the citta which thinks of a being. Loving kindness can be extended to whosoever is in our company and then there is a moment of true friendship. At such a moment there is no thought of self who wants friendship from others, no feeling of loneliness or worry about the attitude of others towards us. If we consider more the reality of loving kindness instead of clinging to an idea of friendship there are more conditions for unselfish love.

Loving kindness is one of the meditation subjects of samatha. Those who have accumulated conditions for the development of calm to the degree of jhāna can attain jhāna with this meditation subject[3]. Loving kindness (mettā) is among the four meditation subjects which are called the "divine abidings" (brahma-vihāras). The other three "divine abidings" are: compassion (karuṇā), sympathetic joy (muditā) and equanimity (upekkhā). They are called divine abidings because they are excellent and of a "faultless nature": those who cultivate them live like the "Brahmā divinities" (*Atthasālinī*, I, Book I, Part V, Chapter XII, 195). The divine abidings are also called "Illimitables" (appamaññās) because they arise in an immeasurable field, their field or object is beings without limits. Loving kindness, for example, can, when jhāna is attained with this subject, be extended to all beings, none excepted.

Loving kindness is sublime and it can be illimitable, but even the most excellent qualities are impermanent and dukkha. Without the development of right understanding good deeds, excellent virtues or even jhāna cannot lead to the end of de-

[3] With this subject different stages of rūpa-jhāna can be attained, but not the highest stage, since the jhānacittas of the highest stage (the fourth in the fourfold system and the fifth in the fivefold system) are accompanied by indifferent feeling. Loving kindness can be accompanied by pleasant feeling or by indifferent feeling and thus it is not the object of the jhānacittas of the highest stage of jhāna.

filements. The final goal of the Buddha's teachings is the eradication of defilements and this means the end of dukkha.

Through the development of right understanding the clinging to the self can gradually decrease, and as a consequence there will be more conditions for loving kindness and patience. One will be more inclined to help others without selfish motives. There are many degrees of non-aversion, adosa, and in the arahat non-aversion has reached perfection. Those who have attained enlightenment, the ariyans, do not have wrong view of people who exist; they have realized that there are only nāma and rūpa, but they can still think of the concept "being". The arahat can think of "being" but he thinks of beings without any defilements. Those who have eradicated defilements are truly kind to all beings.

30.1.1 Questions

1. Why must there be right understanding of the characteristic of loving kindness in order to develop it as a subject of calm?
2. Why is the "near enemy" of loving kindness attachment?
3. Can there be kindness with indifferent feeling?
4. Can there be non-aversion, adosa, towards an object which is not a being?

31 Equanimity

31.1 Equanimity (tatramajjhattatā)

```
The good give up (attachment for) everything;
the saintly prattle notwith thoughts of craving:
whether affected by happiness or by pain,
the wise show neither elation nor depression.

    Dhammapada (Chapter VI, The Wise, vs. 83)
```

We are still susceptible to elation and depression. Those who have highly developed wisdom, the arahats, are not susceptible to elation nor depression, they have equanimity instead. There are many kinds and degrees of this quality and the arahat has the highest degree.

Equanimity, evenmindedness or balance of mind (in Pāli: tatramajjhattatā), is one of the nineteen sobhana cetasikas which accompany each sobhana citta. It is not easy to know the characteristic of equanimity. We may think that there is equanimity whenever there is neither like nor dislike of what we see, hear or experience through the other senses, but at such moments there may be ignorance instead of equanimity. We may confuse equanimity and indifferent feeling, but these are different cetasikas; equanimity is not feeling, the cetasika which is vedanā. The *Visuddhimagga* (XIV, 153) states about equanimity:

It has the characteristic of conveying citta and cetasikas evenly. Its function is to prevent deficiency and excess, or its function is to inhibit partiality. It is manifested as neutrality. It should be regarded as like a conductor (driver) who looks on with equanimity on thoroughbreds progressing evenly.

The *Atthasālinī* (I, Book I, Part IV, Chapter I, 133) gives a similar definition. When there is equanimity there is neither elation nor depression. The object which is experienced is viewed with impartiality and neutrality, just as a charioteer treats with impartiality his well-trained horses. Equanimity effects the balance of the citta and the other cetasikas it arises together with. There is no balance of mind when akusala citta arises, when we are cross, greedy, avaricious or ignorant. Whereas when we are generous, observe morality (sīla), develop calm or develop right understanding of nāma and rūpa, there is balance of mind.

There are different forms and degrees of equanimity. If we know more about them it will help us to understand the characteristic of equanimity. The *Visuddhimagga* (IV, 156-172) deals with different kinds of equanimity[1].

One of the aspects of equanimity mentioned by the *Visuddhimagga* is *equanimity as specific neutrality.* As we have read in the definition of equanimity given by the

[1] The Visuddhimagga uses in this section the term "upekkhā" for equanimity, instead of tatramajjhattatā. Upekkhā can stand for indifferent feeling as well as for equanimity, depending on the context. See also the Atthasālinī, Book I, Part IV, Chapter III, 172, for the different types of equanimity.

Visuddhimagga, it has the characteristic of conveying (carrying on) evenly citta and the accompanying cetasikas, and its function is the preventing of deficiency and excess, or the inhibiting of partiality. Equanimity effects the balance of the citta and the cetasikas it arises together with, so that there is neither deficiency nor excess of any one among them. When the citta is kusala citta it is always accompanied by equanimity which effects the balance of the citta and the accompanying cetasikas. Kusala citta is also accompanied, for example, by energy or effort, viriya, which is balanced: there is neither deficiency nor excess of it, and thus it can assist the kusala citta in accomplishing its task. All cetasikas play their own part in assisting the kusala citta and equanimity has its own specific function in effecting mental balance.

When we abstain from wrong action or wrong speech there is equanimity with the kusala citta. When others, for example, treat us badly or use abusive speech, there can be equanimity, and then there is no impatience, intolerance or anxiety about our own well-being. With evenmindedness one can abstain from answering back harshly or from acts of vengeance. Equanimity is one of the "perfections" the Bodhisatta developed together with right understanding for innumerable lives. When there is mindfulness of nāma and rūpa appearing now there is patience and equanimity, even if the object which is experienced is unpleasant.

There are several other kinds of equanimity. There is equanimity in samatha and equanimity in vipassanā. When calm is developed or when there is right understanding of the present moment there is equanimity which performs its function. The *Visuddhimagga* mentions some aspects of equanimity which are equanimity of samatha and some which are equanimity of vipassanā.

One of the aspects of equanimity mentioned by the *Visuddhimagga* is equanimity as one of the "divine abidings" (brahmavihāra-upekkhā) and this is developed in samatha (Vis. IV, 158). As we have seen, there are four "divine abidings" which are objects of calm: loving kindness, compassion, sympathetic joy and equanimity.

When loving kindness is developed one wishes that other beings may be happy. When compassion is developed one wishes beings to be free from suffering. When sympathetic joy is developed one wishes beings' success. When equanimity is developed one does not think of promoting other beings' happiness, alleviating their misery or wishing their success, but one views them with impartiality.

We read in the *Visuddhimagga* (IX, 96) about the divine abiding of equanimity:

> Equanimity is characterized as promoting the aspect of neutrality towards beings. Its function is to see equality in beings. It is manifested as the quieting of resentment and approval. Its proximate cause is seeing ownership of deeds (kamma) thus: "Beings are owners of their deeds. Whose (if not theirs) is the choice by which they will become happy, or will get free from suffering, or will not fall away from the success they have reached?" It succeeds when it makes resentment and approval subside, and it fails when it produces the equanimity of unknowing, which is that (worldly-minded indifference of ignorance) based on the home-life.

Ignorance is called the "near enemy" of equanimity, because one may think that there is equanimity when there is actually ignorance. Its far enemies are greed and resentment. When there is attachment or aversion there cannot be equanimity at the same time.

If one understands the characteristic of equanimity it can be developed in daily life and condition moments of calm. Sometimes people may be beyond any help, but when we remember that unpleasant results in life they receive are conditioned by kamma, that people are "heirs" to kamma, it will prevent us from being distressed. Sadness about other people's suffering is not helpful, neither for ourselves nor for others, whereas when there is equanimity we can be of comfort to others. Those who have accumulated conditions for the development of calm to the degree of jhāna can, with the divine abiding of equanimity as meditation subject, attain jhāna[2].

The *Visuddhimagga* mentions other aspects of equanimity, which pertain to samatha, namely the specific quality of equanimity in the third stage of rūpa-jhāna (of the fourfold system and the fourth stage of the fivefold system[3]), which is called *equanimity of jhāna* (jhāna-upekkhā)[4], and equanimity in the highest stage of rūpa-jhāna, which is called *purifying equanimity*[5]. At each subsequent stage of jhāna the jhānacitta and its accompanying cetasikas are calmer, purer and more refined.

Each of the aspects of equanimity mentioned by the *Visuddhimagga* is different. Equanimity as "specific neutrality", equanimity as one of the divine abidings, equanimity of jhāna and purifying equanimity are all different aspects of tatramajjhattatā.

The *Visuddhimagga* also mentions aspects of equanimity of vipassanā. *Equanimity as a factor of enlightenment* is an aspect of equanimity in vipassanā mentioned by the *Visuddhimagga* (IV, 159). There are seven factors of enlightenment (sambojjhanga): mindfulness (sati), investigation of Dhamma (Dhamma vicaya, which is paññā), energy (viriya), enthusiasm (pīti), calm (passaddhi), concentration (samādhi) and equanimity (upekkhā). Equanimity is in this case again the cetasika tatramajjhattatā. When the enlightenment factors have been developed they lead to enlightenment. They are not developed separately, but they are developed together with satipaṭṭhāna. The enlightenment factor of equanimity performs its own function while it accompanies citta and the other cetasikas. We read in the *Visuddhimagga* (IV, 159) about the enlightenment factor of equanimity: "He de-

---

[2] With this meditation subject the highest stage of rūpa-jhāna can be attained, but not the lower stages. If someone wants to attain jhāna with this subject he should first develop the divine abidings of loving kindness, compassion and sympathetic joy, by means of which the first, second and third stage of jhāna of the fourfold system (and the fourth stage of the fivefold system) can be attained, but not the highest stage. If he then develops the divine abiding of equanimity he can attain the highest stage of rūpa-jhāna (Vis. IX, 88, 111, 118).

[3] See Chapter 8 for the fourfold system and the fivefold system of jhāna.

[4] See Vis. IV, 177. In this stage of jhāna the grosser jhāna-factors of applied thinking (vitakka), sustained thinking (vicāra) and rapture (pīti) have been abandoned (see Chapter 8 and 11). There is still pleasant feeling (sukha), but no attachment to it; there is equanimity even towards the highest bliss.

[5] In this stage also the jhāna-factor of happy feeling has been abandoned; there is indifferent feeling and "purity of mindfulness due to equanimity" (Book of Analysis, Chapter 12, Analysis of Jhāna, par597, and Vis. IV, 194).

velops the equanimity enlightenment factor depending on relinquishment"[6]. When right understanding sees the unsatisfactoriness of all conditioned realities which arise and then fall away, there will be indifference towards them.

When satipaṭṭhāna is being developed we do not have to aim at the development of equanimity because it develops together with insight. The enlightenment factors reach completion through satipaṭṭhāna. When conditioned realities have been clearly understood as they are, enlightenment can be attained.

There is yet another aspect of equanimity mentioned by the *Visuddhimagga* and this is the *sixfold equanimity* which is actually the equanimity which has reached completion at the attainment of arahatship. We read in the *Visuddhimagga* (IV, 157):

> Herein, six-factored equanimity is a name for the equanimity in one whose cankers are destroyed. It is the mode of non-abandonment of the natural state of purity when desirable or undesirable objects of the six kinds come into focus in the six doors described thus: "Here a bhikkhu whose cankers are destroyed is neither glad nor sad on seeing a visible object with the eye: he dwells in equanimity, mindful and fully aware." (*Gradual Sayings*, Book of the Sixes, Chapter I, par 1).

The arahat has a perfect balance of mind. He is unruffled by the worldly conditions of gain and loss, praise and blame, honour and dishonour, well-being and misery. To us the sixfold equanimity of the arahat seems to be far off. We should remember that this equanimity can only be achieved by understanding, paññā, which has been developed stage by stage. It is useless to have wishful thinking about this perfect equanimity. It cannot be realized by longing for it. The fact that this equanimity is sixfold can remind us that only when understanding of what appears through the six doors has been developed can there be equanimity towards all objects.

Understanding can be developed now, when there is an object presenting itself through one of the six doors. Sometimes the object is pleasant, sometimes unpleasant. When understanding has not been developed it is difficult to be "balanced", to "stay in the middle", without attachment, without aversion. We may tell ourselves time and again that life is only nāma and rūpa, conditioned realities which are beyond control, but we are still impatient and we are still disturbed by the events of life. However, when there is mindfulness, for example, of visible object, understanding can realize it as a rūpa which appears through the eye-door, not a thing, not a person. When there is mindfulness of seeing, understanding can realize it as only an experience, a type of nāma, no self who sees. When realities are clearly known as not a thing, not a person, thus, as anattā, there will be more even-mindedness and impartiality towards them. However, this cannot be realized in the beginning. The arahat has eradicated all defilements and, thus, he can have equanimity which has reached perfection. He is undisturbed, patient and always contented.

We read in the *Kindred Sayings* (II, Nidāna-vagga, Chapter XVI, Kindred Sayings on Kassapa, par 1, Contented) about the arahat Kassapa who was always

---

[6] Relinquishment is twofold: it is the giving up of all defilements and also the inclination to or "entering into" nibbāna (Vis. XXI, 18).

contented. We read that the Buddha, while he was staying at Sāvatthī, said to the monks:

Contented, monks, is this Kassapa with no matter what robe. He commends contentment with no matter what robe, nor because of a robe does he commit anything that is unseemly or unfit. If he has gotten no robe, he is not perturbed; if he has gotten a robe, he enjoys it without clinging or infatuation, committing no fault, discerning danger, wise as to escape[7].

Even so is this Kassapa contented with no matter what alms, with no matter what lodging, with no matter what equipment in medicines.

We then read that the Buddha exhorted the monks to train themselves likewise. We can train ourselves by being mindful of whatever nāma or rūpa appears now. Kassapa had developed the right conditions leading to perfect equanimity.

31.1.1 Questions

1. Why is it difficult to know the characteristic of equanimity?
2. When there is neither like nor dislike is there always equanimity?
3. When we are generous there is equanimity with the kusala citta. What is its function?
4. When one begins to be mindful of nāma and rūpa which appear, is there equanimity with the kusala citta?
5. What is sixfold equanimity and why is it sixfold?
6. In what way can sixfold equanimity be developed?

[7] He enjoys it as sufficing against cold (the commentary to this sutta, the "Sāratthappakāsini").

32 Six Pairs of Beautiful Cetasikas

Among the sobhana cetasikas, beautiful cetasikas, which accompany each sobhana citta, there are twelve cetasikas which are classified as *six pairs*. Of each pair one cetasika is a quality pertaining to the accompanying cetasikas and one a quality pertaining to citta. The first pair is:

- tranquillity of body, kāya-passaddhi
- tranquillity of mind, citta-passaddhi

The Pāli term kāya means body, but it can also stand for the "mental body" which are the cetasikas. According to the *Dhammasangaṇi* (par 40, 41) tranquillity of body is the calming, the tranquillizing of the cetasikas and tranquillity of citta is the calming, the tranquillizing of citta. Thus, tranquillity of body allays agitation of the accompanying cetasikas and conditions the quiet, smooth and even way of their functioning[1]; tranquillity of citta allays agitation of the citta it accompanies.

The *Atthasālinī* (Book I, Part IV, Chapter I, 130) explains about tranquillity of body and tranquillity of mind:

> . . . These two states taken together have the characteristic of pacifying the suffering of both mental factors and of consciousness; the function of crushing the suffering of both; the manifestation of an unwavering and cool state of both; and have mental factors and consciousness as proximate cause. They are the opponents of the corruptions, such as distraction (uddhacca), which cause the disturbance of mental factors and of consciousness.

The *Visuddhimagga* (XIV, 144) gives a similar definition. Tranquillity is the opponent of restlessness or distraction, uddhacca, which prevents the arising of kusala citta. When we, for example, strive after something with attachment, there is also restlessness and there cannot be calm. Not only when we want to have something for ourselves, but also when we merely like something such as a particular colour there is restlessness, and then there is no calm. We keep on being infatuated with pleasant sense objects and we may not notice attachment which is subtle. At such moments there is restlessness.

When the citta is kusala citta there is calm of citta and cetasikas, there is no restlessness nor agitation at that moment. There is a "cool state of mind", no infatuation with the object which is experienced, no restlessness. However, it is not easy to recognize the characteristic of calm. The different types of citta succeed one another very rapidly and shortly after the kusala cittas have fallen away akusala cittas tend to arise. Right understanding has to be keen in order to know the characteristic of calm. If there is no right understanding we may take for calm what is not calm but another reality. For example, when we are alone, in a quiet place, we may think that there is calm while there is actually attachment to silence.

There are likely to be misunderstandings about calm. What we call calm or tranquillity in conventional language is not the same as the realities of tranquillity

[1] See Abhidhamma Studies, by Ven. Nyanaponika, Chapter IV, 10. In this section an explanation is given about the "Six Pairs" (B.P.S. Kandy, 1976).

of cetasikas and tranquillity of citta. Someone may think that he is calm when he is free from worry, but this calm may not be kusala at all. There may be citta rooted in attachment which thinks of something else in order not to worry. At such a moment he cannot at the same time think of the object of his worry since citta can experience only one object at a time. Or people may do breathing exercises in order to become relaxed. Tranquillity of cetasikas and tranquillity of citta which are sobhana cetasikas are not the same as a feeling of relaxation which is connected with attachment. We should know the characteristic of true calm which is wholesome.

There are many degrees of calm. When we are generous or observe the moral precepts there is calm of cetasikas and of citta. At such moments there is no restlessness, agitation or worry. The feeling which accompanies the kusala citta is also calm. We may notice the difference between pleasant feeling which accompanies attachment and pleasant feeling which accompanies generosity; these feelings have different qualities. Those who have accumulated inclinations for higher degrees of calm can develop it if there is right understanding which knows precisely the characteristic of calm. Those who are able to cultivate samatha and attain jhāna experience a high degree of calm since there are at the moments of jhāna no sense impressions and, thus, no enslavement to them. However, even the calm of the highest stage of jhāna cannot eradicate defilements. They will arise again after the jhānacittas have fallen away.

People in the Buddha's time and also people before his time developed calm, even to the degree of jhāna, if they had accumulated the skill and the inclination to do so. The development of calm is not specifically Buddhist. The fact that the Buddha and his disciples developed calm to the stage of jhāna does not mean that everybody has to develop jhāna in order to be able to also develop vipassanā. The Buddha explained that also jhānacitta could be object of insight, in order to help those who were able to attain jhāna not to cling to it, but to understand it as it is: impermanent and not self. We should remember this whenever we read in the scriptures about the attainment of jhāna. If someone has accumulated the capability to reach higher degrees of calm even to the stage of jhāna, they will arise because of conditions. Anything which arises can be object of awareness, and thus also jhāna. The attainment of jhāna is not an aim in itself, neither is it a necessary requirement for the attainment of enlightenment.

We can have moments of calm in our daily life when we study the teachings and reflect on them in a wholesome way. The object of reflection is then actually one of the forty meditation subjects of samatha, that is, recollection of the Dhamma. This meditation subject comprises recollection on the teachings as well as recollection on nibbāna and the eight types of lokuttara cittas which experience it, the "nine supramundane dhammas", included in the Dhamma which is the second of the Triple Gem. There can also be moments of calm when we develop loving kindness or one of the other meditation subjects which suit our inclinations. However, we should remember that it is extremely difficult to attain jhāna or even "access-concentration"[2]. We read in the *Visuddhimagga* (XII, 8) that only very few people, "one in a hundred or a thousand" are able to do so. If someone only wants to

[2] See Chapter 6.

develop calm without right understanding of its characteristic, he is likely to cling to calm without knowing it. If calm arises it does so because of conditions and there is no self who can exert power over it.

Tranquillity of cetasikas and of citta accompany each kusala citta and, thus, they arise also when insight is being developed. When there is right understanding of a nāma or a rūpa which appears there is calm at that moment. When, for example, visible object is known as only a rūpa appearing through the eyesense, not a person, there is calm. At that moment there cannot be disturbance caused by desire nor can there be annoyance. Even when someone treats us badly there can be right understanding of the objects appearing through the six doors, and then we are not perturbed nor afraid.

Calm is one of the factors of enlightenment. We read in the *Book of Analysis* (Chapter 10, Analysis of the Enlightenment Factors, par 469):

> ...That which is calmness of body (cetasikas), that calmness enlightenment factor is for full knowledge, for enlightenment, for full emancipation also. That which is calmness of consciousness, that calmness-enlightenment factor is for full knowledge, for enlightenment, for full emancipation also.

As right understanding develops the enlightenment factor of calm develops as well. We do not have to aim for calm. When the enlightenment factor of calm accompanies at the moment of enlightenment lokuttara citta, it is also lokuttara. As defilements are eradicated at the subsequent stages of enlightenment there will be more peace of mind, less restlessness. The arahat who has eradicated all defilements has reached true calm which cannot be disturbed again by defilements. We read in the *Dhammapada* (verse 96) about the arahat:

```
Calm is his mind,
calm is his speech,
calm is his action,
who, rightly knowing, is wholly freed,
perfectly peaceful, and equiposed.
```

The next pair of sobhana cetasikas is:

- lightness of cetasikas, kāya-lahutā
- lightness of citta, citta-lahutā

According to the *Dhammasangaṇi* (par 42, 43) this pair of cetasikas consists in the absence of sluggishness and inertia, they have "alertness in varying". The meaning of this will be clearer when we read what the "Mūla-Tīkā"[3] states about lightness of citta: "the capacity of the mind to turn very quickly to a wholesome object or to the contemplation of impermanence, etc."

The *Atthasālinī* (I, Book I, Part IV, Chapter I, 30) explains:

[3] A subcommentary quoted by Ven. Nyanaponika in Abhidhamma Studies, Chapter IV, 10.

> Kāya-lightness is buoyancy of mental factors; citta-lightness is buoyancy of consciousness. They have the characteristic of suppressing the heaviness of the one and the other; the function of crushing heaviness in both; the manifestation of opposition to sluggishness in both, and have mental factors and consciousness as proximate cause. They are the opponents of the corruptions, such as sloth and torpor, which cause heaviness and rigidity in mental factors and consciousness.

The *Visuddhimagga* (XIV, 145) gives a similar definition. Lightness is the opponent of sloth and torpor (thīna and middha), which cause heaviness and sluggishness with regard to kusala. When there is akusala citta, there is mental heaviness and we are unable to perform any kind of kusala. Kusala citta needs confidence (saddhā), it needs mindfulness or non-forgetfulness and it also needs mental lightness which suppresses heaviness and rigidity. When there is lightness of cetasikas and of citta they react with alertness so that the opportunity for kusala is not wasted.

There are many moments of unawareness. There are seeing, visible object or hardness time and again, but we may be dull and tired without any interest in awareness. However, when mindfulness arises there are also lightness of cetasikas and of citta which perform their functions: all tiredness is gone and there is alertness. Lightness is needed for the development of right understanding. When understanding of what appears through one of the six doors is being developed, there is also lightness which "crushes" sluggishness. If this moment is not wasted realities can eventually be seen as impermanent and not self.

Another pair of the sobhana cetasikas is:

- pliancy of cetasikas, kāya-mudutā
- pliancy of citta, citta-mudutā

According to the *Dhammasangaṇi* (par 44, 45) this pair of cetasikas consist in suavity, smoothness and absence of rigidity.

The *Atthasālinī* (I, Book I, Part IV, Chapter I, 130) explains:

> They have the characteristic of suppressing the rigidity of mental factors and of consciousness; the function of crushing the same in both; the manifestation or effect of setting up no resistance; and have mental factors and consciousness as proximate cause. They are the opponents of the corruptions, such as opinionatedness (diṭṭhi) and conceit which cause mental rigidity.

The *Visuddhimagga* (XIV, 146) gives a similar definition.

Pliancy of cetasikas and of citta are the opponents of wrong view and conceit. Wrong view causes rigidity and inflexibility. When someone, for example, is attached to wrong practice of the eightfold Path it shows that there is mental rigidity. He may stick to his old habits and way of thinking and then it is very difficult to eradicate wrong view. Someone may, for example, think that he should be at leisure or in a quiet place before he can develop right understanding. Even when we know in theory that this is not right it may happen that we still presume that there cannot be awareness when we are tired or in a hurry. Such presumptions are a hindrance to develop understanding of whatever reality appears in our daily life. When we have listened to the Dhamma and we consider it there can be a beginning of the development of insight. We should not expect understanding to be perfect at once, but at least we can begin to develop it now.

As we have read in the definition, pliancy of cetasikas and of citta are the opponents also of conceit. When there is conceit there is mental rigidity. We are inclined to compare ourselves time and again with others in a conceited way as regards health, appearance, gain, honour or intelligence. Conceit is extremely hard to eradicate, only the arahat has eradicated it completely.

Pliancy of cetasikas and of citta assist the kusala citta so that there is no mental rigidity or intolerance, but open-mindedness to what is right. The *Atthasālinī* (I, Book I Part IV, Chapter II, 151) explains further on about mental pliancy that it is suavity, non-roughness and non-rigidity. When there is loving kindness there is suavity and gentleness. Mental pliancy or malleability is indispensable for each wholesome action. Pliancy is also necessary in order to listen to the Dhamma, to receive it and to be mindful of the reality which appears in order to know it as it is.

We read in the *Gradual Sayings* (IV, Book of the Eights, Chapter II, par 2, Sīha the general) that Sīha visited the Buddha and questioned him on different points. The Buddha knew that Sīha had accumulated right understanding and that it was the right time for him to receive the Dhamma. He did not explain to Sīha immediately the four Noble Truths, but he gave him a gradual discourse. We read:

> Then the Exalted One preached a graduated discourse to Sīha, the general, that is to say: on almsgiving, the precepts and on heaven. He set forth the peril, the folly and the depravity of lusts and the blessedness of renunciation.
>
> And when the Exalted One knew that the heart of Sīha, the general, was clear, malleable, free from hindrance, uplifted and lucid, then he revealed that teaching of Dhamma which Buddhas alone have won, that is to say: Dukkha, its coming to be, its ending and the Way. Just as a clean cloth, free of all stain, will take dye perfectly; even so in Sīha, the general, seated there, there arose the spotless, stainless vision of Dhamma; that whatsoever be conditioned by coming to be, all that is subject to ending.

It was the right time for Sīha to receive the Dhamma. He saw things as they are and attained enlightenment.

Another pair of sobhana cetasikas is:

- wieldiness of cetasikas, kāya-kammaññatā
- wieldiness of citta, citta-kammaññatā

Kammaññatā can be translated as wieldiness or workableness[4]. The *Atthasālinī* (I, Book I, Part IV, Chapter I, 131) explains that they suppress unwieldiness in cetasikas and citta, and that they should be regarded as "bringing faith in objects of faith, and patient application in works of advantage, and are like purity of gold."[5]

When there is wieldiness, citta and cetasikas are like gold which has been made workable. The "Mūla-Tīkā"[6] expresses this as follows:

---

[4] See Dhammasangaṇi, par46, 47.

[5] See also Visuddhimagga, XIV, 147.

[6] See Abhidhamma Studies by Ven. Nyanaponika, Chapter IV, 10.

> Workableness signifies that specific or suitable degree of pliancy or softness which makes the gold, that is, the mind, workable. While the mind is in the flames of passion it is too soft to be workable, as molten gold is. If, on the contrary, the mind is too rigid then it is comparable to untempered gold.

Wieldiness is the opponent of the "hindrances", such as sensuous desire (kāmacchanda) and anger or hate (vyāpāda), which cause mental unwieldiness. We read in the *Kindred Sayings* (V, Mahā-vagga, Book II, Chapter IV, par 3, Corruptions) about five corruptions of gold whereby gold is impure, brittle, not pliant or workable. It is the presence of other metals, of iron, copper, tin, lead and silver which makes it unwieldy. Even so the five hindrances make the mind unwieldy. We read:

> ...Likewise, monks, there are those five defilements of the mind, owing to which the mind is not pliant, not workable, impure, brittle and is not perfectly composed for the extinction of the passions. Which are those five? Sensual desire, ill will, sloth and torpor, agitation and worry, doubt—these are the defilements of the mind owing to which the mind is not pliant, not workable, impure, brittle and is not perfectly composed for the extinction of passions.

As we have seen, according to the *Atthasālinī*, wieldiness brings faith (saddhā) in objects of faith and patient application in kusala. Wieldiness is necessary for each kind of kusala, for generosity (dāna), for morality (sīla), for the development of calm and for the development of insight. Wieldiness makes the mind workable so that one can apply oneself to kusala with confidence and with patience. When someone, for example, wants to develop calm with loving kindness as meditation subject , he cannot be successful when there is no mental wieldiness. When there is ill-will there is rigidity instead of wieldiness. In order to have loving kindness for all beings, not only for dear friends, but also for people one does not know or even for one's enemies, there has to be wieldiness. Without wieldiness one cannot succeed in becoming calm with any meditation subject.

Wieldiness of cetasikas and of citta also perform their functions in the development of insight; they are conditions for patience in the development of right understanding of nāma and rūpa. When there is right understanding of a nāma or a rūpa as only a conditioned reality, not self, there is wieldiness of mind. The development of insight leads to the eradication of the hindrances. The person who has eradicated them has no more unwieldiness but perfect wieldiness.

Another pair of sobhana cetasikas is:

- proficiency of cetasikas, kāya-pāguññatā
- proficiency of citta, citta-pāguññatā

According to the *Dhammasangaṇi* (par 48, 49) this pair of cetasikas consists in fitness, competence and efficiency. Pāguññatā is fitness, competence or efficiency in the performance of kusala.

The *Atthasālinī* (I, Book I, Part IV, Chapter I, 131) explains that proficiency of cetasikas and of citta suppress mental illness and that they are the opponents of the corruptions, such as diffidence, which cause mental illness[7].

When the citta is akusala citta, there is diffidence, lack of confidence in kusala and then there is mental sickness. Mental proficiency assists the kusala citta and then citta and cetasikas are healthy and skilful so that they can perform their functions in the most efficient way.

There are many degrees of efficiency in kusala. When right understanding is being developed, it conditions proficiency and skilfulness in all kinds of kusala. The sotāpanna has eradicated wrong view, doubt and stinginess, and he will never neglect the five moral precepts. His generosity and his observance of morality is purer than the generosity and morality of the non-ariyan, he has no clinging to a wrong idea of "my kusala". His confidence in the Buddha's teachings has become unshakable, it has become a "power". He has, in comparison to the non-ariyan, a higher degree of efficiency and competence with regard to kusala. He can assist others in a competent and efficient way, and thus we see that the development of right understanding also bears on one's relationship with others. We read in the *Gradual Sayings* (V, Book of the Elevens, Chapter II, par 4, Subhūti) that the Buddha spoke to Subhūti about the traditional marks of belief (saddhā) in a believer. One of these "traditional marks" is the following:

> ...Again, in all the undertakings of his fellows in the Brahma-life, be they matters weighty or trivial, he is shrewd and energetic, possessing ability to give proper consideration thereto, as to what is the fit thing to do and how to manage it. In so far as a monk is such, this also is a traditional mark...

There is a higher degree of proficiency as higher stages of enlightenment are attained and defilements eradicated. At the stage of arahatship proficiency has reached perfection.

The last pair of he six pairs of sobhana cetasikas is:

- uprightness of cetasika, kāya-ujukatā
- uprightness of citta, citta-ujukatā

According to the *Dhammasangaṇi* (par 50, 51) this pair of cetasikas consists in straightness and rectitude, being without deflection, twist or crookedness.

The *Atthasālinī* (I, Book I, Part IV, Chapter I, 131) explains that uprightness of cetasikas and of citta crush crookedness and that they are the opponents of the corruptions, such as deception and craftiness, which cause crookedness in mental factors and consciousness[8].

Uprightness is the opponent of deception and craftiness. There may be moments that one's behaviour is insincere. We read in the *Visuddhimagga* (I, 60-84) about the behaviour of the monk who tries to obtain the requisites by hypocrisy, by hinting, flattery, indirect talk, grimaces and gestures. He pretends to be better than he in reality is in order to be admired. We read (I, 70):

---

[7] See also the Visuddhimagga, XIV, 148.

[8] See also the Visuddhimagga, XIV, 149.

> Here someone of evil wishes, a prey to wishes, eager to be admired, (thinking) "Thus people will admire me", composes his way of walking, composes his way of lying down; he walks studiedly, stands studiedly, sits studiedly, lies down studiedly; he walks as though concentrated, stands, sits, lies down as though concentrated; and he is one who meditates in public. . .

We all want to be admired and therefore we may pretend to be better than we really are. Even when it seems that we are generous there tend to be selfish motives for our actions. We may expect something in return, we want to be praised, to be popular. Speech which seems pleasing may be directed towards selfish gain. Uprightness crushes such insincerity. It assists each kusala citta. There are many degrees of uprightness. To the extent that right understanding develops also uprightness develops. The ariyan is called the person who is on the straight, true and proper way (ujupatipanno, Vis. VII, 90-92). He is on the middle Path, avoiding extremes; he is on the Path which leads to the eradication of defilements. One is on the middle Path when there is the development of understanding of whatever reality appears, even if it is akusala. We can develop right understanding in daily life, no matter whether we laugh or cry, no matter whether we are angry or generous. Thus we will learn the truth, we will learn that each reality which arises is conditioned and that it is non-self. In the above quoted explanation of insincerity in the *Visuddhimagga* we read about the monk who walks, stands, sits and lies down as though concentrated. Someone may believe that he is doing these things with concentration which is kusala, although this is not so. When there is mindfulness of realities we can find out whether the citta which presents itself is kusala citta or akusala citta. We will come to know ourselves and, thus, we will become more sincere. The person who is on the middle Way is honest with himself and he does not pretend that he is without defilements. Defilements can only be eradicated if they are known as they are. Straightness of cetasikas and of citta accompany the citta which develops understanding and they assist the citta in this task.

Summarizing the six pairs of sobhana cetasikas, they are:

1. calm of cetasikas, kāya-passaddhi
   calm of citta, citta-passaddhi
2. lightness of cetasikas, kāya-lahutā
   lightness of citta, citta-lahutā
3. pliancy of cetasikas, kāya-mudutā
   pliancy of citta, citta-mudutā
4. wieldiness of cetasikas, kāya-kammaññatā
   wieldiness of citta, citta-kammaññatā
5. proficiency of cetasikas, kāya-pāguññatā
   proficiency of citta, citta-pāguññatā
6. uprightness of cetasikas, kāya-ujukatā
   uprightness of citta, citta-ujukatā

These six pairs accompany all sobhana cittas. They are necessary for each kind of kusala, be it generosity (dāna), morality (sīla), the development of calm (samatha) or insight (vipassanā). They assist the kusala citta and its accompanying cetasikas, so that wholesomeness can be performed in an efficient way. They are counteractive to the hindrances of sensuous desire, ill-will, sloth and torpor, restlessness and regret, and doubt. When the six pairs are present the hindrances do not arise; citta and cetasikas are healthy and skilful in performing their functions. Right understanding is the factor which conditions most of all the development of all the wholesome qualities represented by the six pairs. In the arahat they have reached perfection.

As we have seen, there are at least *nineteen sobhana cetasikas* which accompany each sobhana citta[9]. All these cetasikas accompany the sobhana cittas of the sense-sphere (kāmāvacara sobhana cittas), the sobhana cittas which are rūpa-jhānacittas (of fine-material jhāna) and arūpa-jhānacittas (of immaterial jhāna), and the sobhana cittas which are lokuttara cittas. This does not mean that all these sobhana cittas are accompanied by only nineteen sobhana cetasikas. In addition to the nineteen sobhana cetasikas which accompany each sobhana citta, there are six more, and I shall deal with these in the following chapters.

32.0.1 Questions

1. Why are pliancy of cetasikas and of citta the opponents of wrong view and conceit?
2. Why is it said that there is freedom from illness when there is proficiency of cetasikas and of citta?
3. Why is diffidence, lack of faith (saddhā), the cause of mental illness?
4. Why has the sotāpanna a higher degree of proficiency in kusala than the non-ariyan?
5. Why does uprightness develop to the extent that right understanding of realities develops?
6. Why is the ariyan called a person who walks straight?
7. Which factor conditions most of all the growth of all wholesome qualities?

[9] See Appendix 8 for a summary of them and of the sobhana cittas they accompany.

33 The Three Abstinences

33.1 The Three Abstinences (virati-cetasikas)

There are twentyfive sobhana cetasikas in all which arise only with sobhana cittas. Nineteen among these arise with every sobhana citta, whereas six of them do not arise with every sobhana citta. Among these six sobhana cetasikas there are three which are *abstinences* or *virati-cetasikas*. They are:

- abstinence from wrong speech, vaci-duccarita virati
- abstinence from wrong action, kāya-duccarita virati
- abstinence from wrong livelihood, ājīva-duccarita virati

As regards abstinence from wrong speech, this is abstinence from lying, slandering, harsh speech and idle, frivolous talk. Abstinence from wrong action comprises abstinence from killing, stealing and sexual misconduct. Abstinence from wrong livelihood is abstinence from wrong speech and wrong action committed for the sake of one's livelihood.

We read in the *Atthasālinī* (I, Book I, Part IV, Chapter I, 133) about the three kinds of abstinences:

> ...As regards characteristic, etc., it has been said that each of these three does not trespass nor tread on objects of the other two. They have the function of shrinking from the same; and they have faith (saddhā), sense of shame (hiri), fear of blame (ottappa), contentment and more, as proximate antecedents. They should be regarded as produced by the averted state of the mind from evil action.

The *Visuddhimagga* (XIV, 155) gives a similar definition.

We read that each of the three does not tread on objects of the other two. In the case of cittas of the sense-sphere (kāmāvacara cittas) these three kinds of abstinence arise one at a time, since there is abstinence from one kind of evil at a time. When we, for example, abstain from harsh speech, the cetasika which is abstinence from wrong speech accompanies the mahā-kusala citta and we do not abstain from wrong action at the same time, since there is only one citta at a time. When we are harshly spoken to and we do not answer back there is not always kusala citta with abstinence from wrong speech. We may keep silent with citta rooted in ignorance or with citta rooted in aversion and then there is akusala citta. If we abstain from retorting unpleasant speech with kindness and patience there is kusala citta accompanied by the cetasika which is abstinence from wrong speech.

As we have seen, confidence in wholesomeness (saddhā), shame (hiri), fear of blame (ottappa) and contentment are among the proximate causes of the abstinences. When there is contentment or fewness of wishes there are favourable conditions for observing morality.

As regards abstinence from wrong livelihood for laymen, we read in the *Gradual Sayings* (III, Book of the Fives, Chapter XVIII, par 7) about five kinds of trades laymen should abstain from:

> Monks, these five trades ought not to be plied by a lay-disciple. What five?
>
> Trade in weapons, trade in human beings, trade in flesh, trade in spirits and trade in poison.
>
> Verily, monks, these five trades ought not to be plied by a lay-disciple.

As to trade in flesh, the commentary (Manorathapūraṇi) explains: "He breeds and sells pigs, deer, etc." It is also wrong livelihood to receive bribes for services which are one's duty to perform, or bribes for something one ought not to do.

There is also wrong livelihood for monks. The monk should not try to obtain the requisites of robes, almsfood, dwelling and medicine with unlawful means, such as by way of hinting or talking in a clever way. He should not disparage others in order to obtain gain and honour[1]. The monk's life should be a life of contentment with little. If he realizes that the observance of the Vinaya should not be separated from the development of right understanding he will be able to lead a life of purity.

When someone lies or uses dishonest means in order to obtain something for himself he acts in this way because of selfish desire. He hopes to gain something, but sooner or later he will suffer unpleasant results. Whenever we give in to wrong speech or wrong action we are enslaved and we are blinded, we do not realize the consequences. At that moment there is no shame which shrinks from evil and no fear of the consequences of evil. While we abstain from evil there are confidence in wholesomeness, shame and fear of blame and there is no selfish desire. Understanding, paññā, may or may not accompany the kusala citta which abstains from evil. As right understanding develops there will be less clinging to the concept of self and consequently there will be more conditions to abstain from wrong speech, wrong action and wrong livelihood.

It is not easy to know when there is kusala citta accompanied by one of the three abstinences. So long as it is not known precisely when there is kusala citta and when akusala citta, the characteristics of the cetasikas which are abstention from wrong speech, wrong action and wrong livelihood cannot be known either. It is of no use to try to focus on these realities since there are many sobhana cetasikas accompanying the kusala citta while we abstain from evil and it is difficult to know their different characteristics. When the characteristic of abstinence appears there can be mindfulness of it in order to be able to realize that it is not self who abstains.

There are different degrees of abstinence and the *Atthasālinī* (I, Book I, Part III, Chapter VI, 103, 104) distinguishes between three kinds: abstaining "in spite of opportunity obtained", abstaining because of observance (of precepts) and abstaining by way of eradication. As to the first kind we read:

> When they who have not undertaken to observe any precept, but who reflecting on their own birth, age, experience, etc. and saying "It is not fit for us to do such a bad thing", do not transgress an object actually met with, the abstinence is to be considered as "in spite of opportunity"...

Thus, also those who have not undertaken the precepts can have shame and fear of blame and abstain from wrong speech, wrong action and wrong livelihood.

---

[1] See Visuddhimagga I, 60 and following.

Although the opportunity for wrong speech or wrong action presents itself, they abstain from it when they take into consideration the family they belong to, the education they have had and their experience. They do not want to behave like fools and they fear the consequences of evil conduct.

The second kind of abstention is by way of observance of the precepts. When someone has undertaken the precepts and he considers it beneficial to observe them this can be a condition to abstain from wrong conduct. There are many degrees of observing the precepts. One's morality, sīla, may be limited (Vis. I, 31). Someone may have the intention not to kill living beings, but when his health or his life is in danger, or his relatives insist that he should kill, for example, insects, he may not be able to observe the precept which is abstention from killing. Thus, his morality is limited, it is not enduring. Only through the development of right understanding can morality become enduring.

The sotāpanna has eradicated wrong view and, thus, when he observes the precepts, he does not take the observing for self. He will never transgress the five precepts, even if his life is in danger, and, thus, his morality is of a higher degree than the morality of the non-ariyan. We read about the third kind of abstinence, abstinence by way of eradication, mentioned by the *Atthasālinī*, that it should be understood as associated with the ariyan path:

> . . . When that Path has once arisen, not even the thought, "we will kill a creature", arises in the ariyans.

If right understanding of realities is not developed, all kinds of defilements can arise on account of the objects which are experienced. When a pleasant object is experienced through the eyes, we tend immediately to be infatuated with it. We should realize that what is seen is only visible object, a kind of rūpa which does not last. Visible object can be seen just for a moment, it cannot be owned. Still, we make ourselves believe that we can own it. We want to get it for ourselves and because of it we may even commit evil deeds. In the ultimate sense there are no people or things, only nāma and rūpa which arise and then fall away immediately.

When we realize the consequences of evil conduct we will be urged to develop right understanding which can eradicate defilements. We read in the *Gradual Sayings* (III, Book of the Fives, Chapter XXII, par 3, Morals) about disadvantages of evil conduct:

> Monks, there are five disadvantages to one wanting morals, failing in morals. What five?
>
> Consider, monks, the man without morals, failing in morals—he comes to suffer much loss in wealth through neglect. This, monks, is the first disadvantage to one wanting morals, failing in morals.
>
> Or an evil rumour spreads about him. This is the second disadvantage. . .
>
> Or whatever group he approach, whether nobles or brāhmans, householders or recluses, he does so without confidence and confused. This is the third disadvantage. . .
>
> Or he dies muddled (in thought). This is the fourth disadvantage. . .
>
> Or on the breaking up of the body after death he arises in the wayward way, the ill way, the abyss, hell. This is the fifth disadvantage. . .

> Verily, monks, these are the five disadvantages to one wanting morals, failing in morals.
>
> (The opposite is said of one perfect in morals.)

The *Visuddhimagga* (I, 154) mentions the following dangers of failure in virtue:

> ...Furthermore, on account of his unvirtuousness an unvirtuous person is displeasing to deities and human beings, is uninstructable by his fellows in the life of purity, suffers when unvirtuousness is censured, and is remorseful when the virtuous are praised...

We then read about many other disadvantages. For example, the unvirtuous are always nervous, like a man who is everyone's enemy, he is unfit to live with and incapable of reaching the distinction of attainment. Although he imagines that he is happy, yet he is not, since he reaps suffering.

When we neglect morality we may suffer afterwards from remorse. When we, for example, give in to slandering we may enjoy it at that moment, but afterwards remorse may arise and then there is no joy, no peace of mind. If we abstain from slandering there is no opportunity for remorse. When we abstain from slandering with kindness and consideration for others the citta is quite different from the citta which is forgetful of morality and gives in to slandering. We may be able to learn the different characteristics of such moments.

When one begins to develop insight one cannot expect to have purity of morality immediately. We are still full of attachment, aversion and ignorance, and these unwholesome roots can condition wrong speech, wrong action and wrong livelihood. Only the sotāpanna has no more conditions to commit akusala kamma which can lead to an unhappy rebirth. We should have determination to develop right understanding of whatever reality appears. When we become angry and utter harsh speech there can be moments of awareness of nāma and rūpa in between the moments of anger. Also anger should be known as it is, as only a type of nāma which is conditioned, not "my anger", otherwise it can never be eradicated. We find the unpleasant feeling which accompanies anger very disagreeable and we may have desire for just calm. Then there is clinging again. Also the subtle desire for calm should be known as it is. We should consider what our aim is: only calm, or right understanding of whatever reality appears. We may think that it is too difficult to develop understanding of whatever reality appears, we want to delay it when we are tired, depressed or in an angry mood. However, if there is no beginning of the development of right understanding, even at those moments we consider unfavourable, it will always be difficult. If one perseveres in developing understanding of the present moment, understanding can grow.

One may neglect the precepts because one thinks that they are too difficult to observe. But if one considers the teachings more often and starts to develop understanding, there will be more conditions for remembering what is right and what is wrong in the different situations of one's daily life. The aim of the development of right understanding is the eradication of wrong view, ignorance and all the other defilements. We cannot be perfect immediately, but we may see the danger of neglecting morality and the benefit of observing it.

We may not kill or steal, but we may be forgetful as far as our speech is concerned. A word which can harm ourselves and others is uttered before we realize it. We tend to disparage others because we are attached to talking and want to keep the conversation going. When we are slighted by someone else we are easily inclined to answer back. Our self-esteem may be hurt and then we want to defend ourselves. Most of the time we think of ourselves; we want to be honoured and praised. We forget that it is beneficial to abstain from wrong speech and to speak with kusala citta. How often in a day do we speak with kusala citta?

The Buddha reminded the monks about right speech. We should remember what the Buddha said about right speech in the *Parable of the Saw* (Middle Length Sayings I, no. 21):

> ...Monks, when speaking to others you might speak at a right time or at a wrong time; monks, when speaking to others you might speak according to fact or not according to fact; monks, when speaking to others you might speak gently or harshly; monks, when speaking to others you might speak about what is connected with the goal or about what is not connected with the goal; monks, when speaking to others you might speak with a mind of friendliness or full of hatred. Herein, monks, you should train yourselves thus: "Neither will our minds become perverted nor will we utter an evil speech, but kindly and compassionate will we dwell, with a mind of friendliness, void of hatred; and we will dwell having suffused that person with a mind of friendliness; and, beginning with him, we will dwell having suffused the whole world with a mind of friendliness that is far-reaching, wide-spread, immeasurable, without enmity, without malevolence." This is how you must train yourselves, monks.

When we give in to wrong speech there is no kindness and consideration for other people's welfare. When there is loving kindness there is no opportunity for wrong speech. We can and should develop loving kindness in daily life and we should at the same time see the value of observing morality, otherwise loving kindness cannot be sincere. Many wholesome qualities have to be developed together with right understanding so that eventually defilements can be eradicated.

The abstinences which accompany cittas of the sense-sphere, kāmāvacara cittas, arise only one at a time, but when lokuttara cittas arise, all three abstinences accompany the lokuttara cittas, and then nibbāna is the object. Thus, the object of the abstinences which are lokuttara is different from the object of the abstinences which are of the sense-sphere. The abstinences which are lokuttara are the right speech, right action and right livelihood of the supramundane eightfold Path.

We read in the *Atthasālinī* (II, Part VIII, Chapter I, 219, 220) about the right speech which is lokuttara, that is does not allow the commission of wrong speech, that it cuts off the base of misconduct and fulfils the path-factor. The same is said about right action which cuts off the base of bodily misconduct and fulfils the path-factor, and about right livelihood which cuts off the base of wrong livelihood and fulfils the path-factor[2]. Thus, in cutting off the conditions for wrong conduct the three abstinences which are lokuttara fulfil their functions as path-factors.

---

[2] See Dhammasangaṇi, Part I, Chapter V, par299-301.

Defilements are eradicated subsequently at the different stages of enlightenment. When the path-consciousness, the magga-citta, of the sotāpanna arises, the bases of the three kinds of wrong action which are killing, stealing and sexual misconduct, and of the kind of wrong speech which is lying and also the base of wrong livelihood are cut off. The kinds of wrong speech which are slandering, harsh speech and idle talk have not been eradicated, but they cannot have the intensity anymore of akusala kamma patha (unwholesome course of action) which can produce an unhappy rebirth. The sakadāgāmī, the person who has attained the second stage of enlightenment, has not eradicated these kinds of speech, but at this stage the tendencies to such speech have decreased. The anāgāmī, the person who has attained the third stage of enlightenment, has eradicated the tendency to slandering and harsh speech but not yet the tendency to idle talk. The tendency to idle talk has only been eradicated by the arahat. We may not lie, slander or utter harsh speech, but still, our speech may not be motivated by kusala citta which is generous and intent on helping others or on explaining the Dhamma to others. Instead we may indulge in idle, useless talk. We may, for example, chat with akusala citta about accidents or other events which happen during the day. However, we can also talk with kusala citta about events such as accidents; for example, we may talk about an accident in order to remind ourselves and others of the shortness of life. Idle talk is done with akusala citta. The monk should train himself to speak only about subjects which lead to the goal, such as fewness of wishes and mental development, and he should not indulge in idle talk. A layman does not lead the monk's life, but even while one talks about useless things with akusala citta there can, in between, be moments of awareness of nāma and rūpa. The arahat has no more conditions for the laylife and no more tendencies to idle, useless talk.

Summarizing the cittas which can be accompanied by the abstinences, they are:

- eight mahā-kusala cittas which are of the sense-sphere (kāmāvacara kusala cittas)
- eight (or forty) lokuttara cittas which are accompanied by all three abstinences

In the case of the mahā-kusala cittas, only one kind of abstinence arises at a time, as the occasion presents itself; not every mahā-kusala citta is accompanied by one of the abstinences. The abstinences are not among the nineteen sobhana cetasikas which accompany each sobhana citta; they do not accompany vipākacittas since they are the actual abstinence from wrong conduct. Neither do the three abstinences accompany the mahā-kiriyacittas of the arahat since there are for those who have eradicated all defilements no more opportunities for abstention.

The three abstinences do not accompany rūpāvacara cittas (fine-material jhānacittas) and arūpāvacara cittas (immaterial jhānacittas) since there is no opportunity for abstention when the citta is jhānacitta, the citta which does not experience sense-impressions.

The three abstinences which together accompany the lokuttara cittas are the three factors which are the right speech, right action and right livelihood of the eightfold Path. They accompany the magga-cittas and they also accompany the phala-cittas (fruition-consciousness). The phala-cittas are the results of the magga-cittas, but they are different from other types of vipākacittas. The phala-cittas are lokuttara vipākacittas experiencing nibbāna, and they immediately succeed the magga-citta which produces them, in the same process.

Thus, we see that there are many kinds and degrees of the three abstinences. There is abstinence without right understanding and with right understanding. When lokuttara citta arises all three abstinences accompany the lokuttara citta and they are also lokuttara.

33.1.1 Questions

1. Why can, in the case of cittas of the sense-sphere, only one of the three abstinences arise at a time?
2. At which moment do all three abstinences arise together? Which function do they have in that case?
3. Can the abstinences accompany mahā-vipākacitta of the sense-sphere?
4. Why can the abstinences not accompany jhānacitta?
5. When is wrong livelihood eradicated?
6. What is idle talk?
7. When we talk about an accident is it always motivated by akusala citta?
8. Why is fewness of wishes one of the proximate causes of abstinence from wrong conduct?

34 Compassion and Sympathetic Joy

34.1 Compassion (karuṇā) and Sympathetic Joy (muditā)

Compassion, karuṇā, and sympathetic joy, muditā, are among the six sobhana cetasikas which do not arise with every sobhana citta. They accompany kusala citta only when there is an opportunity for them. They are classified among the four "divine abidings", brahma-vihāras[1]. The other two divine abidings are, as we have seen, loving kindness, mettā, and equanimity, upekkhā[2]. The divine abidings are called "illimitables" (appamaññas), because when they have been developed in samatha as meditation subjects which condition calm and when, by means of them, jhāna has been attained, they can be directed towards innumerable beings.

As regards compassion, we read in the *Visuddhimagga* (IX, 94):

> Compassion is characterized as promoting the aspect of allaying suffering. Its function resides in not bearing others' suffering. It is manifested as non-cruelty. Its proximate cause is to see helplessness in those overwhelmed by suffering. It succeeds when it makes cruelty subside and it fails when it produces sorrow.

The *Atthasālinī* (I, Book I, Part V, Chapter XIII, 193) gives a similar definition.

Compassion has as its near enemy "grief, based on the homelife". This is dosa, conditioned by attachment which is connected with "worldly life", that is, attachment to people and pleasant things. Compassion has as its far enemy cruelty (Vis. IX, 99). One cannot practise compassion while one is cruel.

As regards the near enemy, grief or aversion, we may take for compassion what is actually aversion, dosa. When we see someone else who is in miserable circumstances, there tend to be different types of cittas, not only kusala cittas with compassion but also akusala cittas. There are moments of compassion when we wish to help someone in order to allay his suffering and there can also be moments of aversion about his suffering. Compassion and aversion can arise closely one after the other and it is difficult to know their different characteristics. Through right understanding one can come to know their difference.

Compassion is different from loving kindness. Loving kindness is the cetasika which is non-aversion, adosa. This cetasika arises with every sobhana citta, but when it has the special quality of loving kindness, mettā, it is directed towards beings; it "sees the lovableness of beings", according to the *Visuddhimagga* and promotes their welfare. When there is loving kindness one treats others as friends. Compassion wants to allay beings' suffering. Thus, the objectives of loving kindness and compassion are different. For example, in the case of visiting a sick person, there can be moments of loving kindness when we give him flowers or wish him well, but there can also be moments of compassion when we are aware of his suffering.

---

[1] See also Dhammasangaṇi, par258-261.

[2] The term upekkhā does not, in this case, stand for indifferent feeling, but it stands for equanimity.

We may think that since compassion is directed towards beings who are suffering, there cannot be pleasant feeling accompanying it. However, compassion can arise with pleasant feeling or with indifferent feeling. One can with joy alleviate someone's suffering.

At the moment of compassion there is calm. Compassion can be developed as a meditation subject of samatha by those who have accumulations to do so. The *Visuddhimagga* (Chapter IX, 77-124) describes how compassion as one of the divine abidings is to be developed as meditation subject leading to the attainment of jhāna[3]. Compassion is developed for the purpose of purification from cruelty. When jhāna is attained compassion can be extended to all beings, and then it has become unlimited.

The Buddha who taught Dhamma out of compassion exhorted the monks to be kind and compassionate to others. Compassion can and should be developed in daily life. The Buddha himself visited the sick and asked the monks to do likewise. They should attend to both the physical and the mental needs of the sick. We read in the *Gradual Sayings* (III, Book of the Fives, Chapter XIII, par 4) how one attends to the sick in the wrong way and how in the right way:

> Monks, possessing five qualities one who waits on the sick is not fit to help the sick. What five?
>
> He cannot prepare medicaments; does not know physic from what is not physic, offers what is not, does not offer what is; in hope of gain waits on the sick, not from good-will; loathes to move excrement, urine, puke and spittle; nor can he from time to time instruct, rouse, gladden and satisfy the sick with Dhamma-talk.
>
> Monks, possessing these five qualities one who waits on the sick is not fit to help the sick.
>
> (Possessing the opposite qualities he is fit to help.)

These words of the Buddha were motivated by his great compassion. Whenever he visited the sick he would explain Dhamma to them[4].

We read in the *Gradual Sayings* (III, Book of the Fives, Chapter XXIV, par 5, Taking Pity) that the Buddha explained to the monks about different deeds of compassion towards householders:

> Monks, if a monk in residence follow the course of five things, he takes pity on householders. What five?
>
> He incites them to greater virtue; he makes them live in the mirror of Dhamma; when visiting the sick, he stirs up mindfulness, saying: "Let the venerable ones set up mindfulness, that thing most worth while!"; when many monks of the Order have come, he urges the householders to

[3] With compassion as meditation subject different stages of rūpa-jhāna can be attained, but not the highest stage, since the jhānacittas of the highest stage of rūpa-jhāna are accompanied by indifferent feeling. Compassion can be accompanied by pleasant feeling or by indifferent feeling and, thus, it is not the object of the jhānacittas of the highest stage.

[4] For example in Kindred Sayings V, Mahā-vagga, Book XI, Kindred Sayings on Streamwinning, par3, Dīghāvu.

do good...; and when they give him food, whether mean or choice, he enjoys it by himself, nor frustrates (the effect of that) gift of faith.

Verily, monks, ...he takes pity on householders.

When householders give the monk a gift, no matter whether it is "mean or choice", the monk should accept it out of compassion, in order to help the householders to accumulate wholesomeness.

There are many ways of extending compassion to others. When we understand that we should not hurt or harm others we may out of compassion refrain from wrong speech and wrong action. We read in the *Middle Length Sayings* (I, no. 27, Lesser Discourse on the Simile of the Elephant's Footprint) that the Buddha, while he was staying at Sāvatthī, spoke about the monk who trains himself in order to attain arahatship. The Buddha said about the observing of sīla:

He, being thus one who has gone forth and who is endowed with the training and the way of living of monks, abandoning onslaught on creatures, is one who abstains from onslaught on creatures; the stick laid aside, the knife laid aside, he lives kindly, scrupulous, friendly and compassionate towards all breathing things and creatures...

The Buddha then spoke about the abstinence of the other kinds of akusala kamma. If we see the benefit of compassion it is a condition for developing it in daily life whenever there is an opportunity for it. Sometimes there is an opportunity to alleviate physical suffering and sometimes mental suffering. Someone may treat us in an unjust way by speech or by actions, but, when we consider that he will receive the results of his own deeds, compassion can arise instead of anger. Understanding of kamma and vipāka can condition compassion.

It is the Buddha's greatest deed of compassion to teach Dhamma since in this way beings' greatest suffering, their being in the cycle of birth and death, can be overcome. It is due to the Buddha's great compassion that we today can develop the way leading to the end of suffering.

There are many degrees of compassion. It can arise without right understanding or with right understanding. To the extent that right understanding develops, all good qualities and thus also compassion develop. Compassion can accompany the eight types of mahā-kusala cittas, but it does not arise at all times with these cittas, since there is not always an opportunity for compassion. Compassion does not accompany the mahā-vipākacittas, cittas which are results of kusala kamma of the sense-sphere, because compassion has living beings as object. Compassion can accompany the mahā-kiriyacittas of the arahat.

As regards rūpāvacara cittas, compassion can accompany the rūpāvacara cittas of the first, second and third stage of jhāna of the fourfold system (and the fourth stage of the fivefold system), but not those of the highest stage of jhāna[5].

Compassion does not accompany arūpāvacara cittas nor does it accompany lokuttara cittas, since the object of lokuttara cittas is nibbāna.

[5] Thus, compassion can accompany twelve types of rūpāvacara cittas (Vis. XIV, 157, 181). See Appendix 8.

Sympathetic joy, muditā, is the appreciation of someone else's good fortune. We may think that sympathetic joy is pleasant feeling, but muditā is not feeling. In order to understand its nature we should study what the *Visuddhimagga* (IX, 95) states about muditā which is here translated as gladness:

Gladness is characterized as gladdening (produced by others' success). Its function resides in being unenvious. It is manifested as the elimination of aversion (boredom). Its proximate cause is seeing beings' success. It succeeds when it makes aversion (boredom) subside, and it fails when it produces merriment.

The *Atthasālinī* (I, Book I, Part V, Chapter XIII, 193) gives a similar definition. The function of sympathetic joy is being unenvious. When others receive gifts or when they are praised envy may arise. The proximate cause of both envy and sympathetic joy is the same: someone else's good fortune. Jealousy arises with the akusala citta which is rooted in aversion, dosa-mūla-citta. According to the *Visuddhimagga* (IX, 100) the far enemy of sympathetic joy is aversion (boredom). If there is wise attention sympathetic joy can arise instead of jealousy. The near enemy of sympathetic joy is "joy based on the homelife" (Vis. IX, 100). This is joy connected with the "worldly life" of clinging to pleasant sense objects. As we read in the *Visuddhimagga*, "sympathetic joy fails when it produces merriment", that is, happiness connected with attachment. If there is no right understanding which knows when the citta is kusala citta and when it is akusala citta we may take for sympathetic joy what is actually joy which is akusala. When we say to someone else: "What a beautiful garden you have", there may be moments of sympathetic joy, sincere approval of his good fortune, but there may also be moments with attachment to pleasant objects. Akusala cittas and kusala cittas arise at different moments. Since cittas arise and fall away very rapidly it is hard to know their different characteristics but right understanding of their characteristics can be developed.

At the moment of sympathetic joy there is also calm with the kusala citta. Those who have accumulations to develop calm can develop calm with sympathetic joy as meditation subject. The *Visuddhimagga* (IX, 84-124) describes how the divine abiding of sympathetic joy can be developed as a meditation subject of samatha leading to the attainment of jhāna[6]. It is developed for the purpose of freedom from aversion. When jhāna is attained sympathetic joy can be extended to an unlimited number of beings. We read about the development of the four divine abidings in the *Dīgha Nikāya* (Dialogues of the Buddha III, no. 33, The Recital, 223, 224):

> Four "infinitudes" (appamaññas), to wit:—herein, monks, a monk lets his mind pervade one quarter of the world with thoughts of love. . . pity. . . sympathetic joy. . . equanimity, and so the second quarter, and so the third, and so the fourth. And thus the whole wide world, above, below, around and everywhere does he continue to pervade with

---

[6] With this subject different stages of rūpa-jhāna can be attained, but not the highest stage. Sympathetic joy can be accompanied by pleasant feeling or by indifferent feeling. It is not the subject of the jhānacittas of the highest stage which are accompanied by indifferent feeling.

> heart...far-reaching, grown great and beyond measure, free from anger and ill-will.

Sympathetic joy can be developed in daily life. There are opportunities for its development when we see someone else's good fortune. If we see the disadvantages of jealousy there are conditions for being appreciative when we see that someone is in good health, has success in life and receives honour and praise. We read in the *Dīgha Nikāya* (Dialogues of the Buddha III, no. 31, Sigālovāda Sutta) that the Buddha spoke words of advice to Sigāla which were to be applied in daily life. He spoke to him about the characteristics of bad friends and of good friends. As regards the friend who sympathizes, he is to be reckoned as sound at heart on four grounds (187, par 25):

> ...He does not rejoice over your misfortunes; he rejoices over your prosperity; he refrains anyone who is speaking ill of you; he commends anyone who is praising you.

The good friend is not jealous but he rejoices in someone else's good fortune. One can check oneself whether one really is a good friend to someone else. If we are jealous we are not sincere in our friendship.

If we tend to be jealous it is difficult to cultivate sympathetic joy. Since jealousy has been accumulated there are conditions for its arising when we see that someone else receives praise or other pleasant objects. It is useful to realize such moments of jealousy, even when they are not coarse but more subtle. If right understanding is being developed we will see that someone else's success does not belong to a "person", that it is only vipāka which is conditioned by kamma. Thus, jealousy is in fact groundless. When right understanding sees that there are no people, no things which exist, only nāma and rūpa which arise and fall away, there will gradually be less conditions for jealousy. Envy is one of the "lower fetters" (saṁyojanas) which are eradicated by the sotāpanna. When there is no more jealousy there are more conditions for sympathetic joy. It can gradually become one's nature. The sotāpanna is the true friend who sympathizes and is "sound at heart on four grounds".

Sympathetic joy can arise with the eight types of mahā-kusala cittas. It does not arise at all times with these types of citta since there is not always an opportunity for it. Thus, sympathetic joy can accompany the mahā-kusala cittas associated with pleasant feeling as well as those associated with indifferent feeling. We should remember that sympathetic joy is different from pleasant feeling. The translation of muditā as sympathetic joy or gladness can mislead us. One can be appreciative of someone's success also with indifferent feeling.

Sympathetic joy does not accompany mahā-vipākacittas since it has living beings as object (Vis. IV, 181). It can accompany mahā-kiriyacittas. Also arahats extend sympathetic joy to living beings. They have eradicated all akusala and good qualities have reached perfection in them. Sympathetic joy can accompany rūpa-jhānacittas[7]. Sympathetic joy does not accompany lokuttara cittas since these have nibbāna as their object.

---

[7] It can accompany the rūpāvacara cittas of the first, second and third stage of jhāna of the fourfold system (and the fourth stage of the five-fold system), but not those of

We read in the *Gradual Sayings* (V, Book of the Elevens, Chapter II, par 5, Advantages) about the results of the development of the divine abiding of loving kindness, but, actually the other divine abidings, namely compassion, sympathetic joy and equanimity, lead to the same benefits (Vis. IX, 83, 87, 90). These benefits are the following:

> One sleeps happy and wakes happy; he sees no evil dream; he is dear to human beings and non-human beings alike; the devas guard him; fire, poison or sword affect him not; quickly he concentrates his mind; his complexion is serene; he makes an end without bewilderment; and if he has penetrated no further (to arahatship) he reaches (at death) the Brahma-world...

We read in the *Visuddhimagga* (IX, 97) with regard to the four "divine abidings" that loving kindness is developed to ward off ill-will, compassion to ward off cruelty, sympathetic joy to ward off aversion and equanimity to ward off greed or resentment. However, we should know that defilements cannot be eradicated unless the true nature of realities has been realized. All conditioned realities, even the most excellent qualities, are impermanent, dukkha and anattā. We read in the *Gradual Sayings* (V, Book of the Elevens, Chapter II, par 6, 345) about a monk who has developed the four divine abidings:

> Then he thus ponders: This heart's release by amity...by compassion...by sympathy...by equanimity is just a higher product; it is produced by higher thought. Then he comes to know: Now even that which is a higher product, produced by higher thought, is impermanent, of a nature to end. Fixed on that idea he wins destruction of the cankers; or if not that, yet by his passion for dhamma, by his delight in dhamma, by utterly making and end of the five fetters belonging to this world, he is reborn spontaneously, and in that state passes utterly away, never to return (hither) from that world.

34.1.1 Questions

1. When someone else is hurt we tend to have unpleasant feeling. Can there be compassion at the same time?
2. By what kinds of feeling can compassion be accompanied?
3. Can one extend loving kindness and compassion at the same time to someone else?
4. What is the proximate cause of sympathetic joy?
5. Why is it said that the function of sympathetic joy is being unenvious?
6. Why are loving kindness, compassion, sympathetic joy and equanimity called the "Illimitables"?

---

the highest stage. Thus, sympathetic joy can accompany twelve types of rūpāvacara cittas in all (Vis. IX, 111, and XIV, 157, 182. See Appendix 8.

35 Understanding

35.1 Understanding (paññā)

There are many kinds and degrees of understanding. There can be understanding which is knowing the benefit of wholesomeness and the disadvantages of unwholesomeness, there can be understanding which stems from contemplation on the shortness of life. These kinds of understanding can arise even when one has not listened to the Dhamma. When one has studied the Dhamma there can be intellectual understanding about ultimate realities, about kamma and vipāka, about nāmas and rūpas which can be experienced through six doors, and, when understanding develops further there can be direct understanding of ultimate realities, of nāma and rūpa. Direct understanding of realities can develop to the highest wisdom which eradicates all defilements.

Understanding, paññā or amoha, is among the six sobhana cetasikas which do not accompany every sobhana citta. It is one of the three beautiful roots, sobhana hetus. The two sobhana hetus which are non-attachment, alobha, and non-aversion, adosa, accompany every sobhana citta, but understanding does not. Whenever we perform deeds of generosity or observe morality, understanding may or may not accompany the kusala citta. But when we apply ourselves to mental development, bhāvanā, which comprises studying the teachings and explaining them to others, the development of samatha and the development of vipassanā, understanding has to accompany the kusala citta.

When understanding accompanies the mahā-kusala citta (kusala citta of the sense-sphere) which performs deeds of generosity or observes morality, it may be of the level of intellectual understanding: understanding of the benefit of good deeds and the disadvantages of bad deeds, understanding of kamma and vipāka. However, when we perform deeds of generosity or observe morality, there can also be the development of direct understanding of realities.

As regards mental development, one cannot apply oneself with success to this way of kusala without understanding. Also those who do not know the Buddha's teachings may reflect wisely on the truth that all things in life are susceptible to change and that they do not last, and they may develop calm. There were wise people also before the Buddha's time who understood the characteristic of true calm which is wholesome. Those who understood the characteristic of calm and did not mistakenly think that clinging to quietness was calm, could develop calm with a meditation subject and in this way attain higher degrees of calm. Those who saw the disadvantages of sense-impressions developed jhāna in order to be free of them. Those who saw the disadvantages of rūpa-jhāna, fine-material jhāna, which still has meditation subjects depending on materiality, developed arūpa-jhāna, immaterial jhāna. The person who had become very skilful in jhāna could develop "supernormal powers", abhiññās, such as magical powers, remembrance of former lives and the "Divine Eye", knowledge of the passing away and rebirth of beings. The cittas which develop such powers are accompanied by understanding, but even this kind of understanding cannot eradicate defilements.

The understanding which realizes the true nature of realities can eradicate defilements and its development can only be taught by a Buddha. This kind of understanding does not arise automatically, it has to be developed. When one has listened to the Dhamma and reflected on it, there can first be intellectual understanding of realities. If there is mindfulness of nāma and rūpa when they appear in daily life direct understanding of realities can gradually be developed. Eventually the true nature of realities can be penetrated and defilements can be eradicated at the attainment of enlightenment[1].

Seeing realities as they are is the goal of the Buddha's teachings. Understanding should know what is real in the ultimate sense and what is not real. So long as there is wrong view we cannot see things as they are. People, animals and houses are not real in the ultimate sense, they are only objects of thought. Nāma and rūpa are real in the ultimate sense, they have their own characteristics which can be directly experienced when they appear one at a time, through one of the six doors. We can verify the truth of the Buddha's teachings in being mindful of realities and developing understanding of them. Then we will be able to find out whether realities are permanent or impermanent, whether or not there is a person or self who can control realities.

Every reality has its own specific characteristic by which it can be distinguished from another reality (distinctive mark or visesa lakkhaṇa). Seeing, hearing, hardness or sound have each their own characteristic. However, there are also three general characteristics common to all conditioned realities (samañña lakkhaṇa) and these are: impermanence, dukkha and anattā, non-self. When understanding has been developed it can eventually know realities as impermanent, dukkha and anattā. There cannot, in the beginning, be clear understanding of the true nature of realities. Understanding develops gradually in different stages.

Direct understanding of realities is, as we have seen, different from thinking about them. Direct understanding can only be developed by being mindful of the nāma or rūpa appearing at the present moment. When there is mindfulness of one reality at a time understanding can investigate its characteristic and in that way it can gradually develop. When, for example, hardness appears there can be mindfulness of its characteristic and there is at that moment no thinking of a thing which is hard or of the place on our body where hardness impinges. If we think of the place of its impingement, such as a hand or a leg, we have an idea of "my body" to which we tend to cling. By being aware of one reality at a time we will learn that in the ultimate sense the body as a "whole" does not exist, that there are only different elements which arise and then fall away.

For the development of direct understanding of realities it is not enough to know only the specific characteristics of realities, the characteristics by which they are distinguished from one another. Understanding has to be developed stage by stage,

[1] Intellectual understanding is in Pāli: pariyatti. The development of direct understanding or the "practice" is in Pāli: patipatti. The penetration of the truth is in Pāli: pativedha.

so that it will be able to penetrate the three general characteristics of conditioned realities: the characteristics of impermanence, dukkha and non-self.

When we are absorbed in concepts and there is no mindfulness, we live as in a dream and we do not know what is really there: only ever-changing nāmas and rūpas. We read in the *Middle Length Sayings* (II, no. 54, Discourse to Potaliya) that the Buddha pointed out in different similes the dangers and disadvantages of sense pleasures. One of these similes is the following:

And, householder, it is as if a man might see in a dream delightful parks, delightful woods, delightful stretches of level ground and delightful lakes; but on waking up could see nothing. Even so, householder, an ariyan disciple reflects thus: "Pleasures of the senses have been likened by the Lord to a dream, of much pain, of much tribulation, wherein is more peril." And having seen this thus as it really is by means of perfect wisdom. . . the material things of the world are stopped entirely.

We cannot really see parks, woods and lakes, because what is experienced through the eyes is only the rūpa which is visible object. We can think of the concepts of parks, woods and lakes, and the thinking is conditioned by remembrance of past experiences. When we do not develop understanding of the reality which appears through one of the six doors and only pay attention to "wholes" such as gardens or houses, we believe that we can possess them. When there is mindfulness of one object at a time, such as visible object or hardness, we will understand that in the ultimate sense we cannot own anything. We cannot possess visible object, it can only be seen. We cannot take it with us; it arises just for a moment and then it falls away. We cannot possess hardness, it can be experienced through touch and then it falls away immediately. The development of insight will lead to detachment, it will lead to the eradication of the idea of a self who can exert control over things or events.

When we learn that seeing only sees visible object we may have doubts about the characteristic of seeing. It seems that there is all the time paying attention to the shape and form of things or noticing the dimensions of things. This is thinking, not seeing, the experience of what appears through the eyes. If there were no thinking one could not observe shape and form or dimensions of things. But such moments of thinking are conditioned by seeing, by the experience of what appears through the eyes. There are also moments of just seeing, moments that we are not paying attention to details or focusing on a "thing". It is the same when we read a book. It seems that there are only moments of paying attention to the shape of the letters and their meaning, but there must also in between be moments of experiencing visible object, otherwise we could not read. Before we studied the Dhamma we never considered what seeing is, but if we learn to be mindful of one reality at a time understanding will know realities as they are. We think time and again of concepts and then the reality of thinking can be object of mindfulness so that it will be known as non-self. Gradually we can learn to be mindful of seeing, visible object, hearing, sound and all the other realities which appear through six doors in our daily life.

Understanding is one of the wholesome faculties (indriyas), called the "spiritual faculties", which has to be developed together with the other "spiritual faculties" of confidence, energy, mindfulness and concentration. Through the development of these faculties the four noble Truths can be realized.

Understanding is a controlling faculty, an indriya, in the sense of predominance since it overcomes ignorance (*Atthasālinī* I, Book I, Part IV, Chapter I, 122)[2]. It exercises government over the associated dhammas (the citta and cetasikas it accompanies) by the characteristic of vision, that is, the realization of the three characteristics of impermanence, dukkha and anattā. The *Atthasālinī* states further on (in the same section) that understanding has as characteristic illuminating and understanding. It states (123) that just as a clever surgeon knows which food is suitable and which is not, understanding knows states as "moral or immoral, serviceable or unserviceable, low or exalted, black or pure. . ." Understanding which has been developed knows the four noble Truths.

The *Atthasālinī* then gives another definition of understanding:

> Understanding has the penetration of intrinsic nature, unfaltering penetration as its characteristic, like the penetration of an arrow shot by a skilled archer; illumination of the object as its function, as it were a lamp; non-perplexity as its manifestation, as it were a good guide in the forest.

The *Visuddhimagga* (Chapter XIV, 143) gives a similar definition.

Understanding is also a "power" (bala), because it does not vacillate through ignorance (*Atthasālinī*, I, Book I, Part IV, Chapter II, 148). As we have seen, when the wholesome faculties have been developed they become powers which are unshakable. They cannot be shaken by their opposites.

Right understanding of realities, sammā-diṭṭhi, is a *factor of the Eightfold Path* and as it accompanies the other factors of the eightfold Path they develop together so that the four noble Truths can be penetrated. The object of right understanding which is not lokuttara, supramundane, but "lokiya", mundane, is the nāma or rūpa appearing at the present moment. The object of right understanding which is lokuttara is nibbāna. Right understanding which accompanies the lokuttara magga-citta eradicates defilements; defilements are eradicated at different stages of enlightenment and all of them are eradicated at the attainment of arahatship.

Understanding is classified in several ways and, thus, its different aspects can be seen. It has been classified as one of the seven *factors of enlightenment* (sambojjhangas) and as such it is called *investigation of dhamma*, dhamma vicaya. The factors of enlightenment are mindfulness, investigation of dhamma, energy, enthusiasm, calm, concentration and equanimity. These factors have to be developed together for the purpose of attaining enlightenment. There has to be "investigation" of the reality, the dhamma, appearing at the present moment, over and over again before enlightenment can be attained and defilements eradicated.

Understanding which is supramundane, lokuttara, can be classified by way of three faculties:

1. I-shall-come-to-know-the-unknown" faculty(an-aññātaññassāmī 't'indriya),

[2] See also Dhammasangaṇi (Book I, Chapter I, par16) which describes understanding among others as "searching the Dhamma", that is: the four noble Truths, as a "guide", as a "sword" which cuts off defilements, as a "light", as "glory" or "splendour".

arising at the moment of the magga-citta of the sotāpanna[3].

2. The faculty of final knowledge (aññindriya), which arises at the moment of the phala-citta, fruition-consciousness, of the sotāpanna, and also accompanies the magga-citta and the phala-citta of the sakadāgāmī and of the anāgāmī and the magga-citta of the arahat[4].
3. The final knower faculty (aññātāvindriya), arising at the moment of the phala-citta of the arahat.

The sotāpanna still has to develop right understanding of nāma and rūpa because his understanding has not reached the degree that all defilements can be eradicated. The task of developing understanding is finished only when the "final knower faculty" has arisen[5].

When we learn about the different classifications of understanding we can be reminded that understanding has to be *developed* in order to reach higher stages. It should be developed in whatever situation in our daily life we may be. We are inclined to think that awareness of the present moment is too difficult, but that one day in the future we may reach the goal. If we think that the present situation is not favourable for the development of right understanding, it will not develop. We should remember that each moment is in fact a new situation which is conditioned and which is beyond control, and that it is therefore useless to prefer another situation to the present one. We should not worry about the situation we are in but we should be mindful of whatever reality appears. There is for example time and again heat or cold. Usually we think of a concept of "I am hot" or "I am cold", but heat and cold are only rūpa-elements and they can be objects of mindfulness when they appear. There is no self who experiences heat or cold, it is nāma which arises because of conditions. Through the development of understanding one will be less inclined to cling to a concept of "I feel" or "I experience". It is only a type of nāma which experiences something, a nāma which has arisen and then falls away immediately. There can be a beginning of understanding when there is mindfulness of what has already arisen at this moment because of its appropriate conditions.

35.1.1 Questions

1. Why can there only be direct understanding of realities when there is mindfulness of them?
2. Understanding is an indriya, a controlling faculty. What does it control?
3. What is the object of right understanding of the eightfold Path which is mundane, not supramundane, lokuttara?
4. We may find a particular situation too difficult, not favourable for the development of understanding. What should we do when we are in such a situation?

---

[3] Dhammasangaṇi, par362-364. Vis. XVI, 3.

[4] Dhammasangaṇi, par505.

[5] Dhammasangaṇi, par553.

36 The Stages of Insight

The realities which appear in our daily life are impermanent, dukkha and anattā. We may have theoretical understanding of these three characteristics of realities, but does understanding directly know the truth? There may not be understanding which directly knows the arising and falling away of seeing which appears now or of visible object which appears now. We learn about "arising and falling away of realities", but instead of directly knowing the truth we can only think of the truth. The realization of the impermanence of realities is not thinking: "It does not last". The impermanence of realities cannot be realized in the beginning of the development of understanding. First understanding should clearly know the nāma which appears as nāma and the rūpa which appears as rūpa. Nāma and rūpa are different realities and they can only be object of mindfulness one at a time, but we are still likely to confuse their characteristics. In theory we know that nāma experiences an object and that rūpa does not experience anything, but theoretical understanding is only superficial. In order to develop direct understanding of realities we should first know the difference between the moments of thinking about concepts such as a person, body or house, and the moments of mindfulness of only one reality at a time, such as visible object, hardness or seeing. These are ultimate realities, each with their own characteristic, which does not change, no matter how we name it. One reality at a time impinges on one of the six doors and when mindfulness arises it can be directly aware of that object, and at that moment understanding can investigate its nature. In this way understanding of realities can develop.

The realization of the truth of impermanence, dukkha and anattā does not occur all of a sudden, it is the result of the development of direct understanding in different stages. All through the different stages of development of understanding the object is the same: nāma and rūpa which appear at the present moment, in daily life. The object is the same but understanding develops and sees realities more clearly. Thus, doubt about realities and the wrong view of them are eliminated.

The first stage of insight, which is only a beginning stage, is the understanding of the difference between the characteristic of nāma and the characteristic of rūpa, not merely in theory but through direct understanding of them when they appear. The first stage of insight is called *Defining of nāma and rūpa*, or "Delimitation of Formations" (in Pāli: nāma-rūpa-pariccheda-ñāṇa). The following stages of insight, which are higher stages, cannot be realized before the first stage of insight. Thus, the impermanence of, for example, seeing cannot be realized if there is no clear understanding first of the characteristic of seeing as nāma, different from rūpa. We know in theory that seeing does not stay, that it must have fallen away when we think of a concept, but this does not mean that the arising and falling away of seeing at this moment is directly known. Seeing and visible object may still seem to appear together, and then there is no mindfulness of one reality at a time but only thinking about seeing and visible object.

The understanding of seeing and all the other realities is bound to be vague in the beginning and it is useful to know what one does not understand yet. Seeing arises and then it falls away immediately to be succeeded by other cittas of the eye-door process which experience visible object. When the eye-door process has been completed there is a process of cittas which experience visible object through the mind-door; they do not experience a concept but visible object which has only just fallen away. Later on other mind-door processes of cittas which experience a concept may arise. When one pays attention to the shape and form of something and to the details, the object is a concept. Thus, rūpas which impinge on the five senses are experienced through the corresponding sense-door as well as through the mind-door. We are confused with regard to the truth because it seems that seeing continues for some time and that there is no mind-door process of cittas which also experience the visible object which was experienced by the cittas of the eye-door process. We do not notice the mind-door processes which arise in between the sense-door processes, it seems that the mind-door processes are covered up by the sense-door processes.

When the first stage of insight is reached, paññā which arises in a mind-door process clearly distinguishes the characteristic of nāma from the characteristic of rūpa, there is no confusion about their different characteristics. Neither is there confusion about what the mind-door process is; the mind-door process which follows upon a sense-door process is no longer covered up, as was the case before the first stage of insight occurred. At the moments of insight nāma and rūpa appear one at a time in mind-door processes and at these moments one does not take realities as a "whole", there is no idea of "the world", no idea of a self. There is no self who can direct which nāma and rūpa are the objects of insight, there is no particular order of their appearing. Any nāma and any rūpa can be the object of insight and their different characteristics can be distinguished from each other.

When the moments of insight knowledge, vipassanā ñāṇa, have fallen away it seems again that realities appear as a "whole", as the world. Understanding is still weak. It depends on the accumulated wisdom of the individual which kinds of nāma and rūpa have been penetrated by insight, it may have been only a few kinds. The understanding which was gained at the moments of vipassanā ñāṇa has to be applied again and again and one has to continue to be mindful of all kinds of nāma and rūpa which appear. The concept of self is so deeply rooted that it cannot be eradicated at the first stage of insight. Understanding has to develop further in order to eradicate it.

When the characteristic of nāma and the characteristic of rūpa can be distinguished from each other, nāma and rūpa can be seen more clearly as conditioned realities. Seeing arises, no matter we like it or not, because there are conditions for its arising. Visible object conditions seeing by being its object. If there were no object, seeing could not arise. Seeing is also conditioned by eyesense which is its physical base, a kind of rūpa produced by kamma. If kamma does not produce eyesense there cannot be seeing. Seeing is vipākacitta, the result of kamma. There is seeing of pleasant objects and of unpleasant objects and nobody can cause the experience of objects to be pleasant. Contact, phassa, is another condition for seeing. Contact is a cetasika which arises with each citta and it "contacts" the object so that citta can experience it. If there were no contact there could not be seeing. There is no self who sees and can control the seeing; it is only a conditioned nāma which arises for a moment and then falls away.

Every reality which arises is conditioned by different factors. The seventh book of the "Abhidhamma", the "Book of Conditional Relations" (Paṭṭhāna)[1] deals with twentyfour different types of conditions (paccayas). When we study these we should keep in mind that they occur in daily life. When paññā has been developed more by being mindful of all kinds of realities appearing in daily life, the second stage of insight can be realized. This is *Discerning the Conditions of Nāma and Rūpa* (in Pāli: paccaya-pariggaha-ñāṇa). This is not theoretical understanding of conditions, it is not thinking of all the different conditioning factors for the arising of nāma and rūpa, but it is the direct understanding of nāma and rūpa as conditioned realities. Through direct understanding of the nāma or the rūpa which appears now we will come to understand what our life is and how it is conditioned.

Just as nāma and rūpa which arise at the present moment are conditioned, so they were in the past and so they will be in the future. We have to continue to be born and to receive results of kamma because there is still ignorance and craving and these condition rebirth. There is clinging to the objects which can be experienced through the senses, there is clinging to life. The clinging which arises today is conditioned by clinging which arose in the past and which has been accumulated and carried on from one life to the next life.

We may still doubt whether there is rebirth after the dying-consciousness. If the citta at this moment is clearly understood as a conditioned reality there will also be more understanding about death and rebirth. Each citta which arises now is succeeded by the next one. This also happens at the last moment of our life: the dying-consciousness has to be succeeded by the rebirth-consciousness which is the first citta of the next life. So long as there are conditions for it there will be the arising of nāma and rūpa again and again. Doubts about past life, present life and future life cannot be overcome by theoretical understanding of the conditions for the arising of nāma and rūpa, it can only be overcome by the direct understanding of realities and their conditions.

Life exists in only one moment of experiencing an object. This moment falls away and is gone completely, and then another moment arises. When seeing arises, our life is seeing, when hearing arises, our life is hearing. Each moment of life is impermanent and thus it is dukkha, we cannot take our refuge in it. The cause of dukkha is craving. Very often after seeing, hearing or the other sense-cognitions attachment arises, but it may be so subtle that we do not notice it. We cling to seeing, we also cling to thinking of concepts after the seeing, we want to pay attention to shape and form. When we read there is usually attachment, we have desire to know the meaning of what we read. When we are thinking there are often akusala cittas with attachment, but we do not notice it. When right understanding is being developed attachment can be known as only a conditioned nāma, not self.

We read in the *Kindred Sayings* (II, Nidāna-vagga, Part XII, Chapter V, par 43, Ill) that the Buddha, while he was at Sāvatthī, spoke about the arising of Ill, dukkha, and its cause, and about the ceasing of dukkha and the conditions for its ceasing:

---

[1] Translated by Ven. U. Narada, P.T.S. 1969. See also his Guide to Conditional Relations, P.T.S. 1979.

> ...What, monks, is the arising of dukkha?
>
> Because of sight and visual objects visual consciousness arises, contact is the clash of the three; feeling is conditioned by contact, craving by the feeling. This, monks, is the arising of dukkha.
>
> (We then read the same with regard to the other doorways.)
>
> And what, monks, is the passing away of dukkha?
>
> Because of sight and visible objects visual consciousness arises; contact is the clash of the three; feeling is conditioned by the contact, craving by the feeling. By the utter fading away and ceasing of the craving, grasping ceases, by the ceasing of the grasping, becoming ceases, by the ceasing of becoming, birth ceases, by the ceasing of birth, decay-and-death, grief, lamentation, suffering, despair cease. Such is the ceasing of this entire mass of dukkha.
>
> (The same is said with regard to the other doorways.)
>
> This, monks, is the passing away of dukkha.

We may read this sutta with theoretical understanding of realities, but only through insight, through direct understanding of the truth, can we grasp the deep meaning of this sutta. There are many degrees of knowing the three characteristics of conditioned realities, of impermanence, dukkha and anattā. After the second stage of insight has been reached, understanding investigates more and more these three characteristics. The third stage of insight is *Investigation Knowledge or Comprehension by Groups* (in Pāli: sammasana ñāṇa, Vis. XX, 6). It may seem that investigation knowledge is merely intellectual understanding, but it is a stage of direct understanding, of insight. At this stage paññā clearly realizes the succession of the nāmas and of the rūpas as they arise and fall away very rapidly.

Even after the third stage of insight has been reached, insight is still "tender insight" (taruṇa vipassanā). When insight is merely "tender" a person can still deviate from the eightfold Path. The *Visuddhimagga* (XX, 105) mentions "imperfections" which can arise: someone may cling to his understanding, to tranquillity or to the assurance he has due to this beginning insight. He may forget that also understanding is only a conditioned reality which is not self. Or he may erroneously think that he has attained enlightenment already and, thus, he may get stuck in his development.

The imperfections of insight can only be overcome by continuing to be mindful of all kinds of realities which appear. If one realizes that also insight knowledge is only a conditioned nāma there will be less clinging to it. There is no self who can induce the arising of the stages of insight nor exert control over them. Those who are no longer deluded because of the imperfections of insight, know what is the right path and what is not the right path (Vis. XX, 129). If one does not deviate from the right path anymore insight can develop and then a following stage of insight can be reached. This is the first stage of "principal insight" (mahā-vipassanā), namely, the *Knowledge of the Arising and Falling away of Nāma and Rūpa* (udayabbhayā ñāṇa). As we have seen, at the third stage of "tender insight" paññā realizes the succession of nāmas and rūpas which arise and fall away very rapidly. However, at this stage paññā is not keen enough yet to see the danger and disadvantage of the arising and falling away of realities. At the first stage of principal insight paññā realizes more clearly and more precisely the arising and the falling away of a nāma and a rūpa as it appears one at a time, and there can be more detachment from them. Although realities are more clearly understood at each subsequent stage of insight, the knowledge which was gained has to be applied and one has to continue to be mindful of nāma and rūpa. Only thus the three characteristics of impermanence, dukkha and anattā will be penetrated more deeply.

There are nine stages of principal insight, mahā-vipassanā, in all according to the *Visuddhimagga* (XXI, 1)[2]. In the course of the development of insight there will be more detachment from realities. Wrong views are more and more abandoned and there comes to be a clearer understanding of the fact that conditioned dhammas cannot be true happiness since they are liable to destruction and fall. The following stage of insight, the second stage of "principal insight" is *Knowledge of Dissolution* (in Pāli: bhanga ñāṇa). In order to be able to reach this stage paññā has to investigate thoroughly all the different kinds of realities appearing through the six doors. There must be mindfulness of whatever reality appears in whatever situation one may be. At this stage paññā pays closer attention to the falling away of realities and sees more clearly that they are no refuge. There is a beginning of detachment from the concept of self. The following stage of insight is *Knowledge of Terror* (in Pāli: bhaya ñāṇa). This is not fear which is akusala, it is insight which sees more clearly the danger of all conditioned dhammas which are bound to cease. Each following stage of insight marks a growing understanding of the disadvantages of nāma and rūpa, of conditioned realities, since their true characteristics are seen more clearly. At the moment a stage of insight knowledge arises there is no clinging to nāma and rūpa, but such moments fall away and then there tends to be clinging again. One has to continue being mindful of realities and develop understanding of them until arahatship has been attained. As paññā becomes keener it becomes detached from conditioned realities and it wants to be delivered from them. It sees that conditioned realities are meaningless, void, and that they have no owner, that there is no self who can control them. Understanding brings about more dispassion and equanimity towards conditioned dhammas, although clinging has not been eradicated. When understanding clearly sees the disadvantages of conditioned dhammas, and it has been developed to the degree that enlightenment can be attained, then the stage of insight which is *Adaptation Knowledge* (in Pāli: anuloma ñāṇa) can be reached, and this arises during the process in which enlightenment occurs. This process is as follows[3]:

- mind-door adverting-consciousness (mano-dvārāvajjana-citta)
- preparatory consciousness (parikamma)
- proximity consciousness or access (upacāra)

---

[2] For details see Appendix 9. The way of counting of the stages of insight may vary depending on whether the counting starts at the first stage of principal insight or at the third stage of tender insight, and whether paññā arising in the process during which enlightenment occurs, paññā accompanying the lokuttara cittas and paññā which "reviews" after that process is over, is included or not.

[3] See Abhidhamma in Daily Life, Chapter 24.

- adaptation or conformity (anuloma)
- change of lineage (gotrabhū)
- path-consciousness (magga-citta)
- fruition-consciousness (phala-citta, two or three moments, depending on the individual)

The mind-door adverting-consciousness of this process adverts to one of the three characteristics of the reality which presents itself. The preparatory consciousness, the proximity consciousness and the adaptation which are mahā-kusala cittas accompanied by understanding experience the same object as the mind-door adverting-consciousness. "Adaptation" (anuloma) is the last citta in that process which has as object a conditioned reality and penetrates its true nature. The succeeding citta which is called "change of lineage" (gotrabhū) does not experience the same object anymore as the preceding cittas in that process; it is the first citta experiencing nibbāna (Vis. XXII, 1). It experiences nibbāna but it is not lokuttara citta, it is mahā-kusala citta. Change of lineage is intermediate between cittas of the sense-sphere and the lokuttara cittas which succeed it.

Only one of the three characteristics of reality is penetrated by paññā accompanying the mahā-kusala cittas before the "change of lineage" arises; thus, the reality which appears is either seen as impermanent, or as dukkha or as anattā. In the development of insight understanding investigates the three characteristics, but it depends on the individual's accumulations which of these three is realized more often. There can be thinking of the three characteristics, but when insight develops and different stages of insight have arisen, the three characteristics are seen more clearly by direct understanding.

At the moment of enlightenment the enlightenment factors accompany the lokuttara citta. As we have seen, these are: mindfulness, investigation of dhamma (which is paññā), energy, enthusiasm, tranquillity, concentration and equanimity. The magga-citta eradicates defilements and experiences nibbāna. The phala-citta which is the result of the magga-citta also experiences nibbāna; it does not eradicate defilements[4].

It is useful to learn about the different stages of insight. It reminds us that we have only a limited understanding of realities, but this should not discourage us. The only way to develop insight is to begin at this moment to be mindful of whatever reality appears. We cannot expect the arising of insight-knowledge soon, not even during this life. We have to continue to be mindful of nāma and rūpa and develop understanding of them. Only when understanding has been developed it can distinguish the characteristic of nāma from the characteristic of rūpa. Throughout the development of insight the objects of understanding are nāma and rūpa and one has to continue being mindful of them. Even when the stage of the sotāpanna has been realized one has to continue developing insight. The sotāpanna has realized the four noble Truths, but there are many degrees of realizing them. Only when paññā has been developed to the degree that arahatship is attained, it has reached completion and then all defilements are eradicated.

---

[4] See Abhidhamma in Daily Life, Chapter 24.

As we have seen, there are many kinds and degrees of understanding: intellectual understanding of realities, direct understanding of them, developed in different stages of insight, understanding of the plane of rūpāvacara citta (fine-material jhāna) and of the plane of arūpāvacara citta (immaterial jhāna), and understanding which is lokuttara paññā.

As regards kāmāvacara cittas, cittas of the sense-sphere, which are accompanied by understanding, there are four of the eight types of mahā-kusala cittas, four of the eight types of mahā-vipākacittas and four of the eight types of mahā-kiriyacittas which are accompanied by understanding[5]. If someone is born with mahā-vipākacitta accompanied by understanding he may, if he intends to develop higher degrees of calm, be able to attain jhāna in that life. If someone develops insight he may attain enlightenment in that life. If someone is not born with mahā-vipākacitta accompanied by understanding he can still develop calm or insight, but he cannot attain jhāna or enlightenment in that life. As regards the mahā-kiriyacittas of the arahat, four of the eight types are, as we have seen, accompanied by understanding. The arahat can have mahā-kiriyacittas which are not accompanied by understanding, for example at the moments when he does not preach Dhamma.

All rūpāvacara cittas and all arūpāvacara cittas have to be accompanied by understanding. Without paññā jhāna cannot be attained.

As regards lokuttara citta, the magga-cittas and the phala-cittas of the four stages of enlightenment are accompanied by understanding which is lokuttara paññā. When lokuttara cittas accompanied by jhāna-factors of the different stages of jhāna are not taken into account, there are eight lokuttara cittas accompanied by lokuttara paññā.

When lokuttara cittas accompanied by jhāna-factors of the five stages of jhāna are taken into account, there are forty lokuttara cittas (five times eight) instead of eight[6] which are accompanied by lokuttara paññā. The fact that lokuttara cittas can be counted as eight or forty shows us that accumulations of different ariyans are not the same. They all have eradicated the same kinds of defilements at the subsequent stages of enlightenment, but they have accumulated different inclinations and skills. Some had the ability to develop insight as well as calm to the degree of jhāna and could attain different stages of jhāna, whereas others did not have such skill.

Some types of sobhana cittas are accompanied by understanding, others are not. Understanding is a cetasika, not self, and it arises only when there are the right conditions for its arising. We may find it difficult to grasp how the understanding of the reality appearing at the present moment can develop to the degree that it leads to the eradication of defilements. When someone merely begins to develop understanding he may sometimes have doubts about the benefit of mindfulness of visible object, seeing, sound or hearing which appears now. We should remember that when there is less ignorance of realities there will be less defilements. Ignorance is the root of all that is unwholesome. When there is ignorance we do not know the benefit of kusala and the danger of akusala, we do not know realities as they

---

[5] See the summary in Appendix 8.

[6] See Abhidhamma in Daily Life, Chapter 23.

are. Ignorance conditions wrong view. It is wrong view to take realities for self or to believe that they last. When understanding begins to develop we cannot expect a radical change in our behaviour. We are still selfish, we still cling to the objects we experience, we are still angry, jealous and stingy. We have to be sincere with ourselves when we develop understanding, we should not pretend to be without defilements. Defilements are bound to arise, but we can begin to understand that whatever reality presents itself has arisen because of its appropriate conditions and is not self. We cannot eradicate defilements merely by doing good deeds without developing understanding of realities. Seeing realities as they are is the only way that eventually defilements can be eradicated.

We read in the *Gradual Sayings* (Book of the Tens, Chapter III, par 3, With Body[7]) that wrong bodily action can be abandoned by right bodily action and wrong speech by right speech. However, the three unwholesome roots of lobha, dosa and moha can only be eradicated by understanding. The text states:

> Which are the things, O monks, that can neither be abandoned by bodily acts nor by speech, but can be abandoned by wisely seeing them? Greed can neither be abandoned by bodily acts nor by speech; but it can be abandoned by wisely seeing it. Hatred can neither be abandoned by bodily acts nor by speech; but it can be abandoned by wisely seeing it. Delusion can neither be abandoned by bodily acts nor by speech; but it can be abandoned by wisely seeing it.

Attachment, aversion and ignorance are realities, they arise. They can be object of mindfulness so that understanding can investigate them and see them as they are, as not self. If we avoid being mindful of akusala, it cannot be seen as it is and then it cannot be eradicated. At this moment enlightenment seems far off, but we should not forget that understanding begins by listening, memorizing and considering what one has heard. Considering the nāma and rūpa which appear can condition mindfulness so that there can gradually be direct understanding of realities. Understanding which arises now is conditioned by many moments of studying and considering in the past. It arises and then falls away, but it is never lost since the conditions are accumulated for the arising again of understanding and, thus, it can grow. Understanding which is lokuttara is completely different from past moments of "mundane" understanding, yet, it is conditioned by past moments of insight and also by other good qualities, such as generosity, patience and perseverance, which have been developed together with understanding. Such good qualities should not be neglected, they can be helpful conditions leading to detachment. Understanding develops gradually in the course of many lives and, therefore, we should persevere in considering the Dhamma in daily life and in being mindful of realities.

36.0.1 Questions

1. Why can the arising and falling away of nāma and rūpa not be realized before the difference between nāma and rūpa has been clearly seen?

[7] I am using the translation by Ven. Nyanaponika, in The Roots of Good and Evil, p. 55, Wheel 251/ 253, B.P.S. Kandy, 1978.

2. Through which doorway can insight knowledge realize seeing as it is?
3. Can there be clinging when we perceive a teacup?
4. When is there thinking with akusala citta?
5. What is the object of understanding all through the development of the different stages of insight?
6. Can aversion be the object of insight in the process of cittas during which enlightenment is attained?

37 Wholesome Deeds

As we have seen, nineteen sobhana cetasikas accompany each sobhana citta. In order to perform wholesome deeds the kusala citta needs the assistance of at least these nineteen cetasikas. It needs confidence in kusala, mindfulness which is non-forgetful of kusala, shame which shrinks from akusala and fear of blame which fears its consequences. Each kusala citta has to be rooted in the two beautiful roots, sobhana hetus, of non-attachment, alobha, and non-aversion, adosa. Moreover, there has to be equanimity or mental balance, there has to be calm of cetasikas and calm of citta. There have to be the other "pairs" of mental lightness, pliancy, workableness, proficiency and uprightness, so that there is suppleness and proficiency in the performing of good deeds[1]. In addition to the nineteen sobhana cetasikas which accompany each sobhana citta, there are, as we have seen, six other sobhana cetasikas which do not accompany each sobhana citta. These are the three abstinences of right speech, right action and right livelihood, compassion, sympathetic joy and understanding. Thus, there are twentysix sobhana cetasikas in all. The three abstinences, compassion and sympathetic joy arise when there is an opportunity for them. Understanding does not accompany each sobhana citta, but for mental development, which includes samatha and vipassanā, understanding is indispensable. Each sobhana cetasika has its own function to perform while it assists the kusala citta. Learning about these sobhana cetasikas will help us to see that good qualities do not belong to a self. It is not "I" who is generous, who has kindness or compassion, they are sobhana cetasikas which assist the kusala citta.

We would like to have kusala citta more often but akusala cittas are bound to arise so long as the latent tendencies to akusala have not been eradicated. The eradication of defilements is the goal of the Buddha's teachings and this can be realized through the development of insight. Right understanding should be developed together with all other good qualities. The Buddha, when he was still a Bodhisatta, developed right understanding together with all other kinds of wholesomeness, he developed the wholesome qualities which are the "perfections" (parāmis)[2], during innumerable lives so that in his last life he could attain Buddhahood. This reminds us not to neglect the development of any kind of kusala for which there is an opportunity.

We have learnt about the twentyfive sobhana cetasikas, but now we should apply our knowledge in daily life. When we learn more in detail about the opportunities for the performing of good deeds there are conditions for using such opportunities. Good deeds can be classified as generosity (dāna), morality (sīla) and mental development (bhāvanā). The *Atthasālinī* (I, Book I, Part IV, Chapter VIII, 157) gives, with regard to kusala cittas of the sense-sphere, mahā-kusala cittas, a tenfold classification of good deeds, namely as the "ten bases of meritorious deeds" (puñña-kiriya-vatthus). Learning about these aspects is beneficial for the practice of kusala. We read in the *Atthasālinī* about the following "bases of meritorious deeds":

[1] For the "Six Pairs" see Chapter 31.

[2] The perfections of generosity, sīla, renunciation, wisdom, energy, patience, truthfulness, determination, loving kindness and equanimity.

1. charity or generosity
2. virtue or morality
3. culture or mental development
4. respect
5. dutifulness or helpfulness
6. sharing one's merit
7. thanksgiving or appreciation of someone else's good deeds
8. teaching Dhamma
9. listening to Dhamma
10. rectification of opinion (correction of one's views)

As regards the first "base" or way of kusala, generosity, this is the giving away of useful things or things which give pleasure. True generosity is difficult; while we are giving, there are not kusala cittas all the time, and our motives for giving may not all be pure. Akusala cittas tend to arise in between the kusala cittas, for example, when we wish for a pleasant result, such as a happy rebirth or a good name. We may give because we like to be popular, or we may give with attachment to the receiver. We may give out of fear, we are afraid of other people's opinion and hope to gain their favours by our gifts. Stinginess may arise, we regret getting rid of our money. We understand that we cannot take our possessions with us when we die, but since we have accumulated stinginess it tends to arise. We should remember that life is short and that when there is an opportunity for giving we should use it in order to combat selfishness. In this way the inclination to generosity can be accumulated. We read in the Commentary to the "Cariyāpiṭaka" (the "Paramatthadīpanī VII)[3], which deals with the "perfections" the Bodhisatta accumulated, that the Bodhisatta considered the perfection of generosity as follows:

> Surely, I have not been accustomed to giving in the past, therefore a desire to give does not arise now in my mind. So that my mind will delight in giving in the future, I will give a gift. With an eye for the future let me now relinquish what I have to those in need.

Further on we read in the same commentary:

> When the Great Being is giving a gift, and he sees the loss of the object being given, he reflects thus: "This is the nature of material possessions, that they are subject to loss and to passing away. Moreover, it is because I did not give such gifts in the past that my possessions are now depleted. Let me then give whatever I have as a gift, whether it be limited or abundant. In that way I will, in the future, reach the peak in the perfection of giving."

The *Atthasālinī* explains in the section on "charity", that there can be volition (kamma) which is kusala before the actual giving, namely when one produces the things to be given, at the time of making the gift, and afterwards when one recollects

---

[3] Translated by Ven. Bodhi, included in The All-embracing Net of Views, the Brahmajāla Sutta and its commentaries, B.P.S. Kandy, p. 322.

it "with joyful heart". Thus, giving can be an occasion for kusala cittas in three different periods: before, during and after the giving. It is useful to know that we can recollect our giving afterwards with kusala citta. However, we have to know the difference between kusala citta and akusala citta, otherwise we are likely to take attachment to our kusala or to the pleasant feeling which may arise for kusala. When we are honest with ourselves we can notice that before, during and after the giving there are not kusala cittas all the time, that there are also akusala cittas arising. Instead of being discouraged about akusala there can be mindfulness of it. This is the way to know that it is only a conditioned reality, not self. Before the actual giving we may get tired when we have to buy or prepare the gift and then aversion is likely to arise. While we are giving the gift the receiver may be ungrateful and not respond to our gift in the way we expected and then we may be disappointed. However, when we have right understanding of what kusala is we will be less inclined to mind the reactions of someone else. Kusala is kusala and nobody can change the kusala citta which arises. Before we learnt about the Buddha's teachings we did not consider generosity in this way. We used to pay attention merely to the outward appearance of deeds, we thought of people, of their reactions. Through the Dhamma we learn to investigate the cittas which motivate our deeds, we learn to see realities as they are. Also the recollection of our generosity after the giving can be disturbed by the arising of defilements such as stinginess. Generosity can only become perfected through the development of right understanding of nāma and rūpa. The sotāpanna (streamwinner) has eradicated the wrong view of self and also stinginess. Thus, he has perfect generosity, stinginess cannot arise again.

When we perform acts of generosity, the objects which can be given are the objects which can be experienced through the six doors. The *Atthasālinī* (I, Book I, Part II, 77) illustrates the giving of colour with a story about the treasurer of King Duṭṭhagāmani who presented a dress embroidered with gold at the great shrine, saying, "This dress is golden in appearance, the Supreme Buddha is also golden in appearance; the golden cloth suits the Golden One, and it will be our gift of colour." With the intention to make an offering of sound one can offer a musical instrument such as a drum to the Triple Gem. With the intention to make a gift of flavour one may offer, for example, a root with a captivating flavour.

We read in the same section of the *Atthasālinī* that, when someone makes the gift with his own hands it is an act through the body. When he tells his relatives or friends to present his offering it is an act of speech. When he is considering to make a gift it is an act of thought. Afterwards he will do what is necessary by act or speech in order to accomplish his intention.

The *Atthasālinī* (in the same section, 77) explains that, when someone in giving gifts observes the tradition of his family or observes usage, the giving is accomplished by sīla, morality. Observing rules of tradition which are the foundation of wholesome conduct is sīla.

Even when one does not have things to give there can still be accomplishment of generosity. Another one of the ten "bases" which is also a way of generosity is the "base of thanksgiving" or rejoicing in someone else's kusala. In order to be able to apply ourselves to this way of kusala we should understand the benefit of kusala. When we have confidence ourselves in generosity, in the observance of morality and in the development of insight, we can appreciate these ways of kusala in someone else. We can appreciate the good qualities of someone else and express our appreciation in words so that others may also rejoice in such qualities. When we appreciate someone else's kusala there is generosity, envy does not arise at such moments. When we know about this way of generosity we may remember to speak with kusala citta about the good qualities of other people instead of saying unpleasant things about them.

There is still another way of generosity and this is the "base" which is the "sharing of one's merit". We cannot transfer to others the kusala we perform nor the result it will produce; each person receives the results of his own good deeds. However, we can by performing good deeds be a condition for other people to have kusala cittas as well, namely, when they rejoice in our good deeds. In this way we can "share merit" with others, even with beings in other planes of existence, provided they are in planes where they are able to receive this benefit.

The commentary to the "Without the Walls" sutta (the "Illustrator of Ultimate Meaning", paramatthajotikā, commentary to the "Minor Readings", Khuddakapāṭha) narrates that King Bimbisāra offered a meal to the Buddha and omitted to dedicate his gift to other beings. Ghosts who were his relatives in a former life had hoped for this in vain and because of disappointment and despair they made a horrible screeching in the night. The Buddha explained why the ghosts had screeched. Then King Bimbisāra made again an offering and did not omit to make the dedication, "Let this be for those relatives". The ghosts benefited from his gifts immediately, they had kusala cittas and their suffering was allayed. Lotus-covered pools were generated for them in which they could bathe and drink, and they took on the colour of gold. Moreover, heavenly food, heavenly clothing and heavenly palaces were generated for them. This story illustrates that one can share one's merit with beings who are departed. If one's departed relatives are not able to receive this benefit other beings can. The sutta which has been explained in the commentary ends with the following words:

```
Give gifts then for departed ones,
Recalling what they used to do.
No weeping nor yet sorrowing,
Nor any kind of mourning, aids
Departed Ones, whose kin remain
(Unhelpful to them, acting) thus.
But when this offering is given
Well placed in the Community
For them, then it can serve them long
In future and at once as well.

The true Idea[4] for relatives has thus been
shown,
```

[4] The Dhamma.

```
And how high honour to departed ones is done,
And how the bhikkhus can be given strength as well,
And how great merit can be stored away by you.
```

It is understandable that we are sad when we lose beloved ones, but if we know how to develop what is wholesome it can be a great consolation. Instead of sadness and aversion there can be kusala citta when we dedicate our good deeds to all those who are able to rejoice in it. It can become our custom to share wholesomeness with others.

It is a Buddhist custom when a meal or robes are offered to the monks to pour water over one's hands while the monks recite words of blessing, in order to give expression to one's intention to dedicate this deed to other beings. The water is like a river which fills the ocean and even so a wholesome deed is so plentiful that it can be shared with others.

Some of the "ten bases of meritorious deeds" are included in morality, sīla. Abstinence from ill deeds is sīla. There is abstinence from akusala kamma through the body and this is abstinence from killing, stealing and sexual misconduct. There is abstinence from akusala kamma through speech and this is abstinence from lying, slandering, rude speech and idle talk. When we commit wrong deeds for the sake of our livelihood, there is wrong livelihood. When we abstain from wrong livelihood there is right livelihood. As we have seen (in chapter 32), the three sobhana cetasikas which are abstinence from wrong speech, abstinence from wrong action and abstinence from wrong livelihood perform their functions in assisting the kusala citta while there is an occasion for abstaining from evil conduct. Sīla is not only abstaining from what should not be done, it is also observing what should be done. We can observe moral precepts which are the foundation of wholesome conduct. A layman can make a resolution to observe them. He makes the resolution to undertake the rule of training to abstain from the following unwholesome deeds:

- killing living beings
- stealing
- sexual misbehaviour
- lying
- the taking of intoxicants such as alcoholic drinks

It is a Buddhist custom for laypeople to recite the five precepts when they are assembled in a temple on special occasions. When one recites them with a sincere inclination there is an opportunity for wholesomeness. Conditions are accumulated for wholesome conduct, for observing the precepts also when one is in difficult circumstances which make it hard to observe them. Morality can be considered also under the aspect of generosity, as a form of giving, because when we give up defilements it is also for the benefit and happiness of other beings; we let them live in safety and in peace. When we abstain from killing we give the gift of life. When we see morality as a gift of kindness to others and as a way to have less selfishness we can be inspired to observe it.

As regards abstinence from slandering, rude speech and idle talk, these are not among the five precepts for laypeople. However, engaging in these kinds of speech is akusala, whereas abstaining from them is kusala kamma. We are inclined to be heedless with regard to abstinence from wrong speech. When others speak in an unpleasant way about people we may find it hard not to join in the conversation. Or we may find abstinence of useless, idle talk a way of morality which is hard to observe. So long as one is not an arahat there are still opportunities for speaking with akusala citta. In the development of wholesomeness one has to be farsighted. We should realize that what we accumulate today, wholesomeness or unwholesomeness, can have its effects in the future, even in future lives. We can become more clever in evaluating the circumstances we are in, and the friends we have: we will be able to judge whether surroundings and friends are favourable for the development of wholesomeness or not. We will know what kind of speech should be avoided, what kind of speech is helpful. Since we will be engaged in conversation with others anyway we should learn how we can turn the conversation into an opportunity for wholesomeness. We may remember the way of generosity which is appreciation of other people's kusala while we speak. Or when the conversation tends to be idle talk about pleasant objects, such as good food, nice weather or journeys, there is an opportunity for sympathetic joy. We can rejoice in other people's good fortune of receiving pleasant objects. We should, however, know when the citta is kusala citta and when akusala citta. Otherwise we may erroneously think that there is the sobhana cetasika of sympathetic joy when there is actually attachment.

The *Visuddhimagga* (Chapter I) deals with many aspects of sīla. For the monks there is the observance of the rules of the Order of monks (Paṭimokkha). It is difficult to observe morality perfectly for a layman; he may find himself in circumstances where it is hard not to neglect morality. He may be tempted to kill insects in house and garden, to evade taxes or to accept bribes. The person who has accumulated inclinations for monkhood leaves his home for the homeless life in order to observe morality perfectly and to lead a life of non-violence and of contentment with little. The monk should not delight in gain and honour. He should not give hints nor use other means of scheming in order to obtain the requisites of robes, food, dwelling and medicines, and this is training in livelihood purification, which is an aspect of sīla mentioned in the *Visuddhimagga*. Another aspect of sīla is reflecting wisely on the use of the requisites. The monk should train himself not to be attached to the requisites but he should know that they are not for pleasure, that they are to be used for his health and comfort. Thus, he can dedicate himself to the study and teaching of Dhamma and the development of right understanding. Also laypeople can reflect wisely, for example, on food, while they are eating. Food is most of the time an object of attachment and it can also be an object of aversion. There may be moments that we reflect wisely, with kusala citta, on the use of food: food can be considered as a medicine for the body. Then we will be less inclined to indulge in food. Overeating leads to laziness.

Another aspect of sīla mentioned by the *Visuddhimagga* (I, 42 B) is "virtue of restraint of the sense faculties". We read in this section a quotation from the "Middle Length Sayings" I, 27, the "Lesser Discourse on the Simile of the Elephant's Footprint". The text states:

> . . . On seeing a visible object with the eye, he apprehends neither the signs nor the particulars through which, if he left the eye faculty unguarded, evil and unprofitable states of covetousness and grief might invade him, he enters upon the way of its restraint, he guards the eye faculty, undertakes the restraint of the eye faculty. . .

The same is said of the other doors. When mindfulness arises of one reality at a time as it presents itself through one of the six doors, sīla, good moral conduct, is observed. Moreover, the understanding is being developed which can eradicate defilements. If one separates the observance of sīla from the development of insight sīla cannot become enduring. If one does not develop insight defilements can be temporarily subdued but not eradicated.

Through the development of right understanding sīla can become more perfected. As we have seen, the three cetasikas which are the "abstinences" arise only one at a time when they accompany kusala citta which is not lokuttara but lokiya, "mundane". When enlightenment is attained all three of them accompany the lokuttara citta. At the moment of the path-consciousness, magga-citta, there is "abstinence by way of eradication"; that is the function of the three factors of right speech, right action and right livelihood of the eightfold Path which is lokuttara. Tendencies to evil conduct are eradicated at the subsequent stages of enlightenment, until they are all eradicated at the attainment of arahatship.

The paying of respect to those who deserve respect is another one of the "bases of meritorious deeds" and this is included in sīla. Respect is due to monks, novices, parents, teachers and elderly people. We can express respect and politeness through our conduct in body and speech. We may have selfish motives when we are polite, for example, when we wish for a good reputation or when we want to obtain favours. That is not the way of kusala which is respect. We can pay respect with kusala citta, and then respect is sincere. We should pay respect to the monks because they have left their homes for the homeless life in order to strive after the virtues of the ariyans. The goal of monkhood is arahatship and, thus, the monks can remind us of the virtues of the ariyan Sangha, even if they are not arahats. Laypeople can pay respect to monks by clasping their hands and bowing their head, or by prostrating the body and touching the floor with the forehead, the forearms and knees. When one shows one's respect in this way one should do it thoughtfully and sincerely, remembering that this is another opportunity for kusala citta.

We may pay respect to the Triple Gem in prostrating before a Buddha statue and reciting words of praise while we think of the excellent qualities of the Buddha, the Dhamma and the Sangha. However, there are not kusala cittas all the time. When we experience some bodily discomfort akusala cittas with aversion tend to arise. Or we may think of other things with attachment or aversion. We should know the difference between kusala citta and akusala citta, they arise because of their own conditions and they are not self. While we are reciting words of praise to the Triple Gem there can be mindfulness of realities which appear, even if these are akusala dhammas. Mindfulness of whatever reality appears is the best way of respect we can give to the Buddha since we then follow what he taught.

We read in the *Dhammapada* (verse 109)[5] about the fruits of paying respect:

```
He of respectful nature who
Ever the elders honouring,
Four qualities for him increase:
Long-life and beauty, happiness and strength.
```

The "base of meritorious action" which is dutifulness or helpfulness is also an aspect of sīla. When there are opportunities for helping others we tend to be lazy and forgetful, we are slow in our reactions instead of responding quickly to the needs of someone else. For example, when we are reading an interesting book we may not be inclined to get up and help someone who needs help. If we remember that there are many ways of helping others, that even helping in small matters is beneficial, there will be conditions to use such opportunities for kusala. We may, for example, show someone who got lost the right way, we may help someone in handing him a cup or a dish he needs, or we may help in listening to someone's problems and giving him advice.

Another one of the bases of meritorious deeds is listening to Dhamma and this is included in mental development. When we listen to the Dhamma and study it we learn what is kusala and what akusala, we learn about kamma and vipāka and the way how to develop kusala. Development of calm and of insight starts with listening; there could not be any mental development if one does not know how to apply oneself to it. Listening to the Dhamma or reading the scriptures and considering what we learnt are conditions for the arising of mindfulness of nāma and rūpa. Although we know that listening to the Dhamma and studying it is beneficial we may be inclined to put it off. We believe that we have too many duties to perform or we are distracted by the enjoyment of pleasant objects. When we really see the usefulness of the study of the Dhamma we can accumulate the inclination to listen to the Dhamma or to read the scriptures. Reading even a few lines at a time can be most beneficial.

Teaching or explaining the Dhamma is another one of the ten "bases of meritorious deeds". Both the person who explains the Dhamma and the listener can benefit, since both are reminded of the truth of Dhamma and of the need to apply the Dhamma. Teaching Dhamma is not easy, one should consider the capacity of the listener to receive the Dhamma. One can start with subjects which are more easily understandable such as generosity, and later on explain about the development of understanding which eradicates defilements. It is essential to learn about the ways of developing generosity and to apply them, because if one cannot give up things one possesses how could one give up clinging to self and other defilements? The Buddha preached to general Sīha a graduated discourse on almsgiving, the precepts and on heaven (Gradual Sayings, Book of the Eights, Chapter 2, par 2). When the Buddha saw that Sīha was ready to receive the teaching of the four noble Truths he taught these to him. The teaching of Dhamma should be gradual; in the beginning

[5] I am using the translation by Ven. Khantipalo, in The Buddhist Monk's Discipline, Wheel no. 130/131, B.P.S. Kandy.

one does not see the disadvantages of clinging. When one understands the dangers of defilements one wants to learn to develop the way leading to the eradication of defilements. The gift of Dhamma is the highest gift because through learning the Dhamma one can develop the understanding which eradicates defilements and leads to the end of dukkha. Thus, the teaching of Dhamma can also be considered as an aspect of generosity, dāna.

Both the development of calm and the development of insight are ways of mental development, they are among the "bases of meritorious deeds". As regards calm, this can be developed for the purpose of temporarily subduing defilements. The *Visuddhimagga* (Chapter III-XI) explains how calm can be developed even to the degree of jhāna by means of a meditation subject. It is extremely difficult to develop calm to the stage of jhāna, but some of the meditation subjects which are dealt with in the *Visuddhimagga* can also be used as recollections in daily life and then they can condition mahā-kusala cittas. The "ten bases of meritorious deeds" are objects of mahā-kusala cittas, kusala cittas of the sense-sphere, and, therefore, calm to the degree of jhāna is not dealt with in this context by the *Atthasālinī*. Those who have accumulated conditions for the attainment of jhāna have first to develop, by means of a meditation subject, calm which accompanies mahā-kusala citta.

In order to develop calm we should know when the citta is akusala citta and when kusala citta. When we have studied the akusala cetasikas and sobhana cetasikas we know in theory what is akusala citta and what is kusala citta, but we may not be able yet to apply our knowledge in daily life. We may not know what type of citta arises at the present moment. There are innumerable moments of clinging after seeing, hearing and the other sense-cognitions, but we do not notice them. When clinging is not as coarse as greed or lust it may pass unnoticed. When we make plans what to do next, when we go somewhere, when we want to get something or when we want a rest in the afternoon there are likely to be countless moments of clinging. We have learnt that the development of loving kindness, compassion, sympathetic joy and equanimity in daily life can condition moments of calm, but it is difficult to recognize the characteristic of calm. We may erroneously believe that the citta is kusala citta with calm when it is accompanied by indifferent feeling. However, kusala citta as well as akusala citta can be accompanied by indifferent feeling. It is essential to learn more about our different cittas and this is mental development. When we know the characteristic of true calm which arises with kusala citta, calm can be developed.

As regards vipassanā, insight, this is the understanding of realities which can eradicate the latent tendencies of defilements so that they cannot arise again. If we develop good qualities without developing right understanding of realities defilements cannot be eradicated. Akusala cittas are bound to arise time and again, even in between the moments we are performing good deeds. The eradication of defilements is the goal of the Buddha's teachings. For mindfulness of nāma and rūpa there is an opportunity at any time, but when mindfulness has not been accumulated it does not often arise. We may become impatient and have aversion when there is lack of mindfulness, but then we should remember that the moments of awareness and also the moments of forgetfulness arise because of conditions, that they are not self. Moments of ignorance of realities are real, thus, they can also be object of awareness.

One of the "Perfections", the wholesome qualities the Bodhisatta developed, was determination, the resolution to continue developing understanding in whatever situation he was. We read in the commentary to the "Cariyāpiṭaka" (the Paramatthadīpanī VII)[6] :

> ...For when the Great Man, straining and striving for the fulfilment of the requisites of enlightenment, encounters troubles difficult to endure, depriving him of happiness and his means of support, or when he encounters injuries imposed by beings and formations—difficult to overcome, violent, sapping the vitality— then, since he has surrendered himself to the Buddhas, he reflects: "I have relinquished my very self to the Buddhas. Whatever comes, let it come." For this reason he does not waver, does not quake, does not undergo the least vacillation, but remains absolutely unshaken in his determination to undertake the good.

When we are in very unpleasant circumstances we find it difficult to be mindful of realities. We lack determination. We want to control the experience of sense objects, we want objects to be pleasant. We forget that the experience of sense objects such as seeing or hearing is vipāka, conditioned by kamma. The realities which appear have been conditioned already and if we learn to be mindful of them there will be less inclination to try to exert control over them. Then there will be more patience and more determination to continue developing right understanding in whatever situation.

The tenth "base of meritorious deeds" is "rectification of view". There are many degrees of this way of wholesomeness. Before we studied the Dhamma we may have considered the enjoyment of pleasant sense objects to be the goal of our life. As we gradually come to see that selfishness leads to unhappiness and that kusala is beneficial both for ourselves and for others we start to correct our wrong ideas. We may, for example, be absorbed in the enjoyment of something pleasant such as listening to music, but then, when someone else suddenly needs our help, we may realize that it is more beneficial to help someone than to continue being selfish. However, each situation is conditioned and there is no self who can choose what action he will perform in a given situation. We correct our views when we come to understand that wholesome deeds are kusala kamma which will produce kusala vipāka. We should not cling to pleasant results, that is akusala. Kamma will produce its result, no matter whether or not we think of it. While we are performing good deeds there can be understanding of cause and effect without clinging. We correct our views most of all by developing right understanding of realities. In that way the clinging to the concept of self will decrease, we will be less inclined to take akusala or kusala for self. The "rectification of view" can go together with the other nine "bases of meritorious deeds", thus, with any kind of wholesome action.

The ten "bases of meritorious deeds" are included in generosity, sīla and mental development. The Buddha, when he was a Bodhisatta, developed with perseverance all kinds of wholesomeness together with right understanding. He had no selfish

---

[6] Translated by Ven. Bodhi, included in The All-embracing Net of Views, p. 323.

purposes but he was truly intent on the happiness of all beings. We read in the *Dialogues of the Buddha* (III, no. 30, "The Marks of the Superman") about the good deeds he performed during the lives he was a Bodhisatta, about the results produced by his good deeds, and about the special bodily features which are the "marks" of a Buddha and which are conditioned by these good deeds. I shall quote some passages which deal with his generosity, his purity of conduct and his wisdom:

> ...Whereas in whatsoever former birth, former state of becoming, former sojourning, monks, the Tathāgata, then being human, took on mighty enterprise in all good things, took on unfaltering enterprise in all good things, took on unfaltering enterprise in seemly course of deed and word and thought:—in dispensing gifts, in virtuous undertakings, in keeping of festivals, in filial duties to mother and father, in pious duties to recluse and brahmin, in honour of the head of the house and in other such things of lofty merit...(145) ...Whereas in whatsoever former births...the Tathāgata, then being human, lived for the weal of the great multitudes, dispeller of dread and panic, purveyor of just protection and wardenship and giver of supplies...(148) ...Whereas in former birth...the Tathāgata, then being human, putting away the taking of life, refrained therefrom and laying the scourge and sword aside, dwelt gentle and compassionate, merciful and friendly to all living creatures...(149) ...Whereas in whatsoever former birth...the Tathāgata, then being human, drew near and questioned recluse or brahmin, saying: What sir, is good? What is bad? What is right, what wrong? What ought I to do, or not to do? What when I have done it will long be for my unhappiness...or for my happiness?...(157) ...Whereas in whatsoever former birth...the Tathāgata, then being human, lived without wrath, full of serenity, and even when much had been said, fell not foul of anyone, was neither angry, nor malign, nor enraged, manifesting neither anger nor hate nor melancholy, but was a giver of fine and soft coverlets, and cloaks, and fine linen, fine cotton, fine silken, fine woollen stuffs... (159) ...Whereas in whatsoever former birth...the Tathāgata, then being human, grew desirous for the good of the many, for their welfare, their comfort, their safety, considering how they might increase in confidence, in morality, in education, in charity, in righteousness, and in wisdom, might increase in money and corn, in land, in animals two footed and four footed, in wife and children, in servants and slaves, in kinsfolk and friends and connections... (164) ...Whereas in whatsoever former birth...the Tathāgata, then being human, put away abusive speech, revolted against abusive speech, what he heard here not repeating elsewhere, to raise a quarrel against people here; and what he heard elsewhere not repeating here, to raise a quarrel against people there:—thus becoming a binder together of those who are divided, or fostering those who are friends, a peacemaker, lover of concord, impassioned for peace, a speaker of words that make for peace...(171, 172)

This sutta can encourage us to apply the Buddha's teachings. The Bodhisatta gave us an example to always be eager to listen and to learn, to develop all kinds of good qualities and above all, to develop understanding of realities. When we read about all the virtues the Bodhisatta accumulated in his former lives, we can be reminded that the effect of the development of understanding will eventually be to have less defilements, to become less selfish and more generous, to have more genuine concern for other people.

38 Appendix to Chapter 2

38.1 The Feelings which accompany the different cittas

Pleasant bodily feeling (sukha) arises with only one type of citta: the body-consciousness (kāya-viññāṇa) which is kusala vipāka. This kind of kāya-viññāṇa experiences a pleasant tangible object.

Painful bodily feeling (dukkha) arises with only one type of citta: the kāya-viññāṇa which is akusala vipāka. This kind of kāya-viññāṇa experiences an unpleasant tangible object.

Happy feeling (somanassa) arises with cittas of the four jātis but not with every citta. As regards akusala cittas accompanied by somanassa, four of the eight types of lobha-mūla-citta are accompanied by somanassa. The other types of akusala citta are not accompanied by somanassa.

As regards *ahetuka cittas (cittas without roots, hetus)* , accompanied by somanassa, one type of santīraṇa-citta (investigating consciousness) which is ahetuka kusala vipākacitta, and which investigates an extraordinarily pleasant object, is accompanied by somanassa. One type of santīraṇa-citta which is ahetuka kusala vipākacitta and which investigates a pleasant but not extraordinarily pleasant object, is accompanied by upekkhā. The santīraṇa-citta which is akusala vipākacitta is also accompanied by upekkhā. Thus, only one of the three types of santīraṇa-citta is accompanied by somanassa[1].

The ahetuka kiriyacitta which is the hasituppāda-citta producing the smile of an arahat[2] is accompanied by somanassa.

Of the kāmāvacara sobhana cittas[3] (beautiful cittas of the sense-sphere) four types of mahā-kusala cittas, four types of mahā-vipākacittas and four types of mahā-kiriyacittas are accompanied by somanassa.

The functions of paṭisandhi (rebirth), bhavanga (life-continuum) and cuti (dying) can be performed by mahā-vipākacittas[4]. In that case they are the result of kamma performed by mahā-kusala cittas. Mahā-vipākacittas can be accompanied by somanassa depending on the kamma which produces them. Those who are born with somanassa have bhavanga-cittas accompanied by somanassa throughout life.[5]

As regards rūpāvacara cittas (rūpa-jhānacittas)[6], those of the first, second, third and fourth stages of jhāna (of the fivefold system) are accompanied by somanassa. Thus, four rūpāvacara kusala cittas, four rūpāvacara vipākacittas and

---

1 Abhidhamma in Daily Life Chapter 9

2 Ibidem Chapter 9

3 Ibidem Chapter 19. Kāmāvacara-sobhana cittas, beautiful cittas of the sense-sphere are: eight types of mahā-kusala cittas, eight types of mahā-vipākacittas and eight types of mahā-kiriyacittas (inoperative, neither cause nor result) which are cittas of the arahat.

4 Ibidem Chapter 19

5 The bhavanga-citta is the same type of citta as the paṭisandhi-citta.

6 Ibidem Chapter 22.

four rūpāvacara kiriyacittas are accompanied by somanassa. The rūpāvacara cittas of the fifth stage of jhāna are not accompanied by somanassa but by upekkhā.

As regards arūpāvacara cittas (arūpa-jhānacittas), these are of the same type of citta as the rūpāvacara cittas of the fifth stage of jhāna, thus, they are not accompanied by somanassa but by upekkhā.

Lokuttara cittas can be accompanied by somanassa or by upekkhā, depending on conditions. Lokuttara cittas can be classified as eight, since there are for each of the four stages of enlightenment the magga-citta (path-consciousness) and its result, the phala-citta (fruition-consciousness).

People who have accumulated great skill in jhāna and who have also developed insight, can attain enlightenment with *lokuttara jhāna-cittas*. The lokuttara jhānacittas, which experience nibbāna, are accompanied by jhāna-factors of different the stages of jhāna. When lokuttara jhānacittas are taken into account, there are, instead of eight lokuttara cittas, forty lokuttara cittas (five times eight, since there are five stages of jhāna)[7]. In the case of the lokuttara jhānacittas, the accompanying feeling is in accordance with the accompanying jhāna-factors. In the fifth stage of jhāna there is upekkhā instead of somanassa, and therefore eight lokuttara jhānacittas, accompanied by the jhāna-factors of the fifth stage, are not accompanied by somanassa but by upekkhā. Thus, of the forty lokuttara jhānacittas thirty-two types are accompanied by somanassa. The feeling which accompanies the phala-citta (fruition-consciousness, the result of the magga-citta) is in each case the same type as the feeling which accompanies the magga-citta.

Summarizing the cittas accompanied by somanassa, they are:

- 4 lobha-mūla-cittas
- 1 santīraṇa-citta
- 1 hasituppāda-citta
- 12 kāmāvacara sobhana cittas
- 12 rūpāvacara cittas
- 32 lokuttara jhānacittas

—altogether: 62

Domanassa, unhappy feeling, arises with the two types of dosa-mūla-citta: one type is asaṅkhārika (unprompted) and one type is sasaṅkhārika (prompted)[8]. Domanassa cannot arise with other types of citta except these two.

Upekkhā, indifferent feeling, can arise with cittas of the four jātis but it does not arise with every citta. Thus, upekkhā can be kusala, akusala, vipāka and kiriya. Upekkhā can arise with kāmāvacara cittas (cittas of the sense-sphere), rūpāvacara cittas, arūpāvacara cittas and lokuttara cittas.

As regards upekkhā which accompanies akusala cittas, four of the eight types of lobha-mūla-citta are accompanied by upekkhā. Upekkhā also accompanies the two

[7] This is the reason why cittas can be counted as eighty-nine or as hundred and twenty-one, which include lokuttara jhānacittas.

[8] unprompted: arisen without inducement, spontaneously; prompted: arisen because of inducement either by oneself or by someone else.

types of moha-mūla-citta which are: moha-mūla-citta accompanied by vicikicchā (doubt) and moha-mūla-citta accompanied by uddhacca (restlessness)[9].

As regards *ahetuka cittas,* fourteen among the eighteen types are accompanied by *upekkhā,* namely: twelve ahetuka vipākacittas which are: four pairs of dvi-pañcaviññāṇas (the pair which is body-consciousness is excepted), two types of sampaṭicchana-citta (receiving-consciousness), and two among the three types of santīraṇa (investigating-consciousness). Only santīraṇa-citta which investigates an extraordinarily pleasant object is, as we have seen, accompanied by somanassa. The other two types, one of which is kusala vipāka and one of which is akusala vipāka, are accompanied by upekkhā[10].

The are two types of ahetuka kiriyacittas which are accompanied by upekkhā, namely: the pañcadvārāvajjana-citta (the five-sense-door-adverting-consciousness) and the mano-dvārāvajjana-citta (the mind-door-adverting-consciousness) which performs, in the sense-door process, the function of determining the object (votthapana)[11] and in the mind-door process the function of adverting to the object through the mind-door. Thus, there are fourteen types of ahetuka citta in all which are accompanied by upekkhā.

As regards kāmāvacara sobhana cittas, four of the eight mahā-kusala cittas, four of the eight mahā-vipākacittas and four of the eight mahā-kiriyacittas are accompanied by upekkhā. Thus, twelve kāmāvacara sobhana cittas are accompanied by upekkhā.

As regards rūpāvacara cittas, only the rūpāvacara kusala citta, the rūpāvacara vipāka-citta and the rūpāvacara kiriyacitta of the fifth stage of jhāna are accompanied by upekkhā; thus, there are three rūpāvacara cittas accompanied by upekkhā.

The arūpāvacara cittas are the same types of citta as the rūpāvacara cittas of the fifth stage of jhāna; they all are accompanied by upekkhā. There are twelve arūpāvacara cittas, namely the arūpāvacara kusala citta, the arūpāvacara vipākacitta and the arūpāvacara kiriyacitta of each of the four stages of arūpa-jhāna. At the fourth stage of arūpa-jhāna, the 'Sphere of Neither Perception nor Non-Perception', there is 'neither feeling nor non-feeling', feeling is present 'in a subtle state as a residual formation' (Vis. X, 50)[12].

As regards lokuttara cittas, they can, depending on conditions, be accompanied by upekkhā. When *lokuttara jhāna-cittas* are taken into account, the lokuttara cittas accompanied by the jhāna-factors of the fifth stage of jhāna are accompanied by upekkhā, thus, there are eight types accompanied by upekkhā.

Summarizing, the cittas accompanied by upekkhā are the following :

---

9 *Abhidhamma in Daily Life* Chapter 7

10 Santīraṇa-citta can also perform the function of rebirth. When it is akusala vipāka, accompanied by upekkhā, it can perform the function of rebirth in woeful planes. When it is kusala vipāka, accompanied by upekkhā, it can perform the function of rebirth of those who are handicapped from the first moment of life. The same type of citta which performs the function of rebirth, also performs the functions of bhavanga and cuti, dying, in that life.

11 *Abhidhamma in Daily Life* Chapter 9

12 *Abhidhamma in Daily Life* Chapter 22

- 4 lobha-mūla-cittas
- 2 moha-mūla-cittas
- 1 pañca-dvārāvajjana-citta
- 8 dvi-pañca-viññāṇas
- 2 sampaṭicchana-cittas
- 2 santīraṇa cittas
- 1 mano-dvārāvajjana-citta
- 12 kāmāvacara sobhana cittas
- 3 rūpāvacara cittas
- 12 arūpāvacara cittas
- 8 lokuttara cittas

—altogether: 55 types accompanied by upekkhā.

39 Appendix to Chapter 5

39.1 Cetanā as a link in the "Dependant Origination"

Cetanā as a link in the "Dependant Origination" is called *abhisaṅkhāra*. There are three kinds of *abhisaṅkhāra*:

1. meritorious kamma-formations (puññ'ābhisaṅkhāra)[1]
2. demeritorious kamma-formations (apuññ'ābhisaṅkhāra)
3. imperturbable kamma-formations (āneñj'ābhisaṅkhāra)

Meritorious kamma-formations are the cetanās which accompany the eight kāmāvacara kusala cittas or mahā-kusala cittas (kusala cittas of the sense-sphere)[2], and the five rūpāvacara kusala cittas (rūpa-jhānacittas)[3].

Demeritorious kamma-formations are the cetanās which accompany the twelve akusala cittas, which are: eight lobha-mūla-cittas, two dosa-mūla-cittas and two moha-mūla-cittas.

Imperturbable kamma-formations are the cetanās which accompany the four arūpāvacara kusala cittas (arūpa-jhānacittas). The meritorious kamma-formations and the demeritorious kamma-formations which produce rebirth-consciousness also produce rūpa. The imperturbable kamma-formations do not produce rūpa. Those who cultivate arūpa-jhāna have realized the disadvantages of rūpa. The arūpāvacara kusala cittas which are very tranquil, very refined, produce rebirth-consciousness in the relevant arūpa-brahma planes where there is no rūpa and no sense-impressions. There are four arūpa-brahma planes corresponding to the four stages of arūpa-jhāna.

These three classes of kamma-formations are a link in the Dependent Origination.

---

[1] Puñña means merit, kusala.
[2] *Abhidhamma in Daily Life* Chapter 10.
[3] *Abhidhamma in Daily Life* Chapter 22

40 Appendix to Chapter 8

40.1 The cittas which are accompanied by vitakka and vicāra

Both vitakka and vicāra arise with 44 kāmāvacara cittas, the ten dvi-pañcaviññāṇas are excluded.

As regards jhānacittas, vitakka accompanies only the three rūpāvacara cittas of the first stage of jhāna, whereas vicāra accompanies the three rūpāvacara cittas of the first stage of jhāna and the three rūpāvacara cittas of the second stage of jhāna (of the five-fold system), thus, altogether six rūpāvacara cittas. In the cases that the function of paṭisandhi is performed by rūpāvacara vipākacitta, the citta is not always accompanied by vitakka and vicāra. The rūpāvacara vipākacitta of the second stage of jhāna (of the five-fold system) is not accompanied by vitakka, but it is accompanied by vicāra. The rūpāvacara vipākacittas of the subsequent stages of jhāna are not accompanied by vitakka nor by vicāra. As regards arūpāvacara cittas, they are of the same type of citta as the rūpāvacara cittas of the fifth stage of rūpa-jhāna, thus, they are not accompanied by vitakka nor by vicāra.

When lokuttara jhānacittas, lokuttara cittas accompanied by jhāna-factors of the different stages of jhāna, are taken into account, there are forty lokuttara cittas instead of eight. Among these there are eight lokuttara cittas accompanied by the jhāna-factors of the first stage of jhāna, thus these are accompanied by both vitakka and vicāra. The lokuttara cittas accompanied by the jhāna-factors of the second stage of jhāna (of the five-fold system) are accompanied by vicāra but not by vitakka. The lokuttara cittas accompanied by the jhāna-factors of the higher stages of jhāna are without vicāra, since vicāra has been abandoned at those stages. Thus, there are sixteen lokuttara cittas accompanied by vicāra. When cittas are counted as 121 (including forty lokuttara cittas), *vitakka* accompanies:

- 44 kāmāvacara cittas
- 3 rūpāvacara cittas
- 8 lokuttara cittas

—altogether: 55 cittas

As regards *vicāra*, this cetasika accompanies:

- 44 kāmāvacara cittas
- 6 rūpāvacara cittas
- 16 lokuttara cittas

—altogether: 66 cittas

41 Appendix to Chapter 9

41.1 Cittas which are accompanied by viriya

The cittas which are accompanied by viriya are: all akusala cittas and all sobhana cittas, which include sobhana cittas of the sense-sphere, rūpāvacara cittas, arūpāvacara cittas and lokuttara cittas. Moreover, out of the eighteen types of ahetuka cittas there are two types which are accompanied by viriya: the *mano-dvārāvajjana-citta* which in the sense-door process performs the function of determining the object (votthapana) and in the mind-door process the function of adverting to the object, and the *hasituppāda-citta* which causes smiling in the case of arahats. The other sixteen types of ahetuka cittas are not accompanied by viriya. Thus, 16 types of citta out of 89 cittas are not accompanied by viriya. Altogether there are *73 types of citta accompanied by viriya.*

The paṭisandhi-citta, the bhavanga-citta and the cuti-citta are not accompanied by viriya if their functions are performed by santīraṇa-citta (two types, one kusala vipāka and one akusala vipāka)[1]. If their functions are performed by mahā-vipākacitta they are accompanied by viriya.

Summarizing the cittas which are accompanied by viriya, they are:

- 12 akusala cittas
- 2 ahetuka cittas
- 8 mahā- kusala cittas
- 8 mahā-vipākacittas
- 8 mahā-kiriyacittas
- 5 rūpāvacara kusala cittas
- 5 rūpāvacara vipākacittas
- 5 rūpāvacara kiriyacittas
- 4 arūpāvacara kusala cittas
- 4 arūpāvacara vipākacittas
- 4 arūpāvacara kiriyacittas
- 8 lokuttara cittas

—altogether: 73

When lokuttara cittas accompanied by the jhānafactors of the different stages of jhāna are taken into account, there are forty lokuttara cittas instead of eight; thus, in that case there are hundred-and-five cittas accompanied by viriya.

[1] *Abhidhamma in Daily Life*, Chapter 11.

42 Appendix to Chapter 11

42.1 The different cittas accompanied by pīti

Four types of lobha-mūla-citta are accompanied by pīti, namely the types which are accompanied by somanassa. Two types of ahetuka citta are accompanied by pīti, the santīraṇa-citta which is kusala vipāka and which investigates an extraordinarily pleasant object and the hasituppāda-citta, the smile-producing ahetuka kiriyacitta of the arahat. Moreover, pīti accompanies four types of mahā-kusala cittas, four types of mahā-vipākacittas and four types of mahā-kiriyacittas, thus, twelve types of kāmāvacara sobhana cittas. As regards jhānacittas, pīti accompanies the rūpāvacara kusala cittas, the rūpāvacara vipākacittas and the rūpāvacara kiriyacittas of the first three stages of jhāna (of the five-fold system), thus, nine types of rūpāvacara cittas. When lokuttara jhānacittas, lokuttara cittas accompanied by jhāna-factors of the different stages of jhāna, are taken into account, lokuttara cittas are classified as forty. Since pīti does not arise in the fourth and fifth stage of jhāna, only the lokuttara cittas arising with jhāna-factors of three stages of jhāna are accompanied by pīti. Thus, twenty-four types of lokuttara cittas in all (three times eight) are accompanied by pīti.

If we count cittas as hundred and twenty-one (including forty lokuttara cittas), the cittas accompanied by pīti are summarized as follows:

- 4 akusala cittas
- 2 ahetuka cittas
- 12 kāmāvacara sobhana cittas
- 9 rūpāvacara cittas
- 24 lokuttara cittas

—altogether: 51 cittas

43 Appendix to Chapter 12

43.1 The cittas accompanied by chanda, zeal or wish-to-do

Chanda can be of all four jātis, but as regards the jāti which is vipāka, chanda accompanies only mahā-vipākacittas, not ahetuka vipākacittas; as regards the jāti which is kiriya, chanda accompanies only mahā-kiriyacittas, not ahetuka kiriyacittas. Out of the eighty-nine cittas, twenty cittas are not accompanied by chanda: the two types of moha-mūla-citta and the eighteen ahetuka cittas.

Summarizing the cittas which are accompanied by chanda, they are the following , when cittas are counted as eighty-nine:

- 10 akusala cittas
- 24 kāmāvacara sobhana cittas
- 15 rūpāvacara cittas
- 12 arūpāvacara cittas
- 8 lokuttara cittas

—altogether: 69 cittas

When lokuttara cittas accompanied by the jhānafactors of the different stages of jhāna are taken into account, there are forty lokuttara cittas instead of eight. In that case there are hundred-and-one cittas accompanied by chanda.

44 Appendix to Chapter 20

44.1 Summary of Akusala Cetasikas

44.1.1 Summarizing the fourteen akusala cetasikas, they are:

1. ignorance (moha)
2. shamelessness (ahirika)
3. recklessness or fear of blame (anottappa)
4. restlessness (uddhacca)

   The above 4 arise with all akusala cittas
5. attachment (lobha), arising with eight types of citta, the cittas which are lobha-mūla-cittas, cittas rooted in attachment.
6. wrong view (diṭṭhi), arising with four types of cittas rooted in attachment.
7. conceit (māna), arising with the four types of cittas rooted in attachment which are unaccompanied by wrong view.
8. aversion (dosa), arising with two types of citta, the cittas which are dosa-mūla-cittas, cittas rooted in aversion.
9. envy (issā)
10. stinginess (macchariya)
11. regret (kukkucca)

    The above 3 may or may not arise with the two types of citta rooted in aversion, but they never arise together.
12. sloth (thīna)
13. torpor (middha)

    The above 2, may or may not arise with four types of citta rooted in attachment which are prompted, and with one type of citta rooted in aversion which is prompted. Sloth and torpor always arise together.
14. doubt (vicikicchā) arising with one type of moha-mūla-citta, citta rooted in ignorance

44.1.2 Summary of the Akusala Cittas and their accompanying Cetasikas

1. *citta rooted in attachment* (lobha-mūla-citta), accompanied by pleasant feeling, with wrong view, unprompted, is accompanied by: 7 universals, 6 particulars, the four akusala cetasikas arising with every akusala citta, which are ignorance, shamelessness, recklessness and restlessness, and by attachment and wrong view, thus, by *19 cetasikas.*
2. *citta rooted in attachment,* accompanied by pleasant feeling, with wrong view, prompted, is accompanied by: 7 universals, 6 particulars, by the four akusala

cetasikas arising with every akusala citta, by attachment and wrong view, and it may or may not be accompanied by sloth and torpor, thus by *19 or 21 cetasikas.*

3. *citta rooted in attachment*, accompanied by pleasant feeling, without wrong view, unprompted, is accompanied by: 7 universals, 6 particulars, the four akusala cetasikas arising with every akusala citta, and by attachment. Conceit may or may not arise, thus, by *18 or 19 cetasikas.*

4. *citta rooted in attachment*, accompanied by pleasant feeling, without wrong view, prompted, is accompanied by the same cetasikas as the third type, and in addition, it may or may not be accompanied by sloth and torpor. Thus, it can be accompanied *by 18* cetasikas if sloth, torpor and conceit do not arise, *by 19* if conceit arises, *by 20* if sloth and torpor arise but no conceit, or *by 21 cetasikas* if sloth, torpor and conceit arise.

5. *citta rooted in attachment*, accompanied by indifferent feeling, with wrong view, unprompted, is accompanied by: 7 universals, 5 particulars (less enthusiasm, pīti), the four akusala cetasikas arising with every akusala citta, by attachment and wrong view, thus, *by 18 cetasikas.*

6. *citta rooted in attachment*, accompanied by indifferent feeling, with wrong view, prompted, is accompanied by: the same types of cetasikas (18) as the fifth type of citta rooted in attachment, but, sloth and torpor my or may not arise, thus, by *18 or 20 cetasikas.*

7. *citta rooted in attachment*, accompanied by indifferent feeling, without wrong view, unprompted, is accompanied by: the same types of cetasikas as the fifth type of citta rooted in attachment, but not by wrong view, thus, by 17 types of cetasikas; however, conceit may or may not arise, thus, by *17 or 18 cetasikas.*

8. *citta rooted in attachment*, accompanied by indifferent feeling, without wrong view, prompted, is accompanied by the same types of cetasikas as the seventh type of citta rooted in attachment, and moreover, sloth and torpor may or may not arise; thus, by at least *17 cetasikas*, or, if conceit arises, *by 18 cetasikas*; *by 19 cetasikas* if sloth and torpor arise but no conceit, *by 20 cetasikas* if conceit, sloth and torpor arise.

9. *citta rooted in aversion* (dosa-mūla-citta), accompanied by unpleasant feeling, unprompted is accompanied by: 7 universals, 5 particulars (less enthusiasm), the four akusala cetasikas arising with every akusala citta and by aversion, thus, by at least *17 cetasikas.* Moreover, envy, stinginess or regret may or may not arise; if they arise they do so one at a time, and thus, this type of citta may be accompanied *by 17 or 18 cetasikas.*

10. 1*citta rooted in aversion*, accompanied by unpleasant feeling, prompted, is accompanied by the same types of cetasikas as the ninth type of citta, thus, *by 17 or 18 cetasikas*, and moreover, sloth and torpor may or may not arise. If they arise the citta can be accompanied *by 19 or 20 cetasikas.*

11. *citta rooted in ignorance*, accompanied by indifferent feeling,associated with doubt, is accompanied by: 7 universals, 3 particulars (no enthusiasm, deter-

mination and wish-to-do) and the four akusala cetasikas arising with every akusala citta, and doubt, thus, *by 15 cetasikas.*

12. *citta rooted in ignorance*, accompanied by indifferent feeling, associated with restlessness (uddhacca-sampayutta), is accompanied by: 7 universals, 4 particulars (no enthusiasm and wish-to-do) and the four akusala cetasikas arising with every akusala citta, thus, *by 15 cetasikas.*

45 Appendix to Chapter 31

45.0.1 Nineteen Sobhana Cetasikas accompanying each Sobhana Citta

- confidence, saddhā
- mindfulness, sati
- shame, hiri
- fear of blame, ottapa
- non-attachment, alobha
- non-aversion, adosa
- equanimity, tatramajjhattatā

Six Pairs

- calm of cetasikas, kāya-passaddhi
  calm of citta, citta-passaddhi
- lightness of cetasikas, kāya-lahutā
  lightness of citta, citta-lahutā
- pliancy of cetasikas, kāya-mudutā
  pliancy of citta, citta-mudutā
- wieldiness of cetasikas, kāya-kammaññatā
  wieldiness of citta, citta-kammaññatā
- proficiency of cetasikas, kāya-pāguññatā
  proficiency of citta, citta-pāguññatā
- uprightness of cetasikas, kāya-ujukatā
  uprightness of citta, citta-ujukatā

These sobhana cetasikas accompany: twentyfour sobhana cittas of the sense-sphere, kāmāvacara sobhana cittas.

- eight mahā-kusala cittas
- eight mahā-vipākacittas
- eight mahā-kiriyacittas

fifteen rūpa-jhānacittas of five stages

- five rūpāvacara kusala cittas
- five rūpāvacara vipākacittas
- five rūpāvacara kiriyacittas

12 arūpāvacara-jhānacittas of fourstages

- four arūpāvacara kusala cittas
- four arūpāvacara vipākacittas
- four arūpāvacara kiriyacittas
- eight lokuttara cittas
  (or forty, when lokuttara cittas accompanied by the jhāna-factors of the different stages of jhāna are taken into account.)

45.0.2 Six Sobhana Cetasikas which do not accompany each Sobhana Citta:

- abstinence from wrong speech, vacīduccarita virati
- abstinence from wrong action, kāyaduccarita virati
- abstinence from wrong livelihood, ājīvaduccarita virati
- compassion, karuṇā
- sympathetic joy, muditā
- understanding or wisdom, paññā

Thus, altogether there are *twenty-five sobhana cetasikas*, of which nineteen arise with each sobhana citta and six do not arise with each sobhana citta.

The three abstinences (the virati cetasikas) can accompany the following cittas:

- eight mahā-kusala cittas which are of the sense-sphere (kamāvacara cittas)
- eight (or forty) lokuttara cittas which are always accompanied by all three abstinences
- Compassion (karuṇā) can accompany the following cittas:
- eight mahā-kusala cittas
- eight mahā-kiriyacittas
- twelve rūpāvacara cittas (the rūpāvacara kusala cittas, vipākacittas and kiriyacittas of the first, second, third and fourth stage of jhāna (of the fivefold system)

thus, compassion can accompany twenty-eight types of citta

Sympathetic joy (muditā) can accompany the following cittas:

- eight mahā-kusala cittas
- eight mahā-kiriyacittas
- twelve rūpāvacara cittas

thus, sympathetic joy can accompany twenty-eight types of citta in all.

Understanding (paññā) accompanies the following cittas:

- four mahā-kusala cittas (those which are called: ñāṇa-sampayutta, accompanied by understanding)
- four mahā-vipākacittas (ñāṇa-sampayutta)
- four mahā-kiriyacittas (ñāṇa-sampayutta)
- five rūpāvacara kusala cittas (of the five stages of rūpa-jhāna)
- five rūpāvacara vipākacittas
- five rūpāvacara kiriyacittas
- four arūpāvacara kusala cittas (of the four stages of arūpa-jhāna)
- four arūpāvacara vipākacittas
- four arūpāvacara kiriyacittas
- eight lokuttara cittas

Thus, understanding accompanies fortyseven types of citta in all: twelve kāmāvacara cittas, fifteen rūpāvacara cittas, twelve arūpāvacara cittas and eight lokuttara cittas

When forty lokuttara cittas are counted instead of eight, namely, lokuttara cittas accompanied by the jhāna-factors of the five stages of jhāna, there are seventynine cittas in all accompanied by understanding.

46 Appendix to chapter 34

46.1 Three stages of "tender insight" (taruṇa vipassanā):

- Defining of Nāma and Rūpa (nāma-rūpa-pariccheda ñāṇa)
- Discerning the Conditions of Nāma and Rūpa (paccaya-pariggaha ñāṇa)
- Investigation Knowledge or Comprehension by Groups (sammasana ñāṇa)

46.2 Eight Stages of Principal Insight (Mahā-Vipassanā ñāṇa):

- Knowledge of the Arising and Falling Away of Nāma and Rūpa (udayabbhayā ñāṇa)
- Knowledge of Dissolution (bhanga ñāṇa)
- Knowledge of Terror (bhaya ñāṇa)
- Knowledge of Danger (ādīnava ñāṇa)
- Knowledge of Dispassion (nibbida ñāṇa)
- Knowledge of Desire for Deliverance (muccitukamyatā ñāṇa)
- Knowledge of Reflection (paṭisankhā ñāṇa)
- Knowledge of Equanimity about Saṅkhāra Dhammas (saṅkhārupekkhā ñāṇa)
- Adaptation Knowledge (anuloma ñāṇa)

47 Glossary

abhidhamma
: the higher teachings of Buddhism, teachings on ultimate realities

abhijjā covetousness

abhiññā supernormal powers

abhisaṉkhāra
: kammic activity giving preponderance in the conditioning of rebirth

adhimāna over-estimating conceit

adhimokkha
: determination or resolution

adhipatis "forerunners" of the arising of the ariyan eightfold Path:

adosa non aversion

adukkhamasukha
: neutral feeling

ahetuka cittas
: not accompanied by "beautiful roots" or unwholesome roots

ahetuka kiriyacitta
: inoperative citta without root

ahetuka-diṭṭhi
: The view that here are no causes (in happening)

ahirika shamelessness

ājīva-duccarita
: virati abstinence from wrong livelihood

akiriya-diṭṭhi
: The view that there is no such thing as kamma

akusala kamma
: a bad deed

akusala citta
: unwholesome consciousness

akusala unwholesome, unskilful

alobha non attachment, generosity

amoha wisdom or understanding

an-aññātaññassāmī 't'indriya
: I-shall-come-to-know-the-unknown" faculty, arising at the moment of the magga-citta of the sotāpanna

anāgāmī non returner, person who has reached the third stage of enlightenment, he has no aversion (dosa)

Ānanda the chief attendant of the Buddha

anantarika kamma
heinous crimes

anattā not self

aññasamānā cetasikas
Añña means "other" and samānā means "common", the same. The aññasamānās which arise together are of the same jāti as the citta they accompany and they all change, become "other", as they accompany a citta of a different jāti. Akusala is "other" than kusala and kusala is "other" than akusala.

aññātāvindriya
The final knower faculty, arising at the moment of the phala-citta of the arahat

aññindriya
The faculty of final knowledge , which arises at the moment of the phala-citta, fruition-consciousness, of the sotāpanna, and also accompanies the magga-citta and the phala-citta of the sakadāgāmī and of the anāgāmī and the magga-citta of the arahat

anottappa recklessness

anumodana thanksgiving, appreciation of someone else's kusala

anusayas latent tendency or proclivity

arahat noble person who has attained the fourth and last stage of enlightenment

ārammaṇa object which is known by consciousness

ariyan noble person who has attained enlightenment

arūpa-bhūmi
plane of arūpa citta

arūpa-brahma
plane plane of existence attained as a result of arūpa-jhāna. There are no sense impressions, no rūpa experienced in this realm.

arūpa-jhāna
immaterial absorption

arūpāvacara citta
arūpa jhāna citta, consciousness of immaterial jhāna

asaññā-satta
plane plane where there is only rūpa, not nāma

asaṅkhārika
unprompted, not induced, either by oneself or by someone else

asaṅkhata dhamma
unconditioned reality, nibbāna

asappurisa
a bad man

āsavas influxes or intoxicants, group of defilements

asura demon
being of one of the unhappy planes of existence

atīta-bhavanga
past life-continuum, arising and falling away shortly before the start of a process of cittas experiencing an object through one of the sense-doors

attavādupādāna
clinging to personality belief

Atthasālinī
The Expositor, a commentary to the first book of the Abhidhamma Piṭaka

avihiṃsa the thought of non-harming

avijjā ignorance

avijjāsava
the canker of ignorance

avijjogha the flood of ignorance

avyāpāda the thought of non-malevolence

ayoniso manasikāra
unwise attention to an object

balas powers
strengths

bhaṅga khaṇa
dissolution moment of citta

bhaṅga khaṇa
the dissolution moment of citta

bhava-taṇhā
craving for existence

bhāvanā mental development, comprising the development of calm and the development of insight

bhavanga calana
: vibrating bhavanga arising shortly before a process of cittas experiencing an object through one of the six doors

bhavanga-citta
: life-continuum

bhavangupaccheda
: arrest bhavanga, last bhavanga-citta before a process of cittas starts

bhavogha
: the flood of desire for rebirth

bhikkhu
: monk

bhikkhunī
: nun

bhūmi
: existence or plane of citta

bodhisatta
: a being destined to become a Buddha

bojjhangas
: factors of enlightenment,

Brahma
: heavenly being born in the Brahma world, as a result of the attainment of jhāna

brahma-vihāras
: the four divine abidings, meditation subjects which are: loving kindness, compassion, sympathetic joy, equanimity

brahmavihāra-upekkhā
: equanimity, one of the "divine abidings"

Buddha
: a fully enlightened person who has discovered the truth all by himself, without the aid of a teacher

Buddhaghosa
: the greatest of Commentators on the Tipiṭaka, author of the Visuddhimagga in 5 A.D

cakkhu
: eye

cakkhu-dhātu
: eye element

cakkhu-dvāra
: eyedoor

cakkhu-samphassa
: eye contact

cakkhu-vatthu
: eye-base

cakkhu-viññāṇa
seeing-consciousness

cakkhuppasāda-rūpa
eye-sense

cetanā volition

cetasika mental factor arising with consciousness

chanda "wish to do"

citta consciousness, the reality which knows or cognizes an object

citta-kammaññatā
wieldiness of citta

citta-lahutā
lightness of citta

citta-mudutā
pliancy of citta

citta-pāguññatā
proficiency of citta

citta-passaddhi
tranquillity of mind

citta-ujukatā
uprightness of citta

cuti dying

cuti-citta
dying-consciousness

dāna generosity, giving

deva heavenly being

dhamma reality, truth, the teachings

dhamma-vicaya
investigation of Dhamma

Dhammasangaṇi
the first book of the Abhidhamma Piṭaka

dhammavicaya
investigation of the Dhamma

diṭṭhāsava
canker of wrong view

diṭṭhi wrong view, distorted view of realities

diṭṭhigata sampayutta
accompanied by wrong view

diṭṭhigata-vippayutta
attachment which is dissociated from wrong view

diṭṭhogha the flood of wrong view

diṭṭhupādāna
clinging to wrong view

domanassa unpleasant feeling

dosa aversion or ill will

dosa-mūla-citta citta
(consciousness) rooted in aversion

dukkha suffering, unsatisfactoriness of conditioned realities

dukkha vedanā
painful feeling or unpleasant feeling

dvāra doorway through which an object is experienced, the five sense-doors or the mind door

dvi-pañca-viññāṇa
the five pairs of sense-cognitions, which are seeing, hearing, smelling, tasting and body-consciousness. Of each pair one is kusala vipāka and one akusala vipāka

ekaggatā concentration, one-pointedness, a cetasika which has the function to focus on one object

ganthas bonds, a group of defilements

gotrabhū change of lineage, the last citta of the sense-sphere before jhāna, absorption, is attained, or enlightenment is attained

hasituppāda-citta
smile producing consciousness of an arahat

hetu root, which conditions citta to be "beautiful" or unwholesome

hiri moral shame

hiriyati scruples

idaṃ-saccābhinivesa kāyagantha
the bodily tie of dogmatism

idaṃ-saccābhinivesa
the tie of dogmatism

iddhipādas
four "Roads to Success"

indriya faculty. Some are rūpas such as the sense organs, some are nāmas such as feeling. Five 'spiritual faculties' are wholesome faculties which should be cultivated, namely: confidence, energy, awareness, concentration and wisdom.

issā envy

jāti birth, nature, class (of cittas)

javana impulsion, running through the object

javana-citta cittas which 'run through the object', kusala citta or akusala citta in the case of non-arahats

jhāna absorption which can be attained through the development of calm

jhāna factors cetasikas which have to be cultivated for the attainment of jhāna: vitakka, vicāra, pīti, sukha, samādhi

jhāna-cittas absorption consciousness attained through the development of calm

jīvitindriya life-faculty or vitality

kalyāṇa-mitta good friend in Dhamma

kāma-sobhana cittas beautiful cittas of the sense sphere

kāma-taṇhā sensuous craving

kāma-vitakka thought of sense-pleasures

kāmāvacara cittas cittas of the sense sphere

kāmāvacara sobhana cittas beautiful cittas of the sense sphere

kamma intention or volition; deed motivated by volition

kamma patha course of action performed through body, speech or mind which can be wholesome or unwholesome

kāmogha the flood of sensuous desire

kāmupādāna sensuous clinging

`karuṇā` compassion

`kāya` body. It can also stand for the 'mental body', the cetasikas

`kāya-duccarita virati` abstinence from wrong action

`kāya-ujukatā` uprightness of cetasika

`kāya-viññāṇa` body-consciousness

`khandhas` aggregates of conditioned realities classified as five groups: physical phenomena, feelings, perception or remembrance, activities or formations (cetasikas other than feeling or perception), consciousness.

`khanti` patience

`kilesa` defilements

`kiriya citta` inoperative citta, neither cause nor result

`kukkucca` regret or worry

`kusala kamma` a good deed

`kusala` wholesome, skilful

`kusala citta` wholesome consciousness

`lakkhaṇaṃ` characteristic, specific or generic attribute

`lobha` attachment, greed

`lobha-mūla-citta` consciousness rooted in attachment

`lokiya citta` citta which is mundane, not experiencing nibbāna

`lokuttara citta` supramundane citta which experiences nibbāna

`lokuttara dhammas` the unconditioned dhamma which is nibbāna and the cittas which experience nibbāna

`macchariya` stinginess

`magga` path (eightfold Path)

magga-citta path consciousness, supramundane citta which experiences nibbāna and eradicates defilements.

mahā kiriyacitta inoperative sense-sphere citta of the arahat, accompanied by "beautiful" roots.

mahā vipākacitta citta of the sense sphere which is result, accompanied by "beautiful" roots.

mahā-satipaṭṭhāna four applications of mindfulness, see satipaṭṭhāna

mahā-vipassanā "principal insight"

manasikāra attention

mano-dvārāvajjana-citta mind-door-adverting-consciousness

māra the evil one

mettā loving kindness

micchā-diṭṭhi wrong view

micchā-samādhi wrong concentration

middha torpor or languor

moha ignorance

moha-mūla-citta citta rooted in ignorance

moha-mūla-cittas cittas rooted in ignorance

muditā sympathetic joy

nāma kkhandha group of all mental phenomena

nāma mental phenomena,including those which are conditioned and also the unconditioned nāma which is nibbāna.

nāma-rūpa pariccheda-ñāṇa first stage of insight, insight knowledge of the distinction between mental phenomena and physical phenomena

natthika diṭṭhi
: wrong view of annihilation, assumption that there is no result of kamma.

ñāṇa
: wisdom, insight

nekkhamma
: thought of renunciation

nibbāna
: unconditioned reality, the reality which does not arise and fall away. The destruction of lust, hatred and delusion. The deathless. The end of suffering.

nimitta
: mental image one can acquire of a meditation subject in tranquil meditation

nīvaraṇa
: hindrances, a group of defilements

oghas
: group of defilements, the floods

ottappa
: fear of blame

paccaya-pariggaha-ñāṇa
: discerning the Conditions of Nāma and Rūpa

paccayas
: conditions

paccupaṭṭhāna
: manifestation, appearance or effect

padaṭṭhānaṃ
: proximate cause

paṭicca sammuppada
: 'Dependent Origination', the conditional origination of phenomena

Paṭṭhāna
: Conditional Relations, one of the seven books of the Abhidhamma

paṭisandhi citta
: rebirth consciousness

paṭisandhi
: rebirth

pakiṇṇakā
: the particulars

Pāli
: the language of the Buddhist teachings

pañcadvārāvajjana-citta
: five-sense-door-adverting-consciousness

pañcaviññāṇa (or dvi-pañcaviññāṇa)
: the sense cognitions (seeing etc.) of which there five pairs the sense cognitions (seeing etc.) of which there five pairs

paññā
: wisdom or understanding

paññatti
: concepts, conventional terms

paramattha dhamma
: truth in the absolute sense: mental and physical phenomena, each with their own characteristic. Nibbāna is

Paramattha Mañjūsā
: a commentary to the Visuddhimagga

pasāda-rūpas
: rūpas which are capable of receiving sense-objects such as visible object, sound, taste, etc.

passaddhi
: calm

patisanthāro
: courtesy

peta
: ghost

phala-citta
: fruition consciousness experiencing nibbāna. It is result of magga-citta, path-consciousness.

phassa
: contact

pīti
: joy, rapture

puñña-kiriya-vatthus
: "ten bases of meritorious deeds"

puthujjana
: "worldling", a person who has not attained enlightenment

rāga
: greed

rasa
: function or achievement

rūpa
: physical phenomena, realities which do not experience anything

rūpa-brahma
: plane or rūpa-bhūmi fine material realm of existence attained as a result of rūpa-jhāna

rūpa-jhāna
: fine material absorption, developed with a meditation subject which is still dependant on materiality.

rūpa-jīvitindriya
: a kind of rūpa produced by kamma and it maintains the life of the other rūpas it arises together with

rūpa-khandha
: aggregate or group of all physical phenomena (rūpas)

rūpāvacara citta
: type of jhāna citta

`rūpāvacara cittas, rūpa-jhānacittas`
: consciousness of the fine-material sphere

`sabbacitta-sādhāranā`
: the seven cetasikas which have to arise with every citta

`saddhā` confidence

`sahetuka` accompanied by roots

`sakadāgāmī`
: once-returner, a noble person who has attained the second stage of enlightenment

`sakkāya diṭṭhi`
: wrong view of personality, wrong view about the khandhas

`samādhi` concentration or one-pointedness, ekaggatā cetasika

`samādhi-bhāvanā`
: the development of concentration

`samañña lakkhaṇa`
: general characteristics common to all conditioned realities

`samatha` the development of calm

`sambojjhanga`
: seven factors of enlightenment

`sammā` right

`sammā-diṭṭhi`
: right understanding

`sammā-samādhi`
: right concentration

`sammāsambuddha`
: a universal Buddha, a fully enlightened person who has discovered the truth all by himself, without the aid of a teacher and who can proclaim the Truth to others beings

`sammā-saṉkappa`
: right thinking of the eightfold Path

`sammā-sati`
: right mindfulness

`sammā-vāyāma`
: right mindfulness of the eightfold Path

`sampaṭicchana-citta`
: receiving-consciousness

sampajañña discrimination, comprehension

sampayutta associated with

sampayutta dhammas associated dhammas, citta and cetasika which arise together

Sangha community of monks and nuns. As one of the triple Gems it means the community of those people who have attained enlightenment.

sankhata dhammas conditioned dhammas

saññā memory, remembrance or "perception"

saññā-kkhandha memory classified as one of the five khandhas

santīraṇa-citta investigating-consciousness

saṅkāra dhamma conditioned dhamma

saṅkhāra-kkhandha all cetasikas (mental factors) except feeling and memory

saṅkhāradhamma conditioned realities

saṃsāra the cycle of birth and death

sappurisa good man

Sāriputta The First chief disciple of the Buddha

sasaṅkhārika prompted, induced, instigated, either by oneself or someone else

sati awareness, non-forgetfulness, awareness of reality by direct experience

satipaṭṭhāna sutta Middle Length Sayings 1, number 10, also Dīgha Nikāya, dialogues 11, no. 22;

satipaṭṭhāna applications of mindfulness. It can mean the cetasika sati which is aware of realities or the objects of mindfulness which are classified as four applications of mindfulness: Body, Feeling Citta, Dhamma. Or it can mean the development of direct understanding of realities through awareness.

saṃyojanas The Fetters, a group of defilements

sīla morality in action or speech, virtue

sīlabbata-parāmāsā
wrong practice

sīlabbatupādāna
wrong practice, which is clinging to certain rules ("rites and rituals") in one's practice

sobhana (citta and cetasika)
beautiful, accompanied by beautiful roots

sobhana hetus
beautiful roots

sobhana kiriyacittas
kiriyacittas accompanied by sobhana (beautiful) roots

somanassa happy feeling

sotāpanna person who has attained the first stage of enlightenment, and who has eradicated wrong view of realities

sukha happy, pleasant

sutta part of the scriptures containing dialogues at different places on different occasions.

suttanta a sutta text

tadārammaṇa-cittas
registering-consciousness

taruṇa vipassanā
"tender insight"

Tathāgata literally "thus gone", epithet of the Buddha

tatramajjhattatā
equanimity or evenmindedness

Theravāda Buddhism
'Doctrine of the Elders', the oldest tradition of Buddhism

thīna sloth

tiṭṭhi khaṇa
the moment of its presence, or static moment of citta

Tipiṭaka the teachings of the Buddha

titthi khaṇa
static moment of citta

uddhacca restlessness

uddhambhāgiya-saṃyojana
five higher fetters which tie beings to the higher planes of existence the rūpa-brahma planes and the arūpa-brahma planes

ujupatipanno
the straight, true and proper way

upacāra access or proximatory consciousness, the second javana-citta in the process in which absorption or enlightenment is attained

upādāna clinging

upādānakkhandhas
khandhas of clinging

upekkhā indifferent feeling. It can stand for evenmindedness or equanimity and then it is not feeling

Uposatha Uposatha days are days of fasting or vigil; uposatha is observed on the days of full-moon and new-moon, and sometimes also on the days of the first and last moon-quarter. In Buddhist countries there is a tradition for lay-followers to visit temples and to observe eight precepts on these days

uppāda khaṇa
the arising moment of citta

vaci-duccarita virati
abstinence from wrong speech

vatthu base, physical base of citta

vedanā feeling

vedanā-kkhandha
group of all feelings

Vibhaṅga "Book of Analysis", one of the seven books of the Abhidhamma

vibhava-taṇhā
craving for non-existence

vicāra sustained thinking or discursive thinking

vicikicchā
doubt

vihiṃsā-vitakka
thought of harming

vinaya Book of Discipline for the monks

viññāṇa consciousness, citta

viññāṇa-kkhandha
all cittas (consciousness)

vipākacitta
citta which is the result of a wholesome deed (kusala kamma) or an unwholesome deed (akusala kamma). It can arise as rebirth-consciousness, or during life as the experience of pleasant or unpleasant objects through the senses, such as seeing, hearing, etc.

vipallāsas
perversions. Three kinds: saññā perversion of perception, citta of thought, diṭṭhi of views.

vipassanā ñāṇa
moment of insight knowledge

vipassanā wisdom which sees realities as they are

viriya energy

visaṇkāra dhamma
unconditioned dhamma (reality)

Visuddhimagga
an encyclopaedia of the Buddha's teaching, written by Buddhaghosa in the fifth century A.D

vitakka applied thinking

vyāpāda ill-will

vyāpāda-vitakka
thought of malevolence

yoghas The yokes, a group of defilements

yoniso manasikāra
wise attention to the object

Books

Books written by Nina van Gorkom

- *Abhidhamma in Daily Life* is an exposition of absolute realities in detail. Abhidhamma means higher doctrine and the book's purpose is to encourage the right application of Buddhism in order to eradicate wrong view and eventually all defilements.
- *The Buddha's Path* An Introduction to the doctrine of Theravada Buddhism for those who have no previous knowledge. The four noble Truths - suffering - the origin of suffering - the cessation of suffering - and the way leading to the end of suffering - are explained as a philosophy and a practical guide which can be followed in today's world.
- *Buddhism in Daily Life* A general introduction to the main ideas of Theravada Buddhism.The purpose of this book is to help the reader gain insight into the Buddhist scriptures and the way in which the teachings can be used to benefit both ourselves and others in everyday life.
- *The World in the Buddhist Sense* The purpose of this book is to show that the Buddha's Path to true understanding has to be developed in daily life.
- *Cetasikas* Cetasika means 'belonging to the mind'. It is a mental factor which accompanies consciousness (citta) and experiences an object. There are 52 cetasikas. This book gives an outline of each of these 52 cetasikas and shows the relationship they have with each other.
- *The Buddhist Teaching on Physical Phenomena* A general introduction to physical phenomena and the way they are related to each other and to mental phenomena. The purpose of this book is to show that the study of both mental phenomena and physical phenomena is indispensable for the development of the eightfold Path.
- *The Conditionality of Life* By Nina van Gorkom

  This book is an introduction to the seventh book of the Abhidhamma, that deals with the conditionality of life. It explains the deep underlying motives for all actions through body, speech and mind and shows that these are dependent on conditions and cannot be controlled by a 'self'. This book is suitable for those who have already made a study of the Buddha's teachings.

Books translated by Nina van Gorkom

- *Mettā: Loving kindness in Buddhism* by Sujin Boriharnwanaket. An introduction to the basic Buddhist teachings of mettā, loving kindness, and its practical application in todays world.
- *Taking Refuge in Buddhism* by Sujin Boriharnwanaket. Taking Refuge in Buddhism is an introduction to the development of insight meditation.

- *A Survey of Paramattha Dhammas* by Sujin Boriharnwanaket. A Survey of Paramattha Dhammas is a guide to the development of the Buddha's path of wisdom, covering all aspects of human life and human behaviour, good and bad. This study explains that right understanding is indispensable for mental development, the development of calm as well as the development of insight.
- *The Perfections Leading to Enlightenment* by Sujin Boriharnwanaket. The Perfections is a study of the ten good qualities: generosity, morality, renunciation, wisdom, energy, patience, truthfulness, determination, loving-kindness, and equanimity.

These and other articles can be seen at www.zolag.co.uk or www.scribd.com (search for zolag).